Zeffirelli 1975

Zeffirelli

Zeffirelli

THE AUTOBIOGRAPHY OF
FRANCO ZEFFIRELLI

WEIDENFELD & NICOLSON
New York

Published by Weidenfeld & Nicolson, New York
A Division of Wheatland Corporation
10 East 53rd Street
New York, NY 10022

First published in Great Britain in 1986 by
George Weidenfeld & Nicolson Limited

Library of Congress Cataloging-in-Publication Data

Zeffirelli, Franco.
  Zeffirelli : the autobiography of Franco Zeffirelli.

  1. Zeffirelli, Franco. 2. Moving-picture producers and directors—Italy—Biography. I. Title.
PN1998.A3Z4326 1986   791.43'0233'0924 [B] 86-15760
ISBN 1-55584-022-1

Manufactured in the United States of America
by Maple-Vail Book Mfg. Co., Inc.

First American Edition 1986

10 9 8 7 6 5 4 3 2 1

This book is dedicated *in memoriam*
to the three men who taught me most

Donald Downes, 1902–83
Luchino Visconti, 1906–76
Tullio Serafin, 1878–1968

CONTENTS

ILLUSTRATIONS

Illustrations

FOREWORD

I have been close to death three times – twice by firing squad, once in a motorcar accident – so it is hardly surprising that I have a firm belief in God and a superstitious affection for the idea of destiny. Despite all the evidence to the contrary I am loath to accept the fact that one day I will die: like most people I hold to the possibility of a vague immortality. Thus the idea that I should write down my life, as if it was finished and complete, still seems slightly preposterous. I am deeply suspicious of the sort of motives that people offer for this sort of book: either they wish to capture the spirit of the age to which they contributed, or they want to reveal the true natures of the great and famous amongst whom they mingled. Of course some of this will come through, and memoirs, letters and auto-biographies can add to social history or specialist studies of politics, the theatre, literature, and so on. But by and large this is *post facto* justification. There was another problem: no one tells the full truth about themselves. Quite the opposite, we go to great lengths to hide it, tending to recall only what pleases and putting our own gloss on it. Everyone's public persona is a little miracle of invention, everyone tailors their past to meet the needs of the present: the wittier you are the more those dinner-table anecdotes will build up the coral reef of invention around the tiny central core of reality until no one can any longer discern its original form. So what price then the journal of record or the history of the age?

It was only when I decided to accept this fact, that I am a raconteur rather than a writer, that I was able to contemplate producing an auto-biography – but how to 'tell' my story?

The answer came when a BBC television producer, David Sweetman, made a documentary that was shown at the time my film of *La traviata* opened in London. I was impressed by his approach to my portrayal on television, so I asked him to take on the task of recording a series of interviews and then compile a first draft that I could rework in my own way. The value of having an interlocutor has been that I have had to challenge my own memories – or he has challenged them for me. We have often gone over the same ground twice after an interval of months to see whether the two tales correspond or not. I am not pretending that this is

Foreword

cold academic history, I'm not even sure of all the dates, but, having been bullied into doing it, it seemed sensible to try to get the facts right. Conversely, I have been at pains not to write out all the spontaneity. When I began, my memories of the people I have known were coloured by my feelings about them at the present time, yet as I delved back I realized that someone I hated today I had loved yesterday. I hope some of that comes through, because for me the value of writing this book has been that it has allowed a reassessment of my own life, my memories of it, and my reactions to it. For me it is the observation of that process of reconciliation that I think the reader may find more worthwhile than the social and theatrical history or the insights into the ways of the famous. I hope so.

FRANCO ZEFFIRELLI
Rome and Positano, 1986

Zeffirelli

ONE

No Name

I can see myself aged about eight or nine at my first school in Florence. I am coming down the big staircase after classes are over and I recognize all the parents and servants waiting outside to pick up the children. No one has come for me because I live with my aunt only two hundred yards from the school and it is easy for me to walk home by myself. But on this day a woman across the street seems to be looking at me in a strange way. I still have a distinct image of her: she is dressed in a brown fur coat and a black hat with a veil, she is wearing a lot of make-up and eyeshadow, and she looks slightly mad, with fiery eyes. I start to go home, but very quickly realize she is following me down the narrow medieval street that leads from the school. She is muttering something which I can't make out, then I realize she is saying: '*Bastardino*, little bastard, you little bastard. You'll find out. Don't worry, some day you'll find out.' I turn to leave; she follows. I run as fast as I can till I am safely at our door. I race up the stairs calling to my aunt, 'Lide! Lide!' But when she appears I am suddenly afraid to tell her what has happened. Slowly she coaxes it out of me.

'What did she say?'

I tell her the woman called me '*bastardino*, little bastard'. My aunt is angrier than I have ever seen her. She reaches for her hat and coat and storms out of the house. When she returns later that evening I am too embarrassed to ask where she has been but that night I dream about the woman and wake up afraid. I could not imagine why she hated me so much, couldn't make sense of it, couldn't figure out who she was. I was often terrified by nightmares as a child and there was a recurring scene in which the world was coming to an end, heading towards an appalling void, a blackness that I struggled to escape.

Much later I overheard my aunt talking about her and, to my astonishment, realized that the demented creature was my father's wife. That day my aunt had gone directly to my father's house and confronted the mad woman. If she dared do such a thing again, she told her, she should strangle her with her own hands. The woman never followed me or talked to me again, although every once in a while she appeared outside the school. She would throw her head back and fix her gaze at me through her veil,

2   and sometimes she laughed a rasping, mad laugh.

Most children would have been distraught at such an apparition, but for me it was just one amongst the many oddities that comprised my view of the world. 'Who is your mother?' 'Who is your aunt?' 'Who is that girl with your father?' 'Who is that strange lady?' I had no easy answers to these questions. It was true that I received a lot of attention and affection, but I always had a terrible feeling of embarrassment. I know my aunt was very hurt by this, because I sometimes overheard her talking about it. I can remember spying behind doors and listening to the talk about me and the family situation, about how my father's wife couldn't bear the fact that I, although illegitimate, was my father's only son and sooner or later my father might give me his name and make me his legal heir.

Gradually, I pieced together the whole story, though it always seemed quite unreal, as if I was hearing about someone else's life. I never felt sure of my identity. I saw how different the lives of other children were. They had mothers and fathers and big family gatherings at holidays. If my father brought me gifts he would inevitably have to rush off to his wife and family. At an early age I learned that this was somehow wrong, though it was hard to blame the attractive man who came and went so abruptly.

And Ottorino Corsi was an attractive, vigorous man. He was rather short, but well built and strong, and he had a captivating smile which brought his sharp blue eyes to life. He had started to lose his hair when he was young and was already half bald when I was born. Ottorino Corsi was respected in Florence as a merchant who started from scratch, having lost his inheritance through the madness of my grandfather.

Our family had been substantial landowners in the area of Vinci, the home town of Leonardo da Vinci. When it became clear that my grandfather was unbalanced, his mother, who must have been a strong-minded woman, decided to leave their land and possessions to my father, who at that time was still a minor. But, when this eventually happened, my grandfather, who displayed that determination which in some members of my family leads to achievement and success, but in others to self-destruction, refused to work. He loved music, which he had studied, and he decided to become a conductor. He proceeded to hire a full fifty-piece band – fifty musicians with their families and children brought from Puglia in southern Italy to live in Vinci. Even today there are people in the district who have southern Italian names, evidently the descendants of my grandfather's musicians.

My grandfather had guaranteed to house and support these people, but he had no money of his own, only his son's. He borrowed repeatedly from people who were banking on my father's generosity; and he went on conducting, giving concerts in all the neighbouring villages. It certainly must have been from him that I inherited the musical strain in my character. There was nothing else to inherit, for when Grandfather was finally arrested for debt, my father, who was just twenty at the time, bailed him out. Father couldn't face sending him to a squalid debtors' prison, so he signed all the papers, paid all the debts, and was left penniless. Within a matter of days, the family was forced out of the house and everything was lost, yet Grandfather seemed oblivious to it all. He walked the streets alone, conducting, waving his baton with one hand and drinking from his jug of wine with the other.

When my father told me the story many years later, I was very angry and demanded to know why he had gone against the wishes of his grandmother and so lost our inheritance. But the suggestion that a son might abandon his own father, for whatever reason, was hardly the sort of thing he wanted to hear from me and he told me to be silent.

Although far from mad, my father had something of the old man's impetuosity. He met a girl called Corinna in one of the nearby villages, and she soon found herself pregnant. Just as quickly my father decided to marry her and, together with the mad old man, they left Vinci for Florence, where my father hoped for a new start as a businessman.

None of my surviving family can tell me much about those years before the First World War. I know my father began work in the post office and that some relatives eventually lent him enough money to start a business, but he always claimed it was the war itself that gave him his start. He had suffered an injury while horse-riding in 1913, which kept him from being sent to the front. He remained at home, while most of the other young men were away, and that gave him a chance to establish himself, to build a successful business in wool and silk. He also had an ample supply of lonely wives to choose from in Florence; that was his speciality – affairs with married women. He never went after young girls, at least not after he married Corinna. He liked his women buxom, tall and *married*. Though he didn't want the responsibility of getting unmarried girls pregnant, he certainly got many another man's wife pregnant. He would wait for a husband to come home from the front; then, in the days after he went back, Father would approach her. Thus any offspring could be put down to the husband's visit. I don't know how many stepbrothers and stepsisters I've met born in those war years of 1914 to 1918, all my father's children, though with different family names, Gherardini, Martelli, Venturis, Gori, Piccardi ... and God knows how many others I don't know about.

There is little doubt that Corinna knew all about his philandering, but she was one of those women who takes a kind of pride in the idea that her husband is attractive to other women. She simply turned a blind eye. Then he met my mother and it was a very different story.

My mother, Alaide Garosi, was a successful fashion designer with an *atelier* in the centre of the city, in the Piazza Vittorio Emanuele near the cathedral. She had married a lawyer called Cipriani, but he soon became

4   bedridden with a long illness that was eventually diagnosed as incurable tuberculosis. Left alone for much of the time, my mother threw herself into her career. My father was one of the suppliers of her fabrics. When they met she already had three children from her marriage: the eldest a daughter named Adriana, a son called Ubaldo and a younger daughter called Giuliana. I think my father must have sensed her vulnerability, working so hard and with a husband often away at various sanatoriums. My father kept his eye on her, waiting for one of those moments when she was most lonely, when she realized her husband didn't have long to live. This time, however, there was a difference. This was not the usual casual relationship but a stormy love affair that scandalized the close community that was Florence sixty years ago. She was thirty-nine and pregnant, and everyone knew about it. Her eldest daughter Adriana was already married and having her own baby, yet here was Alaide having a baby when she was about to become a grandmother.

When Corinna, my father's wife, found out, she went wild. My mother suffered from all the recriminations, and lost many of her best clients and friends. Everyone told her to get rid of the baby, even her own mother. But she refused. Maybe that's why I'm such a confirmed anti-abortionist: my mother defied so much of the existing social structure to have me. In the determination that I should live, she destroyed much of her own life.

During the last months of her pregnancy, my mother's husband died. She went into hiding on the outskirts of Florence, where I was born in a small clinic on 12 February 1923. Then the recriminations began: the Cipriani family refused to accept that I was the posthumous son of my mother's late husband; they knew well enough that he had been too ill throughout the previous year to have fathered a child. Equally adamant, the Corsi family would not even consider accepting me. Only Lide, my father's cousin, stood by my mother, counselling her to accept God's will and have the child.

'He knows better than we do,' she would say.

After my birth she alone, from both families, came to visit and to do what she could to support my mother, who now had few friends left.

A name had to be invented for me. I couldn't use my mother's surname because she was still married and it would have needed the approval of her husband's family. Naturally I couldn't bear my father's name either. I became what is known in Italy as 'N.N.'. Everyone knew who my parents were, but on the documents it had to be N.N., *nescio nomen* – 'I do not know the name'. I was told later (though I have never had it confirmed) that there was a Florentine law dating back to medieval times which decreed that illegitimate children be named with a different letter of the alphabet every day, rotating from A to Z. On the day I was born the letter was 'Z'. A cousin of my mother later told me that my mother was fond of a Mozart aria in *Cosi fan tutte* which mentions the *Zeffiretti,* the little breezes. She used to call people she liked 'my little *zeffiretto*'. Apparently she intended to name me Zeffiretti, but this was misspelled in the register and came out as the previously unheard-of Zeffirelli.

My mother left me in the country to be raised by a peasant woman, because she was unable to breast-feed me herself and she couldn't openly keep me with her in Florence without the danger of renewed scandal. Through the church she found a family of Tuscan peasants and that is how she picked my wet-nurse. The first two years of my childhood were spent in the care of a remarkable woman, Ersilia Innocenti.

My mother came to visit every week, I was told, usually at weekends. She arrived by coach in a long black veil, afraid that someone might recognize her.

'*Viene la Signora. Viene la Signora,*' the peasant women would whisper when this mysterious woman appeared. My mother would spend a full day with me, chatting with Ersilia and the family, bringing gifts for everybody, and then she would disappear into her coach and return to Florence. I don't remember if my father ever came, though I think it likely. I was his only son and that he must therefore have been more interested in me than in his other children, legitimate or not. One of the reasons he turned against his wife was that she couldn't produce a male heir for him. He was like the Arabs in that regard: Corinna was disgraced because she didn't have a boy. My father desperately wanted a legitimate son to pass on his family name. Ironically, it was my mother who gave him the boy he longed for yet couldn't acknowledge. I was the main link between them, even after they were no longer in love. Even my appearance must have added to the strangeness of their union, for I was golden blond with bright blue eyes and fair skin, a strange cuckoo amongst all the other chicks my father had left in the nests of Florence. Everyone remarked on how striking our resemblance was.

When I was two I was brought back to the city. It was a difficult time for my mother. The scandal had badly damaged her career, and the economic outlook was not good. Her dead husband had not left her much and even the daughters were now rather poor. They never really forgave their mother for the scandal and moved to Milan to get away from her. So we were alone and rather isolated, our only source of consolation my father's cousin Lide, a cheerful young woman who helped create a small family around me, with father visiting us when he could.

My few memories from that period are clear and distinct. There is an image of me playing with my mother's materials and racing around her *atelier*. I remember the seamstresses since I was their favourite diversion. When I was three or four (it must have been in 1926), my mother made a beautiful costume for me and took me to the children's ball at a carnival.

6   I also remember the first time I saw the Fascists in the Piazza Vittorio Emanuele – a mass of black shirts and flags. My mother looked out of the window, shaking her head. I was waving my own three-coloured flag, waving it again and again, an unwitting farewell to a dying age.

Shortly afterwards my father apparently started having other mistresses again. My mother was absolutely appalled; she was beginning to be seriously ill, but I think she suffered most from my father's absence and betrayals. She must have had witches come to the house because I remember some old crones burning the heart of an animal on a charcoal fire and performing spells to bring my father back. In a way they worked, for occasionally he would visit her during the night. I slept in a huge bed with my mother and some nights I would wake up and see them together. I still have an image of my father next to my mother in an unbuttoned shirt. I pretended to be asleep and watched, fascinated, as they made love. My father would give me a big kiss before leaving to go back to his wife or his club.

One day my mother took me to a small house in a quiet bourgeois suburb of Florence. The woman who answered the door was a designer my mother knew well who was married with children of her own. My mother pointed at me.

'This is his son,' she said. 'Do you want to destroy him, destroy our little family?' My mother began to threaten her with scandal. Later I remember waking and listening to her crying, and I began to hate my father.

She clung increasingly to me, she was so fragile and vulnerable now. When my father heard about the incident with his mistress, he told my mother that he would not see her again. She kept sending him urgent messages to visit us, but he refused. One night she took me to his house on the via dell'Orivolo just behind the cathedral. We waited in a kind of niche between the columns in front of the Bank of Italy. It was cold and windy, close to midnight. I was crying and shivering, and my mother had on a black fur coat and a big hat with a black veil that covered her face. Finally my father appeared, and my mother stepped out and confronted him. He tried to dismiss her, but she wouldn't go away. He slapped her, and without hesitation she took a long pin from her hat and tried to stab him. She missed him but their shouting roused the neighbours. They called the police, who sent my mother home. The opera? My destiny? I think there is a case to be made.

My father agreed to drop the matter if she left Florence. Her business was virtually ruined and she was an outcast of sorts, so she had little choice but to take me to Milan, to her daughter Adriana. My father gave us one thousand lire for the journey and we went in November 1928, when I was five. I was upset to find us crowded into a small room in my stepsister's dingy apartment on the outskirts of the city. By a horrible twist of fate her husband, a young bank clerk called Parri, was also tuberculous. I remember the quarrelling that went on there much of the time because my stepsister's husband didn't really want any of us living with them. The economic situation was bleak and the 'crash' was imminent.

Those winter months in Milan were cold and depressing. We only had a narrow single bed and at night my mother would cling to me as if trying to draw warmth and health from the being she had made. During the day I went to a school across the street which was run by nuns, but, when I returned to the house, I could see that my mother was changing. By spring, she was very frail and ill and one day she vanished; I came home from kindergarten and she wasn't there. At first I was told she had gone out to visit some friends, but later they took me to see her. I still remember the day: I was left to play in the garden behind one of the city hospitals until my stepsister came for me. She was crying as she brought me into my mother's room. I hardly recognized her and I realized instantly how ill she was. She told me not to worry, that she would come home soon, but she never did.

It was in school on the afternoon of 8 May 1929 that one of the nuns came over to me in the yard and whispered, 'Your mother is in Heaven.'

At first, I wasn't sure what she meant. All of the children were staring at me and, oddly enough, I felt a kind of pride at being the object of so much attention. I had no idea what dying meant. But when I went home I began to feel lonely and frightened, a lost six-year-old who didn't know what was to become of him. Fortunately, the next day, my father's cousin Lide came to Milan, and quickly saw the hopeless position I was in.

My mother's family did not want me at the funeral, which was on 10 May. Adriana and, of course, her husband were adamant about not having the 'little bastard' there. I remember the stream of flowers which arrived from friends and many of my mother's former clients, who had abandoned her when she needed them but now chose to remember her. Without asking anyone's permission, Lide took me to the graveyard, though she kept me at a distance from the members of the immediate family. She knew I had a right to be there. The hearse, covered with enormous wreaths, passed slowly and I started to cry. Lide told me to say goodbye and taught me the prayer for the dead, '*Requiem aeternam ...*' That same night we packed and left for Florence.

Aunt Lide, whom I always called, in the Italian way, Zia Lide, was a woman who knew her own mind. When she was younger, she had been about to marry a man she didn't really love, but decided she couldn't go through with it. She had fallen in love with a man named Gustavo, who was handsome and well-off but already married. She chose to stay with him and be his mistress, even though she knew he would never be able to leave his wife. She had renounced marriage for love and they lived together for over thirty years. Much of the time Gustavo lived with us, although I remember occasions when he went back to his wife and children. At one point he and his wife separated, but our laws did not permit divorce.

When I first started to live with Lide I was unhappy and kept looking for my mother, but slowly Lide's warmth and love made it easy to transfer to her my search for affection. I've come to realize now that perhaps the only good thing my father ever did for me as a small child was to let Lide become my mother and give her some money to pay for my upkeep and my education. We had little contact, except when he came on Saturdays to take me for walks in those parts of Florence where no one would see us. We walked in the gardens and parks on the outskirts of the city every Saturday afternoon. Before he left, he would hand me a five-lire coin, which seemed to me a tremendous amount. I thought of Saturday as the day of the *aquila,* the eagle on the back of the silver coin, and of my father as the 'nice gentleman' who came every week to give it to me. I could never really communicate with him and would have preferred to spend Saturday with my friends, but at least I had my little coin, which I saved and which made me feel very rich.

I'll always remember my father as he was then, in his late forties, dressed meticulously in grey with a carnation or a gardenia in his buttonhole. He always wore a white handkerchief in his waistcoat pocket which smelled of eau-de-Cologne. His face was well-shaven and his moustache carefully trimmed. I remember his fine teeth which sparkled when he smiled – a smile I'm sure women could not resist. But for all his dash and charm, I could not call him father in public, even though I knew he would have loved to hear that simple word from my lips.

I much preferred the visits of my mad old grandfather, who was still conducting his orchestra in his head. Sometimes I would follow him as he took my father's English setter, Lord, for walks, and I noticed that when he came to Aunt Lide's he would take out a beautiful watch and say: 'Well, it's five o'clock, I'm hungry, let's have something to eat.' One day we played a trick on him; he put the watch on the table and, without his seeing her, my aunt turned back the watch hands. He kept picking up the watch and setting it down, and my aunt kept setting back the time. Finally, the old man could stand it no more. 'I know it's not five,' he said, 'but for heaven's sake, give me something to eat!'

I suppose I should have been angry that the old rascal had ruined our family, but to a child he was a fabulous being. He was always humming music and playing all the parts from violins to trombones. I was very sad when he died of pneumonia on 17 November 1934. And that in itself was a mystery. One thing I soon learned about my father was his superstition about the number 17: that day of the month was always, so he claimed, unlucky for our family.

There really was too much change and sadness during my early life, and the turbulence of those years has left its mark. My confusion became evident when I started elementary school at seven. I remember the first day when we had to write our names in the class register. Everyone had to stand up and say their own name, and the name of their mother and father. Since my name started with 'Z', I was the last to be called. I listened to all the children, at least thirty in the class, answering when the teacher called out: 'Name of mother? Name of father?' 'Mother, Cristina; Father, Carlo. Mother, Luisa; Father, Giovanni. Mother, Francesca; Father, Piero.' As the names went on, I became more and more stifled, almost paralysed. I could picture all those family groups, all those mothers and fathers that the children had mentioned. At last the teacher called out: 'Zeffirelli'. He asked me to spell my name since he had never heard it before. Slowly I forced myself to say: 'Z-E-F-F-I-R-E-L-L-I.' The children started to giggle.

'Father's name?' the teacher asked. But I couldn't answer. The children giggled again until the teacher repeated the question. I looked at him, but still couldn't speak. Then I lowered my head and said, 'N.N.' The children didn't seem to understand, but the teacher did. He realized the situation he had put me in and quickly asked me the name of my mother. But again I stood silent. There was more giggling from some of the children. I finally forced out the word 'dead'. Strangely, I felt again what I had felt in Milan – that my mother's death somehow made me different, even special.

Overall, the effects of these upheavals were far from positive. I had had three 'mothers' by now – Ersilia, my wet-nurse; Alaide, my real mother; and now Lide, my aunt. Yet every time I offered love to one of these women I was forced to take it back and give it to another. Soon I stopped looking for affection and became very uncommunicative emotionally. My days were silent and my nights were often haunted by the recurring nightmare of the strange woman following me from school. I still have difficulty in trusting love when it is offered. This is something that has marked my entire life. I still search – no doubt I always will – but even when love *is* given to me, I seldom manage to fully absorb it or to believe that it will last.

TWO

The Florentines

It was only with Ersilia Innocenti, my wet-nurse, that I had a sense of permanence. This was renewed every Christmas and Easter when she came to see me in Florence, and every summer when I visited her in the country. Her home was at Borselli, about forty-five miles from Florence, a simple peasant town. I remember the house, whose kitchen seemed so huge to me as a child. The Tuscan peasants of Borselli were very poor, and many were old and sick, bent by years of hard labour in the fields. What I learned from them has stayed with me all my life and explains the strong association I have with a world that has now disappeared, yet which then had changed little since the Middle Ages. It was a way of life that had existed in Tuscany even before the rise of the Renaissance cities.

I used to arrive in Borselli in June at the end of the school year and the first thing I did was to throw away my shoes for the summer. Work was done barefoot; no one wore shoes except for heavy work in the woods, when boots were needed. I helped in the fields with the sheep and the pigs, or went to the fountain with the other children to fetch water. The fountain was situated about two hundred yards down the valley and I remember coming back up the hill with the beautiful copper *mezzina* filled with water. I felt as though I were grasping the earth with my feet, almost sinking deep into it. We woke with the dawn, or even earlier to the light of oil lamps, and went to bed when the sky reddened and night fell.

Once a week, usually on Friday, there was the 'day of the bread', when the ovens were heated with wood we brought from the forest. The work in the kitchen went on for hours, and then came that wonderful fresh smell of baking. On special occasions there was the luxury of fresh pizza made with olive oil, salt, pepper and garlic. There was also the 'day of the laundry' on Mondays, when the women used the ashes left in the ovens after the bread had baked. The oven was cooled for a day, and then the wood ash was taken away and put into big terracotta containers to mature and create a bleach by adding a handful of caustic soda. This was poured over clothes and linen, which the women boiled in the laundry container. The clothes were hauled to the river for rinsing, then hauled back to be hung in the sun to dry. The smell of those clean clothes was fresh and unforgettable.

Mending the clothes with patches began the next day. Except for wedding dresses, which a tailor was asked to create, all of their clothes were hand made, and continually mended. Everyone had a single pair of shoes which they wore only to church and on festivals. The men had one dark suit apart from the old patched clothes. Some of the young men used their army uniforms as work clothes after they came back from military service, but these too were eventually covered with patches. I have tried several times to make costumes like that for the theatre, but never with any success. Such clothes 'grow' with people's lives.

The peasants also wove their own shawls and blankets. Wool was precious, and after they sheared the sheep they washed the fleece carefully and removed any dead ticks. One of the tasks for children was to pick out dead ticks from the clean wool. Then the old women sat at their spinning wheel – *la rocca* – and made thread. The young boys had to cut the grass for the sheep and other animals and bring it to the barn. I remember the smell of that grass, which, like the smell of the bread and the clean clothes, still haunts me. There was also the smell of the fields and the smells that came with certain hours of the day: the smell of the morning dew, for example, just before dawn. At the time, this was all taken for granted.

Of course, I wasn't really one of the peasants. They considered me a *signorino* – a young gentleman – and my mother, and later my aunt, paid handsomely for my upkeep. But I've always felt strongly that my roots are in the Tuscan countryside. I still love the slice of bread with half a tomato on it and a 'C' of oil, so called because that's all the oil they could spare – a slight golden crescent, with a little salt and pepper over it. I've eaten it countless times and even now it brings back the old associations of the country – the peasants, my childhood, the real Italy of the Middle Ages which I knew and is now lost.

During those summers with the peasants I first discovered the theatre. Strange characters, well known and loved by all the villagers, would come regularly to visit, sometimes once or twice a month. They spent the evening around the fireplace telling stories – fantastic, tragic, classic stories mixed with real facts and items of news. I remember one that dealt with a famous murder of the day. These actors recreated the events blow by blow with great cunning, crying and shouting, pretending to kill or be killed. Each performer had his own personality and his bag of tricks: there was a jovial redhead with a rubbery face he could distort hilariously, while another was lean and frightening. They were masters of dramatic effect and I remember how one of them used to put a lantern on the floor close beside himself in order to create diabolical shadows on the walls – something I often do in my own productions. I've never believed anything at the theatre as much as the fantasies those storytellers brought us. They captured our imaginations fully: our hearts sank and our eyes filled with tears only to be jolted into

12   laughter by the comic stories which always followed, so that we would go
to bed relieved rather than frightened. I still marvel at it: no radio and
no television, just simple storytellers, direct descendants of the world of
Boccaccio, Da Porto and Bandello.

When the summers were over and I returned to Florence, those theatrical
memories stayed with me. I would seek refuge in doing things alone, losing
myself in special toys like the small theatres – *teatrini* – that I made myself.
I built little stages which I filled with puppets and scenery. When my aunt's
lover, Gustavo, noticed this obsession growing, he decided to help. He
was an amateur baritone who knew many singers and went to the opera
frequently. It was he who decided that I should be introduced to the
delights of professional theatre. I was no more than eight or nine when we
went to the Florence Opera House, where one of his best friends, Giacomo
Rimini, was singing Wotan in *Die Walküre*. (I've often wondered why I
wasn't put off opera for ever after that first encounter.) I had already met
Giacomo Rimini, who had been to our house for lunch. I had heard him
sing during that visit, so Lide and Gustavo took a chance on my being
interested in seeing him on the stage. At worst, Lide thought, I would sleep
through most of the performance. Their regular box at the opera was the
only place that Lide and Gustavo could be seen together in public.
Somehow, even to the gossipy Florentines, the Opera House was neutral
territory, so my aunt could enjoy the sensation of being legitimate. Perhaps
it was this relaxed family atmosphere that drew me to opera from the
beginning.

I didn't understand *Die Walküre*, of course, but I was riveted by the
incredible sounds. Our box was directly over the orchestra pit and I couldn't
believe the richness rising up from the musicians. I was delighted by the
metal helmets with horns, by the forest of rocks, the fire, the smoke, the
Valkyries galloping everywhere, and then the spell of Wotan surrounding
Brunhilde. It was hardly a refined appreciation, more like a child of today
gawping at *Star Wars*.

After the performance Gustavo took us backstage to see Rimini. I remember that I became separated from Aunt Lide and wound up on the stage,
where I was dazzled to see the smoke from the final fire scene still pouring
from the steam pipes overhead. I stood there alone and stared at the
backdrops which were being rolled away and at the scenery which the
stagehands were dismantling. It was an experience I was determined to
reproduce at home and, as I stood there, I worked out how I could cut out
coloured pictures from magazines to reconstruct the rocky landscapes. It
still surprises me that, in view of my subsequent career in Italian opera,
my very first stage design was for a miniature *Die Walküre*. I had paper
trees, rocks and figures galore, and my aunt and uncle were so amazed that
they promptly gave my father a full report. I worked for hours and hours

with tremendous dedication. While most of the other children were out playing after school, I was buried in my own cardboard Ring of the Nibelungs.

The other centre of my life, besides the summers in the country, was school. I was restless and naughty, the teachers said that I talked too much and gave me very bad marks for conduct. I can see that I must have been rather a pest but I was smart enough, particularly in history, geography and art, to get by. My father insisted that I should also have private English lessons three times a week, one of the few truly beneficial things he did for me. As he did a lot of trading with a wool firm in Manchester and found difficulty in communicating with them, he got the idea that 'Franco must learn English to help write those letters to England one day'.

Later I came to understand that this was part of his plan that I would eventually inherit his business as if I were his legitimate heir. When I was old enough to realize this, however, it was too late; our differences were too marked. At the time, his interest in my education only served to upset his wife, Corinna. Though I was unaware of it then, she never accepted my role as the 'only son'. When she found out that my mother had died, she hoped that at last I would be sent to an orphanage or foster home. When she learned that my father's cousin had taken me in, she was furious and refused to speak to Lide again. It was then that she began coming to my school and following me home, calling me a bastard. It wasn't until Corinna died that I was allowed to see the inside of my father's house. My stepsister, Corinna's daughter Fanny, had insisted on meeting me when I was about ten or eleven. She came with my father on one of his regular Saturday visits and brought her baby with her. The unexpected appearance of three generations of my family, while well meant, was almost as disturbing as Corinna's little drama outside the school. Worse still, despite this show of family feeling, they had to impress upon me the need for absolute secrecy about the visit. In other words, I was allowed to know that I had a sister but must not tell anyone. The result was a further withdrawal on my part. No matter how many people were there to love me, there was never a direct link with anyone.

In some ways the most important male influence in those early years was Lide's lover, Gustavo, who was nearer to us than my father. Lide and I had to fall in with his life. Not only did he introduce me to opera, he inadvertently made me aware of the upheavals taking place in the world beyond the unchanging streets and squares of Florence. Fascism had been established in Italy following Mussolini's march on Rome in 1922, the year before I was born, but if our blustering leader had any influence on my young life I was not at first aware of it. At school we were obliged to wear the Fascists' black shirt and, though I remember little of it, the party line was parroted by our teachers. But young children can remain remarkably

14 aloof from the attentions of their elders, particularly when, like me, they have a fantasy world into which they escape. Not until 1935, when I was twelve, did I become aware of what was happening in the world. On 2 October of that year Italy invaded Ethiopia, and Gustavo, who was in the naval reserve, was mobilized and sent to Livorno. My aunt and I followed him. Here were revelations of the outside world: the docks, the warships, all the talk of war, Africa, and foreign sanctions. I understood little, but I did become aware that life was changing and that I was somehow growing up. The episode was merely a brief hiccup in our lives, however. By the following May, Ethiopia was conquered and, when the world did nothing, the crisis passed, the reserve was demobilized and we returned home.

When we got home, we expected the usual visit from Ersilia, but this time she did not come. She had died – peacefully, thank God – while we were away. Again, I had lost a mother. There would be no more village summers, no more of that old, immemorial Italy that was about to be swept away. Ersilia was part of feudal Tuscany, where the peasants virtually belonged to the *padrone* in the town. They would come in groups with baskets of produce or craftwork to visit the boss. They would sit in the kitchen or the servants' quarters and the lady of the house would graciously accept their gifts and ask about their children and relatives. It is almost impossible to believe that this was such a short time ago.

When I was thirteen and no longer a child, what little sense of belonging I had centred on the Church and around the Catholic Club. The Church was the counterbalance to the Fascist government's attempts to control our minds. In infant school we had been formed into a *Balilla,* the equivalent of the Hitler Youth; in middle school we became *Avanguardista* and later *Giovani Fascisti.* Some might have found the uniforms and the parades glamorous, but my friends and I were bored by the endless marches and speeches. We preferred the Catholic Club with football in the old cloisters and ping-pong, which I still love today. Our favourite activity was bicycle trips at weekends: I can remember the friars hitching up their *soutanes* and pedalling away with us to the hill villages along the Arno valley. In the summer we would go away for several days on trips as far afield as Siena and Arezzo. The Fascists seemed drab by comparison. I was further saved from their teachings by my father's bizarre image of England – to him a nation of worthy Manchester textile barons – which led him to oppose everything the Fascists said about our supposed enemy.

I served Mass with the other children and remember my first Holy Communion, though I more or less took it for granted. I reserved my passionate feelings for the other activity that the Catholic Club excelled in – plays. We were organized into a drama group, boys only at that time, and we put on little plays with historical or biblical themes in the various parish halls. As we improved we got more ambitious: at one of the annual

Maggio Musicale seasons in Florence we were so stunned by the great open-
air production of Rino Alessi's *Savonarola* in the Piazza della Signoria that
we decided we had to do our own version. I played Savonarola in our
performance in the refectory of the Convent of San Marco, a magnificent
setting. We were quite adventurous; we even put on *The Imposter* by Carlo
Goldoni. I think it was this drama group more than anything else that
determined the course my life was to take. My almost daily visit to the
cinema with Lide and Gustavo was also important. We saw everything and
anything, and I believed in absolutely all of it. I cannot remember the first
film I ever saw, but one of the earliest starred Rudolph Valentino – my
aunt and all our female acquaintances were mad about him. The stars were
central to our lives, and I knew the names of all the Hollywood 'greats'
along with the film gossip about their lives. I can recall someone we knew
changing her hairstyle so that she looked like Janet Gaynor, and my aunt
saying of someone else that she was trying to look like Wilma Banki.

I am still very vulnerable to cinema; even today I laugh and cry openly
and believe quite passionately in what is taking place on the screen. The
early horror movies were a great challenge, and I remember being terrified
throughout *The Phantom of the Opera*. Conversely, *Nosferatu* was too intellectual and I merely giggled. The worst effects were induced by Boris
Karloff and I woke up screaming for a fortnight after I had seen the
first Frankenstein film. One film in particular really upset me and stirred
emotions that have lasted to this day. This happened in 1931, not long
after my mother's death, which was why it proved so traumatic. The film
was *The Champ*, with Wallace Beery as the failed boxer trying to bring up
his son, played by Jackie Cooper, after his wife has left him. The story was
elementary and unashamedly sentimental. The mother returns, the boy is
pulled between them, the father attempts to make a comeback in the ring
and dies at the end of his big fight. The film was enough to make anyone
cry and, because of my history of emotional upheaval, it was a personal
assault course. It wasn't unusual for me to cry at films, but as my aunt
and Gustavo walked me home, I just couldn't stop. They were worried that
I was traumatized by what I'd experienced, and for a while a degree of film
censorship was applied.

Because of its hold over me, cinema-going was used as an effective
punishment for my not infrequent misbehaviour. If I behaved too badly,
I would be made to sit in the car with our fox terrier while Lide and Gustavo
went to the cinema without me. This was a terrible punishment and some
of my worst moments were spent sitting alone longing to know what was
happening inside the cinema. By the late 1930s, however, Fascist control of
film distribution and the predominance of propaganda films made the
cinema less interesting. Theatre became paramount to me, along with a
growing interest in art, fostered by Gustavo. An amateur painter as well as

16   a singer, he would come to collect me in his smock and beret, carrying his easel, to take me out to the countryside, where I would sit contentedly watching him paint. I think I knew from the start that he wasn't much good, but the fact that he used oils, then a seemingly wondrous skill, was enough to hold my interest.

Gustavo had dozens of art books and biographies of artists of different periods. In any case, the Renaissance was all around us. I remember that we had two chairs in the house that were called 'Savonarola' chairs, Renaissance-style folding chairs; and, when visitors came, Lide used to call out, '*Franco, prendi la Savonarola. Portala qua!*' (Franco, take the Savonarola. Bring it here!) So there in my mind was Savonarola going back and forth from one room to the next.

Savonarola had prayed in the San Marco cloisters where we played football and which Lorenzo il Magnifico often visited when this Dominican monastery was heavily supported by the Medici family. There were endless treasures to discover – the Michelozzo library, the works of Fra Bartolomeo and Fra Angelico – in a natural way, as part of daily life. Almost all the cells where the friars lived had been decorated by Fra Angelico. At the top of the steps, leading to the monastery, was the beautiful fresco of the Annunciation that had been greeting the friars for centuries as they made their way to and from their devotions.

The Dominican order has always had a noble tradition of art and culture, and most of the friars were highly cultivated men. There were artists amongst them and one in particular, Father Spinillo, was in charge of the youth association. He was a rather good painter and had turned the attic of the monastery into a studio. I learned more about painting from him in that studio than from anybody at school. Father Spinillo was often asked to decorate churches and by watching him I learned a lot about fresco technique.

Another great personality I had the opportunity to meet in those years was Pietro Annigoni. He had just painted a marvellous crucifixion on the wall of a room in the monastery, and I remember spying on him through peepholes in the walls. He really seemed the reincarnation of the old masters, as if he had inherited their genius. His drawings could easily have been mistaken for those of Leonardo or Michelangelo. I was in awe of his skill, even though the critics snubbed him as a shameless *passatista*. But I wondered what was so wrong in trying to draw as well as our greatest masters did.

Immense crowds gathered in those days at San Marco to hear the sermons of the prior, Father Raffaele Coiro. He was sombre and fierce, a modern Savonarola, except that Coiro was tall and attractive. He wore blue-tinted glasses and always seemed comfortable in the black and white robes of the Dominicans. He had a manly voice which rang round the packed church as he preached his midday Sunday sermons with carefully worded political messages which hinted at the world situation and caused considerable excitement. There were few doubts about what he was saying, and he helped many to resist the insidious propaganda of the government's spokesmen.

Another great man I came to know well in those years at San Marco was Professor Giorgio La Pira, who taught Roman law at the university. Professor La Pira was a layman who lived like a friar in one of the cells of the monastery; after the war he became mayor of Florence. He was a unique figure, an apostle of charity and faith who devoted his entire life to the cause of the poor and underprivileged. He and Father Coiro were, without doubt, the most convincing influences I had as a boy. Of course, they were not political figures; on the contrary, their purpose in life was devotional, to care for souls and to enlighten them. Yet the truth about social and political issues came to me through them, and their influence has lasted throughout my life.

The Florence that I knew was in essence the unchanged Florence of the Middle Ages, which was nearing its final days. It was a city which had resisted the worst excesses of modernization. It had preserved almost intact its character both as a medieval city and one which also embodied the splendours of the Renaissance. There were few cars, the streets were uncluttered, the shops were elegant, and the people dressed with taste and simplicity. The tourists had not yet come in droves, and those who did came for cultural reasons or to study.

The British had adopted Florence as their home and had no intention of leaving because of political squabbles. They even had a cemetery of their own – Il Cimitero degli Inglesi. It was originally built on a low hill just outside the city walls. Today that hill is nothing more than a small island which divides the traffic, but once you pass through the gates you find yourself in a remarkable garden of romantic memories, filled with tombs and splendid statuary of the period, with flowers everywhere and the whole place encircled by centuries-old cypress trees. Elizabeth Browning is buried in that island of peace amidst the horrors of today's congestion and traffic.

The British colony consisted of ageless ladies who dressed as if nothing had changed since the turn of the century. I remember vividly their arrival at certain hours, particularly at teatime. They came in pairs or in small groups, streaming down Via Tornabuoni from the Ponte Santa Trinita, or emerging from the narrow, dark medieval streets which surrounded the area. In spring and summer they caused a sensation with their white lace, cream and lilac colours, parasols and old-fashioned hats, at their meeting place, Doney's tea-room. They were the incarnation of D. H. Lawrence's *Twilight in Italy*.

While each one of them had a different history, a life of sadness or happiness, of wealth or poverty, they had all ended up in Florence, where

18   they could preserve an illusion of being or having been 'great ladies'. There
       was, however, nothing gentle or soft about them. They were excruciatingly
       snobbish. Although they adored Italy, they constantly made us aware that
       we Italians were unworthy of our country and had, whenever possible, to
       be shown a better way of behaving. Peasants would be upbraided for
       mistreating their animals and mothers scolded for failing to keep their
       children's noses wiped. We Florentines tolerated them because they were
       part of our city. But behind their backs we always called them the *scorpioni*.
           They were very taken with Mussolini and seemed to have a crush on him.
       I'm afraid these twittering spinsters were overwhelmed by his strong jaw
       and his 'macho' appeal. They were naturally appalled when he clashed with
       England in the mid-1930s. They couldn't accept the way Chamberlain or
       Eden reacted and felt that the British were very ill-advised about Fascist
       Italy: they should come and see for themselves before taking sides and
       acting like fools. For the moment the ladies went on sipping their tea and
       bossing the waiters and trying to pretend that it would all blow over.
           It was my father who found Mary O'Neill. She used to translate letters
       from England for him, and it led him to arrange for me to study with her
       three times a week. She lived in a small dark bedroom crammed with old
       furniture and memorabilia of all kinds. The whole place had a permanent
       smell of fried fish and onions because she lived frugally and cooked her
       meals there on a little spirit stove. Every inch of her walls was covered
       with portraits or prints of all kinds. On the dresser was a photograph of
       her father, a captain in the British army; next to it a statuette in biscuit-
       ware of William Shakespeare, and on the wall above them a colour print
       of Sargent's portrait of Ellen Terry as Lady Macbeth.
           The world of Mary O'Neill was a new world for me and I liked it very
       much. She must have given my father good reports because he was much
       kinder and much more attentive to me than usual, and occasionally he
       would tell me to take her flowers or cakes. I remember seeing him enter the
       tearoom at Doney's with Mary O'Neill on his arm, dressed like a queen.
       She looked lovely, like a Gainsborough, and I suspect that she must have
       been a great beauty in her youth. Her hair was very fine, more ash than
       blonde, parted in the middle, and she had pale blue eyes and pink cheeks.
       Yet for all her delicacy of appearance, there was no nonsense about her.
       She had an old clock in her room and would be cross with me if I didn't
       appear exactly at the appointed hour. Even a minute late would not be
       tolerated. That was my main problem with her; and even to this day it is
       almost impossible for me to be on time.
           I studied English with Mary O'Neill for about four years. I learned
       grammar and poetry, theatre and history; and when I knew the language
       well enough, I began studying Shakespeare's sonnets and plays. I kept
       agreeing with her that Shakespeare was a great poet, but asked how she

thought he compared to Dante. At that age one always likes to make comparisons. Was Verdi better than Puccini? Was Leonardo greater than Michelangelo? Mary O'Neill used to tell me that comparison are 'odorous', as Dogberry says in *Much Ado About Nothing*. I later learned how right she was.

She and I played the scenes from the great plays together. The balcony scene from Romeo and Juliet was her favourite. She must have played Juliet in school when she was a young girl and, when she recited those divine verses, she seemed to be in the grip of some kind of superhuman rapture. One could see then what a charming young lady she must have been, though I was constantly brought back to earth by the chattering of her false teeth. Occasionally her teeth would fall out during a passionate tirade, but she would quickly replace them with an expert twist of her hand.

Mary O'Neill passed on to me an abiding love of British culture, but with the passage of time the situation became progressively more dangerous for both of us. After the Sanctions of 1936, hatred of the British began to increase and by the end of the decade it was a terrifying national phobia that reached its peak when we linked our destiny with that of Hitler. Unfortunately there were too few in Italy who really understood what joining Hitler was going to mean for us. They thought he was a kind of shield. When Hitler's army had marched into Prague, I was riding on a streetcar and one passenger said proudly: 'We will be able to get anywhere with this man.' But I knew he was wrong; I knew it was not going to turn out that way from the first time I saw Hitler in 1937. He had come on a state visit to Venice, Florence, Naples and Rome to cement the alliance between Nazi Germany and Fascist Italy. All the children were trooped out and I had to get up at five o'clock in the morning to be positioned with our 'battalion' near the railway station. The whole city was covered with flags and incredibly lavish decorations. I glimpsed the two leaders through the blur of a bayonet as they were carried past in an open Mercedes convertible saluting the Roman way. I remember the brown uniform of Hitler and the grey-green uniform of Mussolini, both of them covered with medals.

At that young age I wasn't able to judge Mussolini's intellect or his values, but I knew that he was well loved. The Italians saw things happen that really pleased them, like the building of new roads. Despite the fact that the whole world was against us, we had our colonies, and there was a certain national pride again in being Italian. I preferred to be Florentine, to take pride in the art and civilization we had created all around us, rather than in some madcap African adventures.

It was obvious that some branch of the arts was going to claim me and Gustavo kept sending my father examples of my drawings and telling him

20   how talented I was. Between them they decided I should enrol in the Liceo
      Artistico (the high school for those intending to pursue higher studies in
      the arts) with a view to my eventually studying architecture. My enrolment
      there in October 1938 should have been the fulfilment of my every wish,
      but by now the political situation was so tense that it was impossible, even
      for a dreamy fifteen-year-old, to isolate myself from it. The first entry in a
      diary I kept at that time was written a few days before my sixteenth
      birthday, which, as it turned out, was five days before Italy took yet
      another step along the road to war. The diary entries below show the
      confused way that the heady events of the time were absorbed into my
      self-centred teenage world:

> *9 February 1939*: I didn't sleep well. I dreamt all night of the little white
> hand that we drew yesterday in our anatomy lesson*. I wasn't able to
> get it out of my mind. Instead of passing on to other things I insisted
> on drawing the little hand for the whole of the two hours. It was such a
> fine, delicate hand and Professor Fazzari had adjusted the fingers into
> a natural position as if they were about to pluck a flower or a butterfly.
> It really seemed, as my friend Strocchi said, like a hand by Raphael.
>
> What troubled yet fascinated me was that the hand finished at the
> wrist where it had been cut. Professor Fazzari, perhaps aware of the
> gruesome effect a cut hand would have on us, had placed it so that it
> came out from a piece of light blue cloth. But I was constantly aware of
> the missing arm, indeed of the entire body that was supposed to be
> behind the hand and wasn't there. I was aware of the woman – or of
> the girl – to whom that hand had belonged, a person who was alive only
> a few hours before. Her face, her voice, alas lost. As I was drawing, I
> wasn't thinking of anything else. My mind was elsewhere when Professor
> Fazzari told me to change subjects so I asked him to let me try the
> hand again. I tried and tried but I couldn't draw it. I was constantly
> getting the wrong proportions (and I have always been very good at
> drawing hands). It was as if I had gone back to elementary school. So
> the two hours went by wasting one sheet of paper after the other.
>
> Then we skipped physics and we went back to the park but my heart
> was filled with a melancholy for which I couldn't find a remedy. Last
> night I didn't do anything else but roll around in bed and today I did
> something rather absurd: I couldn't help doing it; I went to Regoli (a
> man employed at the academy who gets the pieces from the hospital
> for our anatomy lessons) and I asked him if that hand had been sent
> back to the hospital to be joined to the rest of the body. He didn't

      * It was the practice at that time for students at the Liceo Artistico to follow
      the Old Masters and study anatomy direct from cadavers brought from the city
      mortuary.

answer straightforwardly, he was never a very talkative man, but I understood that the hand went back and I decided to go to the morgue in via Alfani.

I wanted to see to what face and body that little hand had belonged. But in going there, I felt a deep sense of shame. I went to where the coffins were, five or six of them, most of them with old people. Few flowers, few relatives and friends around them. In one simple coffin in a corner there was the body of a little girl, all alone, except for a very small old woman who was there to keep her company for the last hours. It must have been her grandmother. Seeing me looking with wide eyes at her grand-daughter, she smiled at me and asked me if I knew her, knew her little girl. I nodded and said that, yes, I knew her very well. I couldn't take my eyes away from the hand that had now joined the other, both of them holding a little mother-of-pearl spray. The hand I had been trying to draw all the day before was now back with the other one.

Tonight I went to bed with my head full of gloomy and gruesome thoughts and feelings. I feel a great cold in my back so perhaps I have flu coming on. I wish I did, then tomorrow I wouldn't have to go to school. If Professor Fortini asks me something about mathematics there is going to be trouble because today I couldn't study anything. Luckily the day after tomorrow is a holiday – the 'Conciliation'.

10 February 1939: The Pope is dead! We were at architecture class in the morning. Instead of drawing, I had hidden my mathematics book on the table trying to study something at the last minute. Suddenly we heard a great noise coming from the street. 'Edizione Straordinaria!' 'Edizione Straordinaria!' We opened all the windows and we looked down into the street. The Professor sent Giunti down to buy the news-paper. In the meantime we had been asking the people in the street what happened and so we found out that the Pope was dead. Pius XI, dead.

When the paper arrived we got more details – the Pope had suddenly died overnight. There was great excitement and sadness and nobody went back to work. Then Giunti came back, saying with a funereal face that our lessons were suspended for national mourning. We will go back to school the day after tomorrow. It doesn't really make that much difference because tomorrow was going to be a holiday anyway and we said to one another how strange a coincidence that the Pope died on the anniversary of the Conciliation – just one more day and he would have died on the same date. As a matter of fact, to be truthful, we were a bit disappointed because we could have enjoyed an additional holiday if he had died some other time. But now I must put things down in order because what happened today I would like to remember well.

22   From school I went straight to San Marco with Carmelo and Alfredo to
say a prayer for the Pope. In the church there was great commotion,
Father Domenico was covering everything in sight with black material
and taking away flowers and candles and immediately he asked us to
give him a hand. We helped to place over the main altar the great
portrait of the Pope that usually hangs in the sacristy. Then Father
Spinillo appeared, looking pale and older, as if ten years had passed. He
just looked at us and then disappeared up the stairs leading to the
convent. As we finished our work we went to the cloister without
knowing what to do. At one moment we heard some voices in the
corridor. I heard distinctly one friar who said, 'I tell you they killed
him.' The others were objecting and he raised his voice even higher.
'They killed him, I know, I feel it.' Even Carmelo heard it. Both of us
went to the door to hear better. This apparently is the story, at least it
is the story that most of the friars seem convinced of. The Pope did not
approve of the alliance of Il Duce, Mussolini, with the Germans because
he couldn't forgive Hitler for the persecution of the Church in Germany.
So the Pope wanted to sever relations between the Vatican and our
government unless Mussolini did something to stop Hitler. Pius XI was
determined on denouncing the reconciliation with the Italian state and
he had chosen to do so exactly on the tenth anniversary of the
'Conciliation' made in 1929. Apparently he had already called dozens
of cardinals and bishops to Rome for a sort of emergency conclave and
had prepared a very important speech. Then it seems that the Fascists
killed him overnight with poison, just as they did at the time of the
Borgias (only this time it was the Pope who was dead and not the others).

This news left us very confused. The friars sounded very convincing
so after a while I went to knock at the cell of Father Coiro but he was
locked in there with a couple of other friars and they made us wait. We
tried to hear what they were saying but we couldn't make out anything
precise. Then the friars went out and after a while Father Coiro called
me. He said that he knew that I didn't understand anything now but
one day, with the help of God, my mind would open up. In other words,
I had to remember this date and that was all. It is the tenth of February
1939.

11 February 1939: The story of the death of the Pope is really very
strange and mysterious. This afternoon at the gym I even heard Raul
Ancona talking about it and he is a Jew and shouldn't be as concerned
about this story as us Catholics. But Raul and all the people in his
community are convinced that the Pope has really been killed by Hitler.
Mussolini had nothing to do with it. But Ancona is always on the side

always on the side of Mussolini: with him you can't even tell funny stories about the Fascists. Yet even though he is a Fascist, he becomes scarlet with fury when someone mentions the name Hitler.

My aunt took me to San Marco for a big ceremony for the Pope. Everybody was praying. The friars were all there with very pale and drawn faces. Father Coiro's sermon made a tremendous impact on the congregation. I have never heard his voice so sad and low and intense. Some of what he said hit me: we have to prepare ourselves for days full of sorrow and anguish, we must always be ready to put our life and our faith in the hands of God. My aunt was crying, she is convinced that there will be a war and according to her understanding of Father Coiro's sermon that is exactly what he wanted to tell us. Then there was a collective prayer for the soul of the Pope but I was constantly distracted and started to think again about the little hand at the anatomy lesson and about the face of the little girl I saw at the morgue. I did not dedicate my 'Requiem aeternam' to the memory of the Pope but to the soul of that girl. Tomorrow we go back to school and it is also my birthday.

Re-reading those pages I get a sense again of how confusing the times were, the feeling that something terrible was about to happen. That sense of dread seemed to permeate everything, from our private concerns to great public events. Certainly we all believed then that the Pope had been murdered, although nothing has ever come to light about it.

The year 1939 was certainly one of crisis. Fascist Italy was on the move, and the propaganda against England was building to a feverish pitch. Lessons were no longer important: students were herded through the streets of Florence to demonstrate against the 'pluto-Judaean-democracies' of the West. These mobs always ended up in the via Tornabuoni, where the British consulate and the British colony were located. Our national flag was carried aloft and there were Fascist insignia and posters of all kinds. There were endless denunciations of the British, the French and the Americans.

Oblivious to reality, the old British ladies still came out of Doney's and cheered our flags and emblems, waving their lace handkerchiefs as if blind to the nasty propaganda. One day they were pointed out by some demonstrators and were forced to join in the march. When they began to realize what it all meant they tried to get away, seeking refuge wherever they could. The demonstrations now turned ugly, with jeering and the hurling of insults. Once a group of English ladies was trapped in a corner and the situation got out of control, lace dresses were torn, parasols seized. I remember one of the students snatching a straw hat and wearing it through the streets as the demonstration went on its way. Suddenly the *scorpioni* had become *le nemiche,* the enemy.

24   I got caught up in one of the worst of the demonstrations in May 1939 and was pushed and jostled down street after street unable to free myself from the hysterical mob. Their wild eyes reminded me of my father's wife, Corinna, obsessed, mad, shouting abuse at me. Suddenly I saw a cordoned-off road where the police were sheltering the terrified British ladies, among them a pale, frightened Mary O'Neill. It was the last time I saw her.

The British held on for another year because Italy did not immediately declare war when Germany did, but their lives were intolerably difficult. Unlike the American ladies, whom they rather despised, the British were generally not too well off. The French, whom everyone wickedly assumed to be retired ladies of ill repute, were left alone after the collapse of France, so it was only the British, who had loved Florence best, who really suffered.

I remember 10 June 1940. I was riding my bicycle out in the country with Carmelo, who for years was my best friend at school. It was late in the afternoon and on our way back we stopped at a country village. There we heard over the radio that war had been declared. I raced home, very excited about it all, as if a new adventure was about to start. Lide was there, drawn and pale. When she saw the pleased expression on my face, she slapped me.

'Why did you do that?' I asked.

'You don't know what war is,' she said. 'I had hoped you would never know.'

She was right, of course. But a few days later the full force of what had become of my country, the land of Leonardo and Dante, was brought home to me when I heard that the British community had been given a matter of days to pack up and leave. Most of the old ladies had nowhere to go, no homes in England, no relatives ready to take them in. They did the only thing possible – nothing. They waited out the last days numbly expecting the worst. One day I went to the Via Tornabuoni and realized they were gone. The *scorpioni* who had been such a feature of our city had disappeared. They had been rounded up and taken to hill towns outside Florence, where schools and other buildings had been converted into prison camps. The eccentric spinsters who had so loved Mussolini had paid dearly for their naïvety, as would we all in the years ahead.

THREE

Partisans

To say baldly that great events are less important to us than our personal concerns sounds rather self-centred and petty, but most of us recognize that the opposite is only true of politicians and generals. The outbreak of war did not find me and my friends rushing about in uniform, headily scanning the newspapers for word of distant battles; rather, life went on pretty much as before though in an atmosphere of dull anticipation. Everything seemed to be going well for Mussolini and his ally, Hitler. France was occupied, England was surely being bombed into submission, or so they said, but one didn't have to to be a fortune-teller to sense that this might not last. Uppermost in my mind was the knowledge that I would soon be caught up in a maelstrom that would surely destroy a way of life I had barely glimpsed. Now in our third year at the Liceo Artistico, my friend Carmelo and I agreed that we had to see as much as possible of the old Italy before it disappeared forever. Our plan was to make a grand tour of the south, especially Puglia and Naples, and we made our families promise to let us go if we could pass the third and fourth year exams in one sitting. They agreed, thinking, I suspect, that we could not do it. But determination drove us and we succeeded. Now I would have an automatic scholarship waiting for me at the university and could spend the summer of 1941 in the south.

Lide and my father were worried. Things had changed a great deal since we first had the idea: the Russian campaign was not going well, bombing had started even in Italy, the situation was deteriorating rapidly and the euphoria of a quick triumph was fading. Carmelo and I didn't give a damn. He had a lot of trouble with his family, a typically tight-knit Sicilian family. His father was a colonel, an army doctor, and he warned us about the threat of an invasion and how serious it would be if we were caught in southern Italy and couldn't get home. But we had our bicycles prepared and we had organized in detail how much distance we would cover each day, what we would visit and where we would sleep. We had relatives or friends in certain cities and the Dominican friars had monasteries scattered all over Italy where we could have food and rooms for a night.

At that time there were no foreign tourists, and we were all alone on the

Zeffirelli

roads. We had little money, but the financial system had not yet collapsed and, even with wartime rationing, it was possible to get by for a few lire a day.

After visiting Tarquinia, Viterbo, Rome and the royal palace of Caserta, we arrived in Naples on the morning of 19 July 1941. I had pains in my stomach from something I'd eaten and wasn't at all well, but we were anxious to see Naples. We booked into the Hotel Turistico near the station, left our papers there and set off to explore the city. We headed south from the station towards Mount Vesuvius, unaware that the centre of the city was in the opposite direction and that we were leaving the city behind us. Although we cycled on and on, determined to get to the centre, we were in fact in the outskirts of the city. The road became rougher and by this time the pain in my stomach was becoming unbearable. Carmelo insisted we go to a chemist, who diagnosed food poisoning and told me to get to a bed as soon as possible. We found out then that we were going in the wrong direction, away from the city, but it was too late to go back.

We headed for a Dominican monastery on the slopes of Vesuvius which housed a popular shrine of the Virgin, the Madonna dell'Arco. The last stage of the journey nearly finished me, and the friars gave me a mammoth dose of aspirin and put me to bed in one of their cells, where I immediately passed out. I woke in the middle of the night with a raging fever, perspiring heavily, and suddenly saw something unbelievable through the window. First an orange sky, then a red sky. I thought I was delirious until I heard voices and saw the friars silhouetted on the terrace overlooking the valley. I knew it couldn't be sunset, so I got out of bed wrapped myself in a blanket and joined the others on the balcony. It was like a nightmare. Then, all at once, I realized that Naples was under attack, that flares were being thrown over the entire Bay of Naples as the British prepared for a bombing raid. I had never seen anything like it. I could take in the whole gulf, the sea jet black, and the coast and city bathed in this brilliant orange light.

The friars were like birds, flapping their white gowns as they ran along the vast terrace or kneeled to pray to their miraculous Madonna. Something terrible was about to happen. The peasants from the village had rushed into the church to pray and light candles as if the apocalypse was nigh.

I was still running a fever with a temperature of over 100°F so I don't think I fully understood it all, I asked Carmelo what was happening. 'They think they will bomb Naples,' he said.

But I couldn't hear any noise; there was only the lurid glow of the silent flares. Then there was a slow, rumbling, increasingly menacing roar as countless bombers flew over in waves. This was followed by the shattering thunder of their bombs, anti-aircraft fire – an unbelievable noise and sight – and fire bursting out everywhere, a vision of hell. I passed out and someone carried me back to my bed.

When I woke the next morning I felt well again. I opened the window on to the balcony, but I couldn't see anything. The whole gulf of Naples was covered by an immense blanket of smoke and dust from which only the peak of Vesuvius emerged. Carmelo and I decided to leave the monastery to see what had happened. Throughout the war we would see many much worse sights, but it is terrifying to experience these things for the first time, especially in the midst of what was supposed to be a journey for pleasure. Our peaceful dream of beautiful cathedrals, churches and villages was shattered. There were ambulances everywhere, gruesome, dismembered bodies, and demented relatives trying to find missing people. We saw the remains of children who had been blasted to pieces, people with bleeding hands digging in the rubble, searching for relatives and friends. I remember someone pulling at an arm stuck in the rubble and a voice crying from below.

We tried to get back to the station and to our hotel to collect our documents but all the roads and streets were blocked. We had to leave our bicycles and make our way on foot over mountains of rubble. As we approached the central station we slowly realized that our hotel had been destroyed, the whole building completely flattened. Not merely were our documents lost, but all 122 guests, who had sought refuge in the hotel's cellars, were dead. We realized that we would have been killed too had my illness not forced us to stay overnight at the monastery. We felt that the Madonna dell'Arco had worked another miracle. Hardly able to speak, we went back to our bicycles and set off from Naples, heading south away from the destruction. The sheer effort of pedalling helped to clear our minds. We passed Vesuvius again and set off across the peninsula towards Amalfi. When you are young, it is easier to look forward, to put even the horrors of war behind you. It was a beautiful July day, the sea was shimmering and magical. We turned a corner and suddenly saw the village of Positano below us bathed in the rose-orange light of the sunset. I had never seen anything so lovely, a vision of peace after the night before. We coasted down the narrow streets of this totally unspoilt, perfect little fishing village. Most of the peasants were still wearing their colourful traditional costumes and living as they had for thousands of years. There were no strangers there, no tourists; the only outsiders were Carmelo and me. We remained on that incredible coast for a week, eating fish, fruit and vegetables, everything fresh and wholesome, as if somehow we had been transported into the Garden of Eden. We stayed with the family of a fisherman and forgot our journey. We swam in the deep blue sea and lazed on the rocks, selfishly determined to enjoy what we saw as the last days of peace in our life.

We had forgotten our families, who were terribly worried. The last postcards they had received had been sent on 19 July, just before the bombing of Naples, and carried on the last train to reach Florence. After that nothing got through, because communications between north and south were cut. Our families knew we were in Naples when the raid occurred, but they had no word of our survival as the postcards we sent from Sorrento and Positano never reached them. Over 3,000 people had been killed during the attack on the Bay of Naples, the whole of Italy was in mourning, and they received no word from us. Oblivious to all this, we made our way from Positano to Amalfi, on to Salerno, then to Eboli and beyond, towards that part of Italy which is little known, the region of magnificent monasteries and ancient, Spanish-looking towns.

It was in one of those towns that the family of our teacher Father Spinillo lived. He happened to be there visiting his relatives, and when he saw us he looked as if he had seen two ghosts. From him we learned that our family and friends in Florence thought we had been killed in the bombing. Father Spinillo insisted we telephone home, an event of high emotion which predictably resulted in our families insisting that we return immediately. Father Spinillo calmed them down and convinced them that it would be all right for us to continue as planned. We would, he said, be away from main ports and industrial areas, and therefore safe from bombing raids.

While on our way to Puglia we were stopped by a patrol and, when we were unable to produce any documents, we were arrested and kept in prison for three days. When they discovered that Carmelo's father was a colonel in the army, they released us, and we reluctantly decided it was really time to head back north along the Adriatic Coast. As we neared home, we began to speculate about what was in store for us and to realize that the war would not end as quickly as we had thought. Fairly soon we would have to make a major decision: to join the army or face being conscripted.

When we arrived in Florence in the middle of September we were allowed to start at the university, but things there were very insecure. All of Italy's institutions were crumbling, and with many of the faculty away in the army, the situation quickly became worse. I remember something that startled me that term: many of our friends like Raul Ancona were not there with us. We kept asking: 'What happened to Ancona? What happened to Levi? Why are they not here?' Eventually we realized that all the missing students were Jews and, though there were a lot of whispers, nobody gave us a direct answer.

I was beginning to change profoundly in those first months at the university of Florence. I had discovered Italy during my travels with Carmelo and had learned what it was like to be away from home. Now I was beginning to have a clear idea of what was going on in the world. I listened secretly to the broadcasts from London and by Radio Free Europe. We were all faithful listeners. Though the Fascists tried in every way to censor the broadcasts, we heard the famous Churchill speeches over the BBC and

I translated them for my friends. It was now that I started to think seriously about what I was going to do with my immediate future. Slowly, through the Church, we came to realize that what the Fascists were telling us bore no relation to what was actually happening. We all began to sense that Italy was on the edge of total disaster. I was almost nineteen and ripe to become one of the 'slaughtered generation', as we called ourselves. Most of us didn't want to fight a war that was already lost, to fight for ideals that none of us believed in.

As a student I had been able to avoid conscription, but now the time was approaching when deferments of any kind would not be permitted. Gradually we heard about our Jewish friends like Raul Ancona, who had fled to Switzerland, and we agonized over the case of a nobleman's son who had been hidden in a secret room in the family palace in Florence until the Fascists found and killed him. We knew we had to make plans for the moment when we would be forced to join the army. Should we hide in the mountains? Could we escape to Switzerland? Could one pretend to be a friar? But even young novices were being sent to the front.

We lived from day to day until, on 18 July 1943, the Allies landed in Sicily. Mussolini was overthrown a week later, on 25 July, but the illusion of freedom and democracy lasted for only forty days. The Italians should have immediately opened their arms to the Allies once Mussolini fell and before the Germans had a chance to reorganize. Instead our generals and the King tried to outsmart the Allies by asking for certain conditions before surrendering. They wanted to be recognized as a sovereign power, which of course the Americans and the British would not hear of. By this time the Germans had pulled together their scattered divisions and invaded Italy. The King fled and the Italian army made a vain attempt at fighting back, but the Germans slaughtered tens of thousands of our best people.

It was then that the Italian Resistance started. The Americans and the English had both been shockingly slow to take advantage of the situation. Had they moved quickly, they could have conquered Italy without blood-shed. Instead, they stubbornly adhered to a plan which cost them hundreds of thousands of lives, prolonged our anguish in Italy for two more years, and virtually destroyed us. Allied Generals Mark Clark and Harold Alexander could have shortened the war had they landed at Anzio then, instead of in January 1944.

I remember seeing the line of German tanks in my Piazza San Marco when they rumbled back into Florence on 11 September. The tanks were positioned right in front of the church of the monastery of Beato Angelico. From that moment on, for me and for my circle of friends at the university, the Germans were our enemies and the Allies our friends. But at that point all young people were ordered to join the Fascist army. We were given five days to show up, and if we didn't, we were to be shot.

Zeffirelli

My best friends Alfredo and Carmelo had already been conscripted and I talked for hours with my closest remaining friend, Aristo Ciruzzi, about the situation. At the time the partisan movement was very disorganized and we knew little about it, but I liked the idea of living freely in the mountains. At the same time, to join the partisans would be a clear political choice.

We made our decision. Putting it into effect was almost comically simple. A bus took us to a small village in the foothills north of Florence. Then, travelling mainly on side roads, we went higher and higher into the hills. At first we were greeted by peasants who did not speak much, but who indicated with gestures where it was we were supposed to go. We reached the forest area and were met by a foot patrol who had already received a signal that we were coming. There were about five or six of us: Aristo, me and three or four other students. One of them did not stay with us for long; he cried much of the time and made us feel depressed and scared. We travelled on without him.

Eventually we reached a clearing where we were welcomed in a cursory way, given a tent, some bedding, and a few tools, and told to get some rest. They were blunt with us and not particularly kind, which surprised me. I suppose I hadn't fully appreciated that we were in the midst of a dangerous war. It was also not clear to me that most of them were there for reasons rather different from mine. Most of the early partisans were members of the outlawed Communist party, and they despised those whom they saw as latecomers to the cause. There was one exception, however – a man whom everyone called Potente or 'powerful'. He was clearly the overall commander, but, unlike the others, he was pleasant and softly spoken. Although he was not especially tall, his blond hair and grey eyes made him stand out from the test. He was only in his early thirties, but he was already a legend. His real name was Aligi Barducci; he had been born in Florence of a working family and had done quite well as a student of accountancy, but in 1939 he'd been drafted in the Fascist Green Berets and had distinguished himself fighting on the Yugoslav border. The German invasion found him in Santa Marinella, just north of Rome, where he refused to surrender. After a shoot-out with the enemy, he was obliged to take to the hills and was soon a leading figure in the underground. At some point he transferred his allegiance from Fascism to Communism, but in truth patriotism was his main impulse. The partisans were organized into what were called Garibaldi Divisions, the red shirts of the original Garibaldini being thought appropriate by the Communists. Potente led the division named after a victim of the Fascists in the 1920s, Lancillotto Ballerini, and it was this group which I had met up with.

The leaders began to question us about our politics views. They wanted to know what kind of people we were and what political views we held. I told them about the friars, about Father Coiro and Professor La Pira, but this only made them more suspicious. It was ironic that I had joined the partisans to avoid the Nazis only to find myself among Stalinists.

Shortly after we arrived, we met a number of British and American prisoners who had escaped from German camps and had settled with us in the mountains. Because I knew English, the partisan leaders sent them to live in our quarters yet, astonishingly, we were ordered not to fraternize with them. Our Communist leaders, with the exception of Potente, mistrusted our allies as much as our enemies. Naturally, I did everything I could to show the escaped prisoners my gratitude and solidarity.

Living conditions in the mountains were extremely arduous. We were based, overlooking Florence, on the Monte Morello (the dark mountain), so-called because it is covered in pines. When they could, our families sent food and warm clothes for the winter months, which my friends and I shared with the boys from Britain and America. They seemed to us like heroes.

The Germans tolerated the partisans in that area as long as we didn't create trouble. They had enough problems to deal with without worrying about us, and they only did so when they were forced to. One day we made the mistake of attracting their attention. My group was in one of the first tents, hidden in the forest. I was there with two American pilots who had just escaped from a prisoner-of-war camp. It was a beautiful Saturday afternoon in November, and we were polishing our weapons and had started a cooking fire. Suddenly, down in the valley, we caught sight of two German soldiers. They had their coats over their shoulders and it was obvious that they had no weapons, or for that matter anything else with them. They must have decided to spend the day exploring the Italian countryside, and they were laughing, quite oblivious of any danger. We hid behind our tent and the two Americans with us took up their rifles.

I can still remember the smiling faces of those two young Germans as they moved closer to us. When they saw us, instead of heading back, they kept walking forward, pretending they had seen nothing, perhaps hoping that ours was the only tent and that they had stumbled upon a small, isolated group. Within minutes they realized their mistake, the alarm went up and dozens of other partisans rushed towards them. Too late, the Germans turned and began to run down the hill. Shots rang out and they fell, killed instantly.

For a long time I stayed where I was, stunned by my first direct experience of war. By the time I went to see what was happening, a silent group was digging a grave, trying to act as if taking two lives had no meaning. I knew the partisans felt that they had to kill those boys because they would have told their officers where we were. But I couldn't forget those smiling faces and I started to cry. I wanted to leave, but where could I go?

32   The day after the killing a priest from a nearby village walked up the mountain and found us, asking if we knew where the soldiers were.

'The Germans came to me', he said, 'hoping that the two soldiers are still alive, being held prisoner by you.'

One of the older leaders played the innocent and said that we hadn't seen anyone, we knew nothing.

The priest looked uncertain. 'I hate to go back to the Germans', he said, 'and tell them that I haven't found their boys. I promised I would find them and bring them back. They wanted to come themselves right away and burn the whole forest, but I told them that there are many peasant homes in the area, that it would be better to avoid a confrontation.'

When the priest left we hastily packed everything. There were about eighty or ninety of us, and that night we dispersed in small groups and climbed higher to the next chain of mountains. When we stopped we were ordered to burn all the documents we had that might be useful to the enemy in case we were either captured or killed. At first I refused to give up the photographs of my family, my mother, of Lide and of myself as a child, and pictures which Carmelo and I had taken during our bicycle tour. I walked away from the group and looked down at the ancient forest below. Finally, after standing there for a long time, I accepted the fact that the orders were sensible; but, when I set a match to the photos, it was as if my whole life was going up in flames. There was a light wind coming up from the valley and before I knew what had happened I saw sparks in the forest among the trees. It was a very dry November and there had been no rain for weeks; the first sparks caught swiftly. My desperate attempts to stamp out the fire were useless; within seconds the forest around me was ablaze. I had set fire to Monte Morello.

Our new destination took us into the mountains north-east of Florence, near the source of the Arno. On our way we had to cross the major highway that connects Florence to Bologna, Milan and Germany, the main route for the German army and its supplies. Because we had two Americans, one Englishman and seven Poles, our group was called the 'Foreign Legion'.

The Poles had run away from a forced labour camp in the valley. They arrived with two horses they'd stolen, which gave them the air of adventurers from another century. They were certainly a romantic group, full of high spirits, very attractive and dashing. When they first joined us, they seemed to be well kitted out with roll-necked sweaters under their work jackets, yet they were all shivering with cold. They knew little English so, since I spoke French, I asked them what the matter was; after all, it was surely far colder in their native Poland. In answer they opened their jackets and showed how the woollen sweater was just a collar and front panel, and in effect they were naked underneath. This cruelty of the Germans was quite refined; to the Italian peasants the Polish prisoners who were marched through their villages looked better equipped than they, yet the truth was that the poor men were dying of exposure. No wonder the Poles hated the Germans more than any of us. When they attacked a German patrol they did so in a frenzy of hatred. They would scream out 'son of a whore' in Polish as they hacked their victims to death. My principal friend in the group was called Zbigniek. His French was better than that of the others, so we could converse more easily. They were incredibly useful in the hills because they knew which roots and berries were edible, but they had the classic weakness of their people – a love of wine with no head for it. Two of them managed to get into a village where they got blind drunk and were shot while staggering along the main street singing to their heart's content. Another slept with a peasant girl and was killed by her brothers. The Poles were uncontrollable, but they were also immensely brave. By the end of the war only Zbigniek survived. I kept some of their identity documents and after the war I sent them to General Anders, the leader of the Polish government in exile, with an account of their heroism. I remained friends with Zbigniek for a while, though he eventually moved on. Then, much later, I met some Poles in Rome who had known him and claimed that he had been a German spy. I found this unbelievable, yet, strangely, he was the only one of them who had not died. Inevitably, this soured my memories of those brave young fools.

I prefer to remember our 'Foreign Legion' as we were then, just after sunset, waiting to cross the highway between Florence and Bologna. Our foreign legion was the last to cross and as we were about to move, we saw a Mercedes convertible approaching from the direction of Florence. The top was down and riding in it were four high-ranking German officers completely unaware of any danger. We were watching them pass in complete silence but the Poles, who hated the Germans so much, could not resist the opportunity. One of them jumped out screaming like a madman. He clutched a grenade and threw it, then another and another, most of which landed in the open Mercedes. The rest of his compatriots came out of hiding and ran towards the car, shouting in Polish, excited and bloodthirsty. There was a tremendous explosion and the Mercedes showered blood and tumbled on its side, its wheels spinning. The Poles crawled over the carnage, grabbing at the German weapons like vultures. What they didn't know was that a few hundred yards away a full German battalion was coming up behind them. Two motorcyclists were the first to appear, followed by a line of trucks. We were on the other side of the road but still vulnerable, and there was nothing to do but carry on. Without orders, we all began to fire our weapons. Several Germans fell to the ground, but I couldn't tell if I killed any of them. Fortunately for us the light was fading and before the Germans could gather their strength and work out how to

34   deal with us, it was dark enough for us to get away. We scattered with the Germans firing after us, though they must have realized that it was pointless to follow us into the hills. We escaped, but – alas – others were punished. We survivors have had to live with the knowledge that the Germans shot 280 innocent people in revenge for our pointless action. They were mostly peasants, though even the priest who had come to enquire about the two missing German soldiers was not spared.

From then on our aim was simply survival. At the same time the partisan movement was growing ever stronger. By winter 1943 hundreds of thousands of deserters and patriots of all kinds were looking for an escape route and many of them joined us. I remember Christmas that year when several hundred of us were up in the mountains with the peasants. We shivered and starved but we survived. Many of the new recruits proudly wore the 'red star' on their berets, but our group refused and were treated like outcasts. When we decided to build a Franciscan crèche at Christmas in a poor peasant's stable, some of the Communists started to make trouble. The old peasant in whose house we were stood up for us, taking his gun in his hands. He was an uneducated, inarticulate man, but he made himself understood and told the troublemakers to clear out and leave us alone.

In the first weeks of the New Year there was another terrible episode, perhaps worse than any of the others. Late one night the alarm was raised and we had to withdraw quickly. Those of us who were old-timers knew exactly what to do and how to get away, but many newcomers weren't as skilful. We knew how to put out the lamps and duck into the bushes. We shouted at them to come with us, to leave their weapons and their belongings, but a number of them panicked and froze on the spot. The Germans rounded them up.

The next morning we came back to the hills above the village in small groups. I remember the most gruesome sight I have ever seen. Looking down into the village, I saw the small main street lined with trees and on each of the naked branches there was a boy who had been hanged with barbed wire. The families had gathered, and I could hear their moaning and wailing. I counted nineteen bodies. Nothing I have ever seen has made such an impression on me. Later, in my work, I have often turned to the Old Masters for images that I have interpreted in films and plays, but when I made *Jesus of Nazareth,* the crucifixion was based on the horrors of that morning – a mother prostrate on the ground keening for her dead son hung Christ-like on the branches, with German soldiers marching back and forth like centurions.

When it seemed safe we crept down to the village. One of the young Poles with me started to pray, then to cry. I had to hold him and to put my hand over his mouth because his sobs were echoing everywhere. No doubt he remembered what the Germans had done in his own country, mixed with the knowledge that each of us could have been one of those boys.

By Easter 1944 the Americans and British were sending us food and weapons, dropping them from the air, and there was little the Germans could do about it. But on Easter Saturday we were roused at four o'clock in the morning by the sound of shots in the valley. We looked down and saw fire and smoke, but, when a reconnaissance patrol went to find out what was happening, there were shots from the opposite direction.

The Germans had sent two divisions to encircle the entire area that extended northwards to Bologna from the mountains north of Florence. They had decided to wipe us out completely, once and for all. German ss troops were everywhere, burning and destroying everything in their path. Whole villages were levelled. They burned the houses of families who had been giving us food. Other women who had been helping us were dragged from their beds and shot while flame-throwers started fire after fire. The Germans were trying to concentrate us in one area where they could surround us. We had become too strong and our formations were much closer to each other than ever before, each group only a few miles from the next. There were partisan brigades stretching as far as Bologna, all the way to what was called the 'Brigate Romagnole'. We were proud of this and believed ourselves to be a real army, but in reality there were no true military leaders among us. Most were political leaders, and few had any substantial military training. It wasn't until much later, when the war moved north, that military officers joined us.

We reverted to our former strategy. We were ordered to split up into small groups and reassemble in areas outside the ring that the Germans were tightening around us. It proved to be a wise move. Our group descended into the valley, each knowing that the Germans wouldn't keep any prisoners. We hid in a ditch just below where they had parked their trucks and waited. At one point a peasant boy saw us, but he was frightened and ran away. We worried whether he would report us, but by a miracle he returned at night with an old man who was his grandfather. They sat with us and the old man, sad and grave, told us that one of his sons had been killed in the war and that another was missing somewhere in the south, God only knew where. He had brought some bread with him which we devoured greedily. He came back again the next night, this time with a lamb. 'This is for you,' he said. 'I trust someone has done the same for my son.'

Although we were hungry, the lamb seemed so gentle and was white all over without a single blemish. Yet we knew he had to be killed if we were to survive. We drew lots; luckily the miserable task of ending the lamb's life did not fall to me, but I have never eaten lamb since then.

We remained hidden in that ditch for two more days. The Germans were still moving up the mountain and we could see them at night when we could leave our hide-out. The mountains above us were all in flames: the Germans were burning everything in their path as they advanced. They were sure that they were going to get all of us, but when they reached the top of the mountain, they found we had gone. While searching, they had destroyed every house and every person in their path – totally innocent families had been wiped out.

The next night we crossed the road one by one, jumping from one ditch to another until we found ourselves on the far side of a forest. Suddenly, I found that night that I could 'see' in total darkness. When forced to, we can sometimes discover dormant skills: I was able to avoid the trunk of an enormous tree as I approached it; I simply 'knew' it was there and I told the others to follow me. I led them throughout the night until, with the dawn, we came to a group of peasant homes. Somehow I felt I knew the houses ahead of us with smoke rising from their chimneys. Here was the greatest miracle: we were in Borselli, and this was Ersilia's house, the home of my idyllic summers in what now seemed like the distant past. We went behind the house to a grotto, where I knew the straw was kept. My friends were amazed at this turn of events, and ecstatic to find themselves in a safe place. There was a momentary scare when we heard footsteps and someone opened the gate. I looked up and saw that it was my 'brother' Guido, Ersilia's son. He was exactly my age and was hiding from the army too. At first he didn't recognize me and tried to run away, but I called out, 'It's me, Franco. It's me. Really!' He looked as if he were about to faint – we hadn't seen each other for years – but slowly, hilariously, the impossible truth dawned on him and we fell into each other's arms.

Guido gave us valuable information, gleaned from the peasants, about what the Germans were doing. Naturally the Fascist radio announced that their mission had been a complete success and that the 'bandits' (which is what they called us) had been totally eliminated. We knew that we should break up into even smaller units and go our separate ways to new areas. Some of us were sent to a new meeting-place in Pratomagno, south-east of Florence, where the Tuscan brigade had its central headquarters.

Here we were joined again by Potente. He was now trying to instil some order into the scattered Garibaldi Divisions. His aim was that the Italian partisan movement should be sufficiently organized to play a significant part in overthrowing the Germans, and thus the Allies would have to recognize the Italians as equals instead of as a defeated enemy.

How different from other Communists he was, tolerant and under-standing. He was very much a realist, who must have seen that the Allies and Russians would divide the world between them and that Italy would be given to the Western camp. I once heard him say: 'We are not yet the strongest force in Italy but we can become the strongest force if only we don't scare the Italians.' Whatever his politics, Potente was a great fighter who had the sense to respect his fellow partisans whatever their views. I can still remember how he rebuked the others for not giving more attention to the Polish, English and American prisoners-of-war, and said that we must rebuild the world 'together'.

In May 1944, Potente began to arrange missions inside Florence itself. I was instructed to join my family in the country, wait for a few days, and then go to the centre of the city on 5 June to meet secretly with the heads of the Comitato di Liberazione Nazionale. It was sad to leave the few Poles left and my other friends, but at least they had Potente's protection, and I would see my family again.

Late one afternoon towards the end of the month, I left the camp and made my way to the River Arno, near Reggello. As I walked along a little stray mongrel began to follow me. I decided to call him Mussolini. Mussolini and I kept to the dirt paths away from the main roads, but when we got to the river there was no way to cross without using one of the public foot bridges, I arrived at the bridge dressed in my usual rags with this stray dog beside me, and I saw that German soldiers were keeping watch on both sides. There was no point in hesitating, so I walked straight ahead, and with all the courage I could muster, I took out half a cigarette and asked one of the Germans if he had a match. He was a young, thick-set blond boy. He looked closely at me and at the dog – then reached for a match. I knew he was studying me, but I tried not to show any fear. Slowly he made up his mind: this scruffy boy with his little dog could not be a dangerous partisan. He even handed me two cigarettes before I crossed the bridge. As I was crossing with 'Mussolini' at my heels, he shouted to his colleagues on the other side to let me pass. The soldier at the far end of the bridge gave me a big smile and bent down to pat the dog. Again I found it hard to believe that I was face to face with an enemy, both boys seemed so friendly, so open.

'What's the name of your dog?' the soldier asked in Italian.

'Mussolini,' I said, then froze as I realized what I'd said. There was an uncomfortable pause as I shuffled from foot to foot. Suddenly, he started to laugh, calling out to his friend at the other end of the bridge to share the joke. I hurried away as soon as I could.

Once over the bridge I kept to minor roads again until I reached the country house in Lucolena where my father, my stepsister Fanny and her son had moved. It was a happy reunion, with hours and hours of talk. I had my first hot bath and my first change of clothes for at least six months. Except for the occasional icy rivers and streams that we had had to cross, there had been few places to bathe in the mountains. I had discovered that after a certain point you don't really smell too bad because the body's acids 'eat up' any odour. There is a kind of animal smell, but not the stench you might imagine. I never enjoyed a bath so much in my entire life as I did that night. I had to shave all the hair from my body, because I was infested with all kinds of parasites. I told Fanny not to touch my clothes, but to burn them instantly.

Mussolini stayed with us and we both settled into the comforts of home. A week later orders came for me to go to Florence. A friend from the Comitato di Liberazione Nazionale, headed by Count Medici-Tornaquinci, got word to me to leave Lucolena and make contact with the partisans in the city. When I met them I was ordered to infiltrate a new company called the Compagnia della Morte – the 'Death Company' – the Fascists' last attempt to fight alongside the Germans. The government had made a desperate appeal for all young people to enlist and to help save the country from the Allied advance, in order to hold off the invasion until the Germans could develop a new weapon we had heard about – a super weapon, the atomic bomb. We all hoped this last throw of the dice was impossible because the final collapse was coming. The Monte Cassino front had collapsed and the Germans had withdrawn, leaving the Allied troops to swarm into Rome. Then the Anzio front had collapsed too. In any case, most of us were ready for total liberation. Yet the Fascists still clung to the vain hope that this new weapon which the Germans were developing would rescue them at the eleventh hour.

At the Fascist headquarters I was given fifteen days to report to the Compagnia della Morte in Florence. I was allowed to return home and was promised that, when I came back, no questions would be asked. They needed young people so much they didn't care what you had done before or what suddenly made you join them. When the day came, I hitched a ride on one of the vegetable trucks going to the city. The driver picked up several of us and we talked about the latest events quite freely because everybody thought that Rome had been liberated. Our van made a brief stop in Strada, a pleasant town in Chianti, where a hunchback asked the driver for a lift. He hopped in and sat in the back with us and we went on talking, bursting with excitement at the liberation of Rome. The hunchback sat quietly, never saying a word during the entire journey.

The next morning, I presented myself at the Fascist headquarters, housed in an old palace in the centre of town. I was talking with some of the other boys in the line when, suddenly, somebody called me. I turned around and there in front of me was the hunchback. He looked at me and asked me if I had ridden on that truck from Strada to Florence. I didn't dare say no; I felt trapped. My instructions were to avoid any incidents or disturbance and to admit things rather than try to run away. This obviously put me in a difficult position.

'Yes, I was there. Why?'

'You sounded rather pro-British and pro-American.' he said. 'To say the least.'

'How can you say that?' I asked. 'Would I be here if I weren't a Fascist?'
But he remembered every word that had been said and quoted me exactly. I told him that he must have me mixed up with someone else. He called one of the Fascists over and for a split second I looked towards the exit. I thought about running but saw that I would have been caught instantly; running away would have confirmed my guilt. So, again, I told him that he had it all wrong, that I was not the person he was talking about. He called a second Fascist over and then a third. They grabbed me and took me into one of the offices. Everyone was packing, getting ready to move out. They wanted to gather the last few recruits and head north. The clerks and secretaries were dirty and unshaven, and on the brink of physical collapse. After a long wait, a young man in a black shirt came into the room. He looked about four or five years older than I, with an air of authority and cold, steel-grey eyes. He began to question me.

'What have you done until now?' the young man asked. 'And why didn't you report a year ago when you were called up? There is a death penalty for anyone who didn't answer the call.'

I said that I had had a nervous breakdown.

In response I was slapped across the face.

'Where do you live?' asked the second officer.

'I lived hidden in the country,' I answered. 'But now I feel better and feel that my duty is to help my country.'

There was another unshaven Fascist standing behind him.

'Don't believe him,' he said. 'He's a pretty good actor. I've seen him. 'Didn't you work with an acting company?'

I nodded my head glumly, aware that any talent I might have shown was now going to work against me.

'I remember you,' the second Fascist said. 'Now you try to fool us with this role of the confused boy who couldn't make up his mind.'

'But it's true,' I said. 'There *has* been so much confusion in all of our minds, in my mind, and it made me ill. Now I have seen what the so-called liberators are doing. After Monte Cassino there can't be any doubt.'

I was banking on their emotional reaction to the Allied destruction of the monastery at Monte Cassino and I almost managed to strike a chord. But then the hunchback came into the room and told them exactly what he had heard on the truck. He said that he had witnesses, that he would go and get them. But the Fascists told him it wasn't necessary; they were convinced that I was lying and the younger of them moved closer to me. He ordered me to pull down my trousers. I did so. He pointed his gun at my genitals. I felt the cold metal.

'You're a spy,' he said, 'and that means the Villa Triste. You know what I mean?'

I knew exactly what he meant. The Villa Triste was the grim nickname for a once pleasant house in the hills above Florence where the Italian ss had established their headquarters. No one came back alive from there.

A clerk joined us with paper and pencil.

'What's your name?'

I told him, but that only made him more irritated.

'What's your father's name?'

'Ottorino Corsi,' I said.

At that point the most senior of the young Fascists intervened. He asked me to repeat my father's name and, when I did so, he looked troubled. He told the others to do nothing, that he was going out, but would be back shortly.

While he was gone, the clerk took down the details of my story and then I was locked in a small room. I had no idea what was to become of me, but I doubted it would be pleasant. I had almost given up hope when the door opened and the young Fascist returned, surprisingly accompanied by my father.

'Yes, that's him,' my father said. 'He's a half-wit, he doesn't know what he's doing most of the time.'

'He ought to go to the Villa Triste for interrogation,' the young man insisted in a low voice. 'He could have been sent here by the partisans.'

My father laughed heartily and protested that this was impossible, I was simply too stupid to be involved in anything of the kind. The young Fascist weighed it all up, looking from me to him as if trying to find some hidden answer. Then he made his decision. I would be spared the Villa Triste, which meant certain death, but would be sent to the Organizzazione Todt, the slave labour force run by the German army. It was likely that I would be transported to Germany and that I might never return, but at least I would have some chance of survival.

My father grasped the young man's hand and kissed his cheek.

'I'm only doing this for you,' the young Fascist said gravely. Turning to me, his eyes narrowed with anger and hatred, he added, 'You are a disgrace and I don't expect to see you again.'

'Thank you. Thank you,' my father said. 'If there's anything you ever want, call me.' Then he kissed his hand again.

Father left, but I had to wait to be given a work-force number before I was released. My first instinct was to head for the Comitato di Liberazione Nazionale. I went to a little bar where messages could be left but no one was there and this made me nervous. I tried to call a doctor who was a friend of one of the partican leaders, but he wasn't there. Everybody on my side seemed to have vanished.

I made my way home wondering if it was safe or if I would be followed. When I arrived home in Via dell'Orivolo, father seemed exhausted. He took me into his study and told me that I had better make sure that I reported to the labour force in the morning. I reminded him that the English would be arriving in a matter of days, but he insisted that I do what I had promised.

'I'm too old for all of this,' he said. 'I'm too old for all this aggravation.' He was packing his papers and the few precious belongings that he had brought with him to the country.

We both knew what turmoil awaited Florence. The Germans had been cheated in Rome and were going to get their revenge. They had respected the 'open city' agreement in Rome whereby both sides would leave the city untouched, but the Allies had reneged and used the bridges over the Tiber to encircle and entrap several retreating German divisions. The Nazis were not going to let the same thing happen again. My father started to talk about the fate that lay in store for Florence, but I wanted to clear up the mystery.

'Can I ask you something?'

My father nodded.

'How did you know that boy?' I went on.

'Don't worry about him,' he answered.

'But he's a Fascist criminal and you kissed him.'

'Don't say that about him,' said my father.

'Why not? It's true.'

'He was a wonderful boy.' My father smiled faintly. 'I don't know what happened to him.'

'That Fascist? That pig? Wonderful?'

My father stood up to leave. 'Forget about him,' he said. 'Be grateful he saved your life.'

'I am perfectly aware of that, but I still wonder why,' I said. 'Anyway he's done for – all of them are going to be killed. It's only a matter of days, maybe hours.'

My father moved towards me with astonishing speed. 'Don't say such things. One day you may regret having wished that on your own brother.'

We both fell completely silent. My father was shaking, overcome by distress, while I, who had always thought of myself as his only son, tried to take in what he had just said. I had softened my childhood loneliness with the fantasy that I was his only true 'love-child', the only son, who had sprung from the one intense relationship of his life rather than the by-product of some casual affair. Now even that had been taken away from me. I left the room; there was nothing more to be said. But I couldn't help thinking of *Il Trovatore* and of the final moment when the old gypsy Azucena reveals that the murderer has killed his own brother. Indeed, in the end my 'brother' did die. He was shot in Florence as one of the snipers fighting to the death over the rooftops of the city. Perhaps it was just as well.

The next morning I reported to the Organizzazione Todt. By a bizarre piece of bureaucratic nonsense I was given five months' back pay and told to wait outside the office. It was all so simple – when I was sure no one was looking, I just started walking. At first I walked as casually as I could, then I started running south to where I hoped the Allied lines were. I knew they were somewhere near Siena, not far from Lucolena, where my father's country house was. I walked for two full days, avoiding the main roads and crossing forests and fields. I met up with part of my old partisan group and eventually there were five of us all together. We knew that our only hope was to get across to the Allied lines, about twenty miles south of where we were.

The following day, shortly after nightfall, we made our move into the no-man's-land between the opposing forces and sought cover in a ditch. When dawn came we saw we were in a little valley. It was a glorious day in early July, when the Tuscan Chianti countryside is at its most appealing. But that day there was a strange stillness in the air, a curious absence of birdsong. Suddenly, we heard the rumbling of artillery, gunfire, and the din of approaching trucks and tanks. As the roar of heavy engines came nearer, we realized to our horror that we had stumbled into the middle of a battle. From our ditch we saw the German tanks passing within yards of us. Then Stukas and Messerschmitts flashed overhead, followed by English and American fighters. We were absolutely terrified and, if prayers are anything to go by, became devoutly Christian within seconds. I remembered my years with the Dominican friars in San Marco, anything that could give me comfort.

After what seemed a lifetime of noise and fire the German tanks withdrew and others with strange markings replaced them; only later did I learn that this was a South African division. After more noise the terrible silence returned, leaving us even more confused. Had we crossed the lines? Or, more correctly, had the lines crossed us? Some of my friends thought we were still on the German side and that the fighting would flare up again. The suspense made me restless. I had been in that ditch for about ten or twelve hours, I was hungry and thirsty, and, although my friends thought it was still too dangerous to move, I jumped out and started to hurry on.

'I can't stay here,' I called back. 'I'd rather die than stay here a minute longer.'

They did not follow and I found myself wandering alone down a narrow pass. The birds were singing noisily now and there was an air of childish innocence about my strolling along in shorts with my hair hanging down to my shoulders. I headed south and climbed a small hill with a clump of oak trees surrounded by red and yellow flowers. Then I heard a voice. I stopped, motionless. The undergrowth rustled – soldiers! It sounded like soldiers in the bushes. I could see the glint of metal and quickly raised my arms above my head, took a deep breath, and began to walk towards them.

'Are you English?' I shouted finally, realizing that just to speak the language was a declaration and that, if they were Germans, I was finished. There was a long silence and then one of them said: 'NO!'

I closed my eyes and died a thousand deaths, my legs went weak and I could barely keep my arms up. A soldier strode up to me, poking his gun out before him and thrust his face close to mine. Through a mask of simulated fury he hissed: 'We're not fucking English, Jimmy – we're fucking *Scottish.*'

FOUR

Liberation

The soldiers were part of the First Battalion of the Scots Guards. They searched me for weapons, quite unaware of the emotions welling up in me and the unbelievable relief that I was out of danger. They were startled to discover that I spoke English and questioned me as we got into their jeep. It was only then, as we drove away, that I fully accepted what had happened – I was liberated! I was free! For the first time in my life I was really free. Since childhood I had lived under Fascism and now it was over.

When we joined the main column I saw that I was at the heart of the advancing Allied forces. Everyone seemed so well turned out, so well fed, so different from our demoralized, chaotic Compagnia della Morte. When the jeep reached the Guards' HQ, I was taken to a tent where I was confronted by a young Scottish gentleman smoking a pipe. As I was blond and very sunburned, he no doubt suspected that I was German.

'How can you prove you're Italian?' he asked. As it was impossible to prove, I began to give him a long, rambling account of my experiences, telling him how happy I was to be liberated. Somehow I found myself explaining how I had learned English – the whole story of Mary O'Neill came tumbling out. He smiled. I must have struck a chord, particularly by the way I described how she cooked her eggs and served tea in the little boarding-house room she had in Florence. Finally, the Scottish gentleman introduced himself.

'Lieutenant Keith,' he said. 'Now, this might sound a bit gruesome, but we lost our interpreter a few days ago– he stepped on a mine near Siena. Would you be willing to work with us?' I nodded.

He called his driver over, a young man named Jimmy. Jimmy's home was on the Firth of Forth; he was stocky with incredibly blond hair and grey-blue eyes and was very calm and reserved. Lieutenant Keith said something that was totally incomprehensible and, when I asked Jimmy what language they were speaking, he told me it was Scottish slang.

'We speak in our own way,' he said. 'It helps preserve our identity.'

Within minutes they changed me into a Scottish soldier with shirt, shorts, belt, gaiters, beret, and the badge of the regiment. Jimmy took me to the regimental barber, who shaved my hair practically to the skull so that I looked exactly like the rest of them. I watched my curls falling to the ground, as I suddenly ceased to be a scruffy Italian refugee and became a spruce Scots Guardsman.

Work started immediately. All kinds of people were coming to headquarters, many of them peasants looking for relatives and badly in need of clothes and food because the Germans had stolen everything they had. I had to translate what they were saying, although when the officers answered they often slipped into their incomprehensible language, making me realize that they still didn't fully trust me. Harry Keith was different from the start, kind and friendly. He told me that his men had captured an Italian truck which had been a canteen for one of the Fascist battalions and that it was full of cigarettes, soap and chocolate, all of which were indescribably precious in those days. He told me his own men wouldn't touch the stuff as it wasn't to Scottish tastes, and that I could take whatever I wanted to share with the people who came to headquarters looking for help. This thoughtful gesture, typical of the man, confirmed all my ideals about the 'English' that I had nurtured since childhood. Later that afternoon, another jeep arrived with the four friends I had left behind in the ditch.They had obviously taken the same route, and I couldn't resist playing a joke on them. I was in full British army uniform, haircut and all, and I pretended that I was an Englishman who spoke some Italian. My friends were very excited. They said they wanted to help, that they knew where the roads were, where the minefields were, exactly the things I had told Harry Keith earlier. I was particularly hard on Mario and told him, in broken Italian, that I didn't believe him.

'We don't trust Italians. They are treacherous,' I said.

Poor Mario was very ashamed. 'We're not all the same,' he said. 'You'll find more good people than bad in our country. I don't like the Fascists. I hate the Germans as much as you do. I've fought against them.'

Harry Keith was watching from inside the tent and, though he didn't understand what we were saying, he could see that it was good fun. I went on attacking the Italians mercilessly until Mario was almost in tears.

'You can't say that about us,' he finally said. 'We want freedom. We want democracy as much as you do; It's not our fault that we were born in a Fascist country.'

Suddenly I was moved by what he said and realized that this was not something to joke about.

'Look at me,' I said, staring straight at him. 'I am Franco.'

I introduced them all to Harry Keith as my best friends and told him that they could be useful; but Lieutenant Keith said that they should return to their families and thanked each of them. I took them over to the truck to show them all the cigarettes inside: Alpha, Macedonia Extra. They couldn't believe their eyes. Cigarettes had been impossible to get during

46   the war and most of us had smoked chestnut or oak leaves. I gave them all they wanted before they left.

That night I bedded down near Lieutenant Keith's jeep. Jimmy and I were wrapped up in a blanket, but I was too excited to sleep. Then I realized that if I stirred too much they would think that I was up to something. After all, why should they trust me yet? So I forced myself to sleep.

The smell of breakfast woke me: eggs, sausage, bacon, toast, the English breakfast that so far I had only read about. I hadn't seen butter for months. They also served a cereal of some sort and, of course, pots of tea. Sergeant Martin, a solid Scotsman with a large moustache, ate with us. He noticed that I hadn't touched my cereal.

'No porridge?' he asked. 'You don't like it? Then how can you stay with us?'

'All right,' I said, and I began to eat. It was totally tasteless, yet with milk and sugar it was far too creamy and sweet. The next day I put butter, salt and tomato in the bowl, making a kind of pasta. I ate every bit of it and quite liked it. Eventually one or two of the others tried it and some even said it wasn't bad, which sent Sergeant Martin into a tizzy.

'Are you going to corrupt our Scottish traditions, laddy?' he bellowed. 'Don't you know that centuries of healthy and sound young Scots and Englishmen have grown up on our sort of porridge!'

Over the following weeks I came to know Lieutenant Keith's men as individuals. Most were the sons of ordinary workers, while their officers were often caricatures, the stiff-upper-lip type. But all of them were there to do what had to be done and, as each day for them could have been their last, I often reminded myself that these extraordinary young men were risking their lives to destroy Hitler and Mussolini, and to give us Italians back our dignity. At the same time they were full of high spirits and in love with life.

By the end of July we were not more than forty kilometres from Florence and I was able to give the Scots considerable information as we advanced. I had mapped out a number of secondary roads for them, roads which I had used when I was roaming the outskirts of Florence on my bicycle – I showed them how to get across several of the rivers without using the main bridges, thus making it possible to take the Germans by surprise.

Before moving on to Florence, I asked Lieutenant Keith if he would come to my father's house in Lucolena to have lunch with my family. He said he thought that was a fine idea, and Jimmy drove us there in the jeep. My father was amazed to see me again, having had no news since my disappearance. He was overjoyed to find me in British uniform as it brought back the image of Manchester that he cherished. We ate and talked for hours and drank so much good Chianti that we were all rather drunk.

Harry Keith wandered off and I found him later, alone, looking down into the valley. I went over and asked him if he was all right. But he just stood there, contemplating the marvels of the Chianti valley, which is as majestic as anything on this earth – the vineyards, olive groves, flowers and cypress trees which surround the picturesque peasant houses. It is one of the characteristics of the Tuscan landscape that, on every hill, the people have built something precious over the centuries. Either a little church, or an abbey, perhaps a marvellous farmhouse, a villa or a castle. On the top of every hill there is always something to greet the eye, even if only a cluster of ancient cypresses. But Harry Keith looked sad because he knew that all of these things had become prime targets for artillery. And there is no way to stop artillery from destroying – even when there were no Germans in sight, artillerymen felt somehow compelled to fire at anything that stuck out. The Germans also did their part, not wanting to leave any turret or campanile standing in case it were used by the English as an observation post. Treasure upon treasure was lost. Harry and I grew melancholy as we talked about this, and I will never forget that moment we shared in Chianti.

Next day the Scots Guards headed directly towards Florence. The German army had withdrawn, creating a line of defence along the Arno, which divides the city, each side connected by a series of ancient bridges. We camped on the hills to the south, in a villa that belonged to a well-known Italian banker named Gualino.

The Germans had ordered all Florentines who lived near the river to be evacuated before they pulled out and I was told later that everything had been left in place. The people had watered the plants before leaving and even left the birds in their cages, certain that it was only a matter of days before they came back. Nobody believed for a single moment that anyone in the whole world would dare touch Florence, for very few had taken in the fact that the Arno had become the front line. The British, on the other hand, were certain that they would be forced to fight and that the Germans would not spare the city. Several informers told us that the Germans were drilling large holes on the bridges and filling them with dynamite, so the British sent a patrol to see at close range what was going on and they asked me to guide them.

'I assume no one needs to tell you how to find your way in your own city,' said the officer with a smile.

I led the five of us through the hills to the Boboli Gardens behind the Pitti Palace, from where we could see the river and the bridges. It looked as if the Germans were drilling and unloading large crates of explosives, but we waited until it grew dark before moving closer. We had almost reached a fresh observation point on Costa San Giorgio when the Germans spotted us from the other side of the river and opened fire with their machine-guns. We ran for cover, but two of our soldiers were hit: the second

48   and fourth in our little column. The other two soldiers and I were untouched. We managed to grab the two wounded men and hurried back to headquarters. I was shocked; the city where I was born and had spent my life had become a battleground.

At three o'clock in the morning of 4 August 1944 there was an ominous silence in the valley of the Arno which reminded me of that fearful night not so long ago in Naples. We heard artillery fire, then something more than the usual rumble of bombs, something fuller, heavier. It went on for at least two hours. I was still exhausted from the strain of our patrol; my muscles ached, my thoughts were racing and I felt feverish – again a reminder of Naples. The terrifying barrage went on and on. Harry Keith came over; he must have been awake most of the night.

'They've done it,' he said. 'They've blown up the bridges. Damn them!'

Perhaps it was inevitable, but it still seemed unreal. At first light I went up on the roof and looked down over the city lying, like Naples three summers earlier, under a blanket of smoke and dust. The sun was coming up behind the hills of Settignano, but only Brunelleschi's cathedral dome, the tower of Giotto and the Palazzo Vecchio were visible. The rest of Florence lay buried under a heavy, funereal shroud. It was hours before anything appeared and, when it did, the sight was gruesome. The whole area around the river was completely destroyed. The Germans blew up not only the bridges but also all the buildings along the banks, and innumerable historical treasures, palaces and churches were ruined and lost.

Later that morning a group of partisans arrived at the villa, Potente among them. They recognized me and we embraced, though I felt a certain coldness as they stared at my British uniform.

It was Potente's intention that the Allied commanders should give his partisans a role in the fighting, but the officers of the American 5th Army would have nothing to do with him. Undaunted, he had come to the British 8th Army to try again. I translated, deeply moved, as he made an impassioned speech to the Scottish officers, claiming his right to lead his men into Florence. He wanted, he said, to spare the Florentines the horrors of a prolonged siege. He had information that Fascist snipers were everywhere, shooting and killing people.

The British commander was sympathetic: 'I suppose if the German Army was in Edinburgh I'd feel the same way myself.'

They agreed to hold a council of war on the southern bank of the Arno to see whether a crossing was feasible.

The next day, the Scots Guards were given leave and for the first time since the fighting at Monte Cassino they had a taste of freedom. I went with them, and so it was only later that I heard what had happened to Potente.

The day I left, Potente had had his meeting in an abandoned house overlooking the river. While genuinely sympathetic, the British felt obliged to point out that the Germans were holding the far bank in strength and that a crossing, even under cover of darkness, would be suicidal. Potente, so I'm told, proudly insisted on going ahead, but, even as he spoke, the Germans began to shell the British positions. Tragically, they scored a direct hit on the building where the meeting was taking place. Potente was terribly wounded, with damage to his stomach and lungs. He was rushed by jeep to a military hospital at Greve, about twenty miles south of Florence. He died within three hours of arrival.

In the end, however, he succeeded in one aim at least: the British recognized him as an ally and buried him with full military honours. He was the bravest of men. Though I know that, as a Communist, Potente could have been an enemy of the democratic ideals I cherished, I mourned him nevertheless. He was larger than life and one of the few true heroes I have ever known. Though it cost him his life, he alone refused to leave the liberation of Florence to foreigners.

At the time we knew nothing of all this. Our thoughts were of how to relax after our hardships. We had been sent to a beautiful villa in Fagnano on the outskirts of Siena, where entertainments were to be laid on. Naturally, I wanted to get involved with anything that was 'theatre', so I volunteered to help with a performance. It was then that I was introduced to that most bizarre of British Army traditions, the drag show. To my amazement, these tough troops who had fought their way from Africa to Florence wanted nothing more than to see some of their number put on dresses and wigs and camp it up like mad. I approached the Scots Guard captain in charge of the show, Richard Buckle, better known as Dicky, who I soon discovered was a music and ballet expert in London. While I helped him organize the show, I pumped him for information about the London theatre. He was my first contact with British culture since Mary O'Neill, and I wanted to know everything. I had heard about Tyrone Guthrie and his 'modern-dress' production of *Hamlet* with Alec Guinness. Dicky told me all about it and described the famous cemetery scene. He also told me about opera, music, ballet, all the things we had lost contact with. Many years later Dicky Buckle wrote his memoirs, and I came across his own recollection of our meeting in Siena:

> The Battalion had picked up an Italian boy partisan in the Chianti hills and the Guardsmen had adopted him. As he spoke some English, he acted as interpreter, made himself useful and was attired in khaki drill. One morning at Fagnano, near Siena, when I was sticking branches of greenery into curtains of camouflage netting hung around a courtyard of the villa to form the background for a concert party, the boy appeared asking, 'Can I help you, Captain Buckle?' . . . and proved

skilful. I drove him to San Gimignano, that towery hilltop town, and we looked together at the frescoes of Benozzo Gozzoli and Ghirlandaio's 'Death of Santa Fina'. Later in August, I wrote: 'There is a bathing place in the River Elsa. . . . The millstream falling from a high rock makes a perfect showerbath. . . . When Franco sits in the middle of the shaft of falling water, it parts and spreads all around him, like the tail of a huge white peacock in glass beads. I told Franco I was a ballet critic and he told me he wanted to be a stage designer. Later, when Florence was free of the Germans, he left us to return to his home there. I had tea with his family and he showed me his designs. After the war . . . he became known throughout the world as Franco Zeffirelli, designer, director of opera, plays and films, one of the great men of theatre of our time.

That was generous of him, but let me say how much *he* seemed a great man to me. He looked nothing like a warrior. He was always well groomed, his uniform impeccable. He had fine, sensitive hands and spoke in an out-rageous upper-class English accent. He was exactly the type of Englishman that Mussolini made fun of. Il Duce prided himself on his Latin *macho* image. For him the English were effeminate weaklings who ate five meals a day and soaked for hours in hot baths. To me Dicky seemed like a gift from heaven, a source of precious information about the British theatre. But my admiration for him was not only due to my love of theatrical chitchat. It was more to do with his loyalty and bravery.

While we were resting in Siena, Florence was liberated on 11 August. The Allied troops crossed the river from the west and east of the city. The Germans had withdrawn a few days earlier, when they knew the Allies were coming, and none of them were left. The British set up Bailey bridges and within a few hours the two halves of Florence were united again. But liberation was far from being the joyful event it had been in Rome, where people had hugged and kissed each other and danced drunk in the streets. In Rome there had been no battle, no bloodshed; but in Florence a large number of Fascists were trapped and skirmishes erupted for days after the arrival of the Allied forces. The Fascists went wild, shooting at innocent women going to the fountains for water or at people who were waiting in a queue for a morsel of food. When the partisans managed to catch them, they would drag them anywhere, even into churches, and kill them like pigs, so that, at the end, it became a fratricidal battle like the old medieval wars – Guelphs against Ghibellines.

A few days after the liberation Lieutenant Keith had to go by jeep to Florence and I went with him. I was so keen to see what had happened to my home, but when we approached the town my enthusiasm turned to distress. Although I had heard the reports of the damage, these had not prepared me for the scale of destruction the Germans had wrought. The endless vista of rubble around the river was a vision of the apocalypse I could never have imagined.

The Ponte Vecchio was the only bridge the Germans had spared. But on both sides 300 metres of medieval streets were smashed. The Germans had laid booby traps in the ruins: toys, boxes, little things that could attract attention so that if you picked one up, it blew you to pieces. I was amazed to see the Uffizi Gallery still standing beside the river. There were two stories about how that 'miracle' happened. One was that the Germans had mined it along with everything else, but that the partisans attacked the ss just as they were about to blow it up. The other is that a German officer with an immense love for Florence and its works of art had refused, at the last minute, to allow the destruction. I've always felt that the second version must be true, that not all Germans were the monsters we imagined them to be.

We drove along the river bank skirting the fallen masonry until we came to the Bailey bridge that had been thrown over the remains of the Ponte Santa Trinita. We crossed it and entered what remained of the Via Torna-buoni, where the British consulate had been and down which the English ladies, our *scorpioni,* had come each day to take tea at Doney's. Harry Keith went about his various commissions as I waited in the jeep numb with sorrow. When he had finished, I asked him if we could go back to my father's house and Aunt Lide's apartment. Although they were safely in the country, I desperately wanted to know if our family homes had been destroyed. Fortunately he agreed, and again we wound our way through areas now rendered virtually unrecognizable. Our homes had been spared, and I returned to our camp near Siena slightly less miserable than I had been for most of that appalling day.

After their rest period the Scots Guards were moved north to join the other regiments gradually pushing the Germans out of our country. In October we made camp north of Prato, where we occupied the abandoned villa of a famous old opera singer, Iva Pacetti. I was in one of the outhouses in a room filled with old trunks. I opened one of them and saw that it contained the soprano's costumes. I remembered her wearing some of them at the Florence opera. When I told some of the younger officers about my find that curious British delight in 'camping it up' broke out again. They planned a candlelit drag ball in the villa with everyone in Iva's costumes. I have to say I was a little puzzled by all this: they were usually such hearty men I could hardly work out what it was about. Still, it sounded as if it might be entertaining and I led them to my discovery. Some of them immediately started to try on the dresses, but were soon overcome with embarrassment. They really didn't have the will to carry it off and the idea of having a ball was quietly dropped.

Zeffirelli

After Prato we moved further up into the mountains to a village above
Vernio on the road to Bologna and thus we, too, met up with the last-ditch
attempt to hold back the inevitable when the German army regrouped to
form the Gothic Line across northern Italy. The advent of winter and the
fact that the Germans were easily supplied from the north, while the Allies
were forced to contend with the scorched earth, the bombed roads and
mined bridges the Germans had left behind them meant, that at first a
stalemate ensued, with the Allies held at bay. This was warfare at its worst –
the cold damp camp sites, the occasional dangerous sorties, the sudden
artillery bombardment that haphazardly killed one's friends. There were
grim memories, such as the farm we discovered where everyone – children,
old people, even dogs – had been butchered weeks before so that we opened
the door to the unbelievable stench of rotting flesh.

Days of freezing cold and empty boredom alternated with sudden out-
bursts of danger. Then, as Christmas approached, something dreadful happened. There was a growing concern in the regiment that someone was
spying for the Germans, and though I was now very friendly with Jimmy,
Harry Keith and Sergeant Martin, I was unaware of the fact that they
were all watching me. One day there was an alarm in the nearby village.
Our soldiers surrounded the church, but I had no idea of what was going
on as nobody would talk to me or tell me what was happening. It turned
out that three Fascists and their transmitter had been found hidden in
the bell tower, and that the local priest was apparently their accomplice.
From that moment the whole situation around me changed. Jimmy con-
fessed how terrible it had been for all of them during those last weeks
in December when they had no choice but to be suspicious of me. He was
so relieved at the outcome that he got rip-roaring drunk. Sergeant Martin,
who also had one too many that night, kept saying that he was the only
one of them with any judgement: 'I always knew this boy would never
betray us.'

I had apparently been under close surveillance for weeks. All my letters
were opened and read before they were sent home. Everything I did, every
step I took, had been watched. At the same time I had been living with
these men as a friend. I am sure that Jimmy had been given orders to
monitor my activities. Then I found out that Dicky Buckle had refused to
take part – he had found the whole thing distasteful and was talking to me
more than ever. He was my friend, and nothing was going to change that.
It was characteristic of him and of the kind of loyalty he was capable of,
but it was something the Guardsmen teased him about. None of them really
understood him. They told jokes about him and mocked his accent behind
his back, but one day they learned their lesson. We were moving from one
area in the mountains to another when there was sudden artillery fire.
Dicky Buckle jumped out of his jeep and told his driver to run for cover.

He directed the other soldiers to lie down in ditches or hide in bushes. Then he set off to make sure that all his men were safe and, with no thought for his own safety, he walked up and down the road in the midst of the gunfire, bullets and shrapnel flying all around him. He stayed out there in the open, impeccable as ever.

'This is scaring the shit out of me,' one of the soldiers said, 'and look at that cunt. What does he think he's up to?'

To me, it was wonderful. Here was an expert on music, theatre and ballet displaying such bravery, while the *macho* Scotsmen were huddled in ditches. Dicky stood there, towering over them, not even blinking as the artillery fire exploded around him.

We were getting so settled into this way of life that headquarters began to allow periods of leave. I was given permission to go home for Christmas and Jimmy was allowed to go with me. We stayed with Aunt Lide, who did the best she could to create a Christmas feast, given the deprivations of the time. When we returned in January, it was clear to me that this waiting would continue and that there was little reason for my being there now that we were out of the part of the country with which I was familiar. Lieutenant Keith agreed with my analysis and it was arranged for me to return home for good. At the last moment I nearly changed my mind: I could hardly bear to leave those who had become such friends.

Harry Keith said he wished he could go home too, and Sergeant Martin shook hands rather formally and said I was the best 'interrupter' the regiment had ever had – a joke he liked. It was hardest saying goodbye to Jimmy, with whom I'd spent most time, but fortunately he was to visit me in Florence whenever he had leave, so our separation wasn't final.

I tried to take up the threads of my life in Florence as quickly as possible but it was a hopeless task. So much clearing up still needed to be done before normal life could resume. One of the first things I did was get in touch with the members of our old drama group to see if we couldn't get going again. Some of them had already begun to make plans and I was happily welcomed back. A young director, Alessandro Brissoni, was planning a production of Barrie's *Dear Brutus,* so I started work on some designs for him. I was still involved in this production in February, when Dicky Buckle came on a visit. Naturally he was interested in anything to do with the theatre, so I proudly showed him my sketches. But his visit aroused in me the urge to know what was going on in the north. Although the Gothic Line still held, it was clear that at some point the Allies would wear down the German resistance and I was desperate not to miss completely this great historic drama that was being played out. After *Dear Brutus* I looked around for some way of joining in with what was happening, rather than simply to eke out the war with nothing to do in Florence. The answer came in the person of an American officer attached to the Fifth Army called Frederick

54   Hartt. He was in Florence to help save whatever could be shored up of our badly damaged buildings and I met him one day as he was working near the Ponte Vecchio. We got talking and I was fascinated to learn that the American army employed an expert on art restoration to save what war had destroyed – it was so wonderfully American – what other army would do such a thing? When Frederick discovered that I studied architecture and was something of an artist, he asked if I would like to work with him, and I instantly agreed. It was a revelation to discover just how much this man knew of our heritage and we Italians owe him an enormous debt of gratitude. This was especially true when, after a few weeks in Florence, we moved to the seaport of Livorno, where I had lived at the beginning of hostilities with Ethiopia, when Gustavo had been posted to the naval base there. By this time it was unrecognizable. The stupendous Renaissance harbour built by the Medicis in the sixteenth century had been badly bombed; yet worse still were the subsequent actions of the Livornese. Seeing this as a heaven-sent opportunity to clear away those unprofitable old buildings, some of the owners were creeping out at night to dynamite what remained of the classic palaces and harbour installations. As soon as we got there, Frederick Hartt called in the troops and sealed off the old quarter, thus removing the risk of further destruction until the task of restoration could begin. By this act alone he saved a great deal of the city's cultural heritage singlehanded.

When we had done what we could in Livorno, I asked Frederick to arrange for me to go as interpreter with some of the OSS (Office of Strategic Services) officers who were moving north. At the beginning of April the Gothic Line began to crumble. I later found out that 'my' Scots Guards had begun to head north and had seen violent action around Lake Comacchio, though fortunately none of my friends were killed. By the time I began to leave with the OSS group the Scots Guards were heading towards Trieste to see if they would be needed in Yugoslavia. I imagine that at some point, though I'm not certain, they must have split up, because I heard that Jimmy and Lieutenant Keith were sent to Palestine for the awful task of keeping the Jews and the Arabs apart, so it was a long time before they saw their beloved Scotland again.

Towards the end of April the OSS group, with me as interpreter, crossed the River Po by a Bailey bridge close to Mantua and we arrived in Brescia. It was 29 April, the day after Mussolini was shot and the war effectively ended. The general headquarters were understandably in a state of some confusion and there was little for us to do. While we were standing around trying to find out what was going on, a large American captain with a booming voice came roaring up and began to bellow above the noise of the mingling armies.

'Who's going to give me a jeep? Do I have to ask Eisenhower for a jeep?'

He thundered up to one of our officers and introduced himself as Donald Downes, an officer with the OSS and a well-known war correspondent for several US newspapers.

'Mussolini's been shot,' he explained, 'and I've got to get to Milan right away. I need a driver and an interpreter.'

He was so loud and self-assured we couldn't help enjoying the act he was putting on and it was decided that I should go with him.

Off the two of us went with Donald asking me in English what I thought of this and that, trying to find out my opinions. He got me to describe my experiences in the hills and then to tell him about my childhood in Florence. It turned out he knew the city well – in fact he had lived in Italy since the 1930s. At one point a bike caused us to swerve and he hurled a stream of abuse in faultless Italian at the hapless cyclist.

'Why do you need an interpreter?' I asked.

'Insurance,' he explained. 'They're less likely to take a shot at us if there's a witness who might survive.'

He was an intriguing man and I listened fascinated as he talked about the stupidities of Fascism, though he went on to say that the democracies were hardly any better. He loathed Roosevelt and said we would all regret having made a deal with Stalin. The real enemy was the Soviet Union, he claimed, and he gave me a crash course in Russian history from the revolution, through the purges and show trials, to Yalta. Although such things are part of history now, at that time they were little known and I felt that this strange man was somehow completing a missing part of my education. He was certainly fearless in his opinions: as a young man in Rome in 1936 he had been arrested for throwing orange peel at the black-and-white marble map of Mussolini's 'Empire' which Il Duce had had erected in the Forum.

'And now we're going to say goodbye to Benito,' he said.

We drove into the outskirts of Milan and threaded our way through the bomb-damaged streets. I told Donald about my awful experiences in Milan before my aunt had saved me: a tale that matched well the grim desolation which the Allied bombers had wrought. There were clouds of ochre dust rising from the ruined stone buildings, so thick that in places it was like a pall of fog. The Sforza castle loomed out of this mist. We skirted the Piazza del Duomo and pulled up outside La Scala. Here was the Mecca of my youth, the wellspring of Gustavo's tales of grand opera and great singers. I had always longed for the day when I would see this temple for the first time. The façade was intact. We passed through the imposing entrance, crossed the foyer, stepped into the auditorium and found ourselves in the open air; bombs had almost completely demolished the place, which was now an open courtyard. Only a slice of the upper seating remained, including the royal box, whose gilded figures and plush hangings looked unspeakably melancholy. Seated in the box was an elderly lady, quite rigid, staring at the remains of the stage. She was dignified and handsome with severely drawn-back blonde hair. Somehow I was absolutely convinced she was an elderly soprano come to mourn the scene of her triumphs – though I had no evidence, then or now, for the notion.

Regrettably, as it transpired, although half the proscenium had collapsed, the stage and the fly-tower had survived. Had the bomb landed only a hundred yards away we would have preserved our glorious theatre and had a new modern stage, but sadly, the reverse was the case, the worst of both worlds. Attempts had already been made to protect what remained: the debris had been organized into heaps, sad little hills of gilded stucco and plush seating, and a makeshift awning had been slung over the roof to keep out the elements. Donald looked down at the people searching among the rubble for souvenirs.

'Dresden's all gone,' he said. 'Now this. Goddam fools.'

There was an elderly couple seated on a pile of debris, holding hands like lovers at the opera. It was all so sad.

'Come on,' said Donald, 'let's go find Benito.'

As we left, there were murmured insults from some of those who saw our uniforms.

'Odd', said Donald, 'that we two who love this place so much should be getting the blame.'

We drove along the Corso Venezia to the dullest of Milan's open spaces, the Piazzale Loreto. How Donald knew so much about what was going on was a mystery to me but sure enough the square was packed with a huge seething mob and an ugly one at that. On one side was a featureless petrol station and strung upside down by wires from the high canopy were the lifeless bodies of Benito Mussolini and his mistress, Clara Petacci. Poor faithful Clara had stayed with her abandoned Duce even though she could have got away. When they were captured by Lake Como and a firing squad of Communist partisans formed up she tried to throw herself between her lover and the guns. Now their badly mutilated bodies were strung up like so much meat. Her skirt had fallen over her head, exposing her lower parts, until one kindly Christian soul pushed through the crowd, ignoring the jeers and insults of the mob, to pin up her clothes between her legs to give her a minimum of decency. Strung up beside her was the body of Pavolini, the Minister of Culture, who despite his politics had been a great lover and supporter of the opera. It seemed hardly possible that we Italians could be doing this to each other. We had betrayed the western democracies, then we had abandoned our German allies, and now we were tearing ourselves apart.

Donald was looking at the scene through binoculars and scribbling reams of notes. He told me how an old woman had been brought up and how she was slapping and beating Mussolini's dead face. He supposed it was someone who had lost a son or a husband. The atmosphere was terrifyingly barbaric. There were threats from the crowd when our uniforms were noticed, so Donald told me to drive back and, as we went, some men gave the Communist salute and promised we would be next.

We made our way to a hotel that had been commandeered as a recreation centre for Allied officers, where Donald left me with a drink and went off to find out what was going on. He returned with a bottle of whisky and a typewriter, and began to drink and type furiously for a couple of hours, pounding out the story of what we had seen that day. Suddenly, he looked up at me, slightly drunk.

'Let's go and see him,' he said.

I asked him who he meant.

'Mussolini,' he replied.

This time Donald drove, weaving and turning as he tried to follow the instructions he had been given. There were gunshots nearby and it was dark before we arrived outside an official-looking building that I could not identify – it most resembled a hospital. There were only a few lamps functioning and the whole thing was almost foolishly melodramatic. Donald identified us and the guards let us in. We half groped our way to a room where we found the bodies of the Duce and Clara Petacci laid out on two tables. Nobody had bothered to clean them and the sight that greeted us was sickening. Mussolini's face was bloated and engorged with blood. Some sort of fluid was seeping out of his eye sockets. I gagged. Worse than the physical horror was the black comedy – rigor mortis had fixed Mussolini's arms straight out above his head. The partisans had bent one back, but every time they forced the other down, it sprang up in a grotesque parody of the Roman salute. I remembered all those years when he had dominated our lives, strutting around saluting his soldiers, haranguing the adoring crowds. I thought about what his mad illusions had brought us to: ruin and humiliation. And yet there he was, a lump of rotting flesh with two young partisans breaking his arm in order finally to dispose of him. I felt my childhood ended in that room.

'Bye, Benito,' said Donald, and away we went.

'Take the jeep back,' he told me. 'Then go home, back to Florence, and get this war out of your system. Forget all this.'

I drove him to the hotel and then headed back to Brescia.

Now it was really over. The Americans were moving on and I decided to return to Florence again. The Germans had abandoned a lot of horses when they withdrew, and one of the partisans had rounded them up. He asked me to help him take them back. We took six horses and headed for Bologna. The boy's name was Angelo; he rode one horse and I rode another while we led the other four. It was exhilarating, something out of the

58   American Wild West, but it was also very difficult and painful. Angelo talked and sang all the time and cracked awful jokes, but I wasn't used to riding and soon ached all over. By the time we reached Piacenza I was happy to part company with him and hitch a ride on a truck that took me as far as Sassuolo, in the heart of Italy's Communist provinces. I was stranded there when the local militia picked me up. I showed them my documents, which Harry Keith and other officers had given me, but a man in a red bandanna said they looked suspicious, that there were Fascists everywhere with forged documents trying to get home, and that I was under arrest. It suddenly dawned on me that after all the agony I had been through I was going to wind up being shot as a Fascist when the war was already over.

There took me to an empty schoolhouse and locked me in one of the classrooms. There were dozens of others there already, some of whom really had been with the Fascists. They were all in a panic, praying and pleading for their lives. I felt I had to find a way out. I asked to be allowed to explain, but the people in charge were peasants with red stars on their shirts and berets who were acting out a kind of proletarian revolution.

'I'm not a Fascist,' I kept shouting. 'I have been working with the English. I was with Potente.' But the guards only laughed.

There was a committee of some sort next door and they called people in one by one. Most of them never came back. When it was my turn, they took me to a football field behind the school. I tried not to panic like the others. I had a sudden instinct and I concentrated on one man who was coming and going from the school to the field. When the guard turned away, I rushed over to him and begged him to listen to me. He was tall and dark with heavy-framed glasses. He inspired confidence and seemed different from the others, an attractive intellectual.

'I'm not a Fascist,' I said. 'I'm a partisan. I joined the English. I was in Florence when Potente was killed. I knew him well. If you want to kill me, do it, but don't kill me as a Fascist!' I got very excited, grabbing at his lapels. 'Here, look at these papers. They are authentic. They're not forged. You can call Florence. Everyone there will know.'

The man didn't answer, I was desperate; perhaps bribery would do it. I took off the little gold ring that I always had with me and gave it to him. They were emptying the classroom now. Everyone was being brought out and I saw the peasants form up a firing squad. The man looked at the ring. Then he looked at me without really focusing.

'You don't have to give me this,' he said with a sort of smile, and led me away.

As we went back into the school I heard the shots from the field. Once inside, I collapsed in a chair, aware of how close I was to death yet again. The man asked me where I had been all this time and I told him about the

Scots Guards and the events in Milan. He examined the papers carefully and seemed relieved to find them in order. He told me to come with him and, to my surprise, took me to a little trattoria nearby. We ate a meal together which wasn't bad considering the conditions in Italy at the time. He told me he was a writer, that he had written plays. I told him I was an actor. We both rambled on, slightly boastful, slightly drunk, the only sort of talk possible between people who have been so near violence and death.

It was late, but we could still hear distant rifle fire – justice? Revenge? He told me it was not wise for me to go around at that time of night. He lived in a house just outside the small town. 'Come, we'll talk more about the theatre.'

The villa was spacious, but with the feel of a family home.

'You live here alone?' I asked him.

'My family is up there . . . we have a house in the mountains.'

I remember seeing a photo of the actress Eleanora Duse and other pictures of great Italian actors and actresses. I was nearly collapsing; I sat on the sofa in the austere living-room and he brought more wine. He was no longer talking. Every now and then I caught him staring at me. All my limbs were numb. Duse, d'Annunzio, Pirandello . . . six characters. I think he asked me to sleep in his room, which would certainly have been more comfortable, but I was already drifting away. I woke up at dawn to find him beside me on the sofa, his shirt open, his shoes scattered on the floor, sound asleep. There, with his face hidden in a pillow and his arm around my waist, was the man who had saved my life and who had in the end been too ashamed to take the reward he desired.

I left quietly and headed along the road to Florence. Just as the light was fading I came within sight of the city. It was suddenly too much for me. I was shaking violently and started vomiting. The incident in Sassuolo had been a last brush with death and only then, within reach of my home, did all that I had been through hit me with a sickening violence. I steadied myself and forced my legs to carry me on.

The next day brought a tremendous sense of relief, but also of foreboding; of dread at the idea of having to start life from scratch again. The war had changed us all drastically, yet almost immediately we had to resume life as if nothing had happened. I moved in with father and my stepsister, Fanny, and after a few days went round to the university to see what was happening. Classes started up almost at once in a brave attempt to get back to normal. It was the same in every walk of life, a determination to start again. Yet, walking round Florence, I felt that something was still missing. I could not put my finger on it but, despite all the evidence – the reunited families and free speech – there was an indefinable element the city now lacked.

Father was supporting me and was eager for me to complete the last three years of the architecture course. I could see at once that there was something peculiar about him, and it slowly dawned on me that he alone had remained unchanged by the war. He was exactly the same man he had always been. He still wore a flower in his lapel every day, often a gardenia, and never forgot a white handkershief soaked in eau-de-Cologne for his breast pocket. He still spruced up every night before going out to his 'club'. I knew that he still had his women as well and was still breaking hearts, perhaps even creating new children wherever he could. It was as if he had lived the war years in a vacuum, much as he must have done during the First World War.

I took refuge in Fanny's company, as the only person I could talk to. We made up for all the years we had lost, and she was a kind of sister-mother figure to me. I was able to talk to her about the future and about what I wanted to do with my life. She, in turn, seemed to understand how difficult it was for me to pick up my books and start at school again. Unlike my father, she recognized how much I had changed and saw the different person I had become.

Fanny even understood how this change affected my relationship with Lide. My aunt expected things to be the same between us when she and Gustavo returned to Florence after the war. But they weren't at all. I was living with my father and sister now, and this upset her despite the fact that she knew Gustavo preferred this – since I had grown up he no longer welcomed my presence in the house, feeling that I turned much of Lide's affection away from him. It was at this time that my father began to hope that I would use his name, Corsi. But I still went on using the name Zeffirelli – how could it be otherwise? Everyone knew me by that name and I couldn't just start calling myself something else. I was Franco Zeffirelli and I felt that the moment had passed for the kind of father–son relationship he now wanted. He didn't understand this and was deeply hurt; my refusal created a barrier which remained until the day he died.

I was twenty-one years old and my life was in turmoil. It was as if the war continued, not in the world, but in my head. Unsure of what I wanted to do with my life, I was pulled this way and that by my family. The summer of 1945 dragged on in this atmosphere of uncertainty. Then, in September, an event occurred which somehow cleared the air. The Entertainments National Service Association (ENSA) decided to bring over Laurence Olivier's film of *Henry V*. It was the most stunning Shakespearean production of its day. The ENSA programmes were open to all and I turned up early to be sure of a good seat. It was while I was waiting for the film to begin that I witnessed a most extraordinary sight: in through the doors, one by one, came the ladies – the old English ladies in their antique lace and straw hats – and they slipped into their seats like ghosts from the past. That's what had been missing from Florence! But where had they been? I went over to talk to one of them whom I vaguely remembered from my Mary O'Neill period. She told me about the dark days of their incarceration and how at first the much despised American ladies had helped them with food – a most painful charity, it was made clear. Later, when the Americans entered the war, the American ladies too were rounded up and the opposing groups of old ladies had four years in which to make each other thoroughly miserable. How extraordinary they were. Sadly, Mary O'Neill had died not long after her imprisonment – perhaps it was just as well, as she was very old. Somehow many survived and had returned, though they normally preferred to keep out of sight, knowing the confusion of those first post-war days. Tonight, however, was different; tonight was Shakespeare, Olivier, England – and here they were. I wanted to stand up and thank them all for simply being there, to apologize for what had been done to them and to tell them how much we needed them. Without them, Florence was not Florence.

Then the lights went down and that glorious film began. There was Olivier at the height of his powers and there were the English defending their honour – King Henry and all that wonderful cast of characters. Suddenly, I thought of Harry Keith, Jimmy, Sergeant Martin, and I knew then what I was going to do. Architecture was not for me; it had to be the stage. I wanted to do something like the production I was witnessing. When the lights went up my head was clearer than it had been for months. As I watched 'our' ladies making their way down the timeless streets of our city, I knew that at last my war was over.

FIVE

Luchino

I was supposed to be painting scenery. A vast canvas backdrop was spread across the floor of the Saloncino, one of the upper rooms in the Teatro della Pergola in Florence. I was working as a junior assistant to one of the highly skilled scenic painters. My problem was that at one end of the Saloncino there was a gallery which looked down on to the main stage of the theatre and, whenever possible, I would sneak away to watch the rehearsals below. It was during one of those idle moments that I got my break – the one all young actors yearn for and so few get; from provincial bit player to a place at the heart of our national culture.

I was leaning on the rail abstractedly drawing on a cigarette, watching the cast assemble for the first rehearsal of a play that was to open in Milan – the Italian version of John Steinbeck's *Tobacco Road*. Out of the wings stepped the man who was to change my life – probably the single most important person I have ever known – Luchino Visconti. And, typically as it turned out, the first thing I ever saw him do was throw a tantrum, and I really do mean a tantrum! A real shouting, foul-mouthed raving fit. I was enthralled, not least because its source was heir to one of the grandest names and titles in my country – Count Luchino Visconti. On the one hand he was something out of our history books, a descendant of Charlemagne, with ancestors who had ruled Milan and whose family was still powerful in that city – on the other hand there he was, only forty years of age, yet already a legend. Rumour and scandal have always surrounded the Viscontis and Luchino, the offspring of a brilliant high-society marriage between his father Giuseppe, the then Duke, and Carla, heiress to the Erba pharmaceutical millions, was inevitably the focus of much attention. He accepted his role by becoming a youthful tearaway, running away from home so often that his despairing father eventually sent him to a cavalry school. For most of his youth and young manhood he was obsessed with horses and, in a curious way, it was this more than his parents' artistic patronage and amateur dabbling in music and drama that led him, almost accidentally, into theatre and films. We young people knew a lot about him because of all the theatre gossip that we made certain we overheard, only some of which seeped into the popular press. It was common knowledge

that he had taken one of his horses to Paris in the 1930s to try his hand at
the Grand Prix; this was his introduction to the chic inter-war world that
has vanished for ever. His whole upbringing had prepared him for it – the
elegant, handsome, wealthy, aristocratic bachelor in his late twenties with
that leaning towards French culture which Milanese society has always
had, just as we Florentines favoured Britain. Having plunged into the
French season, Visconti was taken up by the fashion designer Coco Chanel
and we, all-knowing as we were, heard rumours that they had had an affair.
To a bunch of teenage Florentines who had just come through several years
of austerity and privation, this all sounded unbelievably exotic. The gossip
among the actors was that Chanel had launched him with an introduction
to the film-maker Jean Renoir. Now here was the odd thing, something we
all found hard to understand: Renoir was very left wing in his political
views and so would have had little time for a horse-riding Italian nobleman,
but apparently he took to Visconti because their political views coincided.
Pre-war Paris was the home of left-wing culture, a haven for socialist
thinkers driven from their homes by the rise of Fascism. It was in these
circles that Count Luchino Visconti, who had never known a day's hardship
in his life, acquired an intellectual affinity with the working-class struggle.
The heir to one of the oldest titles in Europe became a Communist.

It was perhaps not as surprising as it seemed to us outsiders, for I learned
later that earlier he had flirted with Nazism, when it masqueraded as
National Socialism. We tend to forget that much of European Fascism was
originally a revolutionary left-wing movement, and for a time Visconti was
attracted by the idea of the marching masses heading towards the bright
new dawn. He was particularly impressed by the 1936 Berlin Olympics
caught by Leni Riefenstal's camera, and this youthful enthusiasm was later
to surface in films like *The Damned* and *Ludwig*. At the time it was merely
a brief flirtation, which was soon followed by a passionate religious phase
when he even considered becoming a priest. There was something extreme
in his nature, something thirsting for a cause, and Jean Renoir helped
provide it.

In 1935 Renoir hired him as third assistant for the filming of *Une Partie
de campagne* and became his mentor, both as film-maker and political tutor.
Visconti fell in love with the movies: he visited Hollywood in 1937, but he
never really fitted in there.

The affair with Chanel had not lasted long, the gossips said, adding a
second affair with an unspecified Russian princess. There were also rumours
of other, less reputable, liaisons – such predilections had not been uncom-
mon in the family's history.

In 1938 Léon Blum's Popular Front, France's first socialist government,
came to power and although it did not last long, the months of ferment
convinced those like Visconti that power could be theirs. Those months

64   were to colour his thinking for the rest of his life.

He returned to Italy with Renoir, who was to make a film of *Tosca*, but with the outbreak of war in 1940 the authorities insisted that the film could not be made by a Frenchman. The job was given to a German called Carl Koch and, surprisingly, Visconti continued to work on the film. Renoir obviously thought this disloyal of him and the two parted company.

After *Tosca*, Visconti was in a difficult position: as a cavalry officer he had no intention of fighting for Mussolini, and his left-wing views were likely to land him in danger. It was at this point that he came across a French translation of James Cain's *The Postman Always Rings Twice*. He rewrote the piece under the title *Ossessione (Obsession)*. The story was straightforward – a simple tale of murder with a nice twist at the end, nothing controversial or political and thus no problem with the Fascist censors. Visconti now set about raising money – hardly difficult considering his family and their financial connections. But it must be said that he took that simple story and did something quite unexpected and extraordinary with it. Instead of using the theatrical studio manner of most cinema at that time he chose to film on location, using run-down places and ordinary people. In fact he emphasized the unlovely and the squalid. Shot in strongly contrasted black and white, the film appeared in stunning opposition to the flippant confections of the Italian studios or the crude propaganda of the official cinema industry at the time. It was dubbed 'neo-realism' and was identifiably left-wing. To the many who were already finding Mussolini and his hoodlums a sick joke, Visconti became a hero. Inevitably, the censors tried to ban it, but a strange characteristic of Italian Fascism was its nationalist pride in our culture, no matter what form it took. Mussolini held a private showing of *Ossessione*, pronounced it 'art' and let it be distributed. Only in the last desperate days of the Salò regime was the negative destroyed. Fortunately Visconti had kept a 'dupe', an inferior fall-back print, which has meant that some shadow of the original remains.

Liberation found Visconti in the enviable position of being one of the few people in Italian cultural life who appeared to have defied the Fascists. He was a beacon to those of us looking for a new start, and he took up the challenge with an energy that was truly astonishing. Starting in 1945 during the Allied occupation, he introduced to an Italian public starved of foreign ideas modern playwrights like Jean Cocteau, John Steinbeck and Jean-Paul Sartre. The theatre company he formed which toured a country eager for whatever he produced was truly water in the desert.

While all this was happening, there were the usual whispers, the scandals that spilled over into the gossip columns or were passed around the theatrical world – in other words, Luchino Visconti was in every sense a star. And there he was, on the stage below me, throwing a tantrum. My problem was how to attract his attention.

The first difficulty was the head scene-painter, my boss, who caught me leaning over the balcony and told me in no uncertain terms to get back to work. I now had to wait until he was safely out of the way in order to continue my eavesdropping. Over a number of rehearsals the reason for Visconti's tantrums gradually became clear. He had an idea for *Tobacco Road* – not originally in Steinbeck's script – which required a sort of mute one-woman Greek chorus who would observe and in a sense symbolize the action: an old grandmother who would never speak but would crawl animal-like round the stage. They produced various young or middle-aged actresses who were vehemently rejected. He wanted the *real* thing, a mad old lady. This was neo-realism in its most extreme sense and Visconti was pushing it to the limits: to find a very old lady capable of playing this extraordinary role would be no easy task. I slipped downstairs to the wings and quizzed someone in the company just to be sure I'd understood the problem. I had, and when the man saw I was interested he begged me to help, so terrified were they all of Visconti's anger.

Telling him I would do what I could, I set off on my search. Fortunately I had an idea of where to begin: as a child I had seen old men and women in a special grey uniform, the inmates of Monte Domini (the Mountain of the Lord), an old people's refuge with the reputation of a nineteenth-century workhouse. When we passed one of these grey-clad people in the streets the older members of my family would start up a regular litany: 'That's how I'll end up, I know it. When I'm no more use to you, you'll put me there.' Though, as they well knew, no member of our family had ever been near such a place.

Not, that is, until the day I arrived in search of – what? An old woman, *any* old woman, or an actress? I wasn't really sure what I was looking for, though I knew that such old people were usually short of money and grateful for the odd cleaning job, especially during the austere post-war years. The building was appropriately forbidding and an impassive nun listened to my request without comment. She left me in the large, chilly vestibule while she went to make her enquiries. After a brief wait the double doors opened and in tripped a little old lady somewhere between eighty and a hundred. I say 'tripped' because she was a lively, bird-like creature, full of sparkle.

She immediately launched into an unstoppable monologue: 'I'm Virginia Garattoni – used to be in a circus, you know – started at the age of nine – I'm eighty-five, yes, I am – I could hop on horses and climb trees – could do everything, dance and juggle – loved the theatre, dream of my life.'

And suddenly she was off, in full performance, a dance here, a snatch of song there, pulling her shawl over her head and playing a drunk, reciting a bit of a play, pretending to be a dangling marionette. It was inspired, brilliant, mad. Some of the old crones gathered at the windows opening out

66   on to a sort of exercise yard. 'She's a bit crazy,' they said, 'but she keeps us happy.'

I grabbed hold of Virginia's scrawny wrist and led her firmly away. 'Come on,' I said. 'This is your big chance!'

It felt strange, leading her into the theatre. Her uniform was based on the robes of nineteenth-century nuns, complete with grey shawl. Why a young man should be leading such an apparition around was a question that obviously occurred to those we passed. We waited in the wings while Visconti continued his rehearsal. My main problem was to keep her quiet. She was rather deaf and unaware of the need for silence, and in her excitement her already high-pitched voice was piercing.

As the rehearsal came to an end, I managed to get my first real look at the man at the centre of all this. That he was slim and handsome I knew from photographs, but the attractive, bad-tempered air that cowed those around him was a revelation. I liked it and didn't feel at all cowed, which surprised me.

The assistant stage manager was telling him that they had another possibility for the old woman's part, so I told Virginia to get on stage and give him the works. On our way to the theatre I had explained that the famous Count Visconti was looking for someone to crawl around the stage. On cue she went into the biggest crawling routine ever. She played a crawling drunk, sang a crawling song and even managed a sort of crawling dance. She was inspired.

Visconti, for once, was speechless. He described a circle around the stage at the periphery of Virginia's performance. When she finally ceased crawling, he recovered his voice to say the only word possible: 'Miraculous.' He obviously meant it. 'Who found her?'

The assistant stage manager stepped forward, beaming all over his face, apparently intent on claiming the credit.

'I did,' I said, stepping out of the wings and helping Virginia to her feet.

'And who are you?'

'An actor.'

'So you should be with your looks.'

'I also study architecture.' But that did not seem to interest him as much as my appearance.

'What made you bring her here?'

I explained about the scene-painting in the upper gallery and how I had overheard what he'd been saying.

'People spy on me!' he bellowed. 'How dare you? Still you found her and that's good. What are you acting in?' I told him we were rehearsing Jean Cocteau's *Les Enfants terribles* at the home of one of our group, the piece he had had such a success with the previous November. He was clearly flattered.

My mother   My father
As an eight-year-old clown
        With Aunt Lide in Florence, 1936

Gustavo in wartime naval uniform

Aged fourteen

At the Liceo Artistico, 1939: I am in the front row right; my friend Carmelo Bordone is behind me

A snapshot given me by Luchino Visconti on
the opening night of *Crime and Punishment*
    My first film role, as the young lead in *L'ono-
revole Angelina*, directed by Luigi Zampa,
1947

Me (bearded) watching Visconti directing *La
terra trema*, 1948

Directing a member of the chorus in *L'italiana in Algeri*, my first opera, at La Scala, Milan, in 1953

The curtain call when *L'italiana in Algeri* opened at the Holland Festival, with Giulietta Simionato and Carlo Maria Giulini on my right, 1955

Watching Maria Callas try on jewellery in
her dressing-room
    Maria Callas as Fiorilla eyeing the jewels on
the Turk (Nicola Rossi-Lemeni) in *Il turco in
Italia*, La Scala, 1955

With Tullio Serafin in Palermo for Don-
izetti's *Linda di Chamounix*, 1957
Vige, holding a rose, and Aunt Lide arrive
at La Piccola Scala, 1959
Joan Sutherland in the title role of *Lucia di
Lammermoor*, Covent Garden, 1959

Before and after: the setting for the opera *Eurydice* by
Jacopo Peri in the Boboli Gardens, Florence, 1960

'I'll come and see you rehearse tomorrow,' he said. And that was that. I'd done it. I'd broken the barrier and caught the attention of the most interesting man in Italian theatre at that time.

The news that Visconti was coming to see us sent our little group into a panic. I was playing the boy, a rather fey, neurotic part, but I knew that he wouldn't be coming in search of great acting. He arrived with two members of his company and, assuming that he'd come to see me, I shed the role and played myself.

He was studiously courteous about our production and took us all out to dinner, being careful to pay no more attention to me than to the others. But before the evening was over, he had managed to invite me to a private lunch and I knew that my audition, for that is what it surely was, had been successful.

To my surprise, so illustrious a personage was quite happy to let a nobody like me prattle on about my life and my dreams. Over lunch he coaxed out of me the story of my war years and the rather dour world that greeted me when I returned to my father's house. Home, as I explained to him, had become a prison. I felt trapped in Florence and could only wait for something to come along to help me blast my way to freedom. My intended career in the theatre was equally vague and not thought out; I wasn't sure whether I wanted to be an actor, a director or a set designer. I had managed to do a bit of everything with our student drama group. There had been that production of *Dear Brutus*, then Alessandro Brissoni had directed an adaptation of Mark Twain's short story 'The Man Who Corrupted Hadleyburg' immediately after the end of the war. I'd had a part in it as well as designing the sets. This was a period of great experiment on the London stage and I asked all my wartime friends to send me magazines and articles which I pillaged for ideas. We also had the British Council library and a memorable visit from the Old Vic touring company.

Despite my love of design, it was as an actor that I'd first begun to make progress. I was given the young male lead in an amateur production of the pre-war French hit *Les Jours heureux* (*Happy Days*). The big international movie star at that time was Montgomery Clift, handsome, smouldering, with a hint of naïve raffishness. Inevitably we all aped his style, as young actors will. I smouldered my way through *Happy Days* for all I was worth and was tremendously pleased on the first night when a girl came up to me and told me I was the 'new' Montgomery Clift. It might seem quite ridiculous now, but at that moment it was all the praise I could ask for – I looked naïvely raffish and thanked her.

How someone enters the professional theatre and then goes on to succeed usually makes a fascinating story. Unfortunately the tale is often romanticized in the telling and not enough credit is given to pure chance. In my case the pure accident of my being young and good-looking helped me on my way. If this sounds vain, I am sorry, but that is the world of the theatre. The public wants attractive actors and actresses, so inevitably we are conscious of our looks and tend to make a narcissistic appraisal of our qualities. What in others would be intolerable vanity is to us merely the professionalism of an engineer studying his bridge, a driver his engine or a writer his words. I was twenty-two, slim, blond, with blue eyes, and ready to project myself at every opportunity. But at any time there are thousands of good-looking young hopefuls, chafing to get started and wondering where to turn. I take no credit for my looks or for any talent I might have been granted, but I can boast that I was bright enough to work out how to make the leap into professional life.

The answer I found was radio. In the years between the end of the war and the sudden, ineluctable burgeoning of television, radio was the commanding popular medium in Italy. Its comedians were household names and its drama serials were followed with the avidity shown for TV soap operas today. Radio has an ever open door, since it is a voracious user of material; all those broadcast hours have to be filled quickly and cheaply. In contrast to today's TV, radio is receptive to newcomers, and even now almost anyone trying for a part at a radio station will probably be given a sympathetic hearing – you've got to have talent in the end, but it isn't hard to get past the receptionist.

Having realized this, and armed with my *curriculum vitae* of student productions, I presented myself at the Florentine office of the RAI, the state broadcasting company. I was given an audition and a number of bit parts followed.

Next, it was a question of being in the right place at the right time. I had to get into one of those big serials that sometimes became major national obsessions, the way a TV series like *Dallas* is today. I soon heard that they were planning an adaptation of Alessandro Manzoni's nineteenth-century classic *I promessi sposi (The Betrothed)*. This is the story of two young peasant lovers who are determined to marry. Though their families approve, a local landlord falls in love with the girl and uses all his power to prevent the marriage. This simple story is set against the complex, elaborate canvas of seventeenth-century northern Italy. It is one of the few great Italian classics to be a popular, widely-read work. Clearly this was going to be a major production and there was one young man who was very determined to be in it, come what may.

The director of *The Betrothed* was to be Umberto Benedetto, one of the station regulars. I found myself with occasional one-line parts in some of his productions, but try as I might there is a limit to how much you can project in a few words. So how could I attract his attention? The answer came with the decision by another director to do *The Flowers are Not for You to Pick*, which Tyrone Guthrie had directed in England. This was a piece of good fortune, as Guthrie was one of those avant-garde stars of the London theatre whom I knew about from the magazines my wartime British friends sent me. I also knew the story of the play, almost a monologue by a young man drowning at sea who recalls his entire life – an absolutely stunning part for a new actor. Because, allied to my growing reputation as a juvenile voice, I was able to talk fluently about Guthrie's work, I was offered the role. It was nicely timed: *Flowers* was broadcast as Benedetto began casting *The Betrothed*, and after my success as the drowning youth he offered me the part of the young peasant lover.

The series was scheduled to run for eight Sunday evenings. In those days there were no taped shows, only live broadcasts, and this meant that if I committed myself to the part I had to guarantee appearing in all the episodes. I gave my word, but naturally I didn't say anything to Father. Getting to the rehearsals in the afternoon was easy enough, but the actual broadcasts on Sunday evenings were another matter, because my father was maniacal about our sitting down together promptly for Sunday dinner. With the help of Fanny I had to come up with all kinds of pretexts for not being there, every week a different one: a friend was ill; I had to study at someone's house for an exam the next day; I had to go to something special at the theatre, or whatever. But the series was very long, and soon it became more difficult to come up with plausible excuses. Then, as the show progressed, it became a tremendous hit. Most of Italy was tuning in and inevitably my father, like everyone else, began to listen. Now commenced the sort of cat-and-mouse game that families often play amongst themselves in order to preserve a fragile unity. Father continued to pretend he knew nothing about it and let me try to mastermind my way out of Sunday dinner every week. But once I was gone he would settle down with Fanny to enjoy the programme, always switching on the radio a little late so as not to hear the cast-list being read out. In the end he never missed a session, which meant, incredibly for him, staying away from his club on Sunday nights.

Obviously he had mixed feelings about it. He was terrified that it would lead to my giving up my studies for the theatre and also realized that I was earning money on my own and becoming less dependent on him. He liked the idea that he controlled the purse-strings and would give money for a pack of cigarettes or for a few extras, but no more. My role in *I promessi sposi* was the beginning of my escape from prison and it was difficult for him to accept that.

There was a party after the last episode of the series and I remember the pure pleasure of being asked for my autograph for the first time. I stayed out very late, but when I got home Father was still up and waiting. All pretence was over and a blazing tirade followed in which he ranted about my stupidity, my utter folly in preferring acting to architecture.

70   There seemed to be a sadistic kind of satisfaction in the way he played this role of the old-fashioned father. It was ironic that *now*, after all his years of neglecting me, he should be so concerned. He talked as if he had no idea that I was almost twenty-three years old. He also had no idea that his obsession with my becoming an architect was turning me against it. I was old enough to know what I wanted and he was driving me closer to it by the minute. I said nothing, let him vent his spleen, and went to bed.

The next day brought a curious sense of let-down. The series was over, gone, and my little moment of glory seemed to have blown away with it. No one was beating a path to my door to offer me those wonderful roles I felt were my due. But it was no use moping – the row with my father had convinced me that I had to stop being financially dependent on him.

I decided it was time to do things for myself, to take odd jobs and earn some money of my own. First, I started to work for a group of craftsmen who specialized in 'ageing' furniture for export to America and England. The idea was to make new furniture look antique. It was fascinating to learn the centuries-old tricks of their trade, to see how they aged wood in their small dark shops on the seedy little side-streets near the centre of the city. The secret, as I discovered, was to go to riding stables and collect horse's urine in buckets. Big containers of it were filled in the shops, and the wood was soaked in it, then exposed in the sun. The wood began to crack and age before our eyes. Then we fired at the wood with scatter-shot from hunting-guns to simulate woodworm. I also made small watercolours which were sold as souvenirs to the American soldiers. The Florentines sold anything they could to their 'liberators'.

While all this was going on, I continued at the university and tried not to neglect my studies, but the call of the theatre was strong and I would do almost anything to get near a production.

My chance came when it was announced that the city intended to revive the Maggio Musicale Fiorentino, the 'Musical May', which had started back in 1933 under the patronage of the crown princess but which had ceased in the last years of the war. The revival was decided at very short notice, and famous directors and performers were brought in from all over Italy to create the works. A general appeal was made for people to come forward and help. I volunteered to join the scene painters who were working at the Teatro della Pergola, and that was how I met the great Visconti.

Luchino – we were soon on first-name terms – took me out a couple of times after rehearsals. They were polite, entertaining meals *à deux*. When he wasn't pumping me for the story of my life, I would listen happily to his reminiscences of a way of life far beyond my *petit bourgeois* experience. He was not boasting, he wasn't that sort of man; he did not talk down to you, but assumed that you too had walked with princes. Today we are perhaps less impressed by the *soigné* aristocrat, but in 1946 so impeccably dressed and well-groomed a figure as Count Visconti was a pleasure in itself. It was reassuring through its own self-assurance. At its most mundane, the first thing I noticed about Luchino Visconti was not the silk handkerchief or the Parisian tie, but his scent, and at our second meeting I was impertinent enough to ask him what it was.

'Hammam Bouquet,' he explained. 'It's made up for a few clients by an old firm called Penhaligon's in London. It's been used by the kings of England for generations and a select group manage to get a bottle or two from time to time.'

Despite this apparent narcissism, the main impression that Luchino Visconti left was his masculine quality, his virility. He looked like his own Renaissance ancestors must have done, a sort of proud warrior. He had a classical profile and strong, mobile features with heavy eyebrows, large dark eyes and a sportsman's physique. Of course, the quality of his clothes, his expensive suits, silk shirts, handmade shoes and discreet jewellery all added to his naturally aristocratic air. Yet he was no dandy; the overall impression was of a rather ruthless self-confidence.

When Luchino left for Milan for the opening of *Tobacco Road* my little world seemed rather flat, but after the first night a telegram arrived telling me what a success it was and how it was all due to the extraordinary Virginia Garattoni and thus to me. It turned out that she really was the star of the show, and she went on to tour Italy for nearly a year, the darling of the company and as happy as could be, hogging the limelight. When it was over, she returned to the old people's home with a comfortable nest egg and a new set of memories with which to entertain her fellow pensioners.

With the play settled in Milan, Luchino returned to Rome, but not before stopping off in Florence to see me. He arrived in a stunning creamy-white BMW sports car. It was the early summer of 1946 and he suggested a tour of the Tuscan countryside, a part of Italy he barely knew and for which I was an excellent guide. I suppose I ought to have been flattered by his attention, but I was nothing if not sure of myself – was I not the Italian Montgomery Clift about to take the road to Hollywood? Nowadays, older and wiser, my younger self quite amazes me. I sometimes wonder what my reaction would be if I were to meet myself as I was then. Would this boy charm me, or would I find him arrogant and pushy? Obviously the former was Luchino's impression as we drove around Tuscany. I discovered, to my surprise, that his appreciation of things was always at one remove – the Florence he wanted to see was the city described by the Communist writer Vasco Pratolini in novels like *A Tale of Poor Lovers* and *Il quartiere* (*A Tale of Santa Croce*). When we visited old churches and castles in the countryside, this otherwise urbane man showed clear signs of his misspent schooldays by an ignorance of an art and history that I took for granted. He often confused the *quattrocento* with the *cinquecento*. But these were

72   minor considerations when strolling round Siena with that athletic figure in his sporty Battistoni monogrammed shirts and his lightweight double-breasted suits (never a waistcoat) from the finest Milanese tailors. He spoke with the French-style 'r', a sign of the northern Italian aristocracy that ensured the best attentions of waiters and hotel receptionists.

Then, suddenly, through all this charm and style the cracks would appear – the fury and the temper if things were not going his way. But I noticed that, if Luchino threw a fit and decided to break something, it was always a cracked cup that he chose to hurl so dramatically at the wall. This observation helped me to accept such moods, while others shook with fear. It was the best lesson I learned from him, the art of a well-timed tantrum. I soon learned that, if I stood up to him, he backed off at once and this realization helped me keep my balance in what was to be a long and turbulent relationship. Of course, there was something calculating about my attitude to Luchino; I was an unknown, small-time actor in search of that big chance everyone needs, and he was at the pinnacle of his stage career. But to see that he, too, was a man who subtly weighed the advantages of every action was comforting.

Inevitably, my friends took it upon themselves to warn me of the dangers of my association with so notoriously volatile and talked-about a character. Politely but firmly I told them to spare me their advice, feeling with some justification that after two firing squads and the proximity of death on several other occasions, the attentions of a forty-year-old nobleman were hardly likely to prove uncontrollably dangerous. There was, in any case, the one great barrier to my being completely enthralled by him – his politics. From the very beginning I found his upper-class Communism faintly ridiculous. Later I was to see how the 'Party' used celebrities and intellectuals like Luchino to burnish its image, and I came to despise his blindness. In our circle of friends we called Luchino 'Philippe Égalité' and would joke with him that he should pray to God that the Communists never came to power lest he end on the scaffold like his namesake.

That first summer of 1946 Luchino went to his family for the holidays. I was to join my father at the seaside, but first I went to Siena to join my mother's cousin Ines Alfani-Tellini. Apart from Gustavo, Aunt Ines was the only member of my family who had any connection with the stage. She had been, in her day, one of Toscanini's favourite singers and, when her voice had gone, she turned to teaching. She had great sympathy for up-and-coming young performers and every September she went to Siena to help the Accademia Musicale organize its master classes for young musicians and singers from all over the world. The teachers were often the finest in their fields and the pupils full of promise.

In those late summer weeks the city was filled with music, every hall taken up with rehearsals and concerts. The high spot of the season was the annual opera production, often a revival of a little-performed work, organized by Ines herself. At first she tried to do everything – directing and singing – but she soon realized that it was too much for her. That year she asked me to go down to Siena to help design her production of Pergolesi's *La contadina astuta*.

Although I had always been 'musical' and had loved opera since my introduction to *Die Walküre,* I had never thought of myself as part of that world. Those few days in Siena were a revelation, as I suddenly began to sense how theatre and music could combine. It must be said that before the war they seldom did – an opera was a set piece for a star singer, the classic soprano/tenor showcase, little more than a costumed concert. We loved it because of the music, but I, for one, had never taken it as seriously as I did the theatre. Now, working close to singers, I began to sense other possibilities.

After Siena, I joined my father on the coast. Twenty-three years old, and conscious that I was at a turning-point in my life, I threw everything into reverse and almost from the first day embarked on an idyllic summer love affair with a girl called Anita, whom I met walking along the endless beach at Viareggio. When I saw Visconti's *Death in Venice* years later with that last scene of the dying von Ashenbach slumped in a deck-chair watching the boys playing innocently on the beach, I could imagine myself among them. It was an attempt to stop the clock, to make those long days of sea and sun go on forever, to opt out of a life in which every move had to be weighed, every action assessed and planned, as if it were still possible to live the way we had before the war, when pleasure was a bicycle ride in the countryside and ambition was a goal in our local football match. But at the summer's end, when I told Anita that I planned to give up architecture for the stage, she reacted exactly as my father had done. She warned, she ridiculed, she failed completely to see what I longed to do. I saw how impossible it was. She kept asking me why and reminding me that I only had five out of twenty-seven examinations left to take. She became associated in my mind with a life at a drawing-board planning bridges, bus stations and co-operatives, the very prison from which I wanted to escape. We returned to Florence, both aware that things had changed between us.

I thought that it was just the end of a summer romance and decided to forget her, heartlessly perhaps. Indeed, it did look as if she too wanted nothing more to do with me, as she made no attempt to get in touch. Then, one day, when a mutual friend telephoned to exchange the usual gossip, she asked why I didn't want to know about Anita, I, in turn, asked her why she wanted to know, but she merely said that I should call back in an hour, when Anita would be there. I didn't do so. What was the point? But, a few days later, that same friend wrote to say that Anita was in trouble, she was frightened of her family and I must see her. I took all this to be

girlish nonsense, just a way of getting me to come back, and I instantly
dismissed it. In any case, I had other, more pressing things to think about.

With his usual impeccable timing, there had been a letter from Luchino
waiting for me when I got back from Viareggio. He told me he was putting
together a new company with a first production of *Crime and Punishment*
to open on 6 November and – saved till last, of course – there was a small
part for me, if I wished it.

Now, at last, my father had to be told that I would be leaving home,
and it was as dramatic as can be imagined. Not for him the careful selection
of the cracked cup – he just broke everything in sight. Having exhausted
the china and glass, he opened a drawer and pulled out a revolver, which
he started to wave about.

'I made you, now I'll unmake you. I'll do it, I will, I will. . . .'

My stepsister, Fanny, started screaming and I ran out of the house to
spend the next few days with friends until the worst of his rage had passed.

Fanny was the only one who stood by me – on the day I left she handed
me an umbrella as a parting gift, and so I arrived in Rome in early October
almost penniless with only a battered suitcase and her present clutched in
my hand. Apart from Luchino, my only contact was Piero Tellini, the son
of my aunt Ines Alfani-Tellini. Finding him was to prove an act of good
fortune in more ways than one. In the first place, he lived in what was then
a rather seedy boarding-house near the Spanish Steps, where he found me
a room. Today the Hotel Inghilterra is one of the most fashionable in Rome,
prominent in what has become a chic area of smart boutiques. Then, all
that could be said of the Inghilterra was that it was cheap and had
character, which means the plumbing was doubtful. Still, I was grateful
for it.

I saw Luchino on the days when I rehearsed, infrequently because of the
smallness of my part, but otherwise it was much as it had been before with
only the occasional evening meal or weekend trip together. He was very
fastidious about work and I was shown no favours, for which I was grateful.
I was proud to be working with what were at that time the greats of the
Italian stage and did not wish to be branded as someone's protégé. Luchino
had certainly put together a remarkable array of talent: Rina Morelli, Paolo
Stoppa, Vittorio Gassman, Memo Benassi. . . .

All together, Luchino had a company of almost forty players, some of
whom (though not myself) were on full contracts, which meant that they
were paid whether or not there was a part for them. This was typical of
Luchino, the grand gesture quite out of proportion to his resources. I loved
this flamboyance; as a young man it seemed appropriate to me that a great
artist should not give a damn about mundane matters.

We rehearsed *Crime and Punishment* every day in the Teatro Eliseo in
the Via Nazionale and I drank in the opportunity to be directed by so great

a figure. The play was splendid, having been adapted for the French stage by Gaston Baty, and further worked on by Luchino in its Italian version. It was a Russian epic with everyone in the company taking part. To cope with what were, in effect, over thirty-five different scenes Luchino had devised a single open set with areas where different actions took place. This was important to me, for although I had only a tiny role as one of the masons redecorating the room where Raskolnikov kills the two women, I was nevertheless on stage the whole time. My fellow mason, played by Giorgio di Lullo, who later became a successful theatre director in Italy, had to be moody and hysterical, while I was tough and carefree.

I was intrigued by the way Luchino worked as a director, playing every part, acting out every line. I must admit he wasn't a very good actor and sometimes his delivery was embarrassing but it was a very effective way of implanting a single person's view on a complex production and one I use myself to this day.

Sometimes at the end of rehearsals he would come over and discreetly invite me to his home in the Via Salaria for dinner. Luchino was a very precise man, typical of the disciplined aristocrat, and these occasions were always identical. At the end of a day's work he would soak in his bath – he never took a shower in his life – and would read scripts or the latest novel. If I was there, I would sit by the bath talking to him. I am not ashamed to admit that as often as possible I tried to steer the conversation in the direction of myself and my future. After his soak, Luchino would put on one of his many elegant dressing-downs and get into bed, where the butler would bring dinner in silver dishes on a tray.

The following morning the mask of professionalism would be resumed and we would make our separate ways to rehearsals.

The one thing that marred the excitement of being in Rome was news from Florence about Anita. That letter from our friend telling me that Anita was in trouble had not been a lover's ploy – she had been pregnant and had had a miscarriage. I was appalled. Why hadn't I done something? I thought of my own mother, what she had gone through that I should have life and now look at me, at the way I had behaved. Observing the theatrical world I had just joined, I knew that the possibility of marriage and family was not for me. Anita had been my one chance and I had rejected it. Whatever longing I had for children would have to be satisfied elsewhere.

I remember *Crime and Punishment* was a success when it opened in November, though I can recall nothing of the opening night. Perhaps my mind was already preoccupied with how I would survive after the run. With typical unconcern, Luchino had completely ignored the vast company he had assembled and decided that his next production would be Tennessee Williams's *The Glass Menagerie,* which has only four parts. Still, I saw no

76   reason to complain. This was the very heart of what mattered in the Italian theatre and I was in it, so what if I missed a meal or two? In every way, from the quality of the players to the treasure trove of foreign drama that Italy had been denied, this was a golden age for the theatre. Television did not yet dominate everything, and the theatre was still the place where you went for ideas and entertainment, where each new production was eagerly awaited and much discussed. But golden age or no, we certainly weren't overpaid. I received 1,000 lire a day, if I was acting, equivalent then to about £5 a week. Admittedly things were cheap, but my room at the Inghilterra still cost half my income. As Luchino was more likely to give me a silk handkerchief than the 10,000 lire it cost, something had to be done.

It was here that Piero Tellini became my real saviour. Piero had inherited his mother's artistic flair. When I arrived in Rome he was beginning to make a reputation as a scriptwriter with the newly revived Italian cinema. Thanks to him I was able to join that other branch of our post-war cultural Renaissance. When I was not with Visconti and the company I would sit up half the night with denizens of the film world like Roberto Rossellini. Rossellini's *Rome, Open City* had taken up the torch lit by Visconti's *Ossessione* in its attempt at a realistic breath of air after the bland Fascist cinema that had wallowed in the conventions of 1930s film-making. Anna Magnani was magnificent in it. It was a surprise to see an actress who had, until then, been heavily made up and glamorously dressed suddenly revealed as an earthy woman. That was the great shock value of neo-realist films after the grey-toned lighting and studio sets of a former generation. Rossellini had used a wonderful scriptwriter, Sergio Amidei, but the element that was perhaps undervalued at the time was that *Rome, Open City* succeeded because immensely experienced performers like Magnani and Aldo Fabrizi, who played the priest, were suddenly allowed honest dramatic roles, an opportunity that they seized with gusto. It was only later that I realized just how much this was an actor's cinema and not, as was thought at the time, a director's.

So there I was, a witness to two cultural explosions. Luchino was on a winning streak and thanks to Piero I eked out my salary with the odd day in Cinecittà dubbing the seemingly endless stream of American films that were flooding the country. There was also the occasional fee to be earned from designing logos for film publicity material, so I managed to get by.

One day, during the run of *Crime and Punishment,* Piero invited me to a restaurant to meet what he described as a fascinating American – 'Very pro-Italian, knows a lot about the new cinema.' I was intrigued by the idea of this paragon but understood at once when I saw him sitting at our table.

'Well, I'll be ... Haven't seen you since we buried Mussolini.'

This had the whole restaurant staring at us, and thus I met Donald Downes again.

He really was an astonishing man, willing to do anything to live in his
beloved Italy. He was now in Rome working as a writer and journalist.
With his articles in the American press, Donald more than anyone else
publicized the new Italian cinema abroad and generated the interest in
what was going on which eventually had Hollywood clamouring for people
like Magnani. Like Piero, he was also doing a bit of scriptwriting and was
eventually to write a film for Charlton Heston, but his true role in life was
to be one of those prescient people who see what is new and good in others
and help make it known. From that evening in the restaurant we were to
remain close friends until his death.

During the meal he was, as always, full of lively, trenchant opinions about
the way the world was going. He was highly critical of his own government,
whom he accused of losing the peace by not understanding the danger to
countries like Italy. At that time politics were everybody's main preoccupation. The first post-war election of 1946 had produced a Christian-
Democrat government, but there was to be another election in 1948 and
the Communists were confident that they would come to power – hence the
importance of men like Visconti in gilding their image. Donald Downes was
scathing about such antics and provided a useful counterbalance to the
band of left-wing activists who surrounded Luchino.

Donald also helped me find dubbing work. He was closely involved in
the new cinema, in fact he was in one way its *deus ex machina*. He did some
work with the American news agencies and, quite simply, he stole from the
rich to give to the poor. The problem for people like Rossellini was finding
film stock and Donald could be relied on to spirit away the necessary reels
of Dupont I or II negative if supplies dried up. At the time, this was the
best negative on the market, and inevitably the American news crews took
if for granted, wasting reels of the precious stuff.

'What do they need it for?' Donald would shout. 'They only tell lies.'

The high definition of that stolen Dupont film accounts for the quality
of the black-and-white contrast in much neo-realist cinema – a fact not
generally acknowledged.

After *The Glass Menagerie* Luchino decided to do Jean Anouilh's
Eurydice, which fortunately had about sixteen parts, one of them for me.
We opened in Florence and, when I came on in my small role as a bus
driver, I could sense the buzz in the gallery as word went round that it was
Zeffirelli down there, and did you know this and had you heard that – I
doubt any of them followed my part at all.

I avoided my father and stayed with Aunt Lide. One reason was that I
didn't want to see him until I was able to prove him wrong. For the
moment, as a mere bit player, I seemed to fulfil all his worst predictions
that if I gave up architecture I would end up a nobody.

That was early in 1947 and we went on to tour other cities before

78   returning to Rome. My cousin Piero Tellini's first big breakthrough came in the summer of 1947 with the acceptance of a full-length script he had written himself, *L'onorevole Angelina* (*The Honourable Angelina*), the story of the struggle of a working woman who eventually becomes a heroine to the poor. It entirely suited the spirit of the times, being both earthy and socialist in spirit. It also offered a marvellous role for a female star and the director, Luigi Zampa, was able to cast Anna Magnani as the lead. Piero fixed me up with the job of designing the logo for the film publicity and it was when I took my sketches round that I first saw the woman regarded as the most interesting Italian actress of the post-war years. Filming had just begun and I was waiting behind camera for Zampa to finish when Magnani walked on set, coolly elegant in a flimsy black dress, her coat over her shoulders and the inevitable dachshund cupped in her left arm.

I was transfixed. There she was, a living legend. To us Italians and indeed the rest of the world she was the archetypal free-wheeling Roman woman – her sentimental songs like *Quanto sei bella Roma* were to Italy what *Lilli Marlene* had been to Britain and Germany. And she really gave the impression of being a true Roman she-wolf – she would quarrel with taxi drivers, haggle like a fishwife in the street markets and had even made rude jokes about the Fascists when they were in power.

Everybody loved her, yet the irony was that she wasn't Roman at all but the illegitimate daughter of an Italian/Jewish mother and an Egyptian father in Alexandria. Only later did she become Roman, when her grandmother brought her from Egypt and raised her in one of the Roman slum districts, from where she'd struggled to get a place in the Academy of Dramatic Art. She paid her way by singing bawdy songs in seedy bars and clubs, which probably accounts for her famous disdain where men were concerned; she ate them up. A marriage to the director Goffredo Alessandrini, who had offered her her first screen role, was a failure. The longest lasting love-affair was with the actor Massimo Serato during the war. Serato was the father of her only child, Luca. The baby boy was the absolute centre of her life, but then tragedy struck: towards the end of the war he contracted polio. This was before Dr Salk's vaccine was available and Anna was completely distraught – she looked on it as a cruel act of fate and none of her friends could calm her down. As soon as the war ended, she began a fruitless pilgrimage to clinics around Europe. Nurses were hired and an endless procession of doctors came to treat the poor little boy. The result was terrible for Anna; nothing worked and ineluctably Luca developed those sad withered legs that were the cruel evidence of the ghastly disease. Worse for her was the boy's reaction. Because the arrival of his mother usually meant the advent of another doctor with another painful operation, he began to scream and struggle whenever she came into his room. She adored him so much and yet he refused to let her near him. Gradually, when she accepted that there was no cure and the doctors stopped coming, he was reconciled to her; in fact he worshipped her. But, when I first met her, she was right in the middle of all this harrowing drama and it was little wonder that her famous short temper was so evident.

That day, when she walked on to our film set, she was raring to show us a first-class example of the art of tantrum-throwing.

'What about the boy?' she demanded of Zampa. 'Have you changed him? I mean you're crazy to put that boy on with me – it's just politics, that's why he's here, he's just nothing.'

Zampa barely protested. 'It's difficult,' he said. 'It isn't easy to find a boy for this role, someone nice and charming.'

'Rome is full of nice, charming kids,' Magnani said walking away. 'Look around, open your eyes, for God's sake.'

She hovered on the edge of the set and Zampa stood there immobile. Thinking he was free, I went up and held out my sketches, but Zampa was too preoccupied and only shook his head. As I stood there wondering what to do next, Magnani returned to the attack.

'I'm not coming tomorrow,' she added.

'Easy, Anna. I can't change an actor just like that. He's trying his best. Then there's his agent. Anyway, who do we get instead?'

'That little idiot there!' she shouted, pointing at me across the studio. 'Isn't that the whole point about our new cinema – anyone can act as long as the face is right? So he'll do.' She turned away.

The director called me over. 'Come here, you. Who are you?'

'He's my cousin,' said Piero, 'he's a designer.'

Zampa looked me straight in the eyes. 'Have you ever acted?'

Miraculously, before I could say that I had, Piero kicked me sharply in the heel. I immediately got the message. In the neo-realist world the ability to act was a definite drawback. I shook my head in a hammy negative.

'All right, let's try it,' he said. He led me to one side of the set, a small room with a table and a cup. I asked for a script but he just smiled ruefully.

'Don't bother,' he said. 'You'll never learn it, just say numbers.'

I said: 'No. Give me the lines. And I want to be made up.'

Zampa sighed, his worst fears realized. He'd got an egomaniac on his hands.

'All right, all right, somebody take him to make-up.'

While they made me up I rapidly memorized the page of script they had reluctantly given me. Then I went back on set and went straight into my Montgomery Clift routine, all charm and corner of the eye tricks. When I finished there was a stony silence. I looked round, trying to see beyond the lights. Then I heard the cameraman whisper to someone with a touch of disappointment: 'He knows how to act.'

They were standing there wondering how to cope with this major flaw in my character when Magnani returned. They explained the problem to her.

'So he can act,' she said. 'If he can act we can't do anything about it. He looks right for the role. Take him on.'

And with that I was hired.

I turned up next morning and started at once, in a suit slightly too large for me. There was no time and no money to get properly kitted out and as I was playing the son of a wealthy property developer I had to borrow bits and pieces – gold watch, etc. – from friends. It's amazing just how homespun and do-it-yourself the cinema was in the 1940s. We all wanted success so much we just did whatever was needed without thinking about it.

It was a splendid role for me. I was an idealistic rich boy who has a tremendous dramatic scene when he challenges his money-grubbing father. I was able to call on memories of my own family squabbles for that necessary touch of realism, but Magnani wasn't fooled.

'Come on,' she said. 'Tell me all about your acting.'

So, during breaks, she got the whole story out of me, Luchino and all. It was the start of our friendship and for a time we were inseparable. She hated being alone and loved staying up late, so there were many nights spent talking till dawn. That first day she decided to tease me.

'I see old Luchino doesn't miss a bit,' she said. 'So you belong to his stable.'

That stung. 'I don't think so,' I said with as much spirit as I could muster. 'I belong to his company.'

'Quite,' she said, laughing in her usual raucous way, her hand on her chest in a typical Magnani theatrical gesture. Then she turned suddenly serious: 'You're ambitious, aren't you? I can tell. In fact, I don't think I've ever met anyone with so much ambition burning inside them. But take care. Though I love Luchino, I know he's a snake. You may be able to get at the good inside him, but you need a very special corkscrew.'

She smiled at her own vulgarity. I sat speechless.

It was a little too incestuous the way everyone was linked together in those days. At first I kept as quiet as possible about the film, suspecting that Luchino would not be happy about it, but before long he and Magnani were working together and the story was out. Tennessee Williams had come over for the première of *The Glass Menagerie* and was so happy he gave Luchino the Italian rights for *A Streetcar Named Desire,* which had just opened on Broadway. The plan was to star Magnani, whom Tennessee adored, and so she was pulled back into the Visconti set. More surprisingly, so was Donald Downes, who knew Tennessee, though I guessed he did not fully approve of him. This was all a bit too much like being *in* a glass menagerie.

Life in Rome was becoming claustrophobic, I needed a breath of fresh
air. My solution was to take a summer break at my favourite bolt-hole,
Positano, the southern fishing village that Carmelo and I had discovered
on our tour in 1941. I had been back several times, sometimes taking friends
along, happy to show them the still unspoilt beauty of those narrow streets
winding down to the imposing church and the little sea-front caught
between two high mountain spurs. The village had retained its charm
because of its inaccessibility – the only way there was to take the perilous
donkey track over the pass from Sorrento or to make the journey by sea,
as rich families from the court of Naples had done in the seventeenth
century when they came for the balmier air of the Costa Amalfitana during
the oppressive summer months. They built their solid, red-washed villas on
the hillsides above the jumbled fishermen's houses or dotted them on the
various promontories overlooking the village. When I had discovered the
place, there was an air of genteel decay about them, a faded beauty that
merged with the older buildings, some of which dated back to Roman times.

I had made various friends on my holidays, including two brothers who
were either sons or nephews, I never found out which, of the Duchess of
Villarosa. She had a house across the bay on the choicest site of all, an
outcrop almost directly opposite Positano, which afforded a view across to
the village that was breathtaking. One day the two boys and I swam from
cove to cove round to the villa, where I saw for the first time the place that
would later become central to my life. We arrived first at a shingle beach,
where we saw a sight hidden from Positano by the spur of limestone rock –
a cascade falling sheer down the cliff to a wheel which still turned in a
dilapidated Roman mill. It was nearly a ruin and the two boys waved to
a strange old fellow who appeared to live there. They explained that he
was Semenoff, a Russian who had once owned the buildings on this outcrop
but who had been forced to sell off all but the mill, where he now eked out
his existence. The Duchess of Villarosa had bought the three villas on the
hillside, known collectively as the Villa Treville, the lowest showing signs
of its Roman origins, the two highest in eighteenth-century style. The
Duchess invited me to stay for lunch and let me explore the decayed
buildings, used only in the hottest weather and hardly maintained at all.
The place was a riot of Mediterranean vegetation, pines, flowers, trees,
cacti. Through the foliage were romantic glimpses of Positano, an opera set
with dramatic mountains behind it, over which the occasional clouds of
summer mist poured like dry ice, so thoroughly unreal was the whole vision.
This was the antidote to the neo-realism of Rome, that black-and-white
world, with its second-hand concern for the human condition promoted
against a backdrop of the rising *dolce vita* that I was already finding too
hypocritical.

The Duchess was a brilliant woman. Fluent in English, she had several

Zeffirelli

British guests that day. Because I understood what was being said, I gathered that she was tired of Treville – it needed a lot of work, which she couldn't be bothered with. She was, in short, keen to sell. It was one of those moments that later, when one sees everything that has sprung from it, seems too accidental for something so important. The reason for my excitement at the Duchess's remarks was that I knew that Donald was looking for a summer house. He had a rich American friend, Bob Ullman, another cultivated Bostonian, who had sold his New York house in Beekman Place so that the two of them could look for an Italian home. Earlier that year, at my suggestion, they had toured the Amalfi coast in Bob's stylish silver-grey Buick and had asked me to look out for a suitable property. When I got back to Rome, I told them about the Duchess and her villas, a discovery from which I was to benefit as much as they.

All in all, those were great times for Donald and one sure sign of his success as a journalist was the attention Hollywood now paid to Italian film-makers. Donald introduced us all to Helen Deutsch, an independent producer and a scout for RKO. She was particularly keen to get Magnani and had asked to see the rushes of *The Honourable Angelina*. That evening Donald introduced me, she remembered seeing me in the film rushes and offered her congratulations. She was most interested in the fact that I spoke English and, when we went on to a night-club, she took the opportunity to pump me for information. The next day I received a summons to the Grand Hotel, where completely unexpectedly she offered me a five-year contract in Hollywood at $500 a week, a sum quite beyond my dreams. Yet for a reason that I could not have explained, something inside me said: 'Wait.' I stammered my thanks, told her how honoured I was, how grateful, proud, humble – said anything to fill the gap while I tried to work out what I really felt. Happily, she was a kindly soul and saw at once the dilemma I was in.

'Take a month,' she said. 'Think it over and let me know, I'll hold it open for you.'

I ran to Donald's apartment to tell him the amazing news and was somewhat taken aback by his reaction.

'It's not for you,' he said. 'Magnani, yes, she's that sort of star material, but you're something else.'

He must have seen how hurt I was, for he quickly explained that it wasn't that I couldn't act; it was that in Hollywood I would be just another pretty boy hanging about waiting in case they needed someone to fill a gap. Magnani they would use, me they might not. The risk was five years of playing the Latin lover in second-rate movies and then what?

Luchino was more abrasive.

'You?' he laughed. 'The new Valentino? Oh, please ...'

That almost made me take up the offer, but in the end I accepted

Donald's advice. He was quite right, of course, but the letter to Helen Deutsch was one of the hardest I've ever had to write.

There was one positive side-effect from this episode. Despite his offhand manner, Luchino had apparently been quite surprised. He always nurtured a secret longing for Hollywood and there was I being offered the chance he desired. Not long afterwards, with all the nonchalance he could muster, he told me he was planning to make another film and might consider making me one of his assistants.

Thus, only one year after coming to Rome I had made my first moves in both theatre and film – and more surprisingly opera, thanks again to Aunt Ines. She invited me back to Siena to design Vivaldi's *Serenade for Three*, but, when I arrived, she asked if I would take over the production. She was an inspired teacher, but knew she had little talent for directing. So the seeds of the three branches of my career were planted with such rapidity that I was hardly able to take stock of where I was heading.

I returned from Siena in late September 1947 to find Luchino in the throes of trying to raise money for his new film, not easy for someone of his political views. The task of finding backers was not helped by the subject of the film, or rather films, virtually a revolutionary tract about poverty in Sicily. Luchino had gone to Sicily earlier that year to make a documentary. He had been entranced by the beauty of the fishing villages and appalled at the poverty and exploitation of the people. It brought back memories of a writer we all read in school, Giovanni Verga, who lived in Catania and Milan at the turn of the century. Though Verga often wrote about Milanese subjects, his greatest works were stories of his native Sicily – *Cavalleria rusticana,* subject of the opera; *La lupa,* which became a famous play, and *I malavoglia,* the story of the ill-fated lives of a village of Sicilian fisherfolk whose wretched conditions lead to an unsuccessful rebellion.

It was this latter story which Luchino wanted to use, but, as Verga had only died in the 1920s, the copyright was not available. That was not a final barrier, however, as Luchino planned a complete ideological revamp, bringing the story up to date as a tale of fishermen and workers abused by the capitalist system. His idea was on the grand scale. He planned a panoramic trilogy under the title *La terra trema (The Earth Trembles)*. The story, drawn from Verga, of the unsuccessful revolt would be part one. The second was never written, but would have dealt with the island's sulphur miners. The final part was to have shown the peasants and workers successfully rising up against the aristocrats and landowners. The roar and noise of their galloping horses as they hastened to occupy the land would cause the earth to tremble, hence the title of the whole trilogy. But as no more than one part was ever made, it became an unfulfilled dream. Verga's heirs wanted nothing to do with this version, which in truth was far removed from the spirit of the original. Verga was very resigned, like Chekhov in a

84 way, accepting misery as a condition of destiny and not at all as a spring-board for political action.

Luchino borrowed a small fortune but even that was not enough. Any potential backers were also put off by the realization that the film might appear at the time of the forthcoming election in 1948, and everybody knew what sort of earth-trembling people like Luchino were hoping for then. In the end help came from an unexpected source. A Sicilian tycoon, Salvo d'Angelo, raised the money from the Bank of Sicily. Luchino appeared on a Monday to say he would have the money in a week and he would start filming in a month. We – for I was instantly confirmed as assistant director – would leave at once for Sicily to search for locations.

Our main base was Verga's own setting, the village of Acitrezza near Catania, then even less changed by time than Positano. The lives of the fisherfolk were primitive, as if our century did not exist. The fish traders certainly abused their position by paying the people only one per cent of the price their catch would eventually realize. Luchino was sincerely moved by the hopeless conditions of the villagers and felt genuinely that his coming would help them. If I was more cautious in my views, it was not because I couldn't see the wrongs that were done to the fishermen, but rather that I worried that people like Luchino had only the ways of the twentieth century to offer in exchange and that it was the very absence of those ways which gave the villagers what slight yet precious dignity they had. Their lives *were* hard and unjust, but they were also balanced and peaceful compared to the squalor of Italy's industrial north. One would have to be very sure of oneself to disturb that balance – Luchino was sure.

The plan he formulated was somewhat worrying. He would continue to its ultimate point what he had begun in *Ossessione* (which others had later taken up) – no actors at all, only the actual locations with the local people being themselves. They would even use the heavy local dialect, closer to Greek than Italian, though no one except the locals could understand it.

We returned to Rome, he excited, me dubious. Donald was persuaded to acquire some Dupont film stock, while we assembled our crew and returned to Acitrezza for six months' filming. Luchino's other assistant was Franco Rosi, who was in charge of continuity, an incredibly important yet tedious task before the invention of the Polaroid camera, because it meant staying close to the film camera and taking endless notes.

I had the apparently happier task of choosing the performers and briefing them on the story, so that they could dream up their words. But from the beginning it was clear that this was to be no easy ride. First I had to master the dialect. That was simple compared to dealing with the 'actors' once it became clear that with the camera ever present there is no such thing as 'reality'. Even in a documentary the participants tend to put on a show. Here the policeman was meant to 'play' a policeman; the lawyer, a lawyer;

the priest, a priest; a peasant, a peasant; and they were utterly lost. They had never had to think through what being themselves meant in the way that an actor does constantly, always imagining himself inside other people.

Curiously, what they did was to fall back on the only acting conventions they were aware of: the popular films they had seen, the little touring theatre groups. The results would have been funny if it hadn't been for the glowering presence of Luchino. Our non-actors fell back on melodramatic gestures, pompous set speeches, anything but the 'reality' he sought. There was nothing for it but to accept the inevitable. If these people were going to act, they would have to be taught the rudiments of the craft. Whenever possible I would collect the next group together as far from Luchino as possible and try to coax them through their scene. It was a little better, but not much.

There was one hilarious interlude while we were filming. Donald Downes arrived in Catania with Tennessee Williams. They had flown from Rome in a rather ancient light aircraft – a hair-raising flight. Never a good air traveller at the best of times, Tennessee had drunk an entire bottle of Scotch and was nearly dead with fear. Donald had practically to sling him over his shoulder to carry him off the plane.

'This cunt,' Donald shouted to us, 'she was so fucking frightened she started screaming and the pilot had to hit her. I gave her a slap or two as well.' Personal pronouns were variable in their relationship and the two of them quarrelled incessantly.

That was my first sight of the great writer, thrown over Donald's back like a sack of potatoes. We got him to the hotel and, after a shower, he revived enough to come down and join us in the restaurant. But he was still pretty befuddled with booze and air sickness, and couldn't quite make out what was going on. The walls of the restaurant were decorated with large photographs of the world's major cathedrals – the Duomo in Milan, St Peter's in Rome, St Basil's in Moscow – and Tennessee, gulping at another drink, walked around the room trying to focus on them.

'Is it a beautiful city, Catania?' he asked.

'Magnificent,' I answered.

'Oh, I must go tomorrow. Will you take me? I'd love to see that church.' I could hardly tell him it was in Moscow.

But, when he eventually sobered up, I was charmed by him. He had a childlike naïvety which counterbalanced his rather *louche* life and which made his opinions fresh and interesting.

If anything saved the film, it was the cinematography. This is my main debt to Luchino in film-making, his passionate attention to detail. Everything was always researched to a point far beyond the needs of the actual scene. You immersed yourself in the period, the place, its culture, so that even though the audience might not take in every detail they would be absolutely convinced of its essential 'rightness'. The cameraman, Aldo Graziati, virtually started a new Italian school. It was thanks to him that the long pauses and languid action of *La terra trema* were counterbalanced by wonderful camera work which made each frame a composed picture. It did much to highlight the sparse beauty of that bleached Sicilian coast.

To me Aldo was important for another reason: he was one of the few non-Communists working on the film, and I needed his support when the elections suddenly confronted us. Luchino and the others were confident that those heady days of the Popular Front in France would resurface in Italy, and filming was stopped so that we could all return to Rome to vote. I was worried, but Donald reassured me.

'Don't doubt it,' he said. 'The Italians are far too intelligent to be taken in by the antics of a lot of rich men playing at being revolutionaries. The ordinary people know about Communism and they know about Russia. You'll see.'

Of course, he was right. The election produced a landslide for the Christian Democrats and almost demolished the left-wing parties. Aldo and I returned to Sicily jubilant, but Luchino and the others had the look of a defeated army. Luchino and I had been living together during the months of filming and now I knew that more than ever I would have to help him through this difficult period. The worst thing for him was the knowledge that almost all the workers in his film, his supposed peasant army that he was going to lead to liberation, must have voted Christian Democrat. The last weeks of filming were heavy going, but I did what I could to minimize his problems, running this way and that, trying to smooth over the difficulties. In the end we were all glad to finish it and return to Rome, where Luchino could begin his editing.

The result was two hours and forty minutes of very uneven film. With the best will in the world Luchino's supporters could only praise it with reservation, and the unfortunate fact was that with the tide running against the Communists there were few enough of them anyway.

The worst by-product of this episode was the fate of Acitrezza and its citizens. Luchino brought some of them to Venice for the film festival and I found out later how unwise it is to introduce a way of life to people who are never going to be able to continue it. The end came when the village was turned into a tourist centre. Today it is buried under tons of concrete – hotels and villas that in their own remorseless way have finally ended a way of life.

Stunned by the set-back to his political hopes and the failure of the film, Luchino came to depend on me increasingly, both as companion and general factotum. After living together for six months in Sicily, it seemed only natural that I should move into his house in Rome. Compared with the Hotel Inghilterra this was a vision of elegance. The imposing entrance led into a hall with a circular staircase lit by Venetian statues holding lanterns. One salon led to another, this in turn to a library. Large arches separated them, and a single beige carpet covered the floor. The furniture was mainly eighteenth century, and the walls of the smaller salon were decorated with his mother's remarkable collection of Staffordshire pottery of the same period. The large salon had two big windows that opened onto the garden and the walls were covered with an eighteenth-century canvas mural of pretty pastel scenes. Apart from these fixtures, the objects scattered around the rooms were a jumble of styles and periods – some precious family heirlooms, others the result of Luchino's compulsive collecting. He had remarkable taste and the whole effect was of a glittering Aladdin's cave. It was a world away from the reproduction Renaissance style favoured by my bourgeois aunts and uncles. The library had been built round a magnificent Delft fireplace taken from one of his family homes. It was there that we would sit on the floor in front of the fire, talking about work, planning projects, making lists of things to do the next day, writing letters or reading scripts.

The thing I liked best was that I could have a dog again – two in fact. Mussolini had been a country animal and had settled into my father's house outside Florence, where I left him. Since then I had not had a pet and now here was a house big enough for two dogs, and I was more than happy to have their company.

After his setback Luchino was more restrained, though still the grand aristocrat, and those were good times, times when I learned most from him – about that broad Italo–French culture with its emphasis on fine things, of which he was so clearly a part. He had to have the best, yet at the same time he was vulnerable, but if he cried or showed any weakness, he quickly plastered over the cracks. In some ways he was out of touch with what ordinary people felt and it showed in his work: he seldom went deeply into a character, except years later with Ludwig of Bavaria – someone he seemed at last to understand. He was a poor judge of people; servants came and went, hired on a whim like one of the young fishermen from Acitrezza, or, another time, a boy picked up on the island of Ischia. There was the fatal attraction of amusing rascals like the interior decorator he sometimes employed who was constantly stealing things and who even organized two burglaries when Luchino was old and a cripple in a wheelchair. Nothing was ever done about it because the man was *so amusing*.

This desire for entertainment made his attachment to the 'comrades' all the more bizarre. They were the largest group at any of his parties, discussing Marxist theory and plotting how to regroup after the débâcle of the election. I kept to one side.

His theatre company had always cost him quite a sum, but the losses from *La terra trema* were grim. His brothers bought out some of his shares in the various family concerns and his doting sister Uberta was very supportive. But none of this was enough for a man with such extravagant habits and, when the tradesmen could no longer be held off with promises, I would be sent out secretly to sell some of his precious things – a Renoir, a silver ashtray. I became quite a competent antique dealer.

It was at such times that the repressed, vulnerable side of him was most apparent. All those projects we planned night after night in the library came to nothing. No one was interested in backing him and his own money had run out. I was one of the few people he could turn to for support, because, despite all my criticisms, my awareness of his faults and foibles, and my aversion to his politics, despite all that, I loved Luchino Visconti for what I knew him truly to be: a complex being whose moments of great insight and creative awareness made him one of the most exciting men of his day and of my life. I might find things to criticize in his work – *La terra trema* in my opinion was not an artistic success – but I would never allow anyone else to say so. When we took the film to the Venice Film Festival, we encountered an organized band of protesters who had come to hurl abuse at Luchino and his film. As soon as they began their antics, shouting and banging and trying to disrupt the screening, I went berserk with fury. Before anyone could stop me I was in amongst them punching and scratching for all I was worth. Before the police could break up the battle at least two of them got bloody noses and a few well-aimed kicks where it matters. As the police took down our details, I was pleased to see the look of pride on Luchino's face, though I thought it was the least that he deserved by way of support.

SIX

The Wide World

When he finally accepted that he was not going to get the money to finish the trilogy, Luchino decided to return to the theatre, and his reputation was such that his faithful troupe immediately rallied to him. Naturally, Luchino wanted to cover his retreat from the cinema with as big a theatrical splash as possible and only something as epic as Shakespeare would do. And even that needed inflating in some way. He settled on *As You Like It* and then conceived the notion of having Salvador Dali design a surrealist version – but how to track him down? The answer was Chanel, who knew everyone in the gallery world. She was delighted to hear from Luchino and brought the two of them together.

Dali came to Rome and he and Luchino were soon deep into fantasies about how the production would look. Dali came up with the most incredible drawings, far too impractical to be called designs: the characters were to be seated on live goats and the entire action was to take place in a high wind with a perpetual shower of autumn leaves. As art, it was sensational; Dali's Forest of Arden was certainly a magic place.

Luchino used Dali's name to raise some of the money, though to pay the artist's large fees I was obliged to become an antique dealer again. Having raised the money, the next problem was how to execute those impossible creations. I begged Luchino to make me responsible for the sets and costumes, and he was glad to hand over what appeared to be a thankless task.

First, I got Dali to agree to dispense with live goats – stuffed ones would have to do, though they were hard enough to find or make. I entered a bizarre world of faded businesses in side-streets, where such obscure items could be acquired; a world almost as surreal as the one we were trying to create. The perpetual shower of leaves was a nuisance, though a fairly manageable one, but the constant high wind was impossible. My solution was to make wired costumes that looked as if they were being blown about. They were a nightmare to construct and the seamstresses were not helped by Dali's constant fiddling with their creations.

As we approached the dress rehearsal I barely slept during the rush to get everything finished, chasing after Luchino to carry out his rapid-fire   89 orders. Then, one day, I went to the company that made the costumes and found the seamstresses working on another production. I demanded to know what was going on: didn't they know how urgent it all was? Yes, they said, they did and they *so* wanted to help Count Visconti, but they *couldn't* that day because the Greek singer's costume had to be completely remade at once.

'And who,' I thundered, thoroughly confused, 'who is this Greek singer?'

They all talked at once: surely I knew, everyone was talking about her, such a voice, singing Kundry in *Parsifal* and the night before the dress rehearsal she had thrown down her costume and refused to sing until the whole thing was remade, and now the Teatro dell'Opera and Maestro Serafin were desperate.

'Who', I repeated patiently, 'is she?'

Thus I first heard the name Maria Callas, and my initial reaction was one of great loathing. I acquired an instant aversion to the 'Greek singer'.

When I told Luchino about this Callas upstart who was playing havoc with our costumes, his reaction was one of bemused interest. He told me to get tickets for her opening night.

Given how exhausted I was, only something extraordinary could have kept me awake during Wagner at that time, but awake I certainly kept. She was extraordinary: plump and unattractive, but with a voice such as I had never heard before. Luchino was as awed as I and we both joined in the general delirium at the end of the performance. Maria Callas had arrived.

Meanwhile, we were nearing our own first night. Throughout the dress rehearsal I sat in front of Luchino, using a tiny flashlight to take notes, while he bellowed at the stage through a megaphone. Changes, changes, changes; new orders, new details, even at that late stage; and I was already so exhausted. After seven nights with almost no sleep we were still changing the details when slowly, unable to prevent it, I slipped into sleep, dreamless and inert. It could only have been for a few minutes, but suddenly I woke up with a terrible bang – Luchino had hit me over the head with his megaphone. He didn't even stop to remark on it, but continued bellowing orders and commanding changes. Like a robot, I started writing them down again.

When the actors had left the stage, I followed Luchino around as he inspected this and ordered an alteration to that. Then, suddenly, he was finished. Without further thought I sank on to a bank of leaves on the stage and resumed my deep sleep. This time no one bothered me. I awoke next day like an orphan in a fairy tale surrounded by unmoving yet wind-blown trees, watched over by lugubrious stuffed goats.

Happily, after all that work, we had a tremendous first night. The Dali magic succeeded and I was truly happy for Luchino. Given what was to happen in the future, it was fateful that our production and that of Callas were now the two most successful in town. It could only be a matter of time before we were brought together.

The agent for this encounter was the conductor Tullio Serafin, whose daughter was a friend of Luchino. She invited us to a reception at her father's house and we were presented to this very plump Greek-American girl with a terrible New York whine allied to a rather prim, matronly manner. She sounded awful and looked worse. She wore a black tailored outfit so tight that it showed her ample hips and bosom, and she topped it off with a Raphael-style velvet hat. Everything seemed too big – eyes, nose, mouth, and her legs were hairy on top of everything else. I didn't dare catch Luchino's eye. Then, aware that she was being judged and found wanting, and being quick to protect his protégée, Serafin said: 'Come on, Maria, let's make some music.'

The old man sat at the piano and started to play an aria from *La traviata*. I closed my eyes because I have always imagined Violetta as a frail lady and didn't wish to be disillusioned, yet, when Callas began to sing, she was just that, she really was La Dame aux Caméllias. The strange thing was that she didn't try to play it lightly, as if she really were a frail consumptive; she sang with everything she had, and it worked.

I looked at Luchino and saw that he was as entranced as I. The next day I sent Maria Callas some flowers and what was almost a love letter. I followed her to Florence to see her *Traviata* and hung around her dressing-room like a love-sick boy.

'You are my camp follower,' she said with unconscious irony (she was unbelievably naïve). 'Can you do me a little favour, *caro?*'

Of course I said yes, anything. The 'little favour' took all day trying to find some trinket she wanted, but I didn't mind. Maria was an all or nothing person when it came to friends. People were in or out of favour with astonishing speed, but I'm happy to say that she and I became close friends. As I got to know her, I came to understand what had bred such instability into her character. The Callas story is now a legend, but then it was fascinating to hear for the first time how this unprepossessing creature had acquired the art that was bringing her the reputation of our century's most dynamic opera star.

Nothing in her background had been particularly auspicious. Her father was an unambitious pharmacist who had taken his wife and first daughter from Athens to New York, where Maria was born in 1923. The father was something of a failure, the eldest daughter was the family favourite and it was only her mother's ambition that drove the unloved and unlovely Maria into a career as a singer. It was the mother who took the girls back to Athens before the outbreak of war. Maria had the good fortune to fall under the influence of Elvira de Hidalgo, a marvellous teacher who realized before anyone that, while Maria's voice would never be 'beautiful'in the perfect classic style the great coloraturas are supposed to have, nevertheless she had something utterly unique, a dramatic quality that made the roles she sang nerve-wracking experiences. You never knew with Maria whether or not she would pull it off. She used to talk about her voice as if it were an independent being that might not do her bidding. But de Hildago gave her the best training she could, and Maria was fantastically disciplined. Despite all the newspaper stories about temperament and tantrums, when it came to work she was a trouper.

She told me a lot of this as we became friends. Her ungainly figure was due to compulsive eating, an overcompensation for the lack of love in her childhood. This need for food made the war years an agony for her. There was little money anyway, and much of what there was went on singing lessons. De Hildago pushed her forward and she made her debut in *Cavalleria rusticana* at the Athens Opera when she was only eighteen. But there was little money in it.

A great friend of mine, the Greek painter Jan Tsaruchis, told me that times were hard for everyone, including the occupying Italian army, most of whom were lonely and unhappy boys. Jan lived next door to the Kalogeropoulos family (Callas's real name) and he often heard the quarrels between Maria and her mother and sister. He could see how Maria made no attempt to look attractive, quite the opposite. He would sometimes hear her scream and yell at her mother, 'Leave me alone.' Then she would run out, banging the door as she went.

There was a small public garden in front of Jan's house, and from his window he could see the poor girl sitting on a bench crying her heart out. It was there that he witnessed one of the most touching episodes in Maria's youth. One of those lonely Italian soldiers, hardly more than her own age, discovered that she was a singer and took to bringing some of his meagre rations – often little more than two small pieces of chocolate — to pay her to sing for him. She would sing her way through *Traviata* or *Tosca* just for that. The boy would sit enraptured, remembering Italy, his family and his home; then the plump girl would devour whatever food he had brought. I used to think of that sometimes when I watched 'La Divina' gathering bouquets at the end of one of her triumphs.

After the war, Maria went back to New York, but her success in Athens didn't carry any weight there, and after a frustrating year she accepted an offer to sing in *La gioconda* that Verona. From the first, people were polarized by her singing. Some hated the imperfections of her voice. Others, like myself, were knocked out by its dramatic power. Happily for her, one of the latter was the leading conductor Tullio Serafin, who promoted her early career in Italy and brought her to Rome for that triumph we had witnessed. The other man in her life was Battista Meneghini, an elderly

The Wide World

businessman she had met in Verona. Despite his age, Meneghini bowled 93
over the dumpy Maria because he was both the first man to pay any
attention to her *as a woman* and the father-figure she so clearly missed.
Less than two years after her Italian début Maria married Meneghini, who
became her mentor and agent. Whether he was more than that is hard to
say. Whenever I was with her he seemed like an elderly relative: he would
go to bed early and leave us talking. But she certainly seemed to rely on
him: he gave her confidence in herself in a way that no one had done before.
From her marriage in 1949 until her American début in 1954 she laid the
foundations of her reputation in Italy in most of her great roles – Norma,
Tosca, Leonora – and whenever possible I was there to hear her.

As for Luchino, he was on top form again and planning more theatre. *As
You Like It* had helped pull him back from the worst excesses of neo-realism,
but it had been a singular event and was not really Luchino's way of doing
things. His way, and this was another lesson I learned from him, was to be
faithful to the setting of a play as its author had conceived it and to render
it in the most precise detail, probably with more attention and fidelity than
when the play was first done. He could never have staged a modern Hamlet
with actors holding umbrellas and wearing tracksuits. If he was doing a
Goldoni play, he would find out everything about Goldoni's Venice in the
eighteenth century – or rather I would do so for him. Then we would spend
evenings in the library looking at engravings or books of paintings, at
objects found in junk shops, at anything that could help us absorb that
particular period. This way of working is my greatest debt to him and is
the sort of 'realism' I admire. The reason Luchino had a reputation for
experimental theatre was that he had so often done new, modern plays,
especially American ones, but in fact he never did anything at all avant-
garde with them.

He now decided to recharge his reputation for modern works by using
his option to produce *A Streetcar Named Desire*. Because of the work I'd done
with Dali, he said I might design it myself. I collected all the information I
could on New Orleans, the look of the place, the buildings with their
wrought-iron façades, the exact street lamps, the clothes. I read everything,
much helped by Donald Downes, naturally. We found photographs of New
Orleans and books about the city. Without waiting for Luchino, I produced
my first sketch: the house where the play is set. Luchino said he thought
it ridiculous. He was concerned that no one should compare his production
with Elia Kazan's original version on Broadway and said everything was
going to be different. For a month we fiddled, first putting a staircase here
and then there, then moving the balcony from left to right, until we'd tried
every possible permutation.

Then I began to sense that Luchino was taking less interest in my
sketches. The risk was that he would decide I wasn't up to the task and

would find another designer. I had no intention of letting that happen and brought all my cunning to bear on the problem. By that time I knew Luchino well and understood the way his mind worked.

'You know,' I said, 'you had such a good idea at the beginning, I can't think why you threw it away.'

'No, it didn't work,' he insisted.

'Oh, I'm sure it did. There was a staircase here and a balcony there and . . .' – I pretended not to remember distinctly.

'There was an upstairs room,' he said, 'and the balcony was over there – yes.'

I told him I'd redraw it and the next day I brought him the original first sketch which I had carefully preserved.

'This is fine,' he said cheerfully. 'This is the way it should be. I'm glad you remembered.'

It saved my skin, perhaps my career. *Streetcar* was the first major production to have my name independently credited to it, and my designs were original enough to cause comment. Kazan's production had used scrims, painted gauzes, to change the mood, while I used a building whose façade rose or fell as necessary, creating a once elegant, though now dilapidated, New Orleans street or the ramshakle interior of the house. I think this added a necessary realism to the play, and certainly Tennessee Williams, who came over for the opening, thought so. It was then that our friendship really formed. He became a frequent visitor and someone to whom I always showed my work in its earliest stages, for his was always the most helpful advice.

Luchino was now in demand again, and he was offered an irresistible project: the major open-air production for the Musical May season in Florence. In some years this would be an opera, something impressive like Wagner, and in other years theatre. Max Reinhardt had started a tradition of doing Shakespeare with *A Midsummer Night's Dream* in 1933. Because of his reputation, Luchino was virtually given carte blanche. He decided to do *Troilus and Cressida* and, probably to prove that he could still do huge productions despite *La terra trema*, he really went to town with a plan to construct a sort of medieval vision of Troy on the terraces of the Boboli Gardens behind the Pitti Palace.

Although nothing was ever said, he seemed to accept that I was now his designer. I was really happy. It was one of the best periods of my life, working alongside him. I was also delighted to be working on my beloved Shakespeare at last, and also in Florence, the home that I had left three years earlier.

Luchino wanted to create an image of Troy based on Persian miniatures, an exotic city invaded by Western barbarians. I threw myself into realizing this magical concept. It was staggering to see the huge city rise as work progressed. It was best after nightfall, white and ghostly in the moonlight: one critic said that not even the Medicis had ever created such a spectacle.

Its effect on the general manager of the Maggio Musicale was less pleasing. The festival was already in debt and Luchino seemed about to ruin them financially. One hot day the manager climbed the hill and arrived in total despair.

'Maestro, please stop building. We can't afford it.'

'What!' bellowed Luchino. 'Don't you like it?'

'Maybe,' said the manager, 'but we only asked you to give us a play, not build the New Jerusalem.'

To me the most satisfying thing was to see the poster with my name on it plastered all over my city, and I was childishly touched to see old friends in the audience. As soon as the posters were printed, I took one to my father's house. It was the first time we had met since my departure in 1946. He must have heard that I was coming to Florence and did not show too much surprise at my appearance, but embraced me rather stiffly, unrolled the poster and stared at it for what seemed an age. Finally, he looked at me.

'I'm very proud of you,' he said. 'Very proud of what you have done in so short a time.'

While I knew he was speaking the truth, I also sensed that something had upset him. As I walked back to the theatre that evening I realized that what he would dearly have liked to see on that poster was his own family name: Corsi – Franco Corsi.

Nevertheless, as far as we could, we had made up. I took Luchino to the house for a meal, and he and my father hit it off at once. It seemed extraordinary to me, but my father, who had always been so sparing, proceeded to lavish gifts on Luchino. He even gave him a superb, twenty-four-place, hand-embroidered tablecloth in fine Florentine linen, which Luchino adored.

Troilus and Cressida certainly showed that scale was a Visconti speciality. But the organizers of the festival had less cause for joy: bad weather and Luchino's overspending made the production outrageously expensive, and it was several years before they could afford another open-air production.

Buoyed by this critical success, Luchino was determined to make a film again. Ideas were tossed back and forth, and various financiers were approached. In the end the best source of finance seemed to be France. If money from the two countries could be put together then his idea was to film *A Tale of Poor Lovers* by Pratolini. Luchino began work on the screenplay and announced that we would both go to Paris to cast the necessary French actors, who, together with the Italian contingent, would make up one of the first Franco-Italian co-productions. I was ecstatic at the thought of seeing Paris at last, and those evenings in the library making our plans were especially exciting.

Luchino made arrangements for us to see all the best young French talent. To be professional about it, we would have to go to the Conservatoire and the other schools as well as the Comedie Française. Then, for some reason, possibly related to his family's business, Luchino was not able to go. I was devastated and thought the whole trip was about to be cancelled. Timidly, I suggested that perhaps I could go ahead and start the work, prepare the ground for him, and he could come over when the work was well advanced. He thought about it for a while and said, 'Yes, you go ahead. I'll give you a couple of letters. It will be good for you to prove yourself on your own.'

He gave me three letters: one to Jean Marais, the most successful actor in France at the time, one to Jean Cocteau and one to Coco Chanel.

It was the first time I had ever been alone in a first-class sleeper, a beautiful old *wagon-lit*. I arrived at the Gare de Lyon, at the end of June 1949, early in the morning, and to my surprise I was extremely disappointed. How grey and filthy the city was. Today you see a different Paris, because it has been cleaned, but at that time it was deep grey, dark and crumbling. I had imagined the Paris of Dufy – all white and blue and green. Even so I couldn't wait to see more of it.

At the Hotel Lutétia I showered quickly and then went out to discover the city. This was the great era of Signoret, Montand, Piaf, Jouvet, Sartre, Barrault and Gide. Post-war affluence had hit Paris and, as in Italy, there was a feeling that this was a new beginning. There was already the 'New Look' of Christian Dior and Jacques Fath, and Paris was on top of the fashion scene again. There were exciting new people everywhere, and I started to make arrangements to see them about our film. I called Jean Marais first and met him that afternoon. He was in between one day's shooting and another, and he came with an extremely handsome companion in a marvellous sports car. Before he left, he said, 'We are going tomorrow night to the opening of the new show at the Lido. I've arranged for a table, so why don't you come with us?' I didn't know much about Paris, but I knew the opening at the Lido was the event of the season.

I tried to reach Jean Cocteau, but could find no way of contacting him. I tried for the fifteen days I was there, but when I returned to Rome I still had the letter Luchino had given me. I was told he was in the country, then I was told he was sick, finally that he was busy writing. I later found out that he had been involved in some emotional drama and there was no way I could have seen him then.

The second day of my visit was to be the most important. I made my way to 31 rue Cambon to see Coco Chanel. When I arrived, one of those famously rude French concièrges deigned to tell me that Mademoiselle Chanel was not there, that she lived at the Ritz. When I said I would go

there to see her, this gorgon asked me if I was crazy, did I imagine that
she would receive anyone at eleven-thirty in the morning! I took the point
and decided to wait till the afternoon. To kill time I went to the Louvre to
see the Mona Lisa and made myself thoroughly depressed with the way
'our' painting was so poorly displayed.

With these rather irritable thoughts in my mind, I went back to the Ritz
and rang Chanel's suite. A woman's voice answered the phone, demanding
to know who I was, and when it became clear that my French was far from
perfect she became even less helpful.

'I have a letter for Madame Chanel,' I attempted to explain.

'Madame?'

'Yes.'

'I think you mean *Mademoiselle* Chanel. You may leave it with the
porter.'

'I can't, it's rather special.'

'And who is this *special* letter from?'

It was a voice that could wither you even down the telephone.

'Luchino Visconti,' I explained.

There was the dead silence of a hand over the speaker and then, after a
pause, the voice returned.

'You may come up.'

Thus I met Maggie van Zuylen, Chanel's great friend and a woman of
immense charm and fun – yes, fun. As I walked into the outer rooms she
was standing swearing like a street-walker at someone through a further
doorway.

'You cow,' she was screaming. 'You don't frighten me, you little bitch.'

And there suddenly was Chanel, standing in the doorway just as I had
imagined her, in one of her tailored outfits with hat and pearls, but altogether unexpectedly waving a riding-crop and matching her friend word
for word in foul-mouthed abuse.

'Whore, bitch, cow,' the words flew back and forth until suddenly they
both collapsed into a fit of giggles and I realized that the whole thing had
been a wild performance. I quickly closed my gaping mouth and tried not
to look like the country boy come to town.

Dismissing the incident, Chanel walked over and held out her hand for
the letter.

'So, you're Luchino's little friend?'

'His associate,' I said, 'his assistant.'

She raised an eyebrow.

'Read it to me,' she said.

So I read Luchino's message asking her to help me and saying that as
soon as I'd prepared everything he would come.

'He'll never come,' she said. 'He's such a liar.'

Zeffirelli

Then she whispered something to Maggie and the two of them were off again swearing and shouting. I stepped back, rather frightened by this second outburst.

'Where are you staying?' she demanded during a lull in the argument. 'Go to your hotel. I'll be in touch.'

Maggie saw me out.

'Don't worry,' she said kindly. 'She'll do what she can, I know.'

I walked out of the Ritz thoroughly confused and made my way slowly back to Saint Germain, dawdling over the sights. I arrived at my hotel three hours later.

'Monsieur Zeffirelli, there is some mail for you.'

I couldn't believe it. Chanel had already sent a messenger with hand-written letters to certain key people. She had a finely tuned sense of whom it would be appropriate for me to meet. Because she recalled that Luchino had worked with Jean Becker when they were both assistants to Renoir on *Une Partie de campagne*, she now sent me to Becker's assistant, Roger Vadim. It was carefully thought out: we were the 'grandsons' of Renoir, as Becker and Luchino had been his 'sons'. She had taken the time to find out about Vadim, who was then a virtual newcomer. As an assistant director, like myself, she had the idea that we might get along. She put the two of us on the same level and knew that would be better than if she sent me to the director himself. There was also a note for me: 'Come back whenever you want. I'd like to talk to you again.'

The next day I went to see Vadim to talk about casting. He had a young girl with him.

'This girl can play that role, Franco. Believe me, she's wonderful.'

She was dressed in a black leotard, having just come from a dance class, and her hair was tied in a ponytail, something I had never seen before and which was apparently the new fashion. Vadim called her to come and meet me, and gave me photographs to take back to Luchino. Her name was Brigitte Bardot.

I tried to reach Jean Marais because I wanted to ask him if Vadim and Bardot could come with me to the opening of the Lido. When he had invited me, he had said to come with friends if I wished, but I couldn't reach him and went alone that night. I mingled somewhat nervously with the cosmopolitan crowd in tuxedos, evening gowns and extraordinary jewels. This was when the Lido was very chic and I remember nervously looking at the press photographers outside as I arrived in my modest blue jacket and tie. One of the doormen asked me to move aside until I told him I was a guest of Monsieur Marais. I was immediately ushered in, and the head waiter showed me to a table right next to the stage. 'Monsieur Marais has telephoned. He will be a little late.'

There I was, at the best table, with people looking at me and wondering who I was. As it turned out, I had the table to myself. The show started, the tables were jammed and the whole place came alive – but no Jean Marais. Every once in a while I would hear people say, 'Who is he? How did he get that table?' They were no doubt confused; in my blue jacket I certainly didn't look important or rich.

Finally the head waiter returned, bowing and overflowing with unctuous apologies: '*Je suis désolé*, but Monsieur Marais cannot come. He has had a problem at work, but begs you to stay as his guest. He insists that you call him tomorrow.'

I wasn't sure what to do, so I turned my attention to the lavish performance, the first time I had ever seen topless women on stage. The Bluebells strutted in front of me, all glitter and feathers. It was like being in a royal box, all alone, with champagne. All those Bluebells came over to look at me, smiling and trying to impress me – the mysterious young man who had the best seat in the house. I was uncertain how to react, but finally resorted to my Montgomery Clift imitation and smouldered seductively at them over the rim of my champagne glass.

Later the *maître d'hôtel* came over again and said, '*Monsieur, je suis désolé*, we have some clients, very important clients. We cannot seat them. There is no room. Would you be so gracious as to permit us to put them at the other side of your table?'

Merry with champagne, I was happy to agree to anything he suggested and could hardly object when he brought over an attractive couple. The man must have been in his late twenties and the woman younger. They must have been Brazilian or Argentinian with their dark good looks. They were friendly, charming people and we chatted and drank champagne as we watched the show together. Then, suddenly, nothing – my mind is a complete blank. One moment I am at the Lido; the next it is morning and I am outside my hotel, sprawled on the steps and looking up at the porter.

The porter picked me up and took me to my room, where I passed out. Obviously, the beautiful couple had given me something either in my champagne or the cigarettes they passed round. I suppose they had their fun, for I was bruised all over and weak for a couple of days. Later I could vaguely recall beautiful bodies, mouths, hands and arms touching and moving – a sort of erotic dream. My only regret was that they had not simply asked me; I would gladly have joined in without coercion – it was Paris after all!

I slept a day and a night. The morning after that the telephone rang. It was Chanel.

'What happened to you? Do you need a doctor?'

An hour later a doctor arrived. I told him the story, and he said I should notify the police.

Zeffirelli

100   'For God's sake, no,' I said. 'Just check my blood to make sure nothing's wrong.'

Later Chanel said she was furious at Jean Marais, that it was all his fault. 'You should have nothing to do with Marais. He's impossible. Impossible!'

But when I finally met Jean Marais later, I found a surprisingly gentle person. He apologized for not having turned up and of course knew nothing about the mysterious couple. There the matter ended – a mystery to this day.

'You need some air,' said Chanel when I went round to see her. So out we went for a stroll. Only later did I find out how kind a gesture this was on her part. She was still in disgrace because of her wartime affair with a German officer and usually preferred to avoid public places where she might be snubbed. She had only recently been pardoned by the government but her career was in ruins and she was unable to work. As we walked along two girls appeared ahead of us, decked out in the very latest fashion – the 'New Look' by Dior with a pinch-waisted, voluminous skirt, precarious heels, floppy-brimmed hat, tiny handbag. The whole ensemble was probably the most impractical ever created, but very, very fashionable. This was what had replaced the straightforward, elegant simplicity of Chanel, and having these two creatures mincing ahead of us was a red rag to a bull.

'Look at them,' Chanel hissed in a voice that carried the length of the boulevard. 'Fools, dressed by queens living out their fantasies. They dream of being women, so they make real women look like transvestites.'

By this time the two girls were trying unsuccessfully to propel themselves out of range of what they must have thought was a lunatic coming up behind them.

'See,' screeched Chanel again in her powerful voice. 'They can barely walk. I made clothes for the new woman. She could move and live naturally in my clothes. Now look what those creatures have done. They don't know women, they've never *had* a woman!'

Presumably caught off balance by this tirade, one of the girls dropped her tiny handbag. She stopped and tried to bend over to retrieve it, but this was an impossible task given the height of her heels, the spread of her dress and the tightness of her wasp-waist corset, which was typical of the style. I was about to leap forward to help when Chanel's hand restrained me. With a tremendous look of triumph she grasped the bag and handed it to the terrified girl.

'*Et voilà!*' she said and began to laugh uncontrollably.

The girls fled and I was proud of Chanel's behaviour. I realized she was planning her revenge and was not to be relegated to the past as her rivals imagined.

As soon as I recovered I worked hard at casting. I kept calling Luchino every day, but he delayed repeatedly and finally said he wouldn't be able to come. I began to suspect there were problems he was hiding from me.

'When you finish, bring me all the photographs, and we can look at them and go back to Paris together later.'

So I stayed a fortnight, visiting all the acting schools and spending every free moment with Chanel. What kept her so interested in me was the relationship with Luchino. She was always trying to find out about him.

'You never stop loving the people you've loved,' she once sadly remarked. 'Even if they betray you, it's not true that love turns into hatred, it turns into resentment, into anger. But the love you had lingers for ever not because of the person – no, it's because of yourself, because of that moment in your life. Whoever the person was doesn't really matter, that moment is always there.'

She suddenly stopped that sad line of thought and began to ask more questions about Luchino. She never said why, though the reason was obvious. She was proud and tough, which was just as well given the hard time she was having. I remember near the end of my stay going to the rue Cambon and finding her in a state of near madness. It took some time to get any sense out of her, but it slowly emerged that the source of her fury was the story of her perfume, the famous Chanel No. 5. She had sold it to an American firm for a very substantial sum, but it now transpired that she had never properly understood the contract. She was about to bring out two more perfumes: one was Mademoiselle Chanel, the other was Numéro Trente-et-un, the number of her shop in the rue Cambon. Now she discovered she could not use them: by selling her rights to Chanel No. 5 she had an obligation never to create any other perfume that bore any connection with her name.

'*Je suis folle*,' she said. 'I was crazy to do that for those Americans, just for money, for dollars. Why did I do it? Why did I do it? And smell it, smell it.' She put a bottle under my nose, and it was an incredible, enchanting perfume. I can still smell it. 'Mademoiselle Chanel' was sweet and crisp, like lily of the valley. 'Trente-et-un' was very hot and steamy. She had crates of them, which she now had to throw away. I asked her if I could have one of each.

'Take as many as you want,' she said, but suddenly changed her mind. 'No, please, people will smell them and want to buy them. They will come back for more, and every time it will be like an arrow in my heart.' Then she became very suspicious. 'Better not,' she added. 'Perfumes like these are so memorable. I don't want to wake up one day to find that Mademoiselle Chanel has become Mademoiselle Dior.'

Nevertheless I secretly pocketed a bottle of each, for the scents seemed just too good to waste – the rest went literally down the drain.

However, there were other things besides perfume that she was involved with. She was interested in jewellery and was one of the first to mix real stones with fake ones to make 'costume jewellery' fashionable. Louis Cartier created something similar at the turn of the century using semi-precious and precious stones together, but he never used anything that wasn't at least semi-precious. No one had ever dared blend a simulated pearl with real diamonds, or fake sapphires with real ones as Chanel did.

Whenever I was with her, I would remind myself that this small, emaciated lady had been the mistress of powerful men and had been the creator of a completely new way of dressing. She was the centre of almost everything artistic in French life this century from Diaghilev and ballet, to Picasso and painting, to Cocteau and poetry. Given what has happened since, it is strange to recall that I then believed that I was at the summit of my ambition. I thought I had made it, working for Visconti and befriended by Chanel. Indeed, it *was* powerful stuff for someone only twenty-six years old to be sitting in Fouquet's in the Champs-Élysées with Coco Chanel and seeing André Gide walk in. Chanel went over to him and introduced us. It was a hot July afternoon and rather disconcertingly Gide had put his handkerchief on his head. He left it there for a few minutes, shifting it from side to side. I had heard he often did things like that, for he could be unnerving at first encounter. After we left, Chanel told me that she only paid her respects to him because he was such a genius. 'But, really, he is the most unpleasant man I know. And I hope you don't like his books.'

Reluctantly I told her I did.

'I must admit', she acknowledged, 'that you can tell they're written by a genius.'

That was what she respected. If she thought you had talent, there was little she wouldn't do for you. I remember how she engineered my meeting with Christian Bérard, the greatest stage-designer at that time. He had worked with Jean-Louis Barrault, and his production of Molière's *Les Fourberies de Scapin*, which I saw in Venice, was perhaps one of the most beautiful set designs I have ever seen. Chanel adored him and knew I would be interested to meet him, because I told her I wanted to be a stage-designer and had already designed *Troilus and Cressida* and *A Streetcar Named Desire*. So, one day after lunch, we casually walked away from the main boulevards down some side streets to a dingy block. She started up the stairs.

'Christian! Christian! *Tu es là?* Are you there?'

Then I heard this voice from upstairs: 'Gabrielle! Gabrielle! Is it you?'

An extraordinary man appeared, like a character in a Russian novel and very like Semenoff in Positano – bearded, dirty, his trousers stained in embarrassing places. He was with an attractive man who turned out to be Boris Kochno, the choreographer and dancer. As I said, it was all very casual and impromptu, which was the way Chanel sometimes chose to be. She didn't say you must meet Christian Bérard, or anything like that. But she knew how much it would mean to me, and she made sure it happened.

The only one who still eluded me was Cocteau.
'I'm desperate to reach Cocteau. I can't find him.'
'Leave him alone now, he's really in trouble. Besides, you are not missing much. If he finds out that you have talent, he will never give you a word of advice. If he gives you advice, *then* you should worry.'

Just before I left there were tremendous celebrations for Bastille Day on 14 July. I remember Chanel railing about the French Revolution, saying that all the confusions of mind and soul, all France's problems began with it. Nevertheless, I guessed she was somehow very proud of it, and she arranged for us to go to the Place de la Bastille, where the main festivities were being held. It was one of the first big *quatorze juillet* celebrations since the war and Chanel decided to plunge into it enthusiastically. She hired a limousine and invited Maggie van Zuylen and a young Danish model who had unexpectedly appeared on the scene. The girl was a typical Chanel 'creation'; she had that slightly lost, elfish look, a sort of starved sleep-walking air that made me feel slightly uneasy. I had already witnessed how these young hopefuls who flocked to Paris in search of modelling jobs could bring out the worst in these fearsome ladies. Both Chanel and Maggie seemed to find the poor young thing a fair butt for their rather savage humour, and we were no sooner settled in the car with the uniformed chauffeur edging us through the crowds than they started to goad and tease her. It was pouring with rain from one of those rare summer storms and a mass of people pressed close to us. The atmosphere inside the car was claustrophobic. The two women kept up the attack, one in French, the other in German. Apparently the girl had found a rich lover and Chanel thoroughly disapproved.

'You know I don't often agree with her,' Maggie said, 'but this time she's right.'

At first the girl tried to defend herself in a rather hopeless way, but this only increased the onslaught. Suddenly Chanel slapped her face with all her strength. There was a stunned silence, then Chanel yelled at the driver to stop and ordered the poor girl out into the crowd and the rain.

Without hesitation, Maggie took the girl's side and began to quarrel with Chanel.

'Go and get her back,' Maggie ordered, and I leapt out towards the girl, who had wisely kept near to the limousine. But, once back inside, the two women set about criticizing the poor creature again, nagging about her lover. Slowly it dawned on me that in a curious way the girl quite liked this treatment, and soon she had become all kittenish and was promising to follow their advice and do exactly as she was told. That achieved, Chanel was instantly bored with the game and began to fidget. She became conscious of the pouring rain and the almost impassable mob, many of whom did indeed look pretty aggressive. Her fine hand touched the jewellery

Zeffirelli

104 she was wearing.

'What am I doing in all these jewels with all these Communists around? she exclaimed, genuinely preoccupied. 'Here, put them in your pockets.'

So I stuffed the pockets of my mackintosh with her necklaces, bangles and rings. We changed places again so that the girl could be beside Chanel She rested her head on the elder woman's shoulder, sobbing so much she dampened Chanel's elegant coat with her tears. Chanel began cooing and comforting her. By now it was midnight. Rain and more rain. Then fireworks, dancing in the streets and marching bands. But Chanel was suddenly fed up with it all.

'I'm going back,' she said. 'Franco, you're young, you stay. You've never seen it. I'm too old for all this.'

I certainly wanted to see it and was quite glad to get out of that hothouse atmosphere. I watched them drive away and found myself alone in a seething mass of people dancing, kissing and hugging. All at once I realized I still had Chanel's jewellery in my pockets, thousands of dollars worth of diamonds. This ruined my evening, because I had to keep my hands in my pockets all the time and was afraid to join in and enjoy the general frenzy Finally I gave up and went back to the hotel. It seemed almost like a de Maupassant story: a poor young boy who has a treasure in his pocket and every knock at the door, every step, every shadow, every voice, means possible danger. I stared at all those diamonds and pearls, unable to sleep In the morning, when I called the Ritz, she merely said: 'Oh, don't worry I have so many. It's better if you understand that jewels are like anything else.'

'But your jewellery is different, it intrigues me. Can I come and bring them back?'

There was a momentary silence, before she replied: 'As you prefer.'

'Actually, I'm leaving tomorrow, I'd like to say goodbye.'

'Come. Come for dinner at number 31.'

And that was how, on my final summer evening, I came to see her most private inner sanctum in the rue Cambon, where very few had the privilege of being invited. The windows were closed, the curtains drawn and just a little evening light filtered through to merge with the candle light. There were the famous Coromandel screens that she had brought into fashion Louis Quatorze in black enamel with gold and silver. Everything else was beige, except for two life-size Chinese gazelles in some sort of metal Eventually a tray was brought. We ate simple things: an omelette, some cheese. she kept talking, and then she said to me, 'As I told you, Luchino has not come to Paris. I'm sorry, I'd like to see him very much. But he betrays people all the time.'

'Really?' I said. She then told me about an episode in the late 1930s There was a very young photographer named Horst, who had done some wonderful pictures of her when Luchino was an assistant to Jean Renoir. She introduced them and then discovered that they had become more than friends. 'But I suppose you can't help forgiving him,' she said. 'He's so attractive, don't you think?'

I felt embarassed. I didn't want to talk about Luchino. I looked at one of her photographs. 'Is it by Horst?' I asked. She blinked for a moment before replying, 'Yes, by Horst, the other "friend".'

That was my last night with her before I left Paris. At the end of the evening she went to her bookshelf and pulled out a leather-bound album. 'Take this as a souvenir of your first visit to Paris.' It was a collection of twelve beautiful signed prints of ballerinas by Matisse.

'Give my love to Luchino,' said Chanel. 'Tell him to prepare himself for hard times. He'll always have hard times because he's an aristocrat. They'll never forgive him until he's dead and then he'll have a state funeral. And don't ever lose your respect for him, even when you become more aware of his shortcomings. God knows, he has them. Always remember two things: he is wonderful but he has no genius.'

'You musn't say that,' I said aghast. 'He's the greatest director we have.'

'Being a director doesn't necessarily mean you're a genius. You'd better understand that. Actually, those who aren't are sometimes more successful because the critics understand them better.'

Sad as I was to leave Paris and Chanel, I was nevertheless eager to tell my news to Luchino. I was excited about the film we would make and had lists of talented new people for him to see when he came to France. But as soon as I saw him, I knew that something was wrong. Even for someone as capricious as Luchino his total amnesia as regards the film he had sent me all the way to France to cast was truly unnerving. He refused to discuss it and was already well into setting up entirely different plans for work.

To this day I don't know what had gone wrong, though I suspect that the financial settlement of the family's business interests may have been disappointing. Perhaps his family had been unwilling to back the film and he hadn't been able to find a producer. Anyway, I still remember how saddened we all were, because it would have been an extraordinary film and there was so much young talent lined up to take part in it. Not that Luchino let me see how disappointed he was. The aristocrat in him would never allow that, but I sensed it. One evening he handed me all the papers to do with the film – the notes and sketches, the scripts – and told me to wrap them up and keep them somewhere. The bundle looked so much like a stillborn child wrapped in a winding sheet that I almost began to cry.

That summer we went to Luchino's villa on Ischia. One morning, while I was swimming, Luchino appeared on the rock we used as a pier and called me to come in. As I came out of the water, he took hold of me very gently. 'You'll have to go to Florence,' he said. 'It's your father, he's very ill.'

106   The incident still haunts me: my father had had a stroke and I could only suppose that he was dying. I had not reckoned on his incredible energy; he was like a caged beast, his mind imprisoned in his unresponsive body. When he saw me free and moving about, a sort of frenzy overcame him. I stayed to help Fanny, taking him to the bathroom, washing him, attending to him in ways only a son can. But I had not realized what forces lurk inside us, dark energies waiting to be released in moments of stress or danger. My help incensed him; it was as if he now hated me. He would stammer out the most terrible things about my mother in order to hurt me and punish me for being healthy and active when he had been brought so low. It became a constant, gruesome attack. Eventually the doctors advised me to leave, and Fanny swore she could cope. Anything was better than his resentment, even hatred, for me.

I left, but later we realized that it was this fire which kept him alive. In an awesome way he had been punished. Determined to enjoy his mistresses when most men would retire from the game, he had taken a cure – a suspect rejuvenation – and this had caused his stroke. Still he refused to give in, forcing his limbs to work. Eventually he could make his way to the office; then he would ignore the lift and walk up four flights. He would reverse the process at lunchtime and, after a brief siesta, do it again. One day the lift broke down and he refused to have it repaired. He survived another thirteen years, and my sister, who was by then a widow with a little boy, sacrificed her life to this extraordinary, obsessed man, who was determined to go on at any cost and fight death like a wrestler in the ring. Only gradually did his hatred of me subside, so that we were able to see each other again without frenzied resentment overcoming him.

Back in Rome, Luchino and I worked apart for the first time since I had moved in with him. He turned to theatre to cover his disappointment over the film's demise. He did *Death of a Salesman*, while I got a job as assistant director on a film being made by Antonio Pietrangeli, a writer with little experience of directing who had asked Luchino to let me help him. He'd dreamed up a pleasant, Italian-style drama with a couple of minor stars shot on location. It was interesting in its way and I rather enjoyed my novel role as an adviser.

Luchino finally got back into films thanks to a script by Cesare Zavattini, the best script-writer of our time. *Bellissima* was a simple but moving story of a mother who tries to escape from her humdrum life by making her tiny daughter a film star. In the end she is duped and humiliated by the false world of movie-making, and is forced to return to her husband. Luckily, Anna Magnani was available for the lead, and *Bellissima* was shot in the summer of 1951. Unlike Luchino's previous films, it was a story with mass appeal, but contained enough of a moral dilemma to satisfy his political conscience. It was Magnani's no-nonsense approach that made *Bellissima*

Luchino's one truly popular film.

To his credit, Visconti brought realism to a story that could have been a mawkish Hollywood-style melodrama of show-biz failure. This was another case of Luchino not really fitting into the Italian 'new cinema'. Every shot was 'painted' and was the antithesis of the slapdash neo-realist documentary style which made a virtue of speed and the rough, unprofessional look that resulted from hasty filming.

Bellissima was the first experience of film work for a young designer who was later to become master of the medium. Piero Tosi was another Florentine who'd followed much the same route as I had, but, as he was younger, we hadn't known each other in any of our various schools. When he came to see me working on *Troilus* in Florence, I was so impressed by his portfolio that I suggested to Luchino he might help me with the enormous workload. Luchino agreed so long as he didn't cost much, and the same condition was applied to *Bellissima*. I ended up paying Piero out of my own pocket to do the costumes for the film. But, when he saw them, even Luchino had to agree that the boy was brilliant.

The best part of the filming was watching Anna Magnani practising her favourite sport: hunt the flea. This involved someone bringing her a filthy kitten off the streets so that she could while away the hours between takes by killing its fleas. She would snap them between her thumb nails – click, click, click – and was incredibly fast. All the time she would be gossiping and flirting, and every sentence would be punctuated with those snappy little clicks.

'This one is clear,' she would finally announce. 'Get me another one.' And off she would go again – click, click, click.

It was quite an emotional time for Anna in several ways. The first concerned the film director Roberto Rossellini. They had both made their names in his 1945 film *Rome, Open City*, and had inevitably shared a stormy relationship. But Rossellini was one of the few men ever to dominate Anna. He certainly had a way with women and there was a succession of famous affairs. I used to try to find out from Anna what his secret was.

'Is he very well endowed?' I rudely enquired.

'Umm, no, it's not that.'

'Well, what is it then?'

'He's a son of a bitch. That's why we all fall for him. He's a cunt.'

He certainly had been to Anna, who hadn't got over the fact that he had ditched her for a far bigger star, Ingrid Bergman. Ingrid nearly wrecked her career when she left her husband and daughter for Rossellini; hypocritical Hollywood was always outraged by that sort of *public* scandal. It was while we were filming *Bellissima* that Ingrid gave birth to their son, Robertino, in a Roman clinic. You may imagine how Anna reacted.

She soon found a way to console herself. One day I was standing beside

Zeffirelli

her on the set discussing the script with her when she looked up at the electricians' gantry and began to stare intently. I followed her gaze and saw a very attractive boy working on the lights.

'Who's he?' she demanded.

'A new electrician.'

'Is he Roman?'

'I suppose so.'

'Why's he got blond hair and blue eyes?'

'I don't know. Perhaps his mother had a German lover.'

She gave one of her famous guffaws; this was just the directness she loved. She was capable of keeping up this sort of meaningless chatter for some time; the real point was her unrelenting, hypnotic stare in the direction of the young electrician. I was hardly surprised to see them together at a nearby restaurant when I left the studios a few nights later. From then on, he became part of our lives as Anna's man. It was not, however, an easy role for him; he had a wife and children, and Anna insisted that he go to her apartment in the centre of Rome every evening. There he would change out of his working clothes, shower and then dress up in the finest clothes from Battistoni. Of course, Anna lavished beautiful things on him, but she was no fool: he had to change out of them again in the morning, dash round to his tiny flat then head off to work. He soon began to show signs of wear and tear!

Inevitably his wife became exceedingly angry at what was obviously going on. When she eventually discovered who was behind her husband's nocturnal absences, the only way to pacify her was to show that some material good would come to the family from this temporary adventure. So Anna was persuaded to help them. The first 'gift' was to be a dining-room suite, but again Anna was no soft touch. First she gave the table, later a couple of chairs, and then, if he behaved, the sideboard. This was too much for the wife. One night the peace of the Roman evening was shattered by the sounds of screaming in the elegant courtyard of Anna's apartment block. It was his wife.

'You bitch, you stole my husband and you didn't even give us the *complete* dining-room.'

Even when we finished filming the saga of the electrician continued. Luchino decided that we should all go to Paris to promote the opening of the film, and the blond-haired young man, at Anna's insistence, accompanied us. Because she hated flying, we were forced to go by train. We'd booked sleepers but, edgy as ever, Anna made us all sit up playing cards throughout the night. As we pulled into Paris, the effects of this were showing; those famous dark patches under her eyes had become puffy bags and she resembled a gargoyle.

As soon as she looked in a mirror she began to get worried, and she

harassed our press man until he promised her there would be no photographers at the station. He said that as far as he was aware no one knew
of our arrival. She did her best to repair the ravages of the night and then
insisted I accompany her off the train. As we stepped down there was a
sudden splash of light and, when our eyes adjusted, we saw dozens of press
photographers dashing down the platform towards us, their flashbulbs
bursting like mad.

'I'll make that press man pay,' Anna hissed. 'Look at me, I'm like my
grandmother in her grave.'

'Come on,' I said. 'Let's brave it out.'

We lifted our heads, put on our best smiles and walked forward, but, to
our astonishment, the photographers simply parted and let us through.

'What's going on?' Anna snarled as we found ourselves alone beyond the
group.

I stood on tiptoe to look over the backs of the press corps and saw them
cluster around the Italian prime minister, who'd arrived on the same train.
I told Anna that this was a piece of luck and that her anonymity was
assured, but by now she was inconsolable over being ignored.

'I'll make that press man pay,' she said again.

She certainly made life difficult when we arrived at the Hotel George V.
She insisted on waiting in the foyer while they arranged for a king-size
bed to be moved into her room. The electrician was to have a small
communicating room, but in order to play down the affair it was to be
officially mine. The result was that all the production calls were answered
by our blond-haired friend, who may have had many attributes but not
much in the way of organizational ability, and the result was a degree of
chaos in our affairs.

Still, we had a wonderful time. Luchino was in his element with Chanel,
Jean Marais, Simone Signoret and Yves Montand. We all went to the Drap
d'Or to hear Piaf sing. It was just after the death in a plane crash of her
great love, the boxer Marcel Cerdan, and her songs seemed more poignant
than ever. Anna cried throughout and after the performance the two
women, so similar in many ways, fell into each other's arms.

The whole *Bellissima* episode was one of my happiest times with Luchino
but, as so often happens, a moment of happiness precedes one of misery.
When we had finished the film in the summer of 1951, we planned to
separate for a brief period. Luchino was going to Ischia for his holiday and
I was going to Siena for the opera. During those last hot days in Rome he
had one of his sisters and her husband staying, so I was using an attic room.

One morning I was woken by a servant who told me that there had been
a burglary. I found the police already there, with everybody gathered in
the main salon. The losses were considerable: gold dishes and works of art.
The burglars had even got into Luchino's bedroom and scooped up the

110   wristwatches, Cartier for the most part, which lay around his bedside table. The house was like an unguarded boutique and the thieves had had a field day.

The scene that greeted me was like something out of a 'B' detective movie. A raincoated, gruff inspector fired questions at us about our movements the night before. There were even rather overdone clues in the yard, where the thieves had walked into the coalstore, then left obvious footprints as they made their getaway.

Luchino and the two members of the family were standing slightly apart, and as the questioning went on, I suddenly wondered why he didn't call me over to him and tell the police that I was all right and needn't be questioned. But he didn't, and to my intense horror I saw that I was going to be taken to police headquarters with the others. Luchino never said a word as we were led away.

We were driven in a police car and, once at the station, were put in separate rooms. I sat alone in a bare, box-like space remembering all those hours of waiting during the war, feeling the dull anticipation of fear, perhaps pain. Eventually a different officer came in.

'Well, we know it was you or at least your friends,' he said, 'so you'd better start by giving us their names.'

It was such a corny ploy – even the cheapest films had stopped using it – that I almost laughed. What prevented me was the realization of what lay behind his words; in Italy you are guilty until you prove yourself innocent, and all he was doing was setting the target. It was up to me to duck.

God knows how long we sat there as I helplessly tried to establish my innocence. What on earth can you say except that you didn't do it? Worst of all is the terrible knowledge that if they decide to charge you, it can be months before you come to trial. The officer could see we were getting nowhere and called a halt. I was left alone again. Somewhere nearby were Luchino's butler, manservant, maids and cooks – all his servants – and what I realized was that I had to count myself as one of them, nothing more and maybe less. Ruefully I was forced to see how I had escaped from a metaphorical prison only to end up behind very real bars.

Eventually, Luchino's lawyers arranged our release, but the day had passed slowly with little to occupy me except my increasing anger. Food had been brought and more questions asked. At one point I was led out to be finger-printed, the results of which may even now be lying in a file somewhere. For the rest of the time I sat in that dismal room and tried to weigh up the past five years: I had broken with my family, I had had some incredible chances in the theatre and had lived in a style and among people beyond my earlier imaginings, but what did it all add up to except that I was the gilded creature of a famous man? I had nothing of my own – no reputation other than as his assistant and no money, for he gave me none.

I had been happy enough, because I had not questioned his attachment to me, but now the reality was all too clear.

I began to remember incidents in the past showing his temper and insensitivity that I had previously dismissed as merely the moods of a great man. Now I saw them as indications of my lesser status. I recalled the time he had hit me during the rehearsals for *As You Like It*, the total absence of any recognition or appreciation of work done for him, and a dozen or more incidents. Worst of all was something that had happened the previous year, which I had shut out of my memory. While Luchino was between projects, one of the actresses in the company had asked me if I would like to try my hand at directing with a small theatre group she ran. They wanted to do a revival of Bertolazzi's *Lulu*, a powerful play set in Italy, but similar in spirit to the better-known Wedekind version. Luchino was dubious about any talents I might have to undertake such a task, but I was used to that and eager to try. It was about this time that Piero Tosi turned up, and he helped me with the designs. It was my first attempt at theatre on my own, without the guidance of my supposed mentor.

The opening night was savaged by the press. The gist of their criticism was that a Visconti upstart had got too big for his boots. The unfairness of it was that, while I received no support from him, I was damned for being his creature. The critics had no conception of just how wide of the mark their notions were. During the dress rehearsal, while I was standing in the wings watching the performance, I began to hear talking and laughing from some members of the invited audience. This obviously mocking laughter grew worse and worse and, when I saw Piero come up from the auditorium, I asked him what was going on. He looked embarrassed and said he didn't know. When the play ended, I joined Luchino and his friends in the foyer. There seemed to be a lot of nudging and whispering among them, but I tried not to be bothered by it. It was only then, in that room in the police station, that I allowed myself to admit what I had really known all the time – that Luchino had led the jeering and he and his cronies had gone to my first production to laugh at me.

Eventually, the lawyer completed all the formalities and we were released. Back at home that night Luchino kept up a monologue on the subject of the Goldoni play he was planning. I answered when he questioned me, but no more. I was not so much sulking as totally absorbed in my thoughts of what to do next. Luchino might think that everything was as before, but I knew otherwise; I had already brooded my way out of my initial depression and was now beginning to make plans. Just as I had turned my father's possessive behaviour into a determination to enter the theatre, so now I decided to look upon that prison interlude as the impetus to break free from Luchino. Those two moments in my life were pitifully

Zeffirelli

112   similar: at neither time did I know precisely what I wanted to do, nor had
       I the money to do anything with. I was back where I started, though just
       a little wiser.

SEVEN

Separation

Years later Luchino and I were reminiscing about old times when at one point he referred to the amusing incident of the burglary and the way I'd been taken off to the police station. I was stunned. Hadn't he realized how I'd felt when he let me be taken away like that? He was genuinely shocked. How could I have thought like that? Didn't I realize what a scandal it would have been if it had got about that I was staying in his house as something *more* than an employee? His obtuseness was total. Hadn't he even wondered what had caused my sudden decision to leave his house? In the weeks between the burglary and his departure for his annual holiday in Ischia, I let it be known that I intended to move out, and he made no attempt to find out why or to stop me. Of course, that sort of aristocratic indifference was part of the armour he always used to protect himself from any emotional distress.

I think he thought I was just being foolish and would eventually come crawling back. In the meantime, it would be amusing to have me out of the way so that other adventures could be enjoyed. He certainly didn't see my leaving as an end to our working together: he had got used to my being a sort of secretary and he thought I would go on doing so. Even after I'd told him I was moving out he offered me the job of designing his production of Chekhov's *The Three Sisters*. I joyfully accepted, but I was still determined to go.

He also planned to use Piero Tosi for his next play, Goldoni's *The Mistress of the Inn*, so we decided to share a small apartment and brought in another childhood friend and theatrical colleague, Mauro Bolognini, to help with the rent. Mauro was a little older and had been a year ahead of us at the School of Architecture. He'd given up his studies and launched out as a set designer two years before we had made the leap. Later he went on to direct films and build a reputation in both France and Italy. Of course, in those days we were all broke, but we managed to find an apartment not far from my old hotel near the Piazza di Spagna and, while Luchino went off to Ischia for his holiday, the Florentine group set up house. The only problem was my two dogs, who pined for the garden at the Via Salaria. Three small rooms with two lively dogs was a real come-down.

Almost the only thing that truly belonged to me was the portfolio of Matisse reproductions Chanel had given me. I pinned them on my wall to cheer up the narrow bedroom I shared with the dogs. They reminded me of happier days when I thought I was on top of the world.

I went on to Siena for the opera again, then back to Rome to scout for work. Some producers shunned me as Visconti's creature, while those who were his friends stood back when they learned that he was displeased at my daring to break away. He is often recorded as treating actors as he once treated horses: they must run or stop at his command; they could have hay aplenty, but they must jump at his bidding.

The only place I could really think of as home was the villa in Positano where Donald and Bob were now living. As the discoverer of their little piece of paradise, it was open house to me and my dogs. I went whenever I could, happy to be an anonymous holiday-maker among the American and English guests who usually made up the villa party. Conversation was bookish with a smattering of politics, a quite different world from Rome and its theatrical gossip.

Light relief was provided by visitors like Tennessee Williams. He didn't actually stay at the villa, preferring to be in Positano itself. 'I like the smell of real people,' he once said. Judging by the outrageous stories he told us when he came over to the villa, he was often successful in his quest for adventure. His favourite hotel was the beautiful Palazzo Murat, then rather elegantly dilapidated. Later, when Positano began to become fashionable, the owners started to modernize it, much to Tennessee's distress. In the end they kept one room untouched just for him, a sign of how much of a famous personality he had become.

On my own visits to Positano I got to know Michael Semenoff, the mythical old Russian who had originally owned the whole of the Villa Treville and who now lived in the ancient Roman mill by the beach. The place looked intriguing, though almost derelict; with no electricity and no glass in the windows, but Semenoff seemed happy enough. I loved to hear him talk about his life, though I never quite knew how much to believe. Looking like Tolstoy with his long white beard, he would sit by the big millstone which dominated the main room and spin tales about his past. He claimed to have 'found' the villas while in exile from Russia after killing a man in a duel over a prima ballerina in the Imperial Theatre. After the Russian Revolution he made Positano his home and he often played host to the stars of the Russian ballet. Anna Pavlova came, as did Karsavina. Later he persuaded Diaghilev, who often visited Naples, to bring Nijinsky. While they were staying, the great dancer wished to practise, so Semenoff and Diaghilev had the interior walls of one of the villas removed and laid a sprung floor. This was in about 1908. They had an early record of

Invitation à la danse and from that they created the short ballet *Le Spectre* 115
de la rose.

Semenoff lived in Treville in gradually declining circumstances, the centre of a circle of gifted émigrés. Stravinsky came in 1937, when his doctors told him he was suffering from the tuberculosis that had just killed his wife and daughter. While he was recuperating in the sun, he composed *Dumbarton Oaks.*

I never knew what to believe of all this, but something happened to convince me that Semenoff wasn't lying after all. When he died in 1957, his wife inherited the mill, but as they had no children she left it to her maid. The place was a junk-shop of precious and worthless things piled up together. When the maid was clearing the place out, she found a set of table napkins with what looked like ink stains on them. They turned out to be portraits of some guests at Treville by Picasso, who must have stayed with Semenoff at the time Stravinsky composed his *Pulcinella*

That summer, however, I was not to enjoy for long my Positano hide-away. Piero and I were summoned to Luchino's villa on Ischia, to work on our two productions. My relationship with Luchino was now what it had been in Florence and the early days in Rome: we were together sometimes, though not permanently. This suited me very well.

I had no work apart from *The Three Sisters* and that would not be staged until after the Goldoni in 1952. For once I had ample time to research the background to a play, and the last months of 1951 I spent immersed in pre-revolutionary Russia and little else. Piero was doing wonderful work on the Goldoni, but he still found time to help me out. I would hardly have eaten if it hadn't been for him.

At the beginning of 1952, I was nearly in despair. I embarked on a self-promotion campaign, determined to find work outside the Visconti circle. Roberto Rossellini employed me for a few weeks as an assistant, and Antonioni hired me to help with pre-production work on a film he was setting up. But my best offer came from the writer Antonio Pietrangeli, who asked me to help him again with his next film, which meant, as before, that I virtually directed it.

However, there was no sign of anything substantial on the horizon. Only *The Three Sisters* offered a real chance for major creative work. My idea was to create not so much a Russia as known to a Russian of the time, but rather a dream Russia, one correct in its details but with a remote, ethereal air. I was trying to develop my own style by paying attention to cultural truth as I'd learnt to do from Luchino, but giving my own imagination free rein. After all, this Russian play was to be spoken in Italian in Rome, scarcely very realistic. It was to Luchino's credit that he let me have my way, though he was hardly the loser as many people still considered me his creature and awarded all merit for anything I achieved to him. One excep-

Zeffirelli

tion was a charming man who came to congratulate me on the opening night, Corrado Pavolini, who introduced himself as a director from La Scala and said how much he had enjoyed my designs. To my astonishment he asked if I would like to design a production he was doing at La Scala the coming year, a revival of Rossini's *The Italian Girl in Algiers*. It was an incredible opportunity, a complete break with the narrow Roman theatrical world that Luchino dominated.

Pavolini's offer not only propelled me into the world of opera, but right on to its topmost peak. For days I walked around in a dream, barely able to believe my luck. Following *The Three Sisters*, Luchino offered me an assistant's job on his next film; since it seemed to fit exactly into the period before the La Scala production, I accepted gratefully.

He planned to get back into epic films with a story of the Italian struggle for unification. He used an episode in the Italo-Austrian War of 1866 to create a major costume drama. Luchino decided to shoot in colour, and as evidence of his lingering desire for international, and especially American, recognition he persuaded Tennessee Williams to script the film, which was titled *Senso*.

The story was based on an interesting novella, *The Wanton Countess*, by Camillo Boito, whose brother Arrigo was the librettist for Verdi's last two operas. The original novel was similar to *Les Liaisons dangereuses*, a sour tale of a Venetian woman who betrays her elderly aristocratic husband in an affair with an Austrian officer. She is an absolute bitch and he is a gambler and a thief. Luchino took this short, violent story and, with the help of Tennessee Williams, transformed it into the tale of a tormented woman torn between her patriotism for Italy and her love for an Austrian monster.

Unfortunately, the script was something of a hotchpotch. Because of Luchino's passion for larger-than-life events the whole thing was punctuated with grandiose battles, ending with one of the last major engagements of the Italo-Austrian War. Lip service was paid to neo-realism by the decision to shoot this scene outside Verona, as near as possible to the actual battlefield. This should have meant that we started in June, when the weather is usually perfect. Instead, there were delays. The summer passed and shooting began in September. First of all, half the budget was spent during the first fifteen days of filming. But worse still was the fact that the Po Valley in September is almost permanently blanketed in mist as the river, warmed by the summer sun, evaporates. When it came to the final battle, this warm, damp fog lay over the valley, rendering the entire site invisible. The money was rapidly evaporating as well, but there was nothing to do except press on and hope the fog would clear.

As usual Luchino had seen to every detail. There would be thousands of participants, each meticulously costumed and made up. The military equipment was exact in every detail down to a full contingent of nineteenth-century field kitchens with cast-iron ovens and stove-pipe chimneys, If the fog cleared, the scene would be a spectacle of considerable power. The ranks of the Austrian army would march down the slope of the valley to engage the irregular mass of Italian citizenry gathered in defence of their homes. From a high crane the camera would record the first skirmishes, the indecisive to and fro of battle, and then the final victory of the citizens and the rout of the Austrian forces. But the fog refused to clear. The field kitchens and the cannons were put into position, the crane was set up, tents for the actors were erected, and every morning Franco Rosi and I would begin at two to supervise the dressing and make-up of the thousands of extras. And every morning at dawn Luchino would drive up, stare at the fog, shake his head, and drive away.

Many of the extras were local people and, as we laboured through the night to see that all was ready at first light, they would quote a Veronese proverb: 'This is the fog of the valley of the Po, it lasts a month and a week.' This was far from comforting. Nor was there much reassurance that things would be all right if the fog lifted, for Luchino had surprisingly arranged for only one camera, the one to be lifted in the crane. This was incredibly risky. We all knew that in Hollywood a once-only scene like this would be covered by as many as five cameras. Part of the battle was a cavalry charge, and to get the maximum effect there ought to be at least three or four cameras set to shoot the big scene from every angle.

For ten days, or rather nights, Franco Rosi and I went through this pointless labour. When the extras were ready, they had to be put in position. The horses had to be fed, brushed, saddled, mounted and ridden to the top of the hill. The Italians had to be positioned behind bales of hay, ready to appear at the first blast of a trumpet. Piero Tosi, who had done the costumes, was running about seeing to repairs and additions. It was a madhouse.

I was beginning to panic. Rehearsals at La Scala were due to begin in January, and now it looked as if the filming would not end in December as planned. I had already broken the news of Pavolini's offer to Luchino, who had as usual feigned indifference, though I suspect that he was astonished that his protégé was about to leap so far. But I knew that if I had to walk off the film before it was finished, he would see it as an unforgivable betrayal. It was a dilemma I would have preferred to avoid.

Then one morning, without any warning, the wind changed and the fog dispersed. As dawn broke, all was clear. Luchino could see the mounted cavalry in the distance and, grabbing his megaphone, he shouted at everyone to get ready. He clambered into the crane with the cameraman and was borne aloft. As soon as he was hovering safely above us, he shouted down for me to order the charge to begin. I relayed the message and waited.

118 It would take some time for cavalry to wheel round and go back to begin their gallop. Now that the order was given the die was cast. Ineluctably, this epic scene would unfold, and nothing any of us could now do would alter its progress. But just as the riders cantered back into view, I heard Luchino bellowing orders through his megaphone.

'The fires!' he was shouting. 'No one's lit the kitchen fires!'

It was true; and it was just the sort of detail he was fanatical about. I quickly sent a runner to tell the actors to light the straw in their portable ovens and turned my attention back to the great spectacle. The camera was rolling, the horses were thundering down the hill, the irregulars were bracing themselves for the battle, when suddenly all the kitchen fires burst into flame and the damp straw sent up a burst of acrid black smoke. Just as the two forces clashed and the great battle began, the breeze blew this impenetrable cloud towards the camera and us. Within seconds we were engulfed by a fog more dense than the one we had waited so long to be rid of. Somewhere unseen beyond it the battle raged, pointless and unfilmable. Down through the smoke, like a vengeful God in a miracle play, Luchino descended – screaming obscenities at me through his megaphone.

'You unspeakable cretin,' he yelled. 'You irresponsible scum. You ruined everybody's work.'

As quickly as it had come, the smoke went. There before us was the finished, lost battle. Thousands of bemused people were rooted to the spot as they watched their director descend, howling crazy nonsense at his assistant. As he came down to my level he continued shouting viciously – he was out of control.

'You ignorant fool! I don't want to see you any more. Get out of my sight.'

It was too much. I was exhausted. I'd done everything I could to help him and here he was insulting me as if I were a criminal. I began to shake, my eyes seemed to be coming out of my head. Without realizing what I was doing, I lifted my own megaphone and, in a bizarre re-run of his attack on me at that rehearsal of *As You Like It* so long ago, I brought it down on his head with a sickening bang. It seemed as if the hollow noise echoed round the silent valley. Everybody froze. Luchino blinked and said nothing. Centuries seemed to pass, and then he tossed his head as if to shake off a fly.

'Right,' he said, as if nothing had happened. 'Let's try one more time.'

And that was it. He didn't refer to the incident then or ever again. He just ordered the crane up and began to marshal the actors back into position, while I stared around me like someone coming out of a coma and seeing the world for the first time.

After the battle scene the production moved to Vicenza, then to Venice and back to Rome. But before that, the day of decision arrived. At the end of December I told Luchino that I had to leave for La Scala, and for once he forgot his own problems and agreed with my decision. Gratefully, I left Venice for Milan.

The irony of what I was about to do was uppermost in my mind. La Scala had been the Viscontis' theatre. Luchino's grandfather had saved it from financial collapse at the turn of the century and had been its most brilliant *sovrintendente*, responsible for the appointment of Arturo Toscanini as artistic director. Luchino had, however, never worked there. Now I, his creature, was going to.

EIGHT

La Divina

Having seen it in ruins, I was better able than most to appreciate the miracle wrought by the Milanese in rebuilding La Scala in only one year. To them it was a symbol of their city and its culture and they had simply rolled up their sleeves and got on with the job. Donald and I had seen it in ruins in April 1945, yet on 11 May 1946 Toscanini, who had returned from exile in America, stood on the podium of his theatre to conduct Verdi's Requiem. When I first saw the restored theatre, I felt one of those rare moments of patriotism at what we Italians can do if we really try. The production facilities had been improved but more noticeable were the changes front-of-house, with a new heating system to make those cold Milan winters more bearable. Unfortunately, little else had changed; La Scala remained the great bastion of the old traditional opera. We in Florence had been used to adventure; the status of the art had changed during those evenings in the 1930s, when Gustavo had taken me to the Teatro Communale to see the stars of the pre-war years or those later idyllic times when, as a student, I had queued to get my seat in the Gods night after night. We had had productions with sets by de Chirico and other avant-garde artists, a real revolution had occurred; but at La Scala all that mattered were voices. They just wanted great singing and never imagined that drama could enter the equation; that was left for the straight theatre to provide. In some ways they were little more than concert performances in fancy dress.

By a miracle I arrived in Milan just as this was about to change. With the reconstruction of the opera house had come a new generation of directors and singers. Opera had become popular again and a new, younger audience was flocking to it. The productions were becoming livelier and better made, and the singers more committed to the drama of the work. Excitement would be generated by such highly publicized battles as the supposed contest between Renata Tebaldi, principal exponent of pure *bel canto* singing, and the more variable but more dramatic performances of Maria Callas. Supporters were as avid and sometimes as unruly as football fans. But life was returning to what had been a dying art form.

It was the most fantastic time for Italian singers. The list of great voices, all at their peak, seemed endless – Tebaldi, Callas, di Stefano, del Monaco, Corelli, Rossi-Lemeni, Barbieri, Simionato, Gobbi, Bechi, Christoff. . . . it was unbelievable. The manager, Antonio Ghiringhelli, while no great artistic figure, was able nevertheless to hold all these thoroughbreds together. Another brilliant new star was the young Carlo Maria Giulini, who would conduct the opera I was to design, while Giulietta Simionato, the greatest mezzo of the moment, would sing the leading role.

It was nervewracking that my first major work without Luchino should be at the most prestigious opera house in the world, which was also the toughest for a new boy. La Scala was naturally a hotbed of gossip and warring factions who were quick to make life hell for anyone who didn't fit their little schemes. I had two disadvantages: I was known as Luchino's upstart, and I was unknown to the world of opera. But there were some advantages: the director Pavolini, who was an extraordinarily kind person, not only gave me a free hand, but also backed me completely.

Corrado Pavolini was the brother of the Pavolini who had been Mussolini's Minister of Popular Culture, whom I'd seen hanging in the Piazzale Loreto with the Duce. But Corrado had kept clear of politics and no one bothered him. He was getting on by this time and had an easy-going manner.

The main advantage we had was that the opera, *The Italian Girl in Algiers*, was not just another production, it was to be the first in a major revival of Rossini, a genius who had been neglected for decades. Only *William Tell* and *The Barber of Seville* were regular repertory pieces around the world – his other works had been forgotten until then. The importance attached to the production by Sovrintendente Ghiringhelli ensured that everyone worked their hardest. Since it was an opera specifically revived for Simionato, a mezzo, we were happily spared the rivalry and bitchiness that would have been flying around if we had been part of the battle of the sopranos. Tebaldi and Callas adored Simionato, who is one of the nicest people in the world of opera.

Given a free hand by Pavolini, I decided to bring to the design some of the adventurousness we young 'Florentines' had put into our theatre work in Rome. I experimented with the stage machinery, which at that time was little used. La Scala was perfectly well equipped with revolves and lifts, but the staid productions of the 1950s tended to shun such tricks. I made a major feature of them, bringing the stage forward with a sliding apron and, as with *Streetcar*, used a fixed set with any changes raised and lowered as needed. First, the walls of Algiers, battered by the storm that brings Isabella in search of her imprisoned lover, lifted away to reveal the fortress and inside that the Sultan's palace, a delicate Moorish pavilion. The whole movement of the set symbolized the action, opening gradually to the heart of the story. Everything was light, simple blues and whites in folk style

122 with billowing Arabic costumes. I set the piece in the 1820s and tried to make it loose and cheerful, a breath of fresh air after the stuffy, overweight pieces the Milanese were used to. Happily, they adored it.

My father was still very ill and couldn't come to the opening, but Aunt Lide and Gustavo appeared, and the pleasure on his face was our reconciliation. Here was the man who had first taken me to the opera, whose smiles now told me that his invitation had borne fruit. We went with the cast to one of the many theatrical restaurants near La Scala, and Gustavo happily pointed out the old signed photographs on the walls, displaying his encyclopaedic knowledge of opera and opera singers – this tenor he had heard, that soprano he had met – he was in heaven!

For myself, that first night gave me the self-confidence I needed. After years of confusion as a young man, first in school, then during the war, and most recently with Luchino, here was something I had truly done on my own. The world of music is hard and blunt: you can sing or you can't, play the violin or not, design well or badly. To succeed in any part of opera you have to be good, and that was the reassurance I now had.

Not that any of this made much difference to my material circumstances. God knows how I survived then! In Milan I lived in the Hotel Marino opposite the opera house. Like the Inghilterra, it is now quite smart, but then it was distinctly seedy. I had a tiny room and all my designs were done on the bed since I had no fancy drawing-board or lamp. I was paid about £200 for the whole thing, a third on signing the contract, a third on handing over the drawings, and the rest when the production opened. It was pitifully little. This way of working went on for years before I ever really made any money worth talking about. I can remember preparing some work, again on a bed, in a run-down hotel in Genoa when the director of the Dallas Opera, Larry Kelly, called on me. He stood at the door of the room watching me and when he spoke he was choked with emotion.

'I'll never forget this,' he said. 'This is real sacrifice, this is how things should be done.'

Curiously, given the success of *The Italian Girl*, I didn't decide then and there to be a set designer. I suspect I thought La Scala an odd, if pleasurable, interlude. Real life to me was still the cinema. I imagined I would soon be back as an assistant director, then the height of my ambition. The real pleasure of La Scala was being near Maria Callas. Her relationship with the place was frenetic and her first peformance there had been disastrous. The story goes back to the Venice opera season of 1948–9, when Maria had taken her second Wagnerian role, Isolde. The other major star of that season was Margherita Carosio as Elvira in Bellini's *I puritani*. No two parts could be more different. That winter Venice had a severe influenza epidemic and, when Carosio succumbed to the illness, it proved impossible to find a replacement. The conductor, Tullio Serafin, then asked Maria to

step in, but one has to remind oneself what he was asking of her: to learn
in a mere seven days a major new role in an entirely different voice and
vocal style. It ought to have been impossible, but she did it. And all the
cast of sub-characters that keeps the world of opera turning, the voice
trainers, the *maestri sostituti*, the dressers and wigmasters and the rest,
were soon buzzing with the news of her astonishing achievement; hence her
summons to Milan.

Unfortunately, Callas was so overwhelmed by the thought of La Scala
that she agreed to appear in a revival of a tired old production of *Aida*. She
had had some notion that the enslaved princess is so ashamed of her
condition that she would never show her face to anybody, and she decided to
appear throughout the production wrapped in a veil, which she occasionally
lifted to reveal herself to the audience. But that audience had come to see
the new diva; what they got was this overweight Greek lady, peeping out
from behind her trailing chiffon, who had decided not to break into that
dramatic singing which they expected from her. All the Milanese heard was
the unevenness, the changes of register between contralto and soprano
which she thought helped reveal the sharpness of the character of the
barbarian princess. Sadly, they compared her unfavourably with Renata
Tebaldi, the reigning star of La Scala. Maria was a revolutionary but that
first *Aida* at La Scala was a rout. Things weren't helped by the fact that
Ghiringhelli couldn't handle her; he was afraid of what she represented, a
singer with a mind and a vision of what opera could be far beyond his, or
in fact anyone else's, conception at that time. As a result, they quarrelled
and Maria walked out, saying that she wouldn't return until they made her
prima donna assoluta.

Maria almost laid siege to La Scala. She stormed around the world having
triumph after triumph, and she always ensured that copies of her reviews
were sent to Ghiringhelli. Both Maria and Tebaldi did a season in Rio, in
which Maria came out the clear winner. Then she began to circle her prey
with performances in Venice, and then the *Traviata* in Florence that I went
to see, where the audience went wild. Then Genoa, then Turin, and finally
there she was on La Scala's doorstep.

Just before I arrived in Milan, Ghiringhelli had to accept that she was
now such a worldwide phenomenon that she would have to be invited back.
She had created her public, the intellectuals saw what she was doing
and supported her – hence the much-publicized rivalry between Callas
supporters and those of Tebaldi. But Maria was the new, while Tebaldi was
the accepted tradition. The battle of the old and the new really was intense.
The old guard were led by Toscanini's clan, who favoured Tebaldi in the
battle, but the new had the precious support of Tullio Serafin, who had
played the violin at the opening night of Verdi's *Falstaff* and was thus
considered an impeccable descendant of the great tradition. Maria was

Zeffirelli

124 Serafin's protégée and his support was a powerful shield against the machinations of the Toscanini set.

Why Toscanini should have so taken against Maria is hard to explain. 'She has vinegar in her voice,' he said on one occasion, and, of course, the remark got back to Maria, who must have been very hurt by it.

Her reaction was for once restrained – she requested an audition from the maestro. Toscanini refused but she went on asking, putting him in a very embarrassing position. But that was Maria: she always faced a problem head on, which was why I loved her so much. No one ever treated the notorious La Scala claque with such contempt as she did. And they really were monsters, those villains in the gods. Organized by their leaders, the students who made up the claque would applaud or hiss on command and could lift up or throw down a singer at will. In consequence most performers were prepared to bribe the ringleaders in order to ensure a safe passage. Maria never did. This was partially because she and her husband Meneghini were notoriously mean, but also because she loved a fight. If I was in Milan, I would try to wait with her in the wings as she prepared to go on. It was an amazing study in human fortitude. She was always nervous and would try to keep up her spirits by arguing with her devoted maid Bruna about trivial domestic matters such as the laundry bill or the price of vegetables, but when her moment came to go on she would take a deep breath, suddenly assume the part she was playing and launch herself into the action on stage. It never failed to entrance me as I watched it night after night.

It must be said that the rivalry between Callas and Tebaldi was all of the public's making. The two singers were perfectly correct in their behaviour towards each other. In fact, that is usually the case with female singers, despite the popular misconception of bitchy prima donnas. It is the male singers, especially the tenors, who really are unforgiving enemies and who never have a good word to say about each other. But despite its artificiality, the Callas-Tebaldi rivalry certainly engaged the imagination of the La Scala audience – one faction in the claque couldn't stand Maria, another would emit mass yawns whenever Tebaldi started an aria. In the end Maria won, if that is the word. Tebaldi had a disastrous opening night in *La Wally*, when even the scenery played against her – the avalanche ended up in the pit. A few nights later Maria opened in a spectacular performance of *Medea*. She had already sung the role in Florence, but this time it was conducted by the young Leonard Bernstein, who was making his début at La Scala, and the evening was vibrant with energy. When it was over, we knew that the world of opera was transformed. There was BC and AC, before and after Callas. Tebaldi pulled out of a contest that was not of her making and I am happy to say went on to great success in America. But from then on the new world of Italian opera revolved around Maria and those of us who were with her.

Maria came to *The Italian Girl* and must have marked me down as a potential member of the 'new' group that had collected around her, though I didn't know it at first. The idea that we might work together didn't even occur to me. Far more important was the part Giulietta Simionato played in convincing me that I had the talent to succeed. She often whispered a compliment while we were working on *The Italian Girl*, and if she sensed that I was suffering from nerves or having a crisis of indecision over something, she would find a way to show her sympathy.

'You know, Franco,' she would say, 'we singers have it easy, we have our golden voices. If there's a flop we still have that and we'll work again. But you production people have a terrible time, there are no schools for you, no exams to show what you know, nothing you can do to demonstrate your talent except each production. But you have the talent, just like my voice, you have it.'

Giulietta and I have remained close friends to this day, and it was because of her that I made the next audacious move forward. Because of that first Rossini revival, Ghiringhelli decided he wanted to do *La Cenerentola* (Cinderella) using the same team of Pavolini, Giulini, Simionato and myself. But Pavolini was not well. He'd been ill during much of the rehearsal of *The Italian Girl* and I had acted almost as a second director. Ghiringhelli knew this and so, when Pavolini dropped out of *Cenerentola* and I, supported by Simionato, had the gall to ask if I could try my hand both as director and designer, he was perhaps less surprised than he might have been. He knew that what I had done with the designs for *The Italian Girl* had made something fresh out of the piece, and he thought I was worth the risk. Even so, I was stunned when he agreed.

Any pride I might have felt was immediately dissipated by other realities. *Cenerentola* was months away and, as usual, I was broke. This always surprises people who imagine that the glamorous world of first nights and superstars must shower its denizens with high rewards. Rarely is that the truth. I returned to Rome and my friends in our little apartment and began to look for work. After a few weeks I was desperate. I was sitting in my room, bored and aimless, when Piero came back with a friend who worked in the antique business. I forget what we talked about, this and that, football probably, when our visitor suddenly got up and began peering at the Matisse reproductions on my wall. After a moment he asked me for a rubber and, when one was produced, he began, very delicately, to rub at an extreme corner of one of the pictures. To our astonishment the line disappeared. There was no need to be an antique dealer to realize what that meant – they weren't reproductions at all. The lovely, other-worldly Chanel had given me a set of original Matisse drawings, all signed by the artist. We stared round the room, at the fortune hanging on the walls. It was agony: how could I sell a gift, yet how could I *not* do so, given my

126   position? In the end I sold two drawings and eked out the money for as long as possible before two more had to go. Over the following years they were like an annuity that helped me survive both the bad periods between work, or those long periods of research and design that I found essential but for which I was never paid. By the time I was able to earn enough not to need to sell the Matisses, I had only four left and these were stolen when my apartment was burgled, so Chanel's gift finally disappeared.

My return to Milan as a director was not easy. On the first morning I found myself confronted by the chorus of La Scala, a formidable group at any time, all dressed in grey overalls for rehearsals, the ladies clutching their handbags like weapons, waiting to see what I was planning. I was late, and they let it be known that their first break would be in precisely fifty minutes' time. Giulini tried to help, Simionato intervened, but I was faced with bored, elderly men and formidable, bosomy ladies whom I was trying to transform into a glittering court for Cinderella's ball.

When the rehearsal was over, my first thought was to get out as quickly as possible. I wasn't ready for them and it would be better to stop now.

Simionato was furious. 'Of course you can't control them,' she said. 'Not as long as you think of them as a grey wall. They're individuals, some of them very talented ones, they have to be to sing in the La Scala chorus, but obviously they are touchy because they didn't become stars. Your job is to deal with that.'

It was a Thursday and my next rehearsal wasn't until Monday. I went to the office of the union and explained that I wanted to save time at rehearsals by familiarizing myself with the chorus and would like to borrow their register. This contained names and photographs, and after they had agreed I was able to spend the weekend memorizing the faces of Signora Mazzoni, Signor Boscolo, Signora Ghisleni – a soprano, a bass and a mezzo. I could only manage a dozen, but that was enough. Back on stage on Monday, I addressed the ones I could remember personally, suggesting moves here and there, and it was immediately obvious how impressed they all were. I called out Signora Mazzoni and she looked round startled, wondering who had spoken.

'You are a soprano, are you not?'

She nodded, pleased.

'Could you stand over here. You'll have a blue costume, while Signor Biscolo will be over there in brown.'

They began to come alive, to take an interest. I put them into blocs by voices, but then I gave them different things to do, individual business of their own. And they responded. In the end they literally made the production. Instead of being bricks in a wall, each one acted. The critics picked up on it, saying what a miracle it was to see the whole cast acting

instead of merely hanging about while the principals performed. Since then
it's something I do everywhere. I respect the chorus, learn their histories
if I can, and work *with* them.

There was certainly plenty for everyone to do in that *Cenerentola*. I went
back to the original Perrault seventeenth-century fairytale. I decided to
create a fantasy, but not in a no-man's-land. Stendhal, who saw nineteen
consecutive performances of the original Rossini production, said that there
were always topical references for the audience to identify with. I set my
version in the crumbling palace of Don Magnifico near Rome, and I left
out the fairy godmother, who was never in the original: it was the prince's
tutor who helped Cinderella go to the ball.

This approach, of looking at the earliest versions and the period they
sprang from, was my inheritance from Visconti. One thing I did not expect
was his appearance at the public dress rehearsal. His last appearance at
one of my rehearsals had been the opening of *Lulù*, when he had laughed
at my first attempt as a director; this time was different. Again I didn't
realize that he was there. The rehearsal was a huge success, the house was
full and the applause loud. I took my bows and left the stage through a
door leading into the corridor behind the first-level boxes. As soon as I
appeared a crowd of friends ran up to congratulate me, but a door to one
of the boxes opened and I found myself caught in a crippling bear hug.
When I recovered sufficiently to see what was going on, I realized that it
was Luchino who was holding me. His left arm was wrapped round me so
that I could hardly breathe and he swung his right hand as if wielding a
sword to hold back the people. He was crying and shouting like a madman:
'Get back, get back! He's mine. He belongs to me. I made him. Stay away,
you have no right to congratulate him. He's mine.'

He kept on and on, while I just hung in his grasp, unsure of what to do
in the midst of this outburst. To my embarrassment I could make out the
venerable de Sabata, La Scala's artistic director, standing with Callas. They
both stared in amazement as Luchino brandished his imaginary sword for
all the world like one of his medieval ancestors. Our friends started cheering – it must have seemed a continuation of the performance. With the
spell broken by the noise, Luchino stopped and let go of me. The crowd
engulfed us and suddenly he was gone.

I was summoned to Ghiringhelli's office, congratulated, and offered two
productions for the next season: Donizetti's *L'elisir d'amore* with the great
tenor Giuseppe di Stefano, and Rossini's *Il turco in Italia*. Then came the
best news of all. Maria Callas had announced to Ghiringhelli that she was
tired of singing only the great tragic roles: she wished to do something
lighter from time to time. You can imagine my joy when he told me that
Maria wanted to sing Donna Fiorilla in the Rossini and had specifically
asked that I should direct it.

Zeffirelli

As I left Ghiringhelli's office, I bumped into Luchino, who was looking very pleased with himself.

'So, we'll be working together,' he said.

'Together?'

'Well, on the same season.'

I couldn't think what he was talking about.

'I've decided it's time I came home, as it were, to La Scala. It's ridiculous that I've never produced anything for the place.'

Now I saw it all. I had trodden on sacred territory and the proprietor was returning to claim it.

'I'll be doing three productions with Maria,' he said. '*La Vestale* will be the first. It hasn't been done here for years. It'll open the new season. Then you'll come with *Elisir*, I hear.'

I consoled myself with the thought that now I was someone he felt he had to reckon with. I could imagine the scene in Ghiringhelli's office, with Luchino telling the Sovrintendente that he would graciously condescend to direct at La Scala, but only if the boy Zeffirelli took second place or none at all. It was the beginning of another famous rivalry to match the Tebaldi-Callas battles, and the gossip columns soon latched on to it.

I decided I needed a break and my thoughts turned to France. The news was that Chanel was planning a comeback, and I was determined to witness an event the entire fashion world was talking about. I arrived in Paris on the day of Chanel's opening and went to the rue Cambon expecting a glorious occasion. It turned out to be one of the cruellest experiences I've ever witnessed. The critics and buyers, the press and her fellow *couturiers* had come to mock a woman they considered dead. The great names of the time, Dior, Fath, Balenciaga, were at the hub of an immense manufacturing empire and Chanel was a threat. She designed classic clothes wearable for years; the production machine wanted a quick turnover in rapid, throwaway fashions. So the design crowd greeted her collection with mocking silence or sniggering rudeness. Eventually, they broke into open laughter. Saddened, I looked into the circle of mirrors lining the famous staircase that her models used to descend and I saw her reflection. Coco was sitting alone on the top step witnessing her own humiliation.

I went to the Ritz afterwards and saw Maggie van Zuylen.

'She won't come, Franco, but she was happy to know you were there. She needed some friends. The British hurt her most, they were so cruel to her and she always had such faith in them.'

I returned to Rome chastened by an increasing awareness of what the world can be like. I began to see what my public rivalry with Luchino might lead to. It was a rivalry not of my own making or choosing, not least because I started with many disadvantages. The Visconti name was magic in Milan – not for Luchino a sullen chorus at his first rehearsal: the heir of the Dukes of Milan could overawe even the most supercilious seamstress or electrician. Worse still, despite the praise for my production, I was not universally accepted in the cliquish world of La Scala. I had even succeeded in alienating the sacred father-figure, Arturo Toscanini. The story of how that happened illustrates better than anything else the situation Luchino had created.

The Visconti-Callas *Vestale* was to open the season on 7th December, while my *Elisir d'amore* would be second on the 9th. This was an impossible position, as everybody was obviously far too involved with the first to give more than a minimum effort to the second. It was compounded by the fact that Luchino had another burst of *folie de grandeur*: his ancient Rome was a place of mammoth columns and arches, lit for the first time by a hundred open-flame torches. It was spectacular and inevitably occupied all the available time of the scene painters, the lighting technicians, etc.

On top of that everyone with a quarter of an hour to spare hung around watching Maria rehearse. She was a spectacle herself, having just achieved – through strenuous dieting – the incredible feat of turning a dumpy Greek lady into a svelte, dark beauty. In every way Maria Callas created herself. We were all terrified that her voice would suffer; after all, the received truth is that big voices need big bodies. But, as with so much else, she gave the lie to the myth.

With all that going on, it is not hard to see why an air of nervous panic surrounded me. Nothing seemed to get done on time and the days swept by remorselessly. To my chagrin I was told that I could only have a two-hour lighting rehearsal and that it would be on the morning of Luchino's opening. This was particularly infuriating as I had placed a lot of emphasis on atmospheric lighting. The key moment in the opera is centred on the famous aria '*Una furtiva lagrima*'. I imagined Nemorino asleep at a table outside the inn on the village square, just before dawn. He wakes and, remembering his love, sings that moving aria while day slowly breaks and people begin to go about their business. We moved from a shaft of warm light coming from the door of the inn, through the cold light of morning, onto the bright sunlit day.

It was ridiculous to have to light such a scene, indeed the entire opera, in two hours, but that was what I had to try to do while all around me the front of house was being spruced up for that night's gala opening and every florist in Milan, it seemed, was arriving laden with bouquets and paniers of flowers.

Through all this chaos I tried to direct my rehearsal. Suddenly all the houselights went up – chandeliers, box lamps, spotlights. The place was ablaze and down the aisle came an extraordinary procession: Ghiringhelli, de Sabata and all the top personnel of the house led by the grand old man of Italian opera, Arturo Toscanini. This was completely unexpected.

Zeffirelli

130   To the new generation like myself Toscanini was a piece of history rather than part of the present La Scala. He was talking rather loudly to this reverential entourage. At first I wondered why he was making so much noise, and then I realized that he was testing the changes in the acoustics that the rebuilding had created. Despite my fascination with his presence, I kept glancing at my watch, aware that my only lighting rehearsal was vanishing by the minute. He seemed to be unaware that he was interrupting anything and went on talking for at least half an hour. Suddenly I couldn't stand it any longer and, unwilling as they were, I made the technicians dim the houselights and go on with our work. As darkness fell Toscanini at last stopped talking, but only momentarily.

'What is this?' he asked.

They told him.

'What?' he exclaimed. 'There are no dark scenes in *L'elisir d'amore*. It is always light, sunlight, full light.'

I tried to ignore this, but as I went on working I heard someone come near me. It was Ghiringhelli.

'Did you hear what the maestro said?' he asked

This was preposterous. 'I don't give a damn,' I said. 'He's forty years out of date and this is my production. He's a great conductor, but he shouldn't come here telling me what to do.'

There was silence in the auditorium, but I was too angry to care.

'And another thing,' I went on. 'I want another hour for my lighting rehearsal. I've lost an hour.'

Toscanini stood up and quietly led them all out.

Ghiringhelli was white with rage. 'Are you mad?' he said. 'You realize what you've done? You've insulted Toscanini!'

'He should have known we were working. I insist on being treated as a professional and, if you don't give me another hour, forget about *Elisir* opening.'

Ghiringhelli stormed out but, as is the way of these things, my tantrums had some effect. Even today conductors, if we have a difference of opinion, will say: 'Well, I'd better watch out, you're the one who told Toscanini where to get off.'

It was the best bouquet I could have given Luchino for his opening night. It set the old guard at La Scala resolutely against me. Indeed, I might have had to leave if it hadn't been for Toscanini's daughter, Wally, who decided that a little diplomacy was needed. She didn't apologize for her father, but she made it clear that she understood my point. She is a remarkably kind person and she invited me often to their home. Before the war they had run a sort of salon on the evenings when the maestro was conducting. Guests used to eat, then leave for the performance. But Toscanini himself would have only a bowl of *minestrone*, and at precisely twelve minutes to nine he would don his cloak, walk across the square to the theatre and into the orchestra pit, lift his baton and begin. He was never late.

Wally was trying to revive something of those days and, although she represented the old guard, she still had enough sense of their position to see the need to introduce the old man to the new talent – singers, directors, designers. On that first visit he let me know that he bore no grudge.

'Your character could push you on or hold you back,' he said cryptically. 'But that's what they said about me when I was your age.' He reminded me that he had not had an easy time when he first came to La Scala and had had to be quite rude to get people to pay attention – though I must say my experience is that all conductors are very rude anyway!

I never did find out what Toscanini thought of my *L'elisir d'amore*, but the audience and the critics were certainly satisfied. Luchino had also been much praised for his *La vestale*, partly for the stunning setting with its mighty columns and sweeping pageantry, but mostly for the way that he had drawn a performance out of Maria that had previously merely been glimpsed. He really directed her, talked her through the role, gave her gestures and actions drawn from neo-classical paintings that she used to give another dimension to the action. Maria, who had completed her physical transformation into the new slim woman, both looked and sounded magnificent. Franco Corelli sang with her that night. He was absolutely magnificent and one cannot expect to see a couple like them again.

It was now up to me to continue the enrichment of Maria's talent and I was helped in this by her own desire to move on from the heavy set pieces that *La vestale* represented. She had felt swamped by the mammoth sets and, when we began to exchange ideas on *Il turco in Italia*, she begged me to keep everything light and frivolous. She wanted to show that she could play comedy as well as big tragic roles. So that January I went to Positano and spent nearly three weeks in Naples, looking at Neapolitan folk art with its bright peasant scenes and watching the traditional Pulcinella shows in the slums. I wanted to recreate a real Neapolitan fiesta and I told Maria she could either be a stately matron or a wild cat, knowing full well she would choose the latter.

Before Maria would do *Il turco* with me in 1955 she had to do *La sonnambula* with Luchino, and for me it was the best thing they both did. Piero Tosi designed the production in pastel colours, silks and frills. It was a romantic vision, which was frequently copied later, but completely original then. I can remember having an argument with two idiots watching a rehearsal who were suggesting that this sort of thing wasn't up to La Scala standards. The young Leonard Bernstein conducted and Maria was exquisitely dressed in Swiss peasant style – though with all her jewels since no diva sang without them, no matter what the role, beggar or peasant. I remember clearly the third act aria: '*Ah, non credea mirarti...*'. She sang

132 with her lips barely apart, almost like a ventriloquist, the ultimate pian
issimo, and everyone was straining to hear her. The tension was incredible
Today, when Lenny Bernstein wants more pianissimo from an orchestra
he asks them for a 'Callas pianissimo'.

Although I'd seen Lenny Bernstein at La Scala when he and Maria did
Medea, it was only now that I got to know hm. He would slip into my
rehearsals to see what 'Visconti's boy' was up to. Opera people are always
on the lookout for new talent and Lenny was as nosey as the rest of us. As
soon as we began to talk and then go about together I realized what a force
he was. Of course I knew about his musical talents – the New York Jewish
boy who'd reversed the usual trend by being a phenomenal success in
Europe and at the same time having a Broadway hit with *On the Town*
Two years later came *West Side Story*, but he was already a legend. It was
his poor background that did it, of course; he was hungry for success and
burning with talent and energy. He was just turned forty and had those
thickset Jewish good looks which, allied to his almost violent gestures and
intense way of engaging your attention, made him very attractive. And
my God, how he worked – he had prepared *Medea* in one week! You can
imagine what life was like with him, Luchino and Maria around. Luchino
could control Maria, Svengali-like, but he'd met his match in Lenny. Both
wanted any evening to be theirs and the creative tension was incredible
These three 'monsters' became the centre of a Milanese cultural clique
involving a number of rich aristocrats. I don't think Maria felt at home
with them: she had basically *petit-bourgeois* longings, but I think she felt
that this was where real life was. In any case, Luchino was there, so she
stayed. I avoided the group, not just to keep my distance from Luchino
but also because I disliked the supercilious bitchiness of it all. My one regret
was that I missed out on Lenny's company because, whatever his other
qualities, his finest attribute was his sense of fun.

We all went out for a meal after the opening of *Sonnambula* and everyone
knew that a peak had been reached. Maria insisted on ordering everyone's
food – cannelloni for this one, spaghetti for that one, rice over there. It
seemed to help with her dieting. I can still see her fork darting out as she
permitted herself a tiny taste of each dish before going back to her steak
and salad. Then Lenny started playing those games I always dread. One
was the Temple Game in which he beat a rhythm, called a name and, if
you missed the beat, you were out. Inevitably, it started a row. Someone
said that Lenny wasn't keeping time properly and he exploded and went
off in a huff. Finally, the notices arrived and they weren't good. The critics
were fools and couldn't see how beautiful the whole concept had been
though they all agreed that Maria was magnificent. To me it was the
definitive production of *Sonnambula*. I've never dared touch that opera, as
I know I'd have nothing to add.

Disappointed with the press, the party broke up and a few of us went
back to Maria's. As usual, Meneghini went to bed, and gradually everyone
drifted away, leaving us alone.
'Don't go,' Maria said, opening a bottle of champagne. 'Let's see in the
dawn.'
'What about the diet?'
'It doesn't matter tonight. I must drink.'
She drank silently for a time and then began to cry, like a child in
uncontrolled sobs. Then there was another long silence.
'Come on,' I said finally. 'This has been the greatest moment in your life.
The peak of your career.'
'Exactly,' she said, and I saw what she meant. I tried to say all the things
one should, about future triumphs and so on, but she just sat there gulping
champagne and snivelling.
'Why this sour note?' I asked.
'Because I've always been very realistic in my life. When something good
is given to me, my first thought is that I am going to lose it.'
While we were talking, dawn broke and I think it was then that I began
to realize what was missing in her life. What she needed as she came down
from the nervous excitement of a performance was someone who would
take hold of her and tell her he loved her, that she was his woman. This is
crude psychology, but true none the less. Upstairs, old Meneghini was
asleep, whereas she was unfulfilled. Once the singing stopped and the
applause ended, there was a void, and she was only just becoming aware
of it. As I walked back to my hotel, I thought about what might happen
if she went a stage further and decided to do something about it.
    Two days later she turned up at our first rehearsal for *Il turco* as promptly
as ever and showed no signs of the misery of two nights before. A lot of
work had been done in advance and she was able to go for costume fittings
immediately. This caused our first problems.
'I made all this sacrifice,' she protested, 'all that dieting and you give
me a waistline up here. No one will see how slim I am.'
    The costumes were 1810, Empire style, with the dress caught up under
the bust. It was true that they did not show how svelte she had become.
Maria used always to put a photograph of Audrey Hepburn in *Roman
Holiday* on her dressing-room mirror as an ideal to aim for; she even used
to practise the famous head back, wide-eyed pose that Hepburn used. Now
she started to go secretly to the seamstress to get her to lower the waistline
and, of course, I would go and have it raised. Eventually we had a mild
argument with my insisting that she would look ravishing in these flowing
dresses.
'All right,' she conceded, 'do whatever you want provided we have fun.'
    And we did. She brought the house down with her unexpected gift

134   for comedy. The second act was a real catfight with Maria throwing her Neapolitan clogs at her rival, her hair streaming behind her. It was wild. A great change from the pompous *diva*. But I think I was able to persuade her to unbend not so much through my directorial skills as through the realization that her mind was elsewhere. She had indeed fallen in love with, of all people, Luchino. She was not unfaithful to Meneghini, not this first time. Of course Luchino did nothing. But he had never been averse to using his undoubted charms to his advantage, and he found it convenient to seduce Maria, after a fashion. Emotionally starved, she fell completely. She started mooning around and was insanely jealous if she caught him alone with anyone. Even rehearsing a tenor was enough to provoke a fit. She would scour the restaurants near La Scala to see whom he was lunching with, and there was an occasional angry scene if she suspected him of 'infidelity'. No wonder she could play the wild cat on stage. Even Meneghini crept into the production in an off-hand way. Because of his stinginess, Maria always complained that he seldom bought her jewels, for which she was rather greedy. So, for the scene where she meets the Turk, I had the bass, Rossi-Lemeni, loaded with gems, a vision out of the Arabian Nights. At rehearsals I told Maria to 'just watch the jewels, that will be fun'.

    In the duet she began to spot his jewels. He would take her hand to kiss it and she would lift his closer the better to see his rings. Gradually throughout the opera the Turk would present her with this diamond and that gem until at last it was she who was loaded with precious stones. The audience loved it. She overacted splendidly, for that was what was wanted. The first night was the tonic I needed after so much stress, but one incident made it perfect: my father was there with Fanny. Every move was agony for him, and sitting for long periods was a great strain, but he was determined to see Callas in his son's production. I decided to introduce him to her and began the laborious process of helping him through the auditorium on to the stage. He was like a child, each step an adventure, and it was obvious it would take a long time to get backstage. I left him with Fanny while I went to tell Maria we were coming.

    She was sitting in her dressing-room surrounded by an admiring mob.

    'Where have you been?' she demanded angrily. 'Everyone is here telling me how wonderful I am, but my precious director can't even come and say thank you.'

    'Please, Maria,' I began, kissing her, 'I had to get my father, he's coming to meet you.'

    'Your father,' she said, getting up. 'But you said he can hardly walk.' And with that she swept out of the dressing-room, leaving the crowd. In full costume and with her beautiful long hair streaming behind her, she hurried through the dark corridors and out on to the stage, where my father

stood propped on his sticks. She offered her hand, he bowed and kissed it,
she curtsied deeply.

'I am so happy you could come,' she said, taking his arm firmly and helping him forward. 'Your impossible son did not tell me you were waiting or I would have come at once. Of course, we love him, he has such talent, but he is sometimes very forgetful.'

It took twenty agonizing minutes for her to lead him to her room. Every step of the way she told him how brilliant a man he must be to have handled so difficult a son, and my father glowed with pride. I walked slowly with them, deeply grateful to her. Whenever Maria and I quarrelled in the future, I would always stop and tell her I forgave her anything. 'I know your heart,' I would say. 'I know you're not the bitch you pretend to be.'

NINE

The World Stage

There was a triumph looming on the horizon for another admired woman friend. After her disastrous reopening, Chanel had experienced a curious twist of fate. Rejected by the French and British fashion worlds, she was unexpectedly taken up by the Americans. The press idolized her, the Chanel look was in and her sales were tremendous. On top of the world again, she invited me to stay at La Pausa, her villa in the south of France. I'd just bought a little sports car, an MG, and it was thrilling to race around Europe. I have seen many wonderful villas, but hers was unparalleled. It was built of grey rock in an ancient olive grove, yet not a single tree had been cut down to build it – rather, the house had been built around the old gnarled trunks. The whole place was carpeted with fresh lavender, whose pale colour matched the silver grey of the olives. Everywhere was suffused with the scent of flowers. To see it by moonlight was a dream, so spare after her rich Paris apartment. But one thing was the same, Chanel herself: always talking about how she had shown them, how she had won. Who could begrudge her that revenge?

'So, you've left Luchino,' she said. 'That'll be hard for him, he needs love more than I need success.'

She was always transparently honest about herself. In a way her triumph over that terrible setback was very reassuring to me, uncertain as I was about myself.

I felt a lot more secure after *Il turco in Italia*, though that was only an emotional reaction; as far as practicalities were concerned I was still in a parlous state. I had been paid £1,000 to direct and design the opera, but it had taken months of work. As soon as the opera was staged, I was effectively unemployed. But I was convinced that success was what mattered and in any case, my basic needs could be satisfied by the bohemian life in my flat in Rome. Our Florentine group shared all we had: one would bring pasta, another salad, another wine or bread; it was always possible to eat.

We were an extraordinary group. Almost everyone was to make a name in the Italian theatre and cinema: Umberto Tirelli, the costume designer who now has perhaps the world's major collection of ancient costumes for

The World Stage

the cinema; Danilo Donati, who went on to win two Oscars for his designs;   137
and Anna Anni, Lila de Nobili, Renzo Mongiardino and Mauro Bolognini.
One spring we all went back to Tuscany together and had a nostalgic trip
around the old towns and villages we had known as children. It was a
strange time in Italy; with American help, the country was finally being
rebuilt after the terrible desolation of the final years of the war. Many
changes were necessary, even inevitable, but many more were simply the
vulgar offshoot of quick money and bad planning. So much of Italy was
despoiled in that boom period it is now hard to remember how it had been
before. Now we can see the damage. At the time, young as we were, it all
seemed part of the excitement of the age.

I must say we all dreamed about making films; it was all that really
mattered to us. Even after directing at La Scala I still couldn't think of
opera as anything other than something to do until a break in films came
along. In any case, La Scala was hardly a secure employment for me now
that this artificial rivalry between Luchino and me had been created.

Following *Il turco*, Maria went into rehearsals for Luchino's *Traviata* and
I waited in vain for another offer from Ghiringhelli. Fortunately, I now
had a reputation and useful contacts with those I'd worked with. The rest
of 1955 was a void, but in 1956 I produced *Carmen* in Genoa and *Falstaff*
at the Holland Festival conducted by Giulini. These were really thin times
for me and I was able to live only by selling some of the Matisse drawings.
In 1957 productions began in Naples and Palermo and then came the offer
to return to La Scala. I imagined I would be given a major production,
perhaps something to open the season, but, when I saw Ghiringhelli, my
dreams were rudely shattered. I was not to direct at La Scala at all but at
a small new theatre near by, the Piccola Scala.

Despite the way I was treated, I am the first to acknowledge that under
Luchino those were golden years for Maria. Her talents demanded the sort
of fulsome productions he could create. He realized more than had any of
her previous producers that she could be led into a part of great subtlety,
and together they extended the art of opera more and more into full drama
in a way that had only been dreamed of before. Added to that was the
tension that always hung over any of Maria's appearances – would she or
wouldn't she pull it off? I can remember in 1955 standing in the wings
before she went on in Luchino's *Traviata*. There was the usual pointless
chatter, but then suddenly she became serious: 'When the curtain goes up,
I'll feel all that hot air, the sweat and breath of all those people. I always
feel it. I cannot see them, but I know they are there – 2,500 monsters all with
hot breath, panting for me. It's as if their minds and souls were steaming
in torment. I feel it like a wave of hatred, as if they wished me dead.'

That's when I understood why she always gave rather a poor first act –
she was teasing the audience, leading them on. They'd stand around in the

138   first interval complaining about her, claiming that she was no good. I put this to her.

'That's right,' she said. 'I do it on purpose. Then I come back and enjoy the satisfaction of proving them all wrong.'

I watched her do it night after night, teasing them along and then bowling them over. Of course, Maria's claim was far from true; she was always scared of facing 'the monster'. She had to feel the ultimate danger in order to summon up her strength and defeat her fears.

Although upset at being denied the chance to work in the main theatre, I had to admit that the philosophy behind the new Piccola Scala was a sound one: to create a company of young singers, designers, musicians under a controlling director, who would all work in repertory. The idea was to nurture new talent, while producing a different sort of opera from the ponderous superstar productions in the main theatre. It turned out to be a marvellous experience. Opera followed opera with an opportunity to experiment that would never have been allowed in a major house. At last we were able to aim at the sort of production which bore no relation to the static set pieces we so despised in classic lyric theatre. Maria was the inspiration; her belief that opera was as much drama as singing was what we were now aiming for.

My greatest support during this period, and indeed my greatest teacher where opera is concerned, was Tullio Serafin. He was a most generous man, to whom opera was a sacred tradition whose mantle he had inherited and whose task, as he saw it, was to nurture the succeeding generation. Many singers who eventually became stars, including Callas, were discovered and trained by him. He was the great modern advocate of Monteverdi's '*prima la parola*' – first the word, then the melody – that Callas used to such devastating effect. But Maestro Serafin also nurtured young directors by persuading opera-house managers to give them a chance and trying to see that they got new challenges when they were ready for them. For even though he came out of the 'great tradition' he had an ear for the new. He was the first to bring *Wozzeck* to Italy in the early 1930s, which caused a riot at the Rome Opera House.

He was a dapper little man, something of a lady-killer. When I first knew him, he was already getting on and always had an elderly maid with him, but his interest in the young was still predominant. Without my fully realizing it at the time, he took it upon himself to see that I got my chances. He was an extraordinary, intuitive man who thought that the greatest instrument in opera was the human voice. He made a cult out of the voice, but he also had a great instinct for dramatic action. 'Take Monteverdi's *Orfeo*,' he would say. 'When he finds out that Eurydice is dead, he sings "*Morta!*", then a pause, then "*Morta!*" again, and another pause, while the organ holds a sustained, deathly note under it. A couple of centuries later

With Maria Callas after a successful performance as Violetta in *La Traviata* in Dallas, 1958

Susan Strasberg as the lead in the play *Camille*, New York, 1963

Liza Minelli in a screen test for *The Lady of the Camellias*, 1973

Teresa Stratas as Violetta in my film of *La Traviata*, 1982

Judi Dench and John Stride in *Romeo and Juliet* at the Old Vic, 1960
Maria Callas and Tito Gobbi in *Tosca* at Covent Garden, 1964

Olivia Hussey and Leonard Whiting in the
film *Romeo and Juliet*, 1967
    Directing Elizabeth Taylor and Richard
Burton in the film of *The Taming of the Shrew*

Rehearsing *La lupa* by Giovanni Verga with
Anna Magnani in Florence in 1965

My design for *La lupa* and (*below*) the finished set

(*Opposite*)
Working with Richard Burton on the commentary for the documentary film *For Florence*, in aid of the flood damage appeal
  With Edward Albee, New York, 1964
    (*Above*)
    Cooking with Aunt Lide, Castiglioncello, 1965
      A visit in hospital from Gina Lollobrigida
      after the car crash, 1969
    A party in Rome for the conductor Leonard
    Bernstein (*right*), 1970

Directing Graham Faulkner as St Francis
(*left*) in *Brother Sun, Sister Moon*, 1971
With playwright Eduardo de Filippo, Naples, 1974

Gluck composed music for the same dramatic moment, but after Orfeo has exclaimed *"Morta!"* he goes on to an elaborate baroque aria. Which is more powerful, the pleasantness of Gluck or the essential drama of Monteverdi?'

I learned innumberable rules and secrets of the operatic trade from Serafin. I remember when we did Donizetti's *Linda di Chamounix* in Palermo in 1957, I was standing during the dress rehearsal at the back of the stalls, watching the great *concertato* at the end of Act II, when suddenly I heard Serafin from the pit.

'Zeffirelli. Where is Zeffirelli?' he shouted.

I flew down the aisle worried: 'What is it, maestro?'

'Where's the tenor?' he asked angrily.

'He's with the other peasants, maestro. There, can you see him?'

'How have you dressed him?' he demanded, conducting all the while.

'Like his friends in the chorus, he's a peasant like them.'

'No, he's not. He's the "tenor"!'

So I gave him a red jacket. Not only did he stand out visually, but he seemed to sing twice as strongly. What Serafin understood was that singers must be identified and seen almost through a magnifying lens. It was a good lesson.

We even did a completely new work, a jazz opera, *Vivi* by Franco Mannino, at the San Carlo in Naples. it was astonishing to see the old man vigorously conducting a samba like a band leader in a night-club.

He never patronized me, never said: 'Now I'll teach you this, my boy.' But I noticed that whenever there was a discussion at rehearsal he would always end by turning to me and asking if I'd taken in everything he'd been saying, as if the most important thing was that I should absorb everything he knew. I really loved him as a father and owe him more than I can ever repay. All he asked of his 'pupils' was that they were serious: no bullshit was countenanced and hard work was expected. He once came to a hotel room where I was working on a production to ask if I would like a lift to the theatre in his car. When I told him I had to finish what I was doing and that I would run round later to join him, he smiled and said he was glad, that that was exactly how he had been when he was my age.

While I was learning my craft with Serafin I still followed Maria as often as I could. She was unstoppable, everything she did seemed to add to the legend. On the first night of Luchino's *Traviata* in 1955 someone threw a bunch of radishes on to the stage. Maria saw little on stage without her spectacles and so at first she approached the bunch assuming it was a bouquet of flowers. As she bent to pick it up, she realized her error, but majestically continued, raising the ragged plants to her nose, sniffed pointedly and then smiled.

'Thank you so much,' she proclaimed. 'I'll have a good salad tonight.'

Of course not all her doings were as popular as that. At one moment she

140   was the most hated person in the world of Italian opera. In December 1958 she was due to sing Norma in Rome at the opening of the season, when she was genuinely taken ill. Her voice was almost lost, but she agreed to go ahead in order not to spoil the gala performance, which was to be attended by the Italian President. Before curtain-up an announcement was made to the effect that, despite her indisposition, Maria Callas would attempt to sing. Even so, the Roman audience immediately gave her a rough ride. As the booing and hissing increased, Maria became more incensed at what she knew was utterly boorish behaviour. When the first interval arrived, she simply walked out and returned to her hotel. The theatre management begged her to return, reminding her of the waiting presence of the President but she was adamant. That night there was a riot outside her hotel and for months she was the object of every conceivable attack in the press. For a time she kept out of the limelight, but in April she was due to appear at La Scala in a revival of the previous year's *Anna Bolena*, which Luchino had produced. Every box was crammed and as a sign of protest no one had dressed up – many men were tieless, the women without jewels. In the opera the heroine appears only briefly in the first act; her real entrance is in the second act, by which time the tension at La Scala was incredible. As she came through the wings, Maria turned to her dresser and, quoting Bette Davis, said: 'Fasten your seat belts, it's going to be a bumpy ride.'

Then on she went. She stood stock still for a moment, her feet planted well apart, almost as if she was going to have a fight. A curious noise like a chill wind swept up from the auditorium. She just stood there until it subsided, then she sang as I had never heard before: absolutely perfectly and with awesome power. When she finished, there was a second's stunned silence; then, completely unexpectedly, the conductor, Gianandrea Gavazzeni, did something I've never seen before or since: he put down his baton and led the applause. The theatre erupted, Maria had won.

Between them, Serafin and Callas ensured that I did not sink without trace at La Piccola Scala. The new, lavishly endowed Civic Opera in Dallas wished to open in 1957 with a concert by Maria, and they asked if I would stage my production of *L'italiana in Algeri* with Teresa Berganza. In terms of world opera this was hardly headline news, but it was to have amazing repercussions for me. The first production was a joy. We were doted on by the wealthy Dallas matrons, treated like stars, and thoroughly spoiled. All this was very good for morale, and it was my first visit to America.

Despite it all, my ambitions were still elsewhere. When I returned to Italy, I was offered the chance to direct a film. It was only a small company that produced light domestic comedies, but that didn't bother me. I didn't have to produce art movies; I just wanted the chance to direct. The story was a charming tale called *Camping*, about the adventures of two young lovers on a motorcycle. It was funny and sentimental, and the critic

lamned it. Even so, the public flocked to see it. Though by rights it should
have had its day and disappeared, the film is occasionally revived on
elevision. It didn't get me the break in films I hoped for, but it was a new
beginning and I loved doing it.

So, all in all, 1957 was a confusing year. I found it hard to see where I
was going, and I certainly didn't think that Dallas would give me my next
push forward. I knew they wanted me to do something, but I was surprised
when they asked me to direct Maria in a new production of *La traviata*.
With all the ballyhoo surrounding her, the world's press would flock to
Texas to see it. I would have to do something that would stand on its own
after her great performance in Luchino's production two years earlier. He
had set *Traviata* at the turn of the century in a style close to Toulouse-
Lautrec, more Nana than Camille, more Zola than Dumas. It was not the
romantic era, but the age of literary realism. Maria was very earthy, almost
vulgar, a *femme du monde* out of Lautrec. Giulini conducted superbly. As
Luchino and I had known from the time we heard her sing the part at that
private party in Rome, Maria *was* Violetta. But I was not overawed by
Luchino's achievement.

Although I felt that his *Sonnambula* was definitive and that I would
never touch it, I was sure that I had something to add to *Traviata*. I'd been
going to productions of the opera all my life and I'd always had an instinctive feeling that this was my opera. One thing that always annoyed me was
the way so vivid a piece could be so often dragged out and made boring.
The usual thing is to have four locations – Violetta's house, the house in
the country, the soirée in Paris and Violetta's bedroom – with three intervals
between them. But I could tell from the music, the great crash that heralds
the party scene, that Verdi didn't want any break between the country
and the return to Paris; that acts two and three should be run together
without an interval. This would mean elaborate stage machinery and
having got it, I reckoned, why stop there? Why not have nine, even ten
situations - Violetta's bedroom, her dining-room, the salon, the countryside,
the country home, the gambling-room, the ballroom, back to the gambling-
room, another part of the ballroom and the bedroom? Rapid, almost cinematic movement. Because of the constraints of singing and the limited
acting abilities of many performers, opera is often far too static, but here
was a way of opening up the action.

For the Dallas *Traviata* I was sure I had conceived a unique way of
interpreting the work, but first I had to win Maria's support. I went with
Nicola Rescigno, the musical director of the Dallas Opera, to Maria's villa
on the shores of Lake Garda to show her my early designs. The villa had a
wonderful location, but was decked out in Maria's usual dubious taste: she
had a passion for what can only be described as chic hotel lounge décor.
She and Meneghini sat together on a pale pink sofa looking at my costume

142   sketches. I had decided to give her the impression that she was making all the decisions, so that I could ease into the conversation my unusual ideas for the production. They sifted through the drawings, making two piles.

'This is very pretty,' she would say.

'How about this one?' Meneghini would add. 'But not this.'

I craned my neck to see why some ended up on the approved pile and some not, and gradually it became clear that it was nothing to do with the costumes; they always picked the drawings where the figure had a pretty face. I could not believe it. I often omitted the face on my costume designs, sometimes I merely scribbled an impression of the basic features. Only rarely and for no particular reason did I bother to draw a recognizable person, yet those were the ones they chose. It was the Audrey Hepburn syndrome again, the desire to resemble an accepted image of feminine beauty.

While they played this pointless game I began to unfold my scheme. The overture to *Traviata*, I explained, was really a foretaste of the very end of the opera. Anyone with an ear could tell that was so musically, but no one had ever used it in a production. My plan was to begin at the end, for the curtain to go up on the first note and for us to find Maria/Violetta dying. She would simply lie there until the music brightens for the opening part scene, when she would be transformed into the young Violetta. The entire opera was thus seen in flashback, to use the cinematic term from which the idea was drawn. At the end she would have come full circle.

Maria looked up from the sketches and made the obvious point that she would be on stage almost from beginning to end, a fantastic strain on any performer. I reassured her that she could do it.

'Oh, well,' she said. 'It's only Dallas.'

They decided to drive Nicola Rescigno and me back to Milan. It was a lovely June afternoon and should have been a pleasant trip had it not been for Maria's behaviour. Something had got into her and she kept flirting with Meneghini in the front seats, whispering endearments to him, nibbling his ear. Nicola and I began to feel uncomfortable.

'Ah, you bachelors,' she said. 'I feel sorry for you. You have no one to love you. Now, Franco, there's that nice girl in Milan: you know the one, Bice. She's just right for you. When are you going to ask her to marry you?'

She kept on like that, pestering away, spoiling the beautiful sunset over the lake. When we came to a pretty olive grove, Meneghini stopped the car and they both got out to go strolling hand in hand through the trees. Nicola and I sat, unable to make any sense of what was going on. After a while they came back and we drove on.

'You haven't asked me why we stopped,' she said.

'That's your business,' I replied.

'We always stop when we get there,' she went on regardless. 'That was 143 where Battista first kissed me and every time we pass we go and look at the lake and kiss again.'

'Even if it's raining?' asked Rescigno.

'Yes,' she said sharply, 'even if it's raining.'

From then on we were able to drive along in peace, but I was thoroughly depressed. She was right, I told myself, perhaps my life was empty and in need of someone. Her words gnawed at me. What I didn't know was that it was all a performance to shore up her own disintegrating life with Meneghini. She had already met Onassis. The first tentative moves in their affair had taken place and the deeply old-fashioned Maria was terrified of what might happen. Her first reaction was to cling to her 'sacred' marriage. The kiss in the olive grove was part of a desperate struggle with her bourgeois conscience.

They were certainly a weird couple. Meneghini handled all her affairs and everything she earned went to him. She didn't even have a bank account. There was something very squalid about their obsession with money, *real* money. Meneghini almost wrecked her career arguing over money with opera-house managers. At one point, Maria sweetly asked that the Met should pay her a mere one cent more than their top fee. It was such a simple demand, but Herman Krawitz saw at once that it would lead to havoc as each *prima donna* asked for a little more and then a little more. It would have been an impossibly expensive cent for the Met. He refused, and so Maria was able to claim that it was they who were unreasonable – after all she'd only asked for one cent more.

I remember when they arrived in Dallas for rehearsals after she had been on a tour of South America, I went to her dressing-room and they both proudly opened a rather ordinary sack which was stuffed with coins like pirate's loot – bolívares, pesos, cruzeros. It was ludicrous how obsessive they both were about being paid in hard cash. As their relationship began to fracture, many people warned Maria about her dependence on Meneghini, but she was totally naive about her financial affairs and was to get a nasty shock when the crisis came.

For the moment, all we could think about were the rehearsals. The Civic Opera in Dallas held its performances in one of the large convention halls, hardly a theatre at all.

My idea required a lot of subtlety in lighting the production and Larry Kelly had brought in Jean Rosenthal, who had lit many of the great Broadway shows. If I can take credit for the notion of beginning *Traviata* at the end, Jean must have all the praise for making it happen. She lit the first moments so that Maria lay in a sepulchral glow with her eyes in shadow like a corpse. Yet, when the party begins, she is able to jump to her feet already dressed in what is no longer a shroud but a beautiful white brocade

144   dress. The transformation was breathtaking, a romantic tale transforme‹ into a religious experience.

The thing I remember most about rehearsals was arguing with Mari. about who would succeed the recently deceased Pope Pius XII. I wa. convinced we would have a non-Italian pontiff at last and thought th Greek Cardinal Athanagoras favourite in the race. Although Maria held t‹ the Eastern rite, she was prejudiced against him, so bets were laid. Mari. was superstitiously religious, but never overawed by ecclesiastical per sonalities. There was a famous occasion years before when she was singinj *Parsifal* in Rome, that first time I saw her, when she had been granted a papal audience by Pius XII. Before his pontificate he had been nuncio it Berlin and was one of those Italians who become immersed in Germa culture. He volunteered a remark that it was a pity Maria was singinj Wagner in Italian instead of in the original German, and that unleashed a blazing response.

'There's a choice to be made between being "arty" and being popular, she told him. She went on to say that she found it unbecoming for the Vica. of Christ to encourage something for the élite rather than for ordinar people. She was really rather rude, but the Holy Father didn't retreat.

'Surely', he insisted, 'you must admit that the sound of Wagner is bes complemented by the German words?'

When I heard about the incident, I had to admit that His Holines. was fighting on weak ground. The Germans themselves acknowledge tha. Wagner's libretti are pretty dreadful. However, that was not Maria's point 'Opera is action, drama,' she continued. 'The drama does not come jus with the music; one half of the emotions are created by dramatic action the word.'

It was a statement of her own philosophy of opera and her manner o expressing it was typical of the woman. She admired those who stood u to those in power and was forever retelling the story of my contretemp with Toscanini. As for her argument with the Pope, there are lots o variables; most translations of the great libretti are so bad it's difficult t‹ defend them. Then again, many Italian operas are in such quaint, stage language that an Italian audience hardly notices the words even when the can hear them. For that's another key point: half of what is sung is los anyway. I think in the end it depends where you are. Because the Britis have traditionally received other nations' operas, they are well used t‹ having performances in the original languages and there are large number of people in Britain who understand operatic Italian, German, etc. Thi doesn't apply in Italy, which obliges us to have translations. Anyway Maria's 'fight' with the Pope was by now one of the many legends tha surrounded her and drew an audience far beyond the usual opera crowd.

On the day of our opening we heard that Cardinal Roncalli had becom‹

The World Stage

John XXIII. The election of a new Pope is always considered a good 145
omen, so despite the fact that nobody knew anything about this obscure
Archbishop of Venice we felt cheered by the news, even though I lost my
bet. It was always good to have Maria in high spirits; anything to combat
the terrible nervous *Angst* that overcame her before a performance. Her
main problem, often not realized by even her greatest fans, was her eyesight.
Without spectacles, the world for Callas was a terrifying haze. Out on stage
she was truly alone in an enveloping mist. For the sleep-walking scene in
Sonnambula, Luchino placed his handkerchief soaked in Hammam Bouquet
at the point where she must stop or fall, and she found her place by smelling
the scent.

We were fêted after *Traviata*, doted on by an oil-rich society that had
suddenly found not only a cultural force but had also become a centre of
world press attention. Maria seemed to draw lightning. I was in her dressing-
room after the opening of the second opera, *Medea*, directed by Minotis,
when the famous telegram arrived from Rudolf Bing firing her from the
Met in New York. That produced an explosion to remember. The tired old
productions Bing had proposed were certainly a disgrace for a talent like
Maria's. She was accustomed to having wonderful new productions created
for her at La Scala. However, the whole thing had been turned into an
impossible wrangle by Meneghini's insane haggling over money. It was all
meaningless anyway. Those close to her could sense that before long contracts and bookings might not mean anything; café society was beginning
to have more appeal to her than the hours of practice and rehearsals the
art required. The once withdrawn Maria was learning to enjoy nightlife
and, whenever she could, she would drag me along with her.

When I said goodbye to Maria after our *Traviata* in Dallas, we began to
see less of each other; things were moving rapidly for her as her public and
private lives began to overlap. Inevitably, as she was drawn increasingly
into the world of Onassis, which I had no part in, we seldom met. I wished
later that I could have seen what was happening and had warned her,
though I doubt it would have helped. As with many of the roles she sang,
there was a tragic inevitability about the events that overtook her: the
yacht trip with Ari, the way he followed her everywhere, his cuckolding of
Meneghini and the vengeful divorce. No one can doubt that she loved
Onassis and, had he married her, the story might have been a fairytale.
But he only wanted to add the world's most famous *diva* to his collection.
He was in love with power, prestige and the fame she brought him rather
than with her.

For me, the saddest thing was the collapse of a project that would have
transformed my life. One of the rich Texan oilmen who hovered round us
wanted to put up \$2½ million for me to film Maria in *Traviata*. It was what
I dreamed of doing and it would have been a stupendous record of the

Zeffirelli

146 century's greatest *diva* at the peak of her career. Sadly, she didn't have the confidence that I could do it. She made every excuse, but underneath them all lay the legitimate fear that I would not be able to handle so large a project. I wrote desperate letters begging her to reconsider, but she was always vague and elusive. So we parted.

I began to work increasingly with Giulini. We'd done a number of productions for the Holland Festival and now he asked me to do *Falstaff* in Israel at the Mann Auditorium. It was a vast hall, which meant staging the opera as if in the open air. Most worrying was the audience, which was full of those brilliant German Jews who had survived the holocaust and who were probably the most musically exacting audience in the world. No corner-cutting there. If they did not approve, you could hear a sort of angry hum like a distant storm, quite terrifying. At least it meant that the orchestra was one of the best in the world, which was why great conductors like Giulini, Bernstein and Mehta loved to go there.

It was while we were rehearsing *Falstaff* that I received a call from London. It was old Maestro Serafin and, without any preliminaries, he asked me if I could come to London to discuss a new production of Donizetti's *Lucia di Lammermoor* for Covent Garden. Of course I said yes. It was a most stunning offer and I assumed that Maria would be singing.

'No,' he said. 'It's someone else, very probably as great a talent as Maria's, but there are some problems, as you'll see. Don't worry, I know you can work miracles. Come soon.'

With those cryptic comments he ended our brief conversation. As soon as *Falstaff* was over, I flew direct from Israel to London and went straight to see Serafin. Those autumn days in 1958 were beautiful and clear. As I went to the Waldorf Hotel in the Aldwych to join him, it dawned on me that at last I was in the England I had dreamed about. I had been rushing around Europe and even further, from opera house to opera house, without stopping to think where I was. Now here were these famous theatres which I had heard so much about as a young actor. Even so, I had little chance to appreciate my surroundings.

'Come and meet our *diva*,' Serafin said, leading me through the streets of Covent Garden. 'You might decide to go back to Israel again.'

I was too enraptured by my surroundings to be worried by what he was saying, and it was only when we got to the rehearsal room at the Opera House that I saw what he meant. Before us was a stout, awkward, badly dressed woman with a cold. My heart sank.

'Franco,' said Serafin, 'this is Joan Sutherland.' Seeing my look of dismay he quickly told her to join him at the piano.

To my amazement it was Serafin and Maria all over again. Not the same voice, but certainly the same miracle happened – the awkward person and the divine singing. I saw at once why I had been brought in; Serafin knew

I was young and ambitious enough to try anything. Later, when I asked him about it, he simply said: 'You've done enough to deserve this.' He used the word 'deserve', because he wanted to make it clear that he was offering me the chance of a major international début. Quietly he had been training me for it, and Covent Garden was my reward.

Of course, Joan Sutherland and her husband Richard Bonynge were more than anxious to have Serafin nurture her career. They knew he would develop her talent, and protect and advise her, as he had done with Callas and so many others. Joan and I talked for a while, and I could see the main problem was her own fears and frustrations: she knew she lacked grace, and was withdrawn and difficult to reach. I moved close and put my arm round her shoulder, and to my surprise she pulled away, frightened, almost angry with me. This was making things very difficult, for I'm a tactile animal, I have to touch people, to feel the physical presence and warmth of a person. I told her how I felt. Wonderful woman that she is, she took a deep breath and gave me a real hug. Serafin did not seem at all surprised.

I had other productions to do first, but, when I returned, I was able to explore London while working out how I would stage the opera. The capital was, as I expected, delightfully underplayed with none of the pomposity of Paris or Rome. That the world's most successful monarchy should be housed so modestly compared to Versailles or the Vatican was perhaps the secret of its survival. I liked the village atmosphere of much of the city, the human scale, the discretion. The sharp chiaroscuro created by the northern light, the sun low in the sky shadowing the cornices and balconies – it's very appealing to those from southern Europe. I kept thinking of Mary O'Neill and how amused she would have been that I was in England to produce an Italian opera about Scotland with an Australian soprano.

If persons from the past were needed, I found one on my next visit to the theatre. Crossing the foyer I saw a familiar figure dressed in Royal Opera House uniform, a big man with a black moustache in a long red coat with gold buttons.

'Good morning, sir,' he said, staring at me impassively.

I stared back; it hardly seemed possible.

'Have we met?' I began and then realized that we had indeed. It was Sergeant Martin of the Scots Guards. He was having more difficulty than I in placing his young 'interrupter', as he had always called me.

There were no cries of joy, no bear hugs or instant reminiscences when he realized that the impossible had occurred: the young kid in his makeshift uniform was now, incredibly, a fully-fledged international opera director. At first I was a bit upset at what I took to be his coolness, and only gradually did I realize that this was part of the man's sense of what constituted good behaviour. One afternoon I was standing at the back of the stalls watching a final rehearsal when I realized he was near by.

148   'Permit me to say, sir, that it is very good,' he said, and that 'sir' was neither obsequious nor ironic. I looked at him and I could see he was pleased with me, the way a close relative might be. I suddenly thought of my own father with his rages and his insane grudges, then I thought of dear old Sergeant Martin, who was proud that his 'laddy' was doing all right. They say the British are cold, but that's wrong. When you've got eyes to see it, you realize just how much affection they have.

'You don't have to call me "sir",' I insisted.

'Yes, sir,' he replied as I went over and put my arms round him and gave him the most embarrassing embrace of his life. He was at pains to make it clear that on duty I was 'sir', but he allowed me to take him and his wife to an Italian restaurant, where the jokes, stories and memories flowed with the wine.

In between rehearsals there were lots of small but important things to do: a visit to the National Gallery to see the Leonardo cartoon, and, by contrast, a trip to Bond Street to find Hammam Bouquet for Luchino. Both told me a lot about the England I was getting to know. The Leonardo cartoon was so beautifully displayed, a tribute to the sensitive men who had it in their keeping, the sort of English people who have often done more to preserve the heritage of Italy than we Italians. The cartoon was certainly better hung and lit than the Mona Lisa in Paris, which at that time was disgracefully presented. Then the two gentlemen who made Penhaligon's perfumes in their premises in Bond Street were also exaggeratedly English. Their business was archaically run and no longer successful, but they felt they had to keep going for Prince Philip! Generations of the Royal Family had used Penhaligon's, so they felt they couldn't let down the husband of their present sovereign.

While enjoying these side-trips, the real reason for my stay in London, *Lucia di Lammermoor*, was proceeding according to plan. Joan Sutherland and our tenor João Gibin were no problem as far as the music was concerned, and Serafin was as usual full of insights into the interpretation of the opera. That said, my aim with Joan was to make something of her. We designed her a flattering, high-waisted dress, and put a gauze drop across the proscenium, which gave a romantic haze to everything. I'd been carefully studying the tartans and trappings of the Scottish romantic revival and felt it coincided well with Italian romantic opera. I'd decided to do a no-holds-barred approach, with every emotional and dramatic moment played to the full. Lucia's dress during the mad scene was to become famous for its lurid bloodstains.

Half-way through rehearsals it suddenly dawned on me that we were due to open on Friday 17 February. Being nothing if not superstitious about what had been my father's unlucky date, I begged the director of Covent Garden, David Webster, to alter the opening, but he pooh-poohed what he

called my Latin hysterics and pointed out that Covent Garden had never
in its entire history changed its dates. I warned him to beware, but he
wouldn't listen. He was very preoccupied with the fact that this production
would launch what he hoped would be the Royal Opera's own world-class
soprano. He was also negotiating an extraordinary agreement in which this
production of *Lucia* would go on to Dallas, where Maria would sing the
lead, while the Civic Opera would send over *Medea*. I was told that this
was why Maria and Meneghini would be coming to the dress rehearsal.
However, I know that Maria was really coming to witness the birth of a
phenomenal new artist. God knows what she must have felt as she listened
to Sutherland's amazing voice just reaching its prime, while Maria knew
that hers was waning. She must have guessed that most of the great opera
houses, including La Scala, were constantly on the phone to Webster,
Serafin and myself asking if Joan was really as good as rumour suggested.

At the end of the rehearsal Maria went backstage and showed that her
reputation for bitchiness was always untrue when she was confronted with
real talent.

'You are a great artist,' she said to Sutherland. 'I would have been
jealous of anyone singing so well, but not of you.' Then she laughed and
took the formality out of the occasion. 'Of course, you owe a lot to others,
and you might include me among them, but we all owe somebody
something.' It was all very graciously done.

Then the infamous 17th arrived. I was fussing about the stage, as I
always do on the afternoon of an opening, when news came that the tenor
João Gibin was not well and had lost his voice. I went to find Webster and
had the pleasure of telling him that I had warned him, and that we Latins
are never to be sneered at with our superstitions. I then went off to comfort
Joan when she arrived.

I needn't have bothered. She was wonderfully in control of the situation.
Gibin decided to go on even though his voice was a shadow of its usual
strength; and then the most extraordinary thing happened. Though this
was Joan's big night, her launch into world-class opera, she reined in her
voice and sang down, reaching extraordinary pianissimos, so as to help
Gibin. She was prepared to sacrifice herself for the good of the production.
In the end virtue was rewarded, for the audience was so much with her
that they gave her a nine-minute standing ovation after her first aria. The
bizarre thing was that, even after Lucia's death in the third act, when there
is only the tenor left to sing, that wonderful London audience carried him
along. They brought the house down when Joan reappeared for her curtain
calls. The British were determined to make her their star that night. And
they certainly did.

I, too, felt buoyant. It was then only six years since I'd started out on
my own without any idea where I was going. Between La Scala in 1953

150   and Covent Garden in 1959, a lot of ground had been covered. It had been, in effect, the Callas era, and that summer she blasted herself into the headlines in a way she had never done as a mere singer. Callas on the yacht, Callas and Onassis kissing, Meneghini looking wounded, etc. I hated it all. To me Maria was opera and opera had given me my chance. I was free of Luchino and of all those who had tried to push me down, because the world of opera had accepted me. Now, as I watched Maria cast herself in a role outside our world, I felt as betrayed as poor old Meneghini.

   If this was the Callas era, as I believed, then I was going to see it out with Maria in *Lucia di Lammermoor* in Dallas. She arrived there pursued by what looked like every photographer in existence. Professional as ever, she threw herself into the first rehearsal, but she seemed to guess that we were all absorbed with the international scandal she had become.

   Later, when we sat and talked about life and work, she said she would make a beautiful exit from opera. She would marry Aristotle and have a family. It would all be wonderful. As for *Lucia di Lammermoor*, well, there would be a few changes. The bloodstained gown was too much, she wanted something less gruesome, and so on. We talked and made our changes. But when rehearsals really got under way, it was obvious that the recent events had taken their toll. There had been too many night-clubs with Ari, too many society parties and too few hours spent practising. Nicola Rescigno and I were both worried and, given what had recently happened, we 'bachelors' allowed ourselves the odd sour comment about our treatment that day by Lake Garda. The opening night of *Lucia* was a mixture of comedy and tragedy which still makes me shudder. The chorus and ballet group of the Dallas opera were both made up of amateur students from local choral and dance schools. One girl was determined to have a picture of the great lady in action and had hidden a camera in her hoop skirt. During the mad scene, she started taking photographs. It always surprises the public to know that there is quite a lot of noise on stage which is never heard in the stalls. People even talk without anyone knowing. Maria hated being photographed when not lit or posed, and as she descended the long staircase carrying her bloodstained veil, she heard the clicks of the camera. Between the sublime phrases of her aria, we in the wings could hear her hissing: 'Stop snapping, stop taking snaps. Stop it, do you hear?'

   The girl was absolutely terrified, which was really very funny, but our amusement soon collapsed. As Maria reached the end of the mad scene, she approached the famous top E of the final aria and disastrously it wasn't there – nothing, just an awful croak. Being a consummate actress she turned the screech into a death-cry as she collapsed. The Dallas audience took it for part of the show and burst into rapturous applause. But we knew, Maria knew, and those people who count, the rehearsal producers and the voice trainers, they all knew. Once off stage she summoned the *maestro sostituto,* the prompter Vasco Naldini and Rescigno to her dressing-room.

'I have the note,' she said. 'I know what happened tonight. All this damn Press on to me. They make me so nervous, I'll kill them,' she shouted. 'I've got the note,'

She went to the piano, struck a few notes, ran through the aria and, to our horror, when she came to the top E, she missed again. She tried once more and missed again. There was long silence. None of us knew what to do or say, not even where to look. Finally, Maria gently closed the lid on the keyboard. Led by Rescigno, the others turned and left. I was so moved that I went over to her and tried to kiss her on the brow. She stopped me by shaking her head in a way that said she knew what I was trying to convey, but she didn't want anybody's sympathy. Then I, too, left the room.

TEN

Romeo and Juliet

Though I can't remember the exact date, I can recall with absolute clarity an evening in New York during the late 1950s that sums up the way Maria and I lived at the time. I was staying with John Roberts, a close friend who was one of those people who always seem to have the right contacts in the Press and the social world. He was always very generous in making sure I met the sort of people who could be helpful: journalists like Elsa Maxwell, whom he was able to call up when necessary. On that particular evening John and I had been invited to the home of Dorothy Strelsin, another friend, who was a wonderfully flamboyant socialite. Her husband Alfred was a very successful businessman dealing in medical equipment who had produced, among other things, a sort of hospital-in-a-bag, a portable medical unit that could be parachuted into war zones, and he was often called to Washington to consult with the White House and the Pentagon. Their apartment on Fifth Avenue overlooking the park was a centre for theatre and showbusiness people, and that night Dorothy had invited Lenny Bernstein, Maria Callas and Joan Crawford to join us. The apartment was pure 1950s, all spindly chairs and pink mirrors, that ought to have been preserved as a museum of the decade. It was an odd evening. Joan Crawford was on edge for some reason. I was cooking a pasta and it was taking me longer than expected, so they all started banging their forks on their plates and shouting, 'Hungry, hungry, hungry. Food, food, food!', like naughty children in an orphanage.

When the food was served, Joan made some rude remarks about it that needled me.

'If you don't like it, you can throw it in my face,' I told her. 'But I'd still smile because it was Joan Crawford who did it. I'd forgive you anything, I've adored you since I was a child.'

'Nonsense,' she said. 'I hadn't even begun my career when you were a child.'

It was a bad start, but after our joint outburst she calmed down and we got along fine. When we had eaten, we sat around talking and John Roberts suggested we go on somewhere. Joan proposed a well-known night-club, but John was utterly scathing about it.

'You don't know what's going on,' he announced. 'The only place to be 153
is the Peppermint Lounge.'

'Why?' Lenny asked, hating to be left out.

'You mean you don't know?' said John, teasing us. 'You mean you
haven't heard about the Twist?'

A chorus of voices began to ask what on earth the Twist was. Then
Dorothy, who always seemed to know what was going on, told us about
Chubby Checker and the new dance craze.

'We've got to go,' Maria exclaimed.

'But we'll never get in,' said John. 'They're turning people away in their
hundreds. There are mounted police closing off the streets round the block.'

'I'll get us in,' Dorothy said. And of course we knew she'd have some
trick up her sleeve.

Joan Crawford and Lenny left, but the rest of us set off for the Peppermint
Lounge. Sure enough, you couldn't get near the place for the milling crowds,
but Dorothy knew what she was doing: she led us round the back of the
building and through a series of courtyards piled with rubbish bins and
boxes until we came to a kitchen door. She knocked and a Chinese cook
who was clearly expecting her let us in. He led us through the kitchens and
storage rooms, opened a service door and admitted us to the frantic,
heaving, twisting world of the Peppermint Lounge, where Chubby Checker
was belting out 'Let's Twist Again Like We Did Last Summer', and all
those on the dance floor were doing just that. We gawped in amazement
like a bunch of country bumpkins. There was a steep staircase around one
wall crammed with onlookers and John pointed to the top step. I peered
up at a solitary woman, alone, jigging to the music – it was Greta Garbo.
Crawford *and* Garbo in the same night! No one was paying the slightest
attention to her. Nor were they to Maria, a fact which did not please her.

'Look,' I told her, 'if no one cares about Garbo, why should they care
about us opera people?'

But things only got worse when we took to the dance floor. There we
were throwing our backsides around, but clearly not as the other dancers
were – we simply didn't know how to do the Twist, it was humiliating.

'We've got to do something about this,' I told Dorothy. 'We're just
making fools of ourselves.'

She took my point immediately and stalked on to the dance floor to yank
back a young dancer. It turned out that the boy was in Noël Coward's *Sail
Away* on Broadway, Dorothy was backing it, and she offered him $50 to
come to her apartment to teach us how to twist.

Off we went again. Through the kitchens, across the grubby courtyards,
back to the elegance of Central Park East and Dorothy's flamboyant pink-
mirrored bathroom, where we could watch ourselves wriggling away to a
Chubby Checker record. Glancing down the line, I could see Maria trying

154 desperately to get it right, her face in that same fixed mask of concentration she had when mastering a new role. Suddenly the door burst open and in came Alfred Strelsin in his pyjamas.

'What the hell's going on? Don't you remember I've got a meeting in Washington tomorrow?'

Dorothy was just explaining what we were up to, when suddenly a shrill voice burst out: 'I've got it! I've got it!' And there was Maria, the great *diva*, twisting away like mad. 'I've got it! I've got it! I've got it!' And indeed she had.

The next night we followed our shadowy route back to the Peppermint Lounge to try out our new-found skill. Watching Maria twisting away it was hard to remember the awkward, dumpy creature I'd first met with Serafin in Rome. We twisted for a week before I went back to La Scala to start rehearsals for a new production, and I was over the moon to be the first in Milan who knew how to twist. I showed everyone the way to do it. Later, as rehearsals for the opera progressed, I began to feel ill. I had pains in my chest and stomach, and I assumed I had a virus. X-rays were taken, I saw several doctors and an osteopath, but they could pinpoint nothing. Eventually they gave me sedatives for the pain, but it seemed as if it would never end. Finally, a friend suggested I try a doctor he knew, a wise old bird who prodded and poked me, and announced that it was only a *twisted* muscle in my abdomen. The Twist had crippled me, happily only temporarily. Hot pads and rest were the cure, and no Twist for a while.

Looking back, that sort of light-hearted nonsense seems typical of the decade. Today, the 1960s so overshadow the 1950s that it is easy to believe the world was remade in the wake of the first Beatles hit. I was lucky to be thirty-seven, with my career already under way, when the explosion occurred, and the decade was to carry me along with it in a way that still leaves me slightly dazed. Even before the roller-coaster got going there was a feeling that change was coming, that those who'd started out before the war and who had come to their prime immediately after it were now about to stand down.

I knew when Maria closed the lid of the piano in her dressing-room in Dallas that an era was ending. Of course it wasn't an immediate rupture – yesterday opera, tomorrow something else. She had other engagements and I too had more productions planned, but something was surely brought to an end that night. And yet, without my realizing it at the time, I had already taken the first step along the path I was to follow in the 1960s when I had directed Sutherland in *Lucia*. Just as Callas was slipping out of my life so Joan was moving in. And the other fall-out from that *Lucia* was an increasing emphasis on London in my life – the Royal Opera House were keen to have me back and what they wanted more than anything was the sense of Italy that my productions carried with them. After the austerity

years and the rather sparse life that had been available to many in the 155
1950s the British were at one of those periodic moments in their history
when they seem to decide *en masse* to let their hair down. They wanted to
have a little colour and a little fun.

I was invited by David Webster to return to the Royal Opera House at
the end of 1959 to create new productions of *Cavalleria rusticana* and
Pagliacci, which, because they are short, would as usual be performed
together. Eventually they were completely to alter the direction of my life
but at the time they seemed to be just another wonderful opportunity to
try out all the ideas that had been rattling around in my head during the
years of apprenticeship with Luchino. Although *Pagliacci* has become one
of those works I've returned to again and again, refining and perfecting, on
this occasion it was *Cavalleria rusticana* that claimed most of my attention, I
suppose because I was happy to rediscover the world of Verga's Sicily that
I had found while working on *La terra trema*. As soon as I got to London
from Dallas I managed in a few days to create a vision of *Cavalleria* that
had been growing in my mind for some time. I started, as I usually try to
do, with a single powerful image. In this case it was a tiny fragile woman
in a black shawl, swept away by the hot Sicilian wind, the woman central
to the whole drama.

Verga's tale is one of a collection of short stories called *Vita dei campi*
(*Life in the Fields*). From this and another, *La lupa*, he created two one-act
tragedies. Mascagni was attracted to the story as a subject in an opera
competition which he won in 1889 when he was only twenty. Surely because
he was so young the piece has a pleasing freshness, an explosive inven-
tiveness and passion. I wanted to harness that, to recreate Sicily, the feel
of it on stage, that special light at dawn, a fresco of peasant life in the last
century. I had an entirely British cast – no Italians were involved – which
was fine because the British entered more easily, without preconceptions,
into the spirit of my interpretation. The British have an instinctive yearning
for Italy, for sunshine and the Mediterranean. We opened in a bleak London
winter and the effect on the audience of the first ten minutes was as if they
had been transported into a distant sunny land.

During that first run we had a Royal Command Performance for Queen
Elizabeth, the Queen Mother, and a few days before a parcel from Italy
was delivered to me at the Opera House. It was from my father and inside
were all kinds of notes and documents – some were copies of legal acts,
registers of births and deaths and family trees. It transpired that in his
enforced idleness my father had decided to trace his ancestry, more often
an Anglo-Saxon preoccupation than an Italian one. He had ferreted about
and somehow worked out a line that went back to our old family village of
Vinci in Tuscany. He wrote me a letter with all these notes that made a
rather triumphant point.

156 'When you are received by one of the Windsors, hold your head high because if in their veins runs the blood of kings and queens, in yours runs the blood of Leonardo, as you can clearly see from these documents.' It was a nice thought, though on reflection hardly a stunning one, given that anyone from Vinci would, mathematically, be able to trace their line back to anyone who had lived there four hundred years ago. But if the interpretation was exaggerated, the spirit behind it was well meant, though unfortunately a little belated: he was trying to bind us together in a family, a family with ancestors, glorious ones at that. The fact that he had tried to do it, rather than my supposed descent from Italy's greatest genius, made me hold my head high as I waited in line after the performance.

I returned to Italy without yet knowing the effect those two productions were to have. I went to Palermo to produce *La Fille du régiment* and during rehearsals I was called to the phone and a woman's voice said she was speaking from London, from the Old Vic Theatre, and that they had an idea that might interest me. The general manager, Michael Benthall, who happened to be in Australia, had liked 'Cav and Pag' and, the voice went on to say, would on his return like to meet me to discuss the idea of my doing Shakespeare for them. In order to understand my reaction it is necessary to know two things: first that the Old Vic was *the* theatre, the undisputed queen of the English stage, which at that time had a world-wide reputation; and second, that among my closest friends in England are some tremendous practical jokers. My instant conclusion was that as the Old Vic would never ask an Italian to direct Shakespeare this was undoubtedly a hoax. I told the kind female voice that I would only come if the Queen of England asked me personally – then put the phone down. It rang again the day after. A call from Australia – it was Michael Benthall in person making the same proposition and asking if I was interested. I now thought this was a really elaborate hoax, involving a fake international call – I even thought I recognized the voice of Victor Spinetti, a friend of mine in London who is famous for indulging in such amazingly convoluted tricks. I told him haughtily that I was in the middle of rehearsals and couldn't talk to him, he'd have to put it in writing. Only after I'd put the phone down did doubt begin to creep in. If it was a joke, it was a rather obscure one – and what if it wasn't?

A few days later a letter arrived and bang, I realized what a fool I'd been. They really *did* want me to produce Shakespeare, and *Romeo and Juliet* at that. As soon as I read the letter I knew that something really important was going to happen. I flew to London and went to see Michael. All my opening remarks were expressions of doubt about my ability to handle the sacred text. I'd never done Shakespeare even in my own language, and the thought of tackling the great poetry in English for all those guardians of the true flame was terrifying. Michael swept away my fears.

He explained that what they wanted was simply what I'd done with   157
Cavalleria Rusticana, to bring to the production the feel of Italy, not
the Victorian interpretation that still dominated the English stage but
something truly Mediterranean: not heavy carved furniture and velvet
drapes, but sunlight on a fountain, wine and olives and garlic. New, different, real, young. Put like that it made some sense for me to do it and
I agreed.

Back in Rome I was once again plagued with doubt and began to ask
everyone I knew for reassurance. I went to see Luchino and we sat as ever
in front of the familiar library fire and discussed my extraordinary venture.
Despite all our differences we still saw each other from time to time.
Whenever we were together everything was usually fine between us; there
was always the memory of our great days together: Luchino's commanding
presence, the aristocratic look, the grand manner mixed with interest and
affection. Sadly, that night, when I needed his impartial advice, his fair
judgement, perhaps even his encouragement, he gave nothing. On the
contrary he played on all my fears – let's face it: I had only done one play
and not successfully, no Shakespeare, not even in Italian, the Old Vic was
the pinnacle of world drama, a flop there would cripple me for ever and the
chances of succeeding were too slim to risk. I listened to him intently, then
suddenly I knew what was going through his mind. I acknowledged the
wisdom of his advice, thanked him and left. If nothing else, that session
finally convinced me, it was the shot in the arm I needed to show me that
I had to go ahead no matter what.

Romeo and Juliet was planned for the autumn of the new year, 1960. I
would start the decade with a radical shift of emphasis in my work. But
first there was opera, opera, opera – there are times during these years
when my production diary looks a bit like a railway timetable or an airline
schedule: there is nothing like being young, ambitious and poor to fill out
the diary! But the early part of the year was different from the usual round,
Serafin having decided that Joan Sutherland was ready for Italy and that
the same team that had made such a triumph of *Lucia* should take on the
task of introducing her to some of the toughest opera audiences in the
world. Nor were we planning to take the easy way out – not for us a pleasing
little production of one of the ever-popular repertory pieces. It was decided
that she should open in Venice with Handel's *Alcina*. It was an unexpected
choice given that Handel's operas don't usually find favour with the normal
opera public because of their static nature. I tried to loosen it up by setting
the opera as a play within a play, making it – as indeed it might have
been – a performance that takes place during a great party at one of
the eighteenth-century German courts. This gave more motivation to the
eighteen dances that punctuate the piece and it allowed us to make Joan
a monumental figure in rich robes and diamonds which suited her Junoesque

Zeffirelli

figure. Vocally the role of Alcina is almost impossible to sing, but Joan's voice had truly unlimited possibilities. Richard Bonynge helped adapt the score and also played the harpsichord for the performance dressed in a costume and wig as if he were Handel himself, while Nicola Rescigno conducted. Because it was Joan's Italian début the opera world turned out in force. People came from every part of Italy, but chiefly from Milan. Serafin was there of course, like a benediction from the past. The reigning queen of La Scala in the 1930s, Toti dal Monte, came to cheer with the rest. And cheer they did. They kept calling Joan back until she gave a sign to Richard, who returned to the harpsichord to accompany her in 'Let the bright Seraphim' – one of the sparkiest Handel pieces. That brought the house down all over again.

Richard was very keen that Joan should work as often as possible with Serafin, who had so much to teach her, and he also wanted to keep the team that had done *Lucia* together. We decided to do a season in Palermo – first *Lucia*, then *I puritani* as the opening production of the 1961–2 season. Then we took *Lucia* to Genoa and Venice, then *I puritani* to Venice and thence to Covent Garden, where Joan was received back as their own international diva. Joan was now in the same league as Maria, though I never compare the two. As singers both were supreme artists but in utterly different ways; to say you liked one more than the other is only to say you prefer blue to red. But at a personal level there were differences. Callas was already an international star when I first worked with her, she was a goddess and I was the cheeky kid who had made it. With Sutherland it was different: we were making our way together, growing side by side and we – Joan, Richard and myself – were, and are, close family friends.

Of course the main reason that Joan was so sane and steady was her marriage to Richard, who, as a fellow musician, was able to support and inspire her professionally. Most important was their son Adam. It was all so different from Maria's passionate yet unfulfilled affair with Onassis. I often read about them in the gossip columns and sometimes I was invited to join them for evenings in smart restaurants and night-clubs. It was a sort of gilded limbo where one could hardly see for the blinding burst of flashlights. I grew to loathe these encounters; I knew Onassis was only using her as a symbol of his wealth and power. My real sorrow was that every time I saw her I could hear that wonderful voice echoing in my memory, yet all I heard when we met was a voice increasingly raucous and weak.

After my season with Joan my thoughts began to concentrate more and more on the move into drama. Whenever I had a free moment I would sit and daydream about *Romeo and Juliet*, dreaming up costumes and sets, imagining bits of business to flesh out the action. There was however to be one last major opera before London and by one of fate's more curious twists

this was to be the first opera of all, Jacopo Peri's *Eurydice*, which was to   159
form the major open-air set piece of the Maggio Musicale in my home town
of Florence. There may be earlier pieces that could claim to be the first
opera but they exist only as fragments, not in the shape of a fully achieved
musical drama, so we can in all fairness give the title to *Eurydice*. The
original documents had been deciphered and transcribed over a number of
years by a talented team of Florentine musicologists who had produced a
working orchestral score using only ancient instruments – no modern brass
but only wooden flutes, reed instruments and a most impressive water-
organ. They all had that wonderful uncertain non-*temperato* sound. This
was summer 1960, just before the great bandwagon of interest in early
music got under way. It was the Florentine musicologists who were keen
to stage the production, as they wanted me to bring this forgotten piece to
life. I can remember a rather nice old man who was deputed to play it for
me on the piano, because that was the only way they could let me have
any notion of what it might be like. I was entranced – far from being a
collection of independent set pieces the arias actually developed the story:
it was clear that opera had been born fully formed. The reason we have
neglected Peri is that Monteverdi took most of *Eurydice* for his better-
known *Orpheus* some years later. Of course Monteverdi advanced the form,
but there is much that Peri discovered first – his work comes from that
spirit of enquiry that flourished in the Florence of the Medicis.

There was no real problem about staging *Eurydice*, as it had originally
been written as a spectacle to celebrate the nuptials of Maria de Medici and
the French Dauphin in 1600. We restaged it 360 years later on the original
site, the Medici palace. We built a set in the beautiful garden using the real
architecture at the rear of the ducal residence. We made casts of other
Renaissance buildings, fountains and statues and added them on – the
proscenium was forty metres wide. It was so realistic it even confused
visiting experts, let alone casual visitors, and during the day you could
overhear tourists who thought it was the palace itself. Piero Tosi came from
Rome to work with me and we felt as if we were paying homage to our
home town for all we had learned. The scene painters did incredible work
blending the false with the real, so much so that there was an unexpected
follow-up – a year later someone sent me a press cutting from America –
an attack on us Italians for not protecting our heritage! It seemed that a
group of American tourists had visited Florence and seen what they took
to be the Medici palace which, inevitably, they photographed. But when,
a year later, they returned they found half of it demolished. It was,
thundered the newspaper, a scandal!

One thing I was determined on was that my father should see it. But it
was no easy task. I had special seats kept to one side of the stage so that
Fanny could get him to the rest-rooms when necessary. It was now becom-

ing difficult to recall the man who so overawed me as a child: the shrunken frame, the dithering hands. I wanted him healthy and elegant again, dashing and cavalier, a gardenia in his buttonhole – that was the man I wanted to be there to acknowledge my success, not a dying man's pathetic satisfaction in a son's achievement. I felt cheated of him, cheated that I would never know on equal terms that stern figure in the pearl-grey suit, with the scent of eau-de-Cologne; everything I remembered from my childhood Saturdays.

The antidote to those sad reflections came that summer of 1960 with the Olympic Games in Rome. The city turned out to be the perfect theatre for the event – joyful, colourful, sunny Rome awash with bright, healthy young people from all over the world. I've never seen the city like it since: everywhere you looked there were cheerful faces and a feeling of togetherness that affected even the most cynical bystander. Of course the Romans are famous for absorbing the mood of a situation – if there is a leader everyone cheers. The whole city can change depending on the calendar: miserable on All Souls' Day, happy for the Assumption of the Virgin. But that summer a sense of fun was everywhere.

Rather than take my usual holiday in Positano with Bob and Donald I decided to rent a house at Castiglioncello on a promontory off the Tuscan coast. I invited friends to stay while I worked on the details of the forthcoming *Romeo* and I also called together such family as I still had. I invited my Aunt Lide and her maid Vige to join me. With all the international coming and going there had been little time for anything resembling a home and when I stated working at La Scala on a regular basis I was obviously more a resident of small hotels in Milan than I was of my shared apartment in Rome. This made for real difficulties in coping with my beloved dogs. At first I persuaded various friends to take them in from time to time but obviously this couldn't last. As my absences became the rule rather than the exception I asked Aunt Lide to look after my little cocker spaniel and I took the big black Belgian Shepherd to live with some farmers in the Tuscan hills. Perfectly sensible in a way, but I have never forgiven myself. I'm so tortured by the idea of being abandoned and lonely that the idea that I inflicted that on a dog, who was more loyal and loving than any human being, still distresses me. It was these thoughts that made me see that, although I knew I would spend much of my life travelling, I would have to have a base. For someone who had been pushed from house to house, mother to mother, as a child it was essential that I had a home. I also began to hear stories that made me realize that in my frantic climb to satisfy my ambitions I was forgetting the very person who had sacrificed so much for me, Aunt Lide. I have a very old close friend, the actor Alfredo Bianchini, another Florentine, who always gave me news of my aunt whenever we met. It gradually became clear that things were not well with her. She lived with her maid Vige, another orphan, originally taken in by Gustavo's father. The two of them, my aunt and Vige, had nursed Gustavo through his last illness until his death in 1957, but doctors and medicines had left Lide with little money. Alfredo reported that the two women were eking out a fairly miserable existence. I hoped that their visit to Castiglioncello would help bring us back together again, but first I had to see how they would react to a way of life some light-years removed from the rather staid Florentine existence they were used to. I needn't have worried: we all got along famously – Vige was a wonderful cook, trained by my aunt, and that quickly endeared her to my ever-hungry friends. Happily they both adored the crazy characters they met that summer. I worked on *Romeo and Juliet* while Aunt Lide 'managed' our lives. There was a real feeling of family at last, with Lide as everyone's mother. At first I was worried that the way I lived might upset her but I needn't have bothered – 'Thank God there are such nice boys round here,' she would say. 'Girls only make trouble.' And of course the boys would spoil her. She loved chocolates, cakes, trinkets, and everyone showered her with them.

It was that spirit of youthful high spirits that I'd been enjoying, first at the Olympics and then throughout that marvellous summer, that I wanted to bring to London, and heaven knows it needed it. After Rome and Castiglioncello, London seemed grey. There was little sunshine to be found in the theatres either, for this was the heyday of the kitchen-sink school at the Royal Court, when anger and a sullen air of rebellion were thought to be the spirit of the times. I had sensed another spirit among young people that summer, a spirit of rebellion certainly but one that carried with it a message of enthusiasm and cheerfulness rather than depression. It seemed to me, even at the very beginning of the 1960s, that young people were about to give everyone a very pleasant jolt, and it was this that I wanted to bring to the London stage. Happily for me these feelings were exactly mirrored by what Michael Benthall was hoping to see.

Because of my lingering nervousness about presuming to do Shakespeare in the land of his birth I probably studied the play more thoroughly than is usual. I had read it in Italian, going behind the text to the sources that Shakespeare had used. Shakespeare had unashamedly based his play on a similar Italian piece. In the original Italian story by Bandello, Romeo is more mature and has already had several love affairs before he meets the child Juliet. The two make love almost at once and it is only afterwards that Romeo becomes enamoured of Juliet. The nurse is only mentioned briefly as a sort of crone who keeps watch, all the while tapping the ground with her stick, as the young couple make love. Yet out of that minor reference Shakespeare built a major character, a creation of genius.

He did the same with Mercutio, who has only a casual mention in one of the tales. The story had a lovely moment where Juliet is dancing with two

162   men at a masked ball – one, Messer Mercuzzo, has a cold, clammy hand; the other, Romeo, has a warm, gentle hand. So by the touch of the two hands she knows their characters. What we sense when we read Shakespeare is the love he had for Italy, even though Italians can tell from his inaccuracies that he was never there. Italy is a dream country for him, just as England as a land of efficient democratic institutions was a dream for nineteenth-century Italians. Of course Shakespeare's London had many contacts with Renaissance Venice. They were two great trading seaports and the London docks were full of Venetian ships and sailors; and Shakespeare scatters versions of Italian naval slang around his plays. One thing is strange: Shakespeare never dealt with Florence, the cultural hub of Italy at that time. Perhaps because his only contacts were men from seaports, Shakespeare deals only with Venice and its tributary cities: Verona and Mantua. His settings sometimes move east into what is now Yugoslavia and west to Milan or very far south to Sicily – but never to what might for him have been a rival centre, Florence.

Although I could penetrate the Italian setting I was of course aware that this was only the *maquette* on which Shakespeare had moulded his poetry. Shakespeare pillaged other people's tales, garbled passages of history or legend for his one central purpose: language, and I was not fool enough to think that I would have much to contribute on that score. This was my greatest worry, and I had to keep reminding myself that Michael Benthall had brought me in precisely because I was not imbued with the classic Shakespearean verse drama tradition which still adhered to the Victorian view that a correct speaking of the immortal lines was of more importance than any dramatic impact the author might have intended. Thus only experienced, and hence elderly, actors and actresses played the principal roles, making *Romeo and Juliet* a near travesty. Two counter-arguments to this tradition occurred to me. The first and lesser was that all cultures from China to Venezuela acknowledge Shakespeare as the world's greatest playwright – even in translation – which would indicate that his dramatic insights are perhaps more valid than his poetic ones and independent from them. Second and more important, Shakespeare used a fourteen-year-old boy to play Juliet and even in his day such boys can hardly have been much good at verse speaking – to the author, youth was more important than enunciation. Once I had realized this, I had the courage to attempt something new. This wish happily coincided with a phenomenon in the English theatre: the sudden emergence of a number of very young, but undoubtedly brilliant, actors and actresses. There was a crop of young talent in the late 1950s and early 1960s and Michael Benthall was one of the first to see that someone should seize the opportunity to use it. I doubt I would have had the nerve to suggest that we dispense with the normally obligatory great names and cast two newcomers in the title roles if I hadn't

been aware that this was precisely what he wanted to hear. Michael was a
good listener and sat patiently as I poured forth my newly acquired theories
on Shakespeare and Italy, about Shakespeare the modern man influenced
by the ideas of the Renaissance, the Elizabethan who understood what was
happening in Europe. But Michael was no fool – it was one thing to have
an enthusiastic newcomer but quite another to risk a major production
with someone who only had a passing knowledge of the English stage.
Sensibly, he took me in hand, guiding me towards those productions he
thought important and arranging auditions at RADA and other schools.

Yes, I could have young new players but he led me. He suggested that
Judi Dench and John Stride, both just starting out, would be ideal for the
play. And how right he was. He took me to see a production of *The Seagull*
with Tom Courtenay and suggested we use him somewhere. As Courtenay
was very much the young man of the moment and the star of the play I
assumed this meant giving him a major role – but no, Michael suggested
Balthasar for him. I was shocked: Constantin one night, Balthasar the
next? Michael explained about the English repertory tradition, the idea of
a company of actors who alternate between leading roles and small parts,
and I began to realize why London always had such fine, selfless players
and provided such good training for newcomers. I tried to spread this idea
in Italy on my return but old methods die hard. Anyway, I saw John Stride
and Judi Dench and was completely sold on both of them. Judi Dench was
small and doll-like and looked even younger than her age, just the way I'd
always imagined Juliet should be. Before rehearsals began I told them all
about my notion of creating a dream of Italy. I took along books of
paintings, postcards, so that they would know what I was seeing in my
mind's eye. I told them I didn't want make-up, no gilded columns, no
balconies with dangling wistaria. This was to be a real story in a plausible
medieval city at the opening of the Renaissance. So no wigs, they would
have to grow their hair long – girls *and* boys. This was 1960, before the
Beatles, and at first the boys were embarrassed, they wore their hair under
berets on the underground and were galled by the jokes their friends made.
But when they started to act they saw the point – instead of the posing
that a wig brings with it they acted freely, moving their heads like lions
tossing their manes. Among my best memories is Mercutio, played by Alec
McCowen, one of the most exciting actors I've ever worked with, who took
to this idea of youthful high spirits with great verve.

It was the balcony, or rather the lack of a balcony, that caused eyebrows
to be raised. The balcony scene was the very centre of the sort of Norma
Shearer/Leslie Howard approach I was determined to demolish. Juliet's
house in my production was as it would have been, not a pleasant place of
Italianate verandas and artificial flowers but a rather bleak fortress meant
to deter a foe and protect the family treasures. In my production, when

164　Juliet came out she walked on the battlements of this fortress and Romeo was obliged to climb a cypress to get near to her so that they were like amorous young animals who had been kept apart, forcing John Stride to do wonderful athletic things to get closer.

From the opening scene – a misty dawn breaking over the town square – I felt sure that we had got it right. It was so touching, and for once believable – young love, impetuous and unstoppable. I felt elated on the opening night: the audience had responded with enthusiasm, the cast were congratulating one another – and then the real dawn broke. The London drama critics savaged our production in terms so damning they beggared belief. I had guessed they might quibble about the verse speaking, but that was the least of it – they condemned everything from the actors to the sets.

I began to wonder if Luchino hadn't been right and to ask myself whether I had overstepped the limits of my abilities. Overcome with a sort of quivering cowardice I rang Michael Benthall and told him I was leaving. He barked at me not to be so stupid and to be at the theatre before that night's performance. When I got there everyone was nervous – some were reading the afternoon reviews, which were just as ugly. Suddenly Michael called us on stage, making me think of the old line-ups with the Scots Guards, and proceeded to give us a full-scale dressing-down and pep talk.

We were fools to take note of critics with no vision and fools not to realize that we had the most wonderful production, the most original vision of Shakespeare since Tyrone Guthrie's *Hamlet*.

'Go on,' he told them, 'and listen to your hearts.'

And they did. That second night was fantastic and we all felt better.

But I was still unsure of what I'd done. I had to leave for Brussels the next day to begin rehearsals for *Rigoletto*. The following Sunday a friend called from London to insist I go out and get a copy of the *Observer*. I ran to an international news-stand and stood in the street excitedly reading Kenneth Tynan. It was a full-page review and what Tynan said was the exact opposite of all the other critics. This was, he said, the new conception of Shakespeare the English stage had been waiting for 'a revelation, perhaps a revolution . . . a masterly production . . . a glorious evening'. I was thunderstruck. Tynan was *the* critic of his day: it no longer mattered what the others had said, the master had spoken. Following that review the Old Vic was swamped, people came from Europe, even America to see the production. The management had to extend the season and in the end Dench and Stride were playing with a revolving cast. What was especially nice was that young people came in droves and, by a strange coincidence, at the end of the run the fashion for long hair was in full swing so our curious cast came to seem more and more in tune with the youngsters who packed the gallery and the gods. *Romeo and Juliet* slotted neatly into the world of the Beatles, of flower-power and peace-and-love. And not just the

young were infected by its charm: I can remember John Gielgud sitting in   165
the audience surrounded by laughing, crying kids. Afterwards he said: 'I've
never had the luck to have an audience like that.'

Looking back at the end of the year, 1960 seemed almost too good to be
true – *Alcina* with Joan, *Eurydice* in Florence and *Romeo and Juliet* to cap
it all. But perhaps the most important thing was that first step in creating
some sort of family life for myself. If anything, 1960 marked the end of the
era of living in scruffy little hotel bedrooms: it had been good while it lasted
but enough was enough. I was back in Italy at the end of the year to direct
Cimarosa's *Le astuzie femminili* at the Piccola Scala and so I was able to
spend Christmas with Aunt Lide, Vige, my father and Fanny in Florence.

The new year saw me in London again rehearsing *Falstaff* at Covent
Garden. Then I made my debut at Glyndebourne with *L'elisir d'amore*. It
almost looked as if England was to be my home – both as an opera and a
theatre director. Following *Romeo* I was approached by the Royal Shakespeare Company to create a production for Stratford – if anything more
awesome for a foreigner than the Old Vic. And not only was I being invited
into the very temple of the Shakespeare cult but I was being offered not
some light Italianized piece but the full weight of *Othello* – I should have
run away!

First it was back to Dallas for two productions, *Thaïs* and then *Don
Giovanni* with Joan Sutherland as Donna Anna, Elisabeth Schwarzkopf
as Donna Elvira and Nicola Rescigno conducting. That production was
important to me as a significant step in my life-long struggle with Mozart's
masterpiece. I'd already done *Don Giovanni* in the little Royal Theatre in
Naples in 1956 but that was almost a chamber production – Dallas was the
first full-scale attempt. I began an interpretation that I developed later, of
setting the opera as if in the wake of some terrible catastrophe, a bombed-
out, burned-out world. In Dallas I used rough textured burlap screens
appliquéd with patches. From the first I saw the work as an allegory,
outside time and place. The character of Don Giovanni himself is a comment
on humanity valid for all periods but somehow especially in a century
where the dark side of our nature has had appalling sway. That Dallas
production was only the start of an attempt to get inside an opera that can
never be fully understood.

I returned to England in the autumn full of confidence and ready to
tackle *Othello*. Would that I had remembered the voice of Mary O'Neill as
she attempted to teach me her useful store of English sayings: 'pride comes
before a fall' was often on her lips and I was to have cause to remember it.
If I had heard her voice when Peter Hall asked me to do *Othello* I might
have stopped to think about the crucial difference between *Romeo and Juliet*
and Shakespeare's brooding tragedy. Whereas *Romeo* has this wonderful
universal story, so mavellously structured it survives any translation,

166   *Othello* is one of the most flimsy and irritatingly simple of Shakespeare's
plots. In the end, with *Othello* the language is all. *Romeo* is, we believe, an
early work where the writing is not yet at its fullest flowering; *Othello* is a
mature piece and woe to anyone who thinks that the poetry is not the
raison d'être of the play. Thus what had been forgivable oversights in my
Romeo when set against the vivacity and the drama would, if I'd only
thought about it, be inflated into major errors in *Othello*.

All that is hindsight. Carried along by the idea of grabbing another
success, I turned all my thoughts to the play. The usual Othello of the day
was a crude jungle creature, a savage all too ready to be goaded into
madness by Iago. I knew this was wrong – he was a Moor by the colour of
his skin, but he was certainly more civilized than most Europeans at that
time. He was also a Venetian by adoption, a man of the Renaissance. It
had to be so, for why else would Shakespeare give him such wonderful
poetry to speak? He begins as a highly refined and controlled soldier/scholar,
and only at the end, when jealousy has spread its poison, are the hateful
forces released. Uppermost in my mind was the elegance of Africans I had
met – the Ashanti, the Nubian peoples. I had noticed that with a natural
grace went a lack of pettiness and a sort of classical humour. They smile
and tell pleasant stories, they value friendship and good manners. How like
Othello, who never disparages anyone, is always positive and ready to see
the best side of someone, until in the play he comes into conflict with the
vileness of Europe, the corrupted white race. It is Iago's 'primitive' poison
that wrecks Othello's civilization. I knew we needed a great and cultivated
speaker for the part, someone scholarly, not the usual brooding hulk. The
obvious choice was John Gielgud, who turned out to be very keen to do it.
And who better than the young Ian Bannen as Iago, the perfect foil . . . or
so it seemed. As it turned out, whatever chemistry makes a director and
his actors work was missing with us three. Nobody seemed to be able to
communicate with anybody – such a difference from *Romeo and Juliet*.
Gielgud and Bannen were like oil and water and somehow Gielgud and I
never seemed to react together. He sailed through the piece, his usual self.
That's wonderful, but it was hardly what I had in mind. The actors were
somehow at odds with the setting I had created: the magnificent Venice of
Tiepolo and Veronese was meant to emphasize the nobility of the character
and the poetry. But in the end even the set worked against me.

The opening night must have been one of the most disastrous and ill-
fated in the history of the English – and possibly the world – stage. Nothing
worked. Apart from the aimless acting, one of the huge columns I had set
up suddenly swung loose on its cable and came perilously to rest against
another. There it hung for the whole of the first act, creating an awesome
atmosphere of ever-present danger. This was counterbalanced in Act Two
by high comedy. To create quick changes I had parts of the sets on traps

below stage. At one point a wall on which someone was sitting suddenly rose unbidden, carrying him aloft like something out of a Mack Sennett movie. Then, in Gielgud's second jealousy scene with Dorothy Tutin, half his beard fell off so that he had to carry on in profile for the rest of the act. At another point Ian Bannen as Iago ran on loudly proclaiming: 'Iago is dead!'

Guess who came all the way from Italy for the opening night? No one less than Luchino. Evidently his informers must have heard that a disaster was in sight or, perhaps, simple premonition. Anyway there he was making it official that he really 'adored' my work.

The only good thing that came out of the débâcle was my discovery of how the English behave in these situations. I received many letters from friends, from the little seamstresses at Covent Garden or from a stagehand at the Old Vic, all telling me I was not to worry. It's so English to ignore you if you're a success, but when something goes wrong to think well-may-be-he-needs-me-now.

I needn't recount what the critics said – the most withering headline began: 'The pity of it, Zeffirelli!' My greatest embarrassment was for John Gielgud. I was staying at his cottage on the Avon and I liked and respected him. He's a shy, retiring person; I'm gregarious and outgoing, I work by touching and shouting, by trial and error. As Alec McCowen once said in an interview: 'Everything with Franco happens in the last three days. Before, we are looking, searching, wondering and then when he sees everything on stage the magic happens.' I'm a pragmatic director, not a theorist who has it all worked out beforehand, and that was no good with John.

This time naturally I was less irritated that the Italian press chose to ignore the fact that one of their fellow countrymen was producing Shakespeare in England than I had been when they greeted *Romeo and Juliet* with a deafening silence. There is something petty and mean-spirited about Italian critics that has infuriated me all my life and which was to come to a head four years later. For the moment I was rather happy to be ignored. I returned to my family, the only audience that never criticizes, which is a blessing everyone needs sometimes. Aunt Lide and Vige had joined me in Castiglioncello again that summer and it now seemed ridiculous that we should be together for only a few weeks in the summer. Also my shared apartment in Rome was beginning to seem claustrophobic with all the visitors that followed this new life as an international director. My solution was to find another, larger apartment, not far from the old one, and to install Aunt Lide and Vige as mother and housekeeper to a shifting population of opera singers and theatre folk from all over the world. We had two large rooms which served as boys' and girls' dormitories and it wasn't unusual to find Joan Sutherland 'warming up' her voice in the kitchen as she prepared Richard Bonynge's breakfast or to hear some ringing Shakespearean voice holding forth in the bathroom.

168   At the end of 1961 Joan, Serafin and I did *I puritani* at Palermo, and I
began the new year with another *Don Giovanni*, this time for Covent
Garden. But undoubtedly the most exciting prospect was the New York
opening of the Old Vic *Romeo and Juliet* in February. The British Council
had already taken it to the Venice Theatre Festival the previous September,
thus obliging my ill-natured compatriots to acknowledge what I had done.
I sent Luchino an invitation but he replied that he would be unable to
come – which was probably just as well as I only wanted to crow.

The opening at the City Centre in New York was a triumph. There was
a huge reception afterwards and I spent hours shaking hands and accepting
congratulations, always a pleasing activity. As the time passed I became
aware that one lady was hanging on when everyone else was beginning to
leave, though she made no move to come up and speak. Eventually I
approached her and as I got nearer I suddenly realized it has Helen Deutsch,
the lady who had tried to persuade me to go to Hollywood as an actor. She
had been waiting patiently to tell me I'd made the right decision when I
wrote to her fifteen years before.

We all went on to a party given by Paula and Lee Strasberg of the
Actors' Studio and they introduced me to their most famous pupils at that
time, an extraordinary selection of magnificent talents. Rather out of place
among them was Marilyn Monroe. Although a Hollywood star, Marilyn was
trying to improve her skills as an actress and was sensitive about her image
as a scatterbrained sex-goddess – though it must be said that that was
the role she adopted most often even off-camera, giving the impression
it was the real one for her. She was particularly simpering that night,
apologizing for not having been at the performance; it was just impossible for her to go anywhere because of the crowds, so she never got to see
anything. She giggled embarrassingly and we all agreed it was an awful
destiny for her and I suggested we might put on a special matinée behind
locked doors for all those deprived stars who otherwise wouldn't get to see
Shakespeare.

However, despite her silly manner, I could sense that there was something
more to Marilyn than a famous pout and a copious bust. Paula and Lee
were proud of having her as a pupil at the Actors' Studio and were always
trying to nudge her towards 'serious' work. Lee tried to convince me she
was suitable for a part in *The Three Sisters*, a play the Actors' Studio wanted
to put together, but I kept pointing out how nervous she was going to be
facing the public, never having worked with a live audience. Then there
was the problem of her voice. But Lee just waved away my objections and
it was arranged for Marilyn and me to have a quiet lunch at 12.30 in The
Inn on the Park the following day. It was February and cold and this was
an odd place to choose, but her reasons were simple: she wanted to be sure
she was left alone and not mobbed.

For once I arrived on time and thus spent a weary hour and a half waiting for her. I had just cancelled an afternoon press conference when she finally arrived. To be certain that she was inconspicuous she wore a huge white fox-fur coat, sun-glasses and a strange beret in silver lamé that slouched down over her forehead. She was all charm and apologies, but, as soon as she took the dark glasses off, I could see she had just woken up. We talked about the play and I was delighted to discover that she was very bright in a cuckoo sort of way. If you were straight with her and took her seriously, she would drop the mask, but only for a moment. Anyway, after a while she said she might feel secure with me, whatever that meant, and she brought up the idea of *The Three Sisters*. I told her it was a big leap and warned her that if she was one of the sisters and she was on stage with actresses like Geraldine Page or Kim Hunter she would be at a dangerous disadvantage. I suggested to Marilyn that she should play Natasha, the sister-in-law, a part central enough not to demean a star like her but a more manageable role. Natasha is a bitch but also a real woman and she wins in the end, even taking over the house and kicking out the boring sisters. I felt Marilyn could have had fun with it and the audience with her. But that wasn't what she wanted to hear. Then I suggested she avoid the classics for her début, do a light piece, or something new – I was sure she could get Tennessee Williams to write something for her – but I knew she had lost interest. She had wanted me to tell her she was great and would be greater, that we'd start rehearsals in forty days and open in Boston before Broadway, but I couldn't. It was five o'clock and dark outside when we parted. As she was getting into her taxi, something seemed to click into place for her, as if what I had said made sense. She told me she would perhaps like to consider Natasha and that maybe I was right.

For some time after she had gone I stood on the pavement shivering slightly in the bitter New York winter evening, yet still entranced by the sparkling skyline above the park. I couldn't help but reflect on the strangeness of people, myself included, who lay ourselves open for public inspection in theatres and cinemas. I suppose it's inevitable that we will be highly strung, perhaps even mad as the world understands it. For people who have to have nerves of steel when it comes to facing an audience, who have to have the self-confidence of twenty in order to convince the public that our vision is right, we are so often over-sensitive and self-doubting that I wonder how we do it. When I think of Monroe or Callas, I'm amazed there is any theatre or cinema at all. And not just those who appear in front of the public – backstage is a maelstrom of mental anguish, from hypersensitive costume designers to lighting experts in the last throes of nervous collapse.

Making my way back to John Roberts' apartment with the image of Marilyn still fresh in my mind I couldn't help reflecting on the sort of life

170   I was leading – dashing about from country to country, production to
production. I could only suppose that this was what I had wanted when I
so ambitiously drew Luchino's attention to myself that day in the Pergola
Theatre. Wasn't this how men like Luchino lived? All those stars I'd
dreamed about as a kid – Laurence Olivier, Montgomery Clift – didn't they
have busy travelling lives? But then there was Marilyn like some sort of
warning. Success tends to anaesthetize analysis – why question what is so
clearly working? But there are some encounters that pierce the protective
shield, and that had been one of them.

One of the few things that helped me keep my own feet on the ground
was contact with the fellow Florentines of my own age with whom I'd
started out. Mauro Bolognini was making a career in films, Piero Tosi in
stage and cinema design, and I could see myself through them clearer than
the reflection given off by the crowds at first-night parties. Observing their
reactions to the pressures of the entertainment business was a salutary
lesson, though some survived the obstacle-course better than others. The
one member of our group who kept stumbling at the fences was in some
ways the most talented of us all, Lila de Nobili. Lila was a designer,
probably the greatest I have known, and I can say it because all the others
I have worked with would agree with me. They would also agree that she
is one of the most tortured, self-doubting creatures alive. There were times
when it was really rather funny, on other occasions it was sad or infuriating.
But its cause was undoubtedly her utter professional integrity, her honesty
about her work and her own impossible standards. She was quite simply
never satisfied with anything she ever did. The rest of the world might be
cheering and applauding but for Lila this only made it worse: she would
stand in the wings besieged by regret and feeling like a sham because she
hadn't been, as she imagined it, found out.

Lila had been one of the group who had worked with Luchino at La Scala
and their *Traviata* had been a miracle of stage and costume design. But
there was one occasion when her abject modesty nearly drove a group of
us insane. After that opening in New York I received an extremely bizarre
commission: to create a spectacle, for one evening only in May 1962, at
London's Albert Hall. I'd been given a budget of £180,000, which in those
days was beyond belief. The sponsors were an international business association who ran the Man-made Fibre Congress. Not the sort of thing most of
us would ever come across and therefore all the more surprising to discover
that this was a very prestigious affair with enormous financial backing. It
was held in a different country each year and, although London was the
venue for 1962, that year's organizers were Sria Viscosa from Milan. They
asked me to invent something memorable: the Queen Mother would be
there and they wanted Italy to gain some prestige from the event. I asked
Lila de Nobili and Renzo Mongiardino to help and with the unbelievable

£180,000 we proceeded to go mad, to exercise our wildest fantasies. We flew in black dancers and singers from New Orleans, the Dance of the Lion from Japan, di Stefano and Joan Sutherland with the entire chorus from La Scala with Sir Malcolm Sargent to conduct, Jean Babilée danced along with an entire Spanish Flamenco troupe and we flew over a rather odd group of Indians with very elaborate instruments. All this plus Anna Russell and Victoria de los Angeles!

To unify the exotic confusion Renzo decorated the vast arena like the pages of a Victorian children's book, where each page was a fantasy of some half-imagined distant land. Lila designed charming costumes for a group of circus children through whose eyes we saw the action, as if it was their dream bringing the pages to life. At one point hundreds of little ballerinas burst forth, at another there was a huge Italian tarantella.

It was bizarre and very fast moving – we could only allow ten minutes per item – until catastrophe struck with the Indians, who had come a long way and were all set for a big number. It was clear that ten minutes were to them merely a warming-up period and they showed no signs of surrendering the stage. They sat in a pool of beautiful blue light, eyes closed, oblivious to everything, playing their extraordinary instruments. Off stage we began to panic: there was no knowing how long they could go on. Someone told a horror story about all-night sessions of Indian ragas, without a break. There was nothing for it but tough action. I decided to give the order to drop the lights, and then brought in the Spanish dancers with a bang. On to the stage they clattered, heels and castanets creating a din to compete with the Indians – a riot of magenta, orange and flame-red follow-spots. At first the squatting musicians tried to carry on regardless but behind the dancers came a group of model bulls with flashing red eyes and that was it. Muttering angrily, the Indians dragged off their instruments and stormed down the back corridors of the Albert Hall complaining furiously about their treatment. The audience cheered, convinced that this mixing of Indian and Spanish was the most brilliant directorial stroke of the evening.

The finale turned out to be inadvertently comic as well. I'd planned something rather grand and pompous, a stirring choral rendition of Verdi's 'Hymn to the Nations'. This little-known work was written for the opening of the International Exhibition in London in 1862 and was intended to celebrate the part played by England and France in the Italian victory against Austria in 1859. Verdi wrote a piece that combined the three national anthems – 'God Save the Queen', 'La Marseillaise' and 'Brothers of Italy'. One after the other the words and tunes of all three become clearly distinguishable and it was this that caused the trouble. Not realizing what they were listening to, the audience were unprepared for a sudden burst of 'God Save the Queen' and when it came many assumed that the evening

172   was over and loyally stood up for their national anthem. But no! Just as
quickly the anthem changed: there was the French national anthem. Some
stood, some sat. Then the Italian, which only a few had ever heard. In and
out came the anthems, up and down went the audience. It was both
uncontrollably funny and appalling in equal measures. People began to
mutter and complain as if some awful joke was being played on them, some
insult to their national pride certainly not intended by Verdi. The thing
ended not a minute too soon and we flooded the stage with the entire cast
waving the flags of all the nations. When the Queen Mother rose to go, the
audience at last had a chance to assuage their *amour propre* with a sustained
rendition of their national hymn.

The Queen Mother had loved it and so had the organizers and when we got
backstage one of them was waiting with a set of envelopes each containing a
handsome bonus. It was then that Lila went into one of her humility
routines – no, she couldn't possibly accept it – why, she'd done nothing –
and the little she had done wasn't very good, she was so sorry, she had
already been paid more than she deserved and couldn't possibly accept
another penny. The rest of us were appalled. If she didn't accept how could
we? Take it, we hissed in Italian, but she only went on dithering. Finally
I had an inspiration 'I know,' I said. 'You could give it to all the young
people who helped you.You know how poor they are.' The only way with
Lila was to play off one neurosis against another. She looked around
confused but I knew she was hooked and sure enough we got our cheques
and just as surely she gave hers away in a series of gifts and parties for
those who had helped her.

I could already see that before long it would be impossible for her to go
on working. Her self-destructive urge stopped her from doing anything in
America. At first she was a great success with Broadway hits like *Gigi* but
then the American Designers' Union insisted she join and asked for proof
of professional status. The usual thing was to send evidence of past pro
ductions and leave it at that. Inevitably the union would ask for a test to
be taken and the normal response was to refuse and stand by one's past
record. It was a charade everyone had to go through to get an American
work permit and eventually the union would back down. Lila, of course
refused to play the game and decided to take the test. When it happened
she was so paralysed with nerves she flunked it and as a result the woman
who had designed some of the best work of Visconti, Peter Hall and myself
and who was without doubt the theatrical design genius of our time, was
barred from working in the United States. Her only comment was that
they were quite right, she knew nothing about designing.

My own experience was the exact opposite. Just as I had found myself
part of the English theatre with *Romeo and Juliet*, so its American success
meant that I was increasingly involved with projects for New York

Romeo and Juliet

Throughout the spring of that year I frequently flew to America for dis- 173
cussions with producers and backers and the one idea that survived was a
plan to do an entirely new stage version of *La Dame aux caméllias* using
the same title as the Garbo film, *Camille*. I was backing my hunch that the
move was away from kitchen-sink drama, away from minimal sets and
gloomy lighting, and that the public would flock to a play that revived all
the romantic virtues: beautiful sets and a tragic heroine. The New York
theatre people took some convincing, given the sort of things that were
currently dominating Broadway, but in America nothing succeeds like
success and I was a guy who had made it with, of all things, Shakespeare.
The reckoning was that I must have some sort of lucky instinct, so why
not go along with my crazy notions? If pressed, I would have said that that
was pretty much my own assessment of the situation. I had no reason to
doubt my instinct, which to date seemed to be serving me well – again
pride before a fall.

That summer I worked on *Camille* while we stayed at Castiglioncello.
Joan and Richard came to stay, as did John Gielgud and Donald Downes,
and there were passing visits from Wally Toscanini and Luchino. He asked
me to get him a supply of Hammam Bouquet on my next visit to London;
which put me in mind of old times. But when the holiday was over bad
news came: the long-expected end to my father's struggle against the
creeping effects of his stroke. He died on 4 September after battling every
inch of the way. I had seen him often in recent years, whenever I was near
Florence, and I'd used some of my new-found money to help him in his
fight: a special left-hand typewriter, an extra-large-screen television. But
it was clear that it was only a matter of time and in the end there was little
surprise, more a sort of awe that he'd kept going for so long.

When I got to Florence and saw him laid out, smart as ever in a dark
blue suit, I knew at once that there was something missing: the inevitable
gardenia he always wore. It was the wrong season for them but I telephoned
to friends in Milan who had villas by the lakes and asked them to scour
their gardens. I told them I wanted an uneven number – a personal superstition – three, five, seven, nine, whatever. Five arrived just in time for the
funeral and we buried him with a gardenia in his buttonhole and a posy in
his hands.

Back at the house after the interment it was hard to comfort my stepsister
Fanny. She had sacrificed her life to him, given up any chance of remarrying.
We sat in his room under the two formal portraits, one of him, the other
of Corinna his wife, the dark nightmare of my childhood. I tried to feel
more compassion but the emotion would have been false. I had liked him
better in recent years, he had been proud of me, as I could see from the
album of press cuttings on his desk, but there was always a coolness, an
awkwardness between us. He was still the man who had treated my mother

174   in a way that destroyed her life. She had loved him and it had ruined her
and no matter how much you grow and mature these are things that will
not heal. I told Fanny I wanted nothing of the inheritance I was now
legally entitled to. She had earned it, she could have it all. Much sadness
and bitterness had to be buried with my father.

ELEVEN

Magnificent Ladies

If, as the French say, vengeance is a dish to be eaten cold, then there was a long-awaited meal coming my way. It still rankled that La Scala had shunted me to one side, offering me productions only in the Piccola Scala and behaving as if I was somehow not up to directing for the main theatre. I knew that this was the result of the insanely jealous politics of the place but I was determined that one day I would come out on top. That day was now at hand thanks to the Austrian conductor Herbert von Karajan, who was then director of the Vienna Opera. He had come up with a marvellous scheme whereby Vienna and La Scala would exchange productions. To launch the idea he proposed to conduct a new staging of *La bohème* in Milan before taking it across the Alps, and he wanted me to direct it. Karajan isn't a man to argue with and they were obliged to invite me back. To rub it in, I insisted they also engage me to direct *Aida* for the following spring.

There was another cause for satisfaction here because the Metropolitan Opera in New York had already asked me to make my début with them by directing a new *Aida*. By rights, I should have jumped at the proposal, but, when Rudolf Bing told me that they wanted Birgit Nilsson in the title role, I was astounded. Why, I demanded, did they want a Swedish soprano, no matter how great an artist she was, when right on their doorstep was the sensational black singer Leontyne Price, who was in every sense born to sing the part? The Met refused to budge and I stood by what I had said and turned down their offer. Now I was able to insist that one of the conditions for my return to La Scala was that Leontyne Price should star in my new production – they, thank heavens, agreed. I eventually saw the Met's *Aida* that October and I'm happy to say it was uninspiring.

By contrast, a few nights later, Paula Strasberg had taken me to see the new sensation on Broadway, the unexpected *Who's Afraid of Virginia Woolf?* by Edward Albee. It was one of those all-too-rare occasions in the theatre when you are completely bowled over. I met Albee and we became great friends, and the next day I set about buying the Italian and French rights to the play, though there were those who thought I was crazy, that so 'New York' a piece would never 'translate' for a European audience. 175

Zeffirelli

There were even doubts it could travel as far as Los Angeles. But I have never been so certain of anything in my life as I was then that Albee's play was a classic which would run anywhere.

The rest of the year was spent plane-hopping: a visit to Chanel in Paris, Karajan in Vienna, back to New York to celebrate Maria Callas's birthday with Lenny Bernstein at Trader Vic's. Inevitably, when our paths crossed I would suggest a production to Maria, but there was always that laugh and a wave of the hand to indicate that she couldn't think of interrupting her sparkling new cosmopolitan lifestyle for something as unrewarding as opera. Sometimes I was taken in by this show of bravado, most times not. While in New York, I began auditioning for *Camille*, which produced one memorable encounter. A young unknown by the name of Dustin Hoffman turned up at the theatre and did his piece. It was immediately obvious that here was someone of astonishing talent, but it was equally clear that he was totally unsuitable for any of the roles on offer. When I asked him about it, he heartily agreed. His explanation was that he had been to see the Old Vic *Romeo and Juliet* and had decided that he had to work with me and that this was as good a way as any of getting to see me. I was flattered at the time and am even more so now when I see what he has gone on to achieve.

I returned to Italy for Christmas, which I spent in Florence with my stepsister Fanny, the first since the death of our father and therefore all the more sentimental. I would have liked to have seen her take some new direction in her life now that the burden of looking after our old man was ended, but I knew in my heart of hearts that this was impossible. Fanny had settled into her quiet Florentine life. But I insisted on one excursion when I took her with Aunt Lide to Milan for the opening of *La Bohème* in the New Year. That first night, on 31 January 1963, was precious to me as it represented a recognition I had been accorded in London and New York but had so far been denied in my own country. To many people in the Italian theatre and opera I was just one of Visconti's boys, someone with no identity of his own. Elsewhere I could be Franco Zeffirelli but not, until that *Bohème*, on my home ground. But if *Bohème* made the point, it was the subsequent *Aida* that rammed it home. *Bohème* ran through the early part of the year and was given as a gala for President Segni on 15 April. A week later *Aida* opened and it was to establish the style that is now associated with the name Zeffirelli, lavish in scale and unashamedly theatrical.

I got Lila de Nobili to design it and she came up with an exquisite re-creation of the original production of 1871. Those sets had been commissioned for the great celebration held in Cairo to mark the opening of the Suez Canal, but they were blocked in Paris, where they were built, by the revolution that followed the French defeat at the Battle of Sedan. Lila was able to bring that vision back to life for the first time. The result was as vast as a Hollywood epic – mammoth sets evoking a fantasy Egypt, huge set pieces with the largest chorus and groups of extras the stage would hold. It was in a way an extension of what we had enjoyed doing at the Albert Hall, opera as spectacle. And why not? I'm always extremely wary of taking opera too literally, of trying for psychological insights through some sort of realism. Any truths that opera may have to teach us seem to me to emerge from the unreality. Short men in armour and large ladies in chiffon singing about ancient Egypt don't make much sense at one level – when elevated by music and grandeur they can absorb us and reveal to us the confusions of emotion and loyalty, the nature of power and pity, that could not be so movingly expressed in any other way.

Whatever emotions were to be expressed on stage they were as nothing to those being agonized over in the wings. The problem was that inevitably I had a large say in how the sets were created: after all the director has to move his characters about and that more than anything must dictate the final designs. Lila did not object to that – far from it. What upset her was that she alone was credited as the designer. She insisted that we share joint billing. Forgetting that this sort of masochistic humility was now the dominant trait in her character, I rather absent-mindedly pooh-poohed the idea. When she saw the posters with her name credited as the sole designer she was indignant. Without warning she left before the dress rehearsal. It was years before we made it up.

To be fair, it wasn't merely weird over-agonizing that caused these reactions, she was also motivated by extreme integrity and generosity. But eventually self-doubt dominated her and she finally abandoned her career, moved to Brussels and went to a school of art to start again from scratch. Naturally she was a brilliant pupil and was top of her year, which absolutely infuriated her as they had failed a girl that she had decided was far better. 'This is not a serious school,' she announced, and left to take up a course in plumbing and electrical work. That was the only thing that ever satisfied her. 'I can do everything now,' she told me after she completed the course. 'I don't depend any more on "them" and I can finally be really helpful to a lot of friends.'

She moved back to Paris and was completely entranced by the events of 1968 and would go to the barricades with a breadbasket full of stones and drawing materials. She would spend all day sketching, though she never threw anything at the police. When her dreams of a new commune collapsed, she virtually withdrew into isolation. She looked after her sick mother until the old lady died many years later and left her a small annuity which has allowed Lila to live quietly in a state of suspension. She has a house full of cats and is currently involved in theories about how to raise children without curbing their creative instincts. Sublime as it may be for her, I find

178   it all rather tragic. If she didn't have that annuity, she might be forced to work again and we would all benefit from her genius. I live in hope that she will return to the theatre one day; God knows we need her.

I wish she had stuck it out with that production of *Aida*, as its success would have done much to restore her confidence. I hasten to add that I too, needed some bolstering, because my own self-confidence had had a nasty jolt a month before. *Camille* had been a disaster on Broadway. My supposedly infallible instinct had proved as dubious as anyone else's. My notion that the New York public were ready for a revival of romance was to be proved right – unfortunately for me – a few years later, when much of Broadway would be awash with tragic heroines. There is simply no satisfaction in being so far ahead of the game that you disappear from sight, which is what happened to my star-crossed *Camille*. Susan Strasberg played the lead and was unfavourably and unfairly compared with Garbo. To an audience conditioned to tough realism our nineteenth-century Paris was like something from outer space. They just didn't know what to make of it. After the opening we had a classic all-night session in Sardi's waiting for the papers to come out. It was the usual bleak dawn as we flicked through the pages and saw how the critics had massacred us. A lot of it was very unjust and much of it was an attempt to cut the Strasbergs down after what was seen as their too successful influence on American theatre. The press did a lot of harm to a beautiful and sensitive actress when they savaged Susan in that way but that's just one of the things you have to take in a business like ours. Only the critic Rex Reed was far-sighted enough to see that *Camille* was a portent of things to come, but even his praise was not enough to save us; our show was doomed. *Camille* had opened on the unlucky date of 17 March!

There was one positive result to be gleaned from that cold New York morning. I woke up to the fact that it was one thing to direct a great classic with all the support of a superbly professional theatre company but quite another to stick one's neck out and tackle a piece with people I had assembled myself. I saw at once that I had entered a new area and that I hadn't been fully conscious of what I was letting myself in for. I decided not to make the same mistake twice: I had thrown myself into *Camille* with my customary zeal as if enthusiasm alone could solve all the problems – that morning found me an older and wiser person than I had been the night before. *Camille* was my last theatrical flop – I may not always have created wonders on stage or screen, but from then on I have managed never to fall below a certain level of competence.

And if that was the main lesson *Camille* taught me the second was: always leave New York as soon as the curtain goes down on the first night – either you're a hit and everyone hustles round making an inflated idiot of you or you're a flop and the ego has to adjust to your being invisible. Unfortunately

it's a lesson I've seldom put into practice. I love New York too much. I've 179
always had such fun with friends like Lenny Bernstein, John and Janet
Roberts, Dorothy Strelsin and many others. Why everyone falls for the
illusory magic of the place is a recurring mystery. We all convince ourselves
that there's something in the atmosphere of New York that is vibrant,
creative and different. Perhaps it's a mass delusion or perhaps because the
place is filled with so many people, all convinced there is a special electricity
around, that they do actually generate it. And that feeling of New York
being *the* place was never more apparent than in the early 1960s when
America burst free from the rather staid Eisenhower years. Being friends
with the Bernsteins helped as they seemed to be at the centre of all the
crazy, exciting things that were going on.

For myself, the obvious effect of this highly charged existence – dashing
from city to city, from continent to continent, leaping from opera to opera,
play to play, was that I never had time to take stock of what I was doing –
or, more to the point, why I was doing it. In retrospect, I think I didn't
want to have to consider things in too much depth. After all, I was doing
what I had always thought I wanted to do. That I might be frantically
running away from something was the sort of gloomy thought that only
crept in when I found myself alone in strange hotel rooms, in airport
lounges, in the midnight cocktail bar or the empty theatre. So what was I
missing – love? That was ever available in temporary bursts. A family? I
had one, my extended, jumbled collection of Lide, Vige, friends and dogs
in Italy. Success? I seemed to have that, so why the occasional nagging
doubts? It was almost like *hubris* – ingratitude to God for the gifts he had
bestowed.

So the frenetic journeying continued. At the end of the year I went to
La Scala for another von Karajan production, *La traviata*. It could be
argued that I can direct that particular opera blindfold; I've done it so
often that for me it really is a case of refinement rather than new creation.
But one thing is always different – the performers – and there the director
always starts afresh. In this case our Violetta, Mirella Freni, was new to
the role and, though she had triumphed as Mimi in the Karajan *Bohème*,
Violetta was a very different matter.

There were two things that worried me. We were due to open on 17
December and nothing I could say could persuade the management to
change the date. Worse still perhaps was the fact that this would be the
first *Traviata* at La Scala since the famous Visconti/Callas production and
the shadow of that mythic interpretation lay across our rehearsals. This
was particularly evident when I noticed that Freni was beginning to look
extremely tired and nervous at rehearsals; when I took her to one side, I
discovered that she was the victim of the most horrendous hate mail sent
by the supporters of other *divas* who had sung the role or wanted to.

180   Inevitably there were poison-pen letters from Callas fanatics – that I
expected – but even the Tebaldi claque had joined in and, most surprising
of all, the crudest threats came from admirers of Scotto and Stella – what
a bunch! I begged Freni's husband to intercept all this hate mail and to
keep it from his wife, who was clearly being destroyed by it, but he chose
to ignore my advice. Despite these worries, my team and I came up with
one of the best stagings of the opera I've ever done. The sets were expensive,
but worth it, conveying a real sense of sumptuous *fin de siècle* Parisian
life.

When I didn't have my time completely taken up with the inevitable
last-minute crisis on costumes, designed by Danilo Donati, and lighting, I
was increasingly aware of other worrying portents. Karajan did not appear
to be planning a full run-through of the opera. He rehearsed a bit here and
there, but at no time did the singers get a full try at the whole piece as they
would on the night. This was particularly worrying in the case of Freni.
Karajan dismissed my worries, insisting that this was his way of keeping
the singers fresh and not over-rehearsed.

The opening night loomed like an accident waiting to happen. Disastrously it was still set for 17 December and, despite all my warnings that
this date was a sure recipe for disaster, as it had been for *Lucia* and *Camille*,
they insisted on going ahead.

Freni arrived at the theatre a wreck; the hate-mail had reached a cre-
scendo in these final days. When she left a restaurant, she would find more
letters stuffed in her coat pockets! She was also unsure how to pace herself,
never having sung the entire opera. I tried my usual safety measure and
went to Karajan to suggest discreetly that the register be brought down,
as many singers often request, in order to help Mirella, but he turned out
to be even more unwilling to consider such a move than I expected. There
was no more I could do, except to find a spot from which to observe what
anyone could see was going to be a disaster. In the event, it happened far
sooner than I expected. During the high '*gioia*' in the first act solo aria her
voice cracked twice; a truly horrible screeching sound was all she could
manage. I've seldom heard anything worse. Naturally there were boos from
the gods – you often get that even when the singing is terrific, and anyone
with any sense ignores it. In fact, most of the audience were rather good
natured about the whole thing and were clearly willing to forgive and
forget. When her voice cracked the second time, there were more boos, but
again nothing too dreadful. But then a self-inflicted disaster struck. If Freni
had had her wits about her, she would have simply joined the entire cast
for their first act bow, kept a sad look on her face and let everybody get
on with it. Instead, she decided on bravado and took a solo curtain call for
all the world as if she had just given the best performance ever. Inevitably
this further provoked the fury of the gods. But still the bulk of the audience

gave her a polite encouraging clap. Instead of counting herself lucky, the poor woman, who must have been on the verge of a nervous breakdown, raised her fist like a fishwife and shook it at her tormentors. The entire audience was stunned and the booing became more general. We dropped the curtain and got her off.

Karajan was furious and felt genuinely insulted, but really he was also to blame and it was pointless at this juncture to start hectoring Freni, who in a short while would have to be back out there in front of what was by now a totally hostile theatre. Karajan returned to the podium and for the first time in his entire career the great man himself was booed. He was shattered. I could see that he was debating whether or not to walk out, but in the end professional pride drove him on. Though the evening was doomed, the rest of the opera went smoothly. Freni sang the lyric parts magnificently and Karajan gave a superb reading of Verdi's score.

The next day, however, Freni pleaded sickness and Anna Moffo coped with the next two performances. Not that the public were any more sympathetic to her; at one point a cat attached to a parachute was launched from the gods and floated, screeching all the way, down on to the stage in front of her. Then, quite senselessly, the La Scala management decided to cancel the rest of the performances and, worse still, to ditch the entire production. All those beautiful sets and costumes, all that work for nothing. I think the idea had taken hold that somehow the whole thing was jinxed and that it was better to lay the curse to rest. Shortly afterwards, I happened to bump into Luchino, who, of course, was quick to pick up on my experiences in New York and Milan.

'My dear,' he said, 'as an old friend, may I suggest you keep away from the Lady of the Camellias, she doesn't seem to be doing you much good.'

I could hardly fault him at the time.

As if one difficult lady wasn't enough, I now turned to another: Anna Magnani.

Anna had had a majestic initial success in Hollywood after those early days we had shared in Rome. She had even won an Oscar for *The Rose Tattoo*, which Tennessee Williams wrote for her; they were great friends. In America she made films with such stars as Marlon Brando, Anthony Quinn and Burt Lancaster; then, slowly, there was a decline. She later made some pleasant pictures, but they were only moderately commercial and word went round that she was no longer box-office. She came home, but Italy was not the same. In her absence, the sort of hard female roles she had played were now being done by Sophia Loren, who was backed by her husband, the producer Carlo Ponti. It had been planned that Anna would take the lead as the mother in Alberto Moravia's *Two Women* with Sophia Loren as her daughter. Anna was far from happy when Ponti told her this.

182   'Don't make me vomit,' she said. 'I know you're in love with your wife, but don't try to suggest that she could play my virgin daughter.' She let out a booming guffaw. 'If anything, that cow should play the mother, not the daughter – she's old enough.'

As Anna was to say later, she should have cut out her tongue, because it was then that Ponti conceived the notion of replacing the old Magnani with a newer, more fiery model – his wife. The film was made and Loren seemed to many people to be playing every gesture, every inflection *à la* Magnani. Anna believed her characterization had been appropriated.

I think in my whole career I have seldom seen anything as tragic as the way Magnani reacted to that experience. Of course, she had a reputation for being a difficult, explosive character, but she was a great original actress and it was senseless to let her drop from public view.

I was determined to help and felt sure I had a solution with *Who's Afraid of Virginia Woolf?* I was certain that Anna would be brilliant as the squabbling wife and, after the opening of *Aida*, I went to Paris to an apartment she kept there to try to win her over. She had, of course, heard of the play; it was the biggest hit on Broadway and was already spoken of as a movie vehicle for Liz Taylor and Richard Burton. She had read the translation I'd sent her, but before long she put it to one side.

'This is not for me,' she said. 'I hate this woman, she's merciless, a fury, she's a bitch. Imagine, I make my comeback in the theatre with that? I'm another kind of woman, earthy. If I have to be a bitch, let me be a classic one – Medea, that's what we should do, eh?'

I was not discouraged; I went on trying to convince her that this play was going to be the biggest hit for years and she mustn't pass up the chance. But she was already daydreaming about other earthy parts we might do together – Cleopatra, things like that.

I left her with her maid and her animals, clicking away at the fleas as ever. She had many cats to practise on; when in Rome, she would go out at night dressed like a beggar to feed the city's army of strays who would gather like an endless, insatiable audience, hungry for her gifts.

I turned my attention to yet another woman in trouble, Maria Callas. I might have left her well alone if the reason for her retirement – her relationship with Onassis – had brought her the happiness she yearned for. But I was increasingly convinced that this was not the case. Whenever I saw them together, she would try to disguise it and she obviously still doted on him. In an unpleasant way, this desperate adoration on her part only brought out the worst in him, tempting him to treat her as badly as he could. There seemed not to be any limit to his sadism. He had a penchant for humiliating her, particularly in front of old friends, and showed absolutely no sign of marrying her. Despite everything, Maria clung to her Greek

Orthodox faith and longed for a church wedding. There were rumours that she had had a miscarriage and, if so, it must have been a shattering blow for her – I cannot pretend that the 'divine' Maria would have made the perfect mother for any child, but that certainly is how she saw herself now that her career was declining, and she felt painfully unfulfilled that it was denied her.

The irregularity of their affair was one more way for Onassis to humiliate her, for although he had used her fame as a means of increasing his social status, there were occasions when he would decide that it was 'improper' for him to be seen with his mistress. However, in the end, it was Ari's children who were his main excuse for not marrying her. They refused to accept Maria, blaming her for their parents' divorce. Once, when I was staying on board Onassis' yacht and Maria was having a siesta, Alexander Onassis started to water-ski round the yacht using the biggest of their motorboats to create a storm that shook everyone out of their beds. It was only one of dozens of ways in which he or his sister Christina attempted to show their distaste for their father's mistress. So Ari was able to fend off her requests that they marry until his children were won over and, of course, they never were.

David Webster at Covent Garden was as determined as I to see her return and very gradually, throughout 1963, we began to sense that she might look favourably on an approach. We saw ourselves as her staunchest friends, determined to protect her from a dubious affair and restore her to her rightful place as the supreme artist of the world of opera. Finally Webster decided to act; he told Callas he wanted her to make a comeback in *Tosca* in 1964 and, to our delight, she agreed to consider it, insisting that I do it with her to provide the warm, friendly and competent support she would need. 'It helps to know you're among friends, you know, David.' When David told me this, I went at once to Paris to the apartment she still kept in the Avenue Foch.

At first she tried a little of her cat-and-mouse routine, telling me how happy and fulfilled she was, that she had lots of plans and that she was working hard every day on her voice. She said that she hadn't promised David anything, only that she'd consider it. I let her run on for a while, and then I leant over and lifted one of her hands from her lap and held up her fingers. Her nails were long and well manicured. She looked at her own hand, puzzled by what I was doing. Then she realized. They were not the hands of someone who has been accompanying herself on the piano every day.

'Well, I've been so busy,' she admitted. But she knew she could no longer go on pretending with an old friend like me. 'Yes, I've been busy,' she said suddenly, very sincere. 'I've been trying to put some order into my life after all the tragedies and disappointments. Of course, I think I've found the right man at last, but perhaps I should come back to work before it's too late.'

184   And with a coy little girl's gesture she waved around her elegant hands, then suddenly tucked them under her arms to hide them and turned to me.

'Now tell me about *Tosca*,' she said.

Maria was always ready to study and rethink a great role no matter how many times she'd done it. She was always full of questions, some quite elementary, about what she was meant to think and feel. She already knew that we would have Tito Gobbi as Scarpia and I explained how I saw the relationship between Tosca and Scarpia as the key to the dramatic structure of the opera. Having someone as attractive and fascinating as Gobbi should make that relationship much more complex, because for me Tosca is a passionate, instinctive person, not the tight, haughty, overdressed *diva* with feathered hat and stick that is usually portrayed. My Tosca would obviously be drawn to an attractive man, even one whose heart is made of steel. This Tosca would be like Anna Magnani, earthy, sexy – when she rushes into the church she has a jealous outburst against Cavaradossi, then suddenly it's over and she starts to kiss him passionately as if they might make love right there. And of course it's that sensuality that makes her confrontation with Scarpia so vibrant. Unknowingly, far from merely hating him, shs's actually mysteriously attracted to him, to his power, to his cruelty. In the end Tosca kills Scarpia not merely to save her lover, but to save herself from herself. I just stopped myself from saying that it was not unlike her own feelings for Onassis. Maria frowned, puzzled yet intrigued, then asked me, 'But do I love him or not?' My heart sank. Couldn't she see what I was getting at?

'You decide,' I said.

'But I have to know if I love him or not.'

'Can't you imagine what your reactions would be, with a man like that, powerful, corrupt, sadistic but with that aura?'

And then she nodded – she had realized to whom I was referring. She had seen who Scarpia was.

Singers, even one of the stature of Maria, need a simplified notion that they can cling to – do I love him or not, is this a friend or an enemy? They have to compartmentalize the character, even when there are supposed subtleties – this man is my friend but he's going to betray me, this man killed my father but he loves me. They have to have a clear-cut vision because they have so much else to worry about, above all the risky, athletic business of producing miraculous sounds from a little inch of flesh in the throat. Everything comes from there and it has to be perfect, so you cannot overload their minds with supposedly sophisticated interpretations. The genius of Callas was that once she had her simplified notions worked out, she would begin to dress them up, just as a child is born from a single cell. And curiously she was always childish when asking about a role; she would

talk in a babyish way – 'Am I good or bad here?', 'Why do I say that, am
I a different woman?' It could be very irritating, mixed in as it usually was
with endless talk about herself – 'Am I looking beautiful today? Isn't this
dress lovely?' – or with ridiculously petty arguments with her maid over
domestic trivia. But then suddenly she would see it, would grasp the point
and would begin to discuss it with intense sophistication. Then she was the
diva, then it was all worth while.

Throughout her career Callas dropped operas from her repertoire if she
felt she could not bring something to the role. She stopped singing *Aida*
because she saw her as a proud, independent spirit whereas Verdi didn't
really create the part in that way and Maria was straining to do something
that wasn't there. Conversely, as Elizabeth in *Don Carlos* she *was* the queen
of Spain without any doubt. What Maria required of her directors was a
vast input of ideas, not merely major suggestions regarding character and
plot but dozens of little touches and even tricks that would help inspire
her. I might tell her that when Tosca runs into the church with her bunch
of flowers, that she has clearly picked at random but with great care, she
suddenly tosses them nonchalantly onto a chair as if they had completely
passed out of her mind – she's an impetuous woman and she's now thinking
of other things. I would plant that idea in her mind and maybe a fortnight
later during rehearsals she would do it. She would have been ruminating
and weighing it up along with all the other bits and pieces I had offered her
and, when it was accepted, it was there. Rehearsing with Callas generated a
kaleidoscope of ideas, images and visions.

With all those elements whirling around – plot, character, theatrical
business, voice and music – it's hardly surprising that a *prima donna* like
Maria should be just that: a *prima donna*. Moody and manic, desperate for
love and praise, self-centred and childish; it could hardly be otherwise.
Maria leaned heavily on those around her. Her chauffeur and Bruna, her
maid, were really her closest friends, who stayed with her all her life. She
also 'inherited' the remarkable Maggie van Zuylen, who had a wonderful
capacity for befriending and amusing the famous. As with Chanel, Maggie
was a sort of close confidante and admirer, always full of sparkle and able
to deal on equal terms with those super egos. She was able to lead the life
of a socialite because of her husband's diplomatic career and his banking
interests, in fact one of her daughters married a Rothschild: Maggie had
distinctive looks, which she passed on to her children. If I remember
correctly she was born Egyptian and had beautiful dark hair and a lovely
smile. But most remarkable were her clear green eyes. I remember, years
later, after her death, the opening night of a *Bohème* I did with Karajan in
Salzburg, I was introduced to a group of elegant people and I noticed a
man with just those eyes, and I knew at once that he was Maggie's son.

As I was leaving Maria's Paris apartment after our 'rehearsal' for *Tosca*, she clung to me and begged me not to let her change her mind.

'You must call me all the time. Keep me warm for this. Don't let me back out.'

I promised and, sensing her change of mood, pressed her into doing a double comeback, the *Tosca* in London and *Norma* in Paris. Miraculously she agreed.

As soon as I told David Webster the good news he got in touch with Paris and began the immensely complex double planning necessary to accommodate this new notion. The plan was to open with *Tosca* in London in the coming January and follow it with *Norma* in Paris the following May. The two productions would then be exchanged the following year. Although it was only June when I met Maria this still left little time as far as organizing an opera goes. In order to fit *Tosca* into the Covent Garden schedule I would have to overlap my rehearsals with those of a new production of *Rigoletto* that we were creating for Geraint Evans that same January. Although I could see how strenuous that was going to be I was nevertheless so overjoyed at the prospect of having Maria back that I merely shrugged away the difficulties.

In any case it was time for our holidays in Castiglioncello again, so it was hardly the moment to be anticipating the problems of the winter. There was enough to be fretting over with the forthcoming *Who's Afraid*, which because of the way Italian theatre productions are organized had to be financed by the troupe putting on the production. I spent a lot of time that summer dealing with the problems of money and of finalizing the casting. After Anna's refusal I picked Andreina Pagnani as the female lead and we started rehearsals in Rome in August. However, it was clear from the beginning that things were not well with her. On 9 September, eleven days after we began, Andreina dropped the bombshell that she felt totally alienated from the part she was trying to play and that she just couldn't go on. We were due to open on 6 October in Venice and there was barely time to find a substitute. I called Anna again, this time out of desperation, and begged her to help. I swore she wouldn't regret it, that it would do as much for her as for me, but it was no use. Finally, another great actress, Sarah Ferrati, came to the rescue, though by the time she had stepped into the role we were already so behind schedule we were forced to rehearse through the weekends, day and night, in order to catch up. We decided to abandon the usual practice of having a series of previews, as there simply wasn't time. When we got to Venice at the beginning of October, we opened cold. Happily, despite any rough edges in the production, my instinct that the play would have universal appeal proved correct and, although we were only giving three performances to close the International Theatre Festival, I was sure we would have a successful run when we later toured the play round the country. We opened in Rome on 8 November and the first act alone received a twenty-five-minute standing ovation. It was ridiculous, we almost couldn't go on. There was virtually a riot at the end. Most of the Italian theatre world was there, and backstage was a dense throng of people shouting their congratulations. And then the wall of bodies suddenly parted to permit the figure of Anna Magnani to burst through. At once she was on top of me punching and screaming, incapable as ever of controlling herself.

'You son of a bitch, you should have strangled me. That role was written for me – I have missed it forever!' She grabbed hold of me and came as close as physically possible. 'What you don't understand', she insisted, 'is that I'm a woman alone. Look at all those whores in the movie business. They'd be skipping from brothel to brothel if it wasn't for their husbands. They've got men to look after them, to tie them down, to help them make decisions. But what about me – me – me?'

Her voice was getting higher and louder. It was becoming rather embarrassing and we forced her into a dressing-room and held her in a seat till the fury abated and she sat, wracked with sobs.

'I've lost it,' she said. 'I've lost it forever. I'll never have a role like that to play. You were right, but you should have forced me, you should have slapped me across the face the way Rossellini did – he knew how to handle a *stronza* like me!'

It was pointless to ask how anyone could force her to anything, since no one ever had, not even Rossellini, if the truth were known. Still, I was resolved to do something for her if I could. What that might be was not yet clear, as I again plunged into a punishing schedule of theatre and opera: an Italian *Hamlet* with Giorgio Albertazzi, *Falstaff* in Rome, and then London after Christmas for the double task of producing *Rigoletto* and *Tosca*.

Sometimes we rehearsed *Rigoletto* in the mornings and *Tosca* in the afternoons and sometimes vice versa – it's a wonder I didn't get them confused. I can remember a recurring nightmare in which I walk into a rehearsal hall to find a cast waiting for me and I can't remember what it is we are supposed to be doing. I ask them to tell me but they are waiting for *me* to tell *them*, and we stare at each other helplessly ... The usually co-operative Covent Garden staff were at first put out by these unprecedented demands but gradually the air of excitement at the idea of Callas's return began to get through to them and things were soon buzzing like mad. As soon as she arrived for rehearsals Maria's presence was enough to ensure that everyone was working flat out. As ever, she herself was the most conscientious person in the production, hard-working and determined to master every detail. She and Gobbi were the perfect foil to each other, and they would meticulously prepare each day's work so as to maximize their time together. She was always searching for her motivation in a scene, and

Zeffirelli

I remember the agonizing over the moments before she kills Scarpia. Gobbi was amazing: it was he who conceived the idea of nearly raping her, of grabbing her wrists and spreading her arms in a crucifix, thus laying her open to him. She then runs to the table.

'But what', she asked, 'am I feeling?'

'You want him,' I said. 'You know you want him to violate you and that's what you can't deal with.'

'So what do I do?' she asked. But then just as quickly she knew, she understood what she herself would have done. She needed to clear her head, to cool herself of those passions – and so we created the most gripping though ludicrously simple piece of business – she frenziedly poured herself a glass of water, drank it in one gulp, stopped with the glass in mid air as she saw the knife on the table, held that frozen profile for what seemed like for ever, lowered the glass and, just as Scarpia came up behind her, she grabbed the knife, turned and stabbed him to death. That was the kiss of Tosca. The suspense was riveting.

The rehearsals were almost as eventful as the real thing would have been. Once when going through that scene the retractor knife jammed and although it had no point Maria certainly knocked the breath out of poor Tito. The dress rehearsal was even more dramatic. We had permission to use real candles. Maria had a long curled wig and when bending back from Scarpia the false hair caught fire. As it was a wig she felt nothing and was somewhat put out to find herself being beaten about the head with the rolled-up parchment that Tito had grabbed.

No such disasters marred the opening night, though Maria was herself a walking disaster area. All her familiar fears for her voice returned and with them her psychosomatic illnesses. By the evening she was hoarse. With anyone else it would have been diagnosed as bronchitis. Of course there was nothing wrong with her except a paralysing nervous attack. We stood in the wings with her gripping my hand and crossing herself over and over in the Orthodox manner. The first chord struck up and I had to push her out onto the stage – 'Mario, Mario' – and she was off, her voice perfect, her nerves conquered. I looked down at my hand, which was bleeding from where her nails had cut into my palm. It was like stigmata and I cherished the wounds for weeks.

There was one detail of that opening scene that really brought out her character – the bunch of flowers she was carrying. The day of the opening the regular opera house florists had delivered a neat bunch of red roses, just the sort of thing a classic *diva* might carry. But this Tosca was different, emotional, erratic. In that hiatus before curtain-up when I always have to do something to take my mind off things, I went out into Covent Garden, which was still the old fruit, vegetable and flower market, and I bought a flower here, another there, in much the same sort of dreamy way I imagined

Tosca would have done, making a big loose bundle of glorious clashing colours. It was that that Maria carried in the crook of her arm and which so perfectly echoed her character.

My other great find during rehearsals was a ten-foot length of gold-embroidered cloth in an Indian shop which became the magnificent stole that Tosca wore when she went to confront Scarpia. I remember Maria trying it on in her dressing-room, starting to practise those gestures – twitching the edge, letting it slide down her arms – that brought such drama to her movements. She also wore a pair of long buttoned gloves that she slowly unfastened and peeled off as the scene evolves. It was almost as if she were stripping, exposing herself, tantalizing Scarpia. This was Maria, the actress at her best. This was what she brought to opera, something far beyond glorious singing.

Everything that opening night was perfect – a far cry from my poor *Rigoletto*, which was dogged with problems. It was due to open on 4 February but at the last minute Geraint Evans completely lost his voice and, unlike Maria's, this was a real illness. It happened so much at the last minute that it was absolutely impossible to put a substitute on stage. It wasn't just the absence of an available baritone; there was also the fact that this was Geraint's production – he'd waited all his life to sing Rigoletto. For such a superb artist and so nice a man it was an unfair blow. The Covent Garden management understood all this and, quite without precedent, they cancelled a first night. Three days later, as Geraint had still not recovered, they were forced to open with Peter Glossop. Meanwhile, I had an entire cast waiting for me in New York and for the first time ever I was obliged to miss one of my own first nights.

The task before me was a most flattering one – Rudolf Bing had asked me to do *Falstaff* as the last new production at the old Metropolitan Opera House before the move to the Lincoln Center. Naturally I was honoured by the offer, but perhaps more than the honour, even more than the chance to do another *Falstaff*, the thing that mattered most was the opportunity to work with Lenny Bernstein for the first time.

Although we had been close friends since La Scala in the 1950s we had nver managed to do a production together. I was really looking forward to the sheer fun of it – Lenny has got such energy, he gives so much, and talks ... a day with him is like four years at Yale. I know there are people who find him overdramatic and showy but that's just the public side of a deeply thoughtful man. I realize that his ultra-liberal politics, Black Panthers and all, might have seemed at that time to be the opposite of my beliefs, but I can understand why he holds them: the tragic Jewish experience and the need to counterbalance the uncaring attitude of so many Americans explains it all. Moreover, I have one sure touchstone in judging people: how they are viewed by those closest to them, their helpers. Maria had Bruna, her devoted maid, and Ferruccio much as I now have my Aunt's cook, Vige; and Lenny was the same – his Chilean people at the house in Park Avenue are adoring friends. You can't fake a thing like that, people choose to give it to you and it reflects what you are.

Lenny and I speak the same language, we love the same things, we understand one another. In some ways we are both isolated in a world of gloom, boredom and arrogance, too often surrounded by people who don't really know what theatre or even life is about. Doing *Falstaff* with him was one of the most riveting, revealing, charming experiences of my life. We had fun like children, real genuine fun, exactly the way old Verdi wanted it, the way Shakespeare imagined it. As the last production at the old Met it had to be, and was, something very special.

My conception was of a rough-hewn rural world, of country folk in home-made clothes, eveything wood, wool, sacking and stone. This was a world of well-off, well-fed peasants with busty wives. All the action was bawdy, skirt-lifting, farting and drinking. I designed the sets and costumes as a deliberate reaction to the sparse metallic look that was currently fashion-able. The costumes were magnificently realized by the ninety-year-old Madame Karinska, who had worked for Diaghilev. She had the waspish intelligence of Chanel, and God how she worked. She had material especially woven, she hand-embroidered it herself just as the good wives of Windsor would have done. The detailing was incredible.

I wondered at first whether Lenny would turn out to be another Luchino when we got down to working together but I needn't have worried. First of all, we are about the same age and there is a mutual respect that ensures that any fireworks have creative results. *Falstaff* has three acts with a scene change in each, so you have to have some sort of machinery or the production drags on interminably. In my designs, interiors became exteriors and back again simply by raising or lowering a ceiling or dropping in some foliage. All very quick except for the last act – the forest. This I wanted to be splendid, a real wood, not just a few stray trees, and so we needed a five-minute break in the middle of Act Three. This caused my only real rift with Lenny, who went on nagging that such a pause went against the music. To him there is a clear musical thread that bridges the two scenes: the secretive voices in the forest, the orchestra introducing the mystery with the distant, plangent note of the hunting-horn. But I wanted a real forest and hypocritically tried to convince him that it would be much more tantalizing for the audience if they had to wait. He let me have my way and at every performance the forest scene received a round of applause. However, I knew from the beginning that he was right – musically that is – and if I ever do *Falstaff* again I'd try to create stage machinery which would let me have a 'real forest' without an interval. Not that I ever will do it again. I'd already done it five or six times before, starting with Giulini at the Holland Festival in 1956, but, to me, that production with Lenny was as near to a definitive statement as I could manage. It's still revived at the new Met but it's not really the same: a warehouse fire destroyed Karinska's costumes and the replacements are inevitably inferior. Today the production looks to me a bit like a ghost stalking the paths of its earlier life, though it still fills the Met whenever it is revived.

After *Falstaff* it was back to London to arrange for the transfer to Covent Garden of the Palermo production of *I puritani* with Joan Sutherland. This was to be the spring of both my *divas*, as the next opera was the Callas *Norma* in May. Given the success of *Tosca* I had no reason to expect anything but good of the affair, but as soon as we assembled in April I realized that the greatest problem ahead would be Maria's voice. *Tosca* is difficult enough but *Norma* is the worst challenge of all. Maria had often been compared to Giuditta Pasta, who created the role. Pasta too was reported to have an uneven voice and 'off nights', yet Stendhal records that he went to see many consecutive performances of her *Norma*. Given that today's singers like today's athletes are stronger than they used to be, how on earth did Pasta do it? The answer was probably that in a sense she simply didn't – one night she'd sing her heart out in the first act, then coast through the rest, the next she'd go easy in the first but sing out in the second and so on, conserving and then using her strength. Thus no two performances were ever the same, which may have been why Stendhal went so often: the only way to get a whole opera.

Nowadays the public would never accept such behaviour, hence the intense strain on a singer. Worse still, the *Norma* Maria would sing is tougher than that which confronted Pasta because it is now sung slightly higher. The pitch has been raised – that is to say the note that the orchestra uses to tune its instruments has moved higher over the decades and singers have had to follow.

All this was in the back of my mind, but my first concern was the interpretation of the piece. Again Maria had done *Norma* many times and again she wanted to clear her mind and start again. I told her to close her eyes, sing the music to herself, then tell me what she saw. What became clear as she hummed the arias and talked was the change that had come over her. The original Callas Norma had been a virginal creature, almost the Casta Diva she invokes. Now she saw an altogether more romantic creature, someone who has loved and who is now a passionate woman, not an untouched priestess. Norma, as I saw her for Maria, appears in a clearing of a lush, mysterious forest, overhung with branches through which light filtered. Here was the mythical forest of ancient Gaul, the sacred vale of the Druids, a place not barren and cool but verdant and rich. As the opera is in four acts I decided to set it over a year, beginning in spring with everything green, then hot summer when she has arranged a tent for shade,

Zeffirelli

192   then a third act of red and yellow autumn as the tragedy begins and finally
a burned-out, blackened winter.

It was the right setting for her. Here Maria, denied children of her own,
could sing her heart out for Norma and the children they were trying to
tear from her. It was the other half of the passionate Maria in *Tosca* and
could never have been done before the episode with Onassis. In an awesome
way she had become the parts she was singing.

Just as clearly, her voice reflected the strain of her life. Once again, as
the first night on 14 May drew nearer, that famous instrument began to
show signs of stress. I begged her to take it easy, to skip some of the more
trying coloratura, to consider bringing down the entire register to what it
would have been in Bellini's day; but she was adamant in her refusal.

'No one will know,' I argued. 'And those that do won't care.'

'You might be right, but I'll know,' she said fiercely, 'and I'll care.'

We approached the opening like circus performers about to try a complex
and dangerous feat for the first time. It was undoubtedly the night of
nights with *le tout* Paris in attendance, including an entire Onassis party.
Regrettably it was also the opera equivalent of an international football
match with two rival groups of supporters – pro- and anti-Callas claques
waiting to cheer or hiss as the opportunity arose.

For me it was the evening of 'my ladies' – not only was Maria on stage
but most of the others were out there in the audience. I had brought Aunt
Lide and Vige with my stepsister Fanny. They were dressed for the great
occasion – Lide had made a stunning robe out of a length of gold brocade
curtain she'd bought in the flea-market in Florence, she'd borrowed a white
mink stole and was bedecked with magnificent costume jewellery, huge
'emeralds' and other stones that I bought at a theatrical suppliers for her.
She looked regal and everyone in the theatre was wondering who she was.
People kept coming up and talking to her, convinced that she was a great
opera star of the past whom they couldn't quite place, attended by her two
ladies-in-waiting. Her air of mystery was confirmed when Anna Magnani,
flamboyantly dressed in red, entered the auditorium. She caught the attention of the entire audience, but, when she saw Aunt Lide, she walked
straight over and embraced her.

'You old cunt,' she yelled, laughing raucously, 'What are you playing –
the queen of a high-class brothel?' To everyone in the theatre who could
only see and not hear this was a sure sign of Aunt Lide's stature.

As soon as I got backstage, all my thoughts were with Maria. It was clear
from the start that the voice really was not in top form. Not only were we
witnessing Norma's struggle with her emotions; there was a conflict between
Maria and every note in that challenging score. To those of us who appreciated what Callas stood for, difficulties with the highest notes were irrelevant.
Her acting interpretation and general vocal creativity were at a peak. That

night, her Norma was one of the finest moments of music theatre I have ever experienced; she could at will pick us up and dash us down emotionally. Even today I shudder when I remember the nervewracking tension of that first act – would she make it or not, would her voice hold out, would she triumph over the odds?

In the end, she didn't; her voice failed in the first act *cabaletta*. The anti-Callas claque began to rumble and some booed. The pro-Callas claque defended her. Most of us simply willed her on. Summoning all her courage, she continued. Sadly, there were a few fools who could not see that what had happened was irrelevant. I was furious. Could these idiots not tell that, despite a minor accident, hers was a great interpretation of Norma, certainly the greatest ever in our time?

When the interval came, I peeped through the spy-hole in the great curtain to try to gauge the audience's reactions and that was how I made out a frail figure all in white sitting near the front. I hurried down into the stalls to speak to her.

'Mademoiselle Chanel,' I said, lifting her hand. 'How marvellous you've come.'

'I just wanted to see what's become of you,' she said, and then launched into one of her usual monologues telling me how she had been travelling, but had hurried back for this. 'You came all the way from Italy for my flop – how could I not cross Paris for your triumph?' I was delighted to hear all her news, but, while she was talking, I suddenly realized I had a confession to make and, as soon as there was a pause, I spoke.

'The reason we're all here', I said, 'is because of you.'

She looked puzzled.

'I've never told you before,' I continued, 'but when I left Luchino I had quite a hard time before I got started. Even when I got work I had very little money and one thing saved me – your gift.'

She looked even more confused.

'The Matisse drawings,' I said. 'At first I thought they were repro-ductions. When someone told me they were real, I was forced to sell some of them to stay alive. It was a sad way to treat a gift.'

She didn't seem to remember the episode at all. 'But no, *mon cher*,' she laughed. 'Don't think about it. Come and see me soon and I'll look out a really special present for you.'

The lights were dimming and I had to go. I meant to take up her invitation, perhaps go to La Pausa again, but it was not to be. I was not able to visit her before her death, but I am so grateful she came that night to see what had become of me and that I had a last opportunity to thank her.

Maria coped with the challenges of the second act with unparalleled skill, but in the third act there is a particularly dangerous high C and, for all to

194   hear, Maria's voice cracked again. This was not *Lucia* in Dallas, where she could make the noise into her death scream and collapse in a sudden dramatic gesture. This was undisguised, right there out on the huge stage of that vast opera house in front of everyone. Again the idiots took to shouting and booing. It was so stupid. Great opera is not merely a question of vocal athletics. To me and to those who love opera Maria had triumphed. And nothing could alter that.

   Backstage everybody seemed to be affected by an insane gaiety, a release of tension. I barely had time to make the usual gestures to Maria before she was whisked away by Onassis and the beautiful people who considered the evening theirs. We were all bidden to Maxim's, where Onassis had taken over an entire floor for the party of the season and, when I entered with my three ladies, Lide, Vige and Fanny, the sheer crush of the rich and famous was overpowering. At the centre, the bull-like figure of Ari stood beside his Norma, who looked drained after her ordeal. Wasn't this what she wanted, I wondered? Wasn't it what I wanted? The endless congratulations, the praise heaped on me in front of my adoring family. And then I looked again at Maria and saw what it could do. My confusion was total: like Maria I seemed to have everything and nothing. What on earth were these people to us? – just the super-rich Monte Carlo jet set to whom we were classy entertainers. My problem was that I could see short distances ahead, could decide that I wanted to direct this or that opera or play, but the overall picture kept blurring like the faces passing before me, speaking their praise and moving on. I manœuvred my ladies to our table, where they could survey the glittering mob. To them, at least, it was all simple fun. Aunt Lide was still quivering in her 'mink' and 'jewels', while Fanny just looked straight ahead as if in a dream. It was dear Vige who best caught my own feelings.

   'Signora Fanny,' she said, leaning across and slightly slurring her speech as a result of two unaccustomed glasses of champagne. 'Signora Fanny, please look at everything carefully so that you can tell me all about it tomorrow. Don't tell me now, tell me tomorrow, because I don't think I shall remember anything.'

TWELVE

Poor and Famous

Somewhere along the line, it's hard to say exactly when, I had become newsworthy. Journalists asked my opinions, interviewed me and singled me out at the events I went to. I was asked to sit for well-known photographers like Richard Avedon, Lord Snowdon, David Bailey and, most bizarre of all, Horst, the cause of Chanel's rupture with Luchino. I did not let on that I knew about the episode, but, while he was arranging his shots, I had a close look: he was still a very attractive man and I could see why Coco had been so jealous.

I was no longer just someone near the famous, I was famous. Of course, this realization changes the way you behave – it is bound to when you are no longer one of the crowd – but, because it happened gradually, it was less disorienting than it often is for people like pop singers who suddenly go from total obscurity to world-wide stardom in a matter of weeks. I'd been around famous, glamorous, rich people for fifteen years before I became aware that I, too, had entered that curious domain occupied by those whose names and faces are known to those that they themselves do not know.

It is stupid to denigrate fame, when ultimately it is what all artists and entertainers work towards. And it must be said that the pleasures of being famous outweigh the often-expressed drawbacks. However, there was an unusual element to my success – I was famous and poor, a rare combination. One of the reasons I continued to dash around working so insanely hard was that I needed the money. I was paid only a straight fee for directing an opera or a play and, what with my expenses and the constant cost of setting up new projects, a good proportion of which never saw the light of day, I was often barely in pocket by the time a show opened. In fact, I was still selling the Matisse drawings during the mid-1960s and there were often occasions when it took all of my Aunt's and Vige's skills at producing inexpensive Tuscan peasant food to ensure that we all sat down to a decent meal. Jet-set my life may have been, but one may discount any thoughts that it was all done on a tide of cash.

Financially my worst failing was a passion for live theatre. I enjoyed introducing the best of modern drama to Italy and I followed the tradition that Luchino had established of bringing in the best new plays, usually   195

196   from the States, and maintaining a theatre company to tour them round the principal Italian cities. But even Luchino had beggared himself trying to keep that up and he had family resources I could never hope to match. Anyway, even if it was madness, most of 1964 was taken up with theatre work, touring my Compagnia di Prosa Franco Zeffirelli both in Italy and abroad.

We took our Italian version of *Hamlet* to Paris for the Festival des Nations a week after *Norma,* and then went on to Vienna. I then started rehearsals at the Roman theatre in Verona for an open-air version of *Romeo and Juliet* in Italian with Anna Maria Guarnieri and Giancarlo Giannini. This was to prove the delight of the summer when it toured the various Roman amphitheatres and other ancient open-air sites which abound in Italy. *Hamlet,* meanwhile, was visiting the capitals of Eastern Europe, including Russia, where I joined the group for the opening in Moscow.

It was after our summer holidays at Castiglioncello that Monica Vitti opened in my Italian version of Arthur Miller's *After the Fall* and then we took our *Hamlet* to London, where it ran for two weeks during the World Theatre season at the Old Vic. Then came a production which was to give me more fun and more misery than any other at this time.

I went to Paris to begin rehearsing the French version of *Who's Afraid of Virginia Woolf?* This was to become one of the greatest successes of the Paris theatre in our day, but hardly for reasons that anyone could have predicted. In fact, at first, all seemed to be almost boringly normal. Madeleine Robinson and Raymond Gérome were both superbly professional and I had no trouble at all in knocking the production into shape. So easy was it that I was able to take long weekends in London in order to set up a production of *Much Ado About Nothing* which Laurence Olivier wanted for his new National Theatre Company at The Old Vic.

Liz Taylor and Richard Burton were in France to film scenes for *The Sandpiper,* and they asked if they could sit in on one of our rehearsals for *Who's Afraid.* They slipped in and out without my meeting them and even came to one of the previews at the end of the month. Despite our not having any contact, these visits were later to produce results for all of us.

When we finally opened, we knew at once that we had a success. This was important to me because, unlike the Italian system, a play can run for ever in France if it is a success and, better still, the director receives a percentage for every performance.

The producer of *Who's Afraid* was Lars Schmidt, who'd married Ingrid Bergman after the Rossellini episode, and this was the start of a friendship that lasted until her death a few years ago. We had plenty of time to get to know each other, for the play ran for an amazing three years. Normally I would have had little to do with it after the opening, but this was to turn

Poor and Famous

out to be no ordinary run, though the trouble that was to come had not 197
yet surfaced. For me the greatest pleasure was the weekly cheque – by
today's standards a quite modest £200, but then a pleasing sum and
certainly the first real money I'd ever made.

A few months after we opened, Lars Schmidt rang to beg me to come
back to Paris to help deal with serious problems with the cast. When I
arrived at the theatre, it was immediately apparent that everyone had
fallen out with everyone else. But a brief investigation revealed that the
root of the trouble was Madeleine Robinson's conviction that her co-star,
Raymond Gérome, was somehow a scene-stealer who was robbing her of
the credit she felt she merited. It was all pretty childish, but there was
always the risk that it would affect the actual performances, particularly
as Madeleine had used her persuasive powers to stir up the young actor
Claude Giraud against the older man. With Claude and Raymond not on
speaking terms, life was very difficult for everyone. I did what I could to
clear the air, letting them all have their say to me, sympathizing with their
grievances and then offering to mediate a compromise. As the grievances
were entirely illusory in the first place, it wasn't that difficult to negotiate
a settlement, but I had the curious feeling that whatever patching up I had
achieved would only be temporary and that there was worse to come. Both
Lars and Ingrid shared my concern, but we were all somewhat amused by
the fact that what was happening in the play was so grimly reflected in the
way the actors were behaving towards each other, as if Albee's powerful
drama had somehow infected our players. Lars pointed out that, despite
the risk of backstage trouble, he could hardly be sorry about the relationship
which had developed between Madeleine and Raymond, as no couple could
have better played out all the venom needed on stage than the two of them.
I took his point, but hoped it would all go no further.

As if to ensure that 1964 ended with all my over-emotional ladies duly
visited I called on Anna Magnani at her Paris apartment. The success of
the French version of *Who's Afraid* had rubbed in even further her stupidity
in turning down the role and she had been mortified to see just how well
Madeleine Robinson had taken to the part. This was just what I wanted,
because I had again decided to try to bring her back to the Italian stage,
not out of purely altruistic motives but rather because I now felt we could
help each other. My reasoning was simple: it was proving more and more
difficult to keep my Italian theatre company going. The irony was that,
despite success after success, the way the theatre system was organized,
with ridiculously heavy taxes and not one penny of subsidy for a private
company, we were never able to have a fully profitable run. Even our
foreign successes were a two-edged sword as we struggled to pay the
enormous costs involved in transporting plays as far afield as Poland and
London. Prestige was one thing, but the reality was that much of the year

Zeffirelli

198   I was obliged to disband the company. Many of the players were loyal and enjoyed doing the sort of modern work we specialized in, and were forced to mark time, doing odd film dubbing jobs, in order to be available whenever we started up again. This was clearly unsatisfactory for all concerned, not least for myself as I had to waste countless hours trying to deal with the financial side of things, never my strong point. A solution had come to me when I had seen how well the summer audiences had taken to our open-air *Romeo and Juliet*. What I wanted to do was to re-stage that production for indoor performances and to tour it again. But I knew that Shakespeare played by young actors would never be a sufficient draw to ensure our financial well-being – what we needed was a star vehicle and, obviously, a star, to run in tandem with our Shakespeare in order to draw the crowds. Hence Magnani. I also had what I knew would be the perfect part for her, *La lupa*, the other play, along with *Cavalleria rusticana*, that had been taken from Verga's *Vita dei campi*. What a part for a woman like Anna, the she-wolf of the title. Who else could play it?

I began 1965 with rehearsals for *Much Ado About Nothing* in London, but I flew to Rome one weekend in the middle of January to see Anna. She still lived in that stunning roof-top apartment in the centre of the city and as soon as I arrived I remembered the story of the aggrieved wife screaming abuse from the courtyard below. There was plenty to remind me, in fact, because when the maid showed me in I could hear the most appalling row taking place. I knew that she often had intensely emotional arguments with her son Luca and I assumed that I had intruded on one of them. This seemed to be a particuarly bad quarrel: she swore at him, she ranted and raved, and I began to wonder if I shouldn't just slip away and come back later. Then suddenly she walked into the room, quite calm, showing no sign of having been worked up – and I noticed that somewhere in the background the argument was still going on, I could hear her screaming at Luca! Anna turned to her maid and asked her to put the birds on another terrace. It was then that I realized what was going on – they were Mynah birds which she had picked up somewhere and they had learned to mimic exactly Anna's quarrels with Luca; they'd even distilled them so that only the choicest bits were offered, making it a lot worse than the reality, which, heaven knows, was bad enough. It was very funny, if a little alarming.

When we settled down to talk I decided not to waste time and told her straight out that I wanted to do *La lupa*, that she was ideal for the part and that this was a chance to mend the *Who's Afraid of Virginia Woolf?* mistake. I put that a little more delicately, but the message was there. She took the point and after a minimum of humming and hawing, she agreed. I don't think she was a hundred per cent convinced about either the play or her role, and I know she was worried about making a comeback after so long an absence, but what could she do? She had to trust me now that she

had seen *Who's Afraid* go from triumph to triumph.
I returned to my rehearsals in London with the sense of a job well done and then, on 24 January, one of those public events took place that manages to shunt aside all one's own concerns – everything just seemed to stop with the announcement that Churchill had died. To those of us who had resisted the blandishments of Mussolini's Fascism, Churchill more than anyone had represented hope during the worst years of the war. He had seemed so indestructible then that it was impossible to believe that he was no more. The following night an old friend, Lord Drogheda, took me to Westminster Hall to see the great man lying in state. I was very moved by the dignified solemnity, the guards at the four corners of the catafalque, the sense of history about the great beamed room. Just as there have been British people with more awareness of Italian culture than most Italians so it does appear to require a foreigner fully to savour the best that Britain offers. I think that everything surrounding the death of Churchill, his lying in state, the magnificent funeral, were in some ways the last act in a great national drama. It was the end of something – a great imperial era? – a sense of national purpose? I know many of my British friends resent this sort of foreign idealization of a Britain that never quite matched up to the illusion we had of it. But sometimes you need a national myth and without one you can end up with nothing towards which to work. I know that theatre people often have a very simplistic view of politics and tend to express very black and white patriotic sentiments but perhaps that is because we know the value of illusion, how it can help strengthen the weak and stimulate the weary. I think Shakespeare understood that very well and it is interesting to speculate on how he would have dealt with a life like Churchill's – what a work of theatre he could have made out of that.

Because I was staying at the Waldorf in the Aldwych, I was able to see the opening preparations for the state funeral on the morning of Saturday 30 January. I remember setting out to cross Waterloo Bridge for my rehearsals at the Old Vic and seeing the Israeli delegation led by David Ben-Gurion, who, because it was Saturday, the Jewish Sabbath, felt obliged to walk all the way from the Savoy to St Paul's Cathedral. The soldiers were being lined up as I passed and I knew this was going to be one of those events that the British do better than anyone else. This was confirmed that lunchtime when I went back to the Waldorf and watched a little of the magnificent ceremony on television. As I recrossed Waterloo Bridge for the afternoon rehearsals I saw the awesome sight as all the river cranes were dipped in salute to the sirens of the ships along the Thames while the barge brought Churchill's coffin to the South Bank. I dashed into Waterloo Station and was able to see the formal leave-taking before the great man's mortal remains were entrusted to his family for their journey to his final resting place near where he had been born.

Zeffirelli

200   At about this time ITV broadcast the second act of *Tosca* with Maria. Although I was not directly involved in the transmission, I did meet Lew Grade, who as well as being involved in television was at that time one of the world's major film producers. It was a meeting which was to foreshadow later major events. The cinema was much on my mind because I had never doubted that films were in some ways my ultimate goal; after all, I'd started out in films and, despite all the success in opera and theatre, I still had a deep-seated belief that they were somehow only a preparation for the world of the big screen. This was especially in my thoughts at that time because my London agent and friend Dennis van Thal was even more keen than I to see me work in films. Although that had been my original ambition the success of my theatrical work had pushed the idea to the back of my mind. Now when Dennis talked about cinema I tended to insist that I would have to keep on with what I was doing by filming a stage classic. So Dennis began to come up with suggestions from Shakespeare and that triggered off the idea of remaking the Douglas Fairbanks/Mary Pickford version of *The Taming of the Shrew*, which I had thought could be done amusingly with a couple like Mastroianni and Loren. But Dennis waved away the idea and insisted I think about British actors if I really intended to make my début in movies as a director of international stature. But with whom? Which couple had the stature to take on such a piece? It was only then that I realized that the answer was staring us in the face – the Burtons, though I hardly expected them to be willing to work with a new director. Dennis, however, saw a way in – he knew that Burton longed to get back into Shakespeare and might just be persuaded. Tenaciously, Dennis managed to track the famous couple to a hotel in Dublin, where they were staying during filming in Ireland. He arranged a meeting and I flew there on 6 February. My first impressions of Ireland were far from good: there were flags out and a general air of festivity and on enquiring I was told that people were still celebrating the death of the old enemy Churchill. People had actually been singing and dancing in the streets when the news first broke and some had kept up the jollity for over a week. It left me with a poor impression of the place and I decided to get my meeting with Liz and Richard over as soon as possible and return with all speed to London.

   I made my way to the appointed hotel wondering what I should find, and certainly my fantasies hardly approached the bizarre reality.

   While writing this book I have come to realize that there is an odd feature about my first encounters with the famous – Visconti, Chanel, Magnani: they always seemed to be throwing a tantrum in some dramatic way. Liz Taylor and Richard Burton were a new variation on this theme. When I first met them in their hotel suite in Dublin, pandemonium had broken out. Liz Taylor had somehow acquired a bush baby and the unhappy creature had not taken to its luxurious imprisonment. It had rampaged round the rooms knocking over lights and vases, had ripped curtains and cushions before finally taking refuge near the ceiling of the bathroom, clinging to one of the hotwater pipes. Various members of the hotel staff were dashing about trying to resolve the problem, Liz's maid had withdrawn, her face scratched and bleeding, while Liz herself stood at the door yelling at Richard to come and help.

Richard kept his back turned to the whole performance. Constantly sipping at his drink, he preferred to discuss Shakespeare with me. He certainly knew what he was talking about and that famous voice was mesmeric enough to ride above the cacophony emanating from the bathroom.

Liz came storming back into the drawing-room. 'Will you please stop talking about your damned Shakespeare and give me a hand.'

He slammed down his drink and yelled back: 'Will you please stop this bloody nonsense with that horrendous little monster and come and talk to this man. He's a superb Shakespearean director and you might be lucky enough to work with him one day. Can't you be more pleasant to him?'

'I don't care what he thinks of me. All I want is some help for my bush baby.'

On and on they quarrelled, like Katherine and Petruchio in *The Taming of the Shrew* ... I stopped, suddenly aware of what I was thinking: that they would be perfect in the roles if only they could be persuaded to do it. I could see that Richard would be no problem – he was desperate to get back into a classic part – it was Liz I would have to win over.

'Can't you help me?' she asked, looking at me with her hypnotic sapphire eyes. 'I couldn't get along with someone who doesn't like animals.'

I started telling her about my dogs and cats as I followed her into the bathroom. I looked at the poor terrified bush baby and could see at once that it was now exhausted. I had arrived at just the right moment, and wrapping a towel round my hand I reached up and prised it free. When I deposited the docile creature in Liz's arms I could tell that from now on she would take little persuading to go along with any plan Richard and I might dream up.

I returned to London elated and settled into *Much Ado*. The main pleasure for me in doing the play was that it brought me close to Larry Olivier, who had been my hero since I was a boy. Of course we had met before, when I was working at the Old Vic, but now that he was running the National I had a chance to get to know him better. It is strange, given how much I was in awe of the man who had been the Hamlet and Henry V of my youth, that I cannot for the life of me remember when or on what occasion we first met. It must have been at the time of *Romeo and Juliet* at the Old Vic and there had certainly been several encounters after that one, but what ought to have been that first unforgettable meeting has simply vanished

202 from my memory as if it had never occurred – or rather, as if we had always known each other, which was possibly wish-fulfilment on the part of my subconscious.

We had been preparing *Much Ado* for some time and I had tried to persuade Larry to be my Don Pedro, which he would have made into a memorable performance. He demurred as he now had a lot of administration to handle and was in any case contracted to play a certain number of major roles per season and, not surprisingly, he began to be very careful with his time and to hoard whatever free evenings he could. However, he rang me up, I think in Paris, while I was rehearsing *Who's Afraid of Virginia Woolf?* to suggest a suitable actor – the young Albert Finney. Young he might have been but *Tom Jones* had already made him an immensely successful international star and I assumed he would want the lead. I had forgotten that wonderful English ensemble tradition. We had already cast Robert Stephens and Maggie Smith in the leading roles and Larry was far from trying to change that, rather it was his intention to let Finney earn his passage in the company. Of course, in the end Finney had the last laugh when he almost stole the show.

At the first rehearsal I told everyone they were going to have fun: this was to be a *Much Ado* in Sicilian comedy style. I decided to make Finney a sort of jokey Spanish Don Pedro – we strapped him in a corset to keep him pompously rigid and gave him a cigar throughout rehearsals and he hammed it up superbly with a Spanish accent, making the character so striking that in the end he almost became the main attraction. But he wasn't alone; everyone in the company let rip as if relieved to be enjoying themselves after all the recent bout of depression that had struck the English stage. This was the only light relief in the National's rather heavy season – *The Seagull, A Long Day's Journey into Night, The Crucible, The Dance of Death* – it's a wonder the audience weren't committing suicide in the aisles. Our first night audience laughed so much that Penelope Gilliat had to be rushed to hospital after the performance – she was pregnant and had been shaking so much she gave birth shortly after.

Richard Burton came to see one of the performances. I wasn't there but he left a very nice note – 'I would give my right arm to work in a production like this'. Of course it was now up to me to see that he did.

Three nights after the opening of *Much Ado* the Paris opening of Maria's *Tosca* conducted by Georges Prêtre took place. I now commuted between the two capitals to check up on the productions, though I must admit that my heart was in London with my wonderful, vivacious team rather than in that hothouse atmosphere that always surrounded La Divina. But all Maria's eccentric ways were as nothing compared to the unbelievably insane behaviour of the cast of *Who's Afraid of Virginia Woolf?* That March I was again summoned to Paris by Lars, only this time things were really serious

So deeply were the two leads into their role of hating one another on stage that Madeleine had taken to physically assaulting Raymond whenever possible. The script calls for her to give him the odd shove and the occasional tap but she had begun to lay about her with a will. The poor man was getting hurt and she seemed impervious to all attempts to get her to calm down. Then one night it happened: pushed beyond endurance Raymond picked up a bottle on stage and smashed it over her head. The show was stopped and the theatre closed down till she recovered. It was the scandal of Paris and Lars and Ingrid were at their wits' end as to how to deal with it. Again I played the father confessor, listening patiently to all sides, but this time I sensed that perhaps it wasn't quite so necessary, and that Raymond Gérome's pre-emptive strike was about the best thing that could have happened. It was a somewhat chastened Madeleine Robinson who agreed to return after her wounds had healed. She also agreed to try to curb her temper. Of course, no one would deny that it was all wonderful for business: people kept coming back time and time again as no two performances were ever the same. There was hardly a word of Albee's original play left as the two swore at each other, getting ever more creative in the way they insulted and cursed. I sat watching one of the performances wondering how on earth it had got to that point, you really did think they were going to murder each other right there on stage. But I had to admit it did keep up the tension to a remarkable degree.

Having calmed them down as far as I could, I flew from Paris to New York. With the success of *Falstaff* the Metropolitan Opera wanted me to complete the circle and give them the first opera to open the new theatre at the Lincoln Centre. When Rudolf Bing first asked me, I was stunned; we had always had an excellent relationship and I'd done one of my best productions for him, but I, as a foreigner, hardly expected such an honour. I went to New York to watch the building going up. I wanted to be as familiar as possible with the elaborate stage equipment that was being installed under the supervision of Herman Krawitz, Bing's right-hand man and a brilliant theatrical organizer. Bing had chosen to open the new theatre with a new opera based on Shakespeare's *Antony and Cleopatra*. He asked me to write the libretto and design and direct the production. He also commissioned the music from the prestigious American composer Sam Barber. Given the subject and the scale of the occasion, I assumed that what he was planning to compose was something akin to *Aida* and I was all set to rise to the occasion with mammoth sets, a vast cast and sumptuous costumes – the sort of spectacle that would honour such an important event in America's cultural life. This turned out to be a dangerous assumption, but for the moment I was happily planning all manner of wonders with the extraordinary machinery that I had watched being installed.

While in New York I saw Callas singing *Tosca* at the Old Met. It was not

Zeffirelli

204 a particularly exciting production, but the New York audience was so pleased to have Maria back that there was a general air of good-will about the evening. They applauded her just for being Callas, which after all her years of fighting to win over audiences must have given her some satisfaction at last.

It was inevitably quite a glittering evening. The funniest thing was to watch all the glorious old ladies, sparkling in their diamonds, hanging about in the foyer trying to be the last to make an entrance before the lights went down; it must have been nerve-wracking for them: wait too long and all would be darkness, the great moment lost. One by one, they gave up, went in and were applauded to their seats. The last to hold out was Zinka Milanov, a great soprano of the 1950s and 1960s who was absolutely armoured with jewels. Seizing her moment, she entered and was greeted by a tidal wave of clapping and cheering. For a moment she walked on, graciously acknowledging what she took to be her right, but slowly it dawned on her that the applause was not for her. Glancing up, she saw entering a box the demure figure of the widowed Jacqueline Kennedy and knew, to her horror, that she had been upstaged.

Mrs Kennedy had come with the Bernsteins and Mike Nichols, the film director. After the opera, they went backstage to congratulate Maria. Given what was to come later, it was a fateful encounter.

I was more interested in Maria's performance than in all the surrounding antics. The Callas magic worked again, though it was clearer than ever that her voice was not at its best. I wondered how she would stand up to the revival of the Paris *Norma* and the final run of *Tosca* in London.

I began rehearsals for *La lupa* in Rome in May, so I was unable to be in Paris for *Norma*. Five performances were planned, but after the opening night on 14 May, when Maria apparently struggled to the end, it was suddenly announced that there would only be three more, the last being cancelled. I supposed I must have realized that there would be problems ahead with the move to Covent Garden, but for the moment I had enough on my plate trying to handle Magnani. She had been so long away from the live stage that she virtually had to relearn every element of the actor's craft. At least there were no problems over the role itself. Anna fitted perfectly into the part of the loose-living peasant woman cursed by the other women in her village, a sort of Carmen figure, who was probably the first of the anti-heroines.

She has a daughter, a quiet girl living in the shadow of this vibrant mother who she believes is more beautiful, more sexy than she is. Eventually the daughter finds a young man who loves her and wants to marry her. The mother is horrified to discover that this, of all the men in her life, is the one she loves – really loves. She decides she must get away and, after the wedding, she disappears into the Sicilian wilderness and becomes a wild creature, a lone She-wolf roaming the hills searching for peace. Several years on she can bear it no longer and returns for one last look. But then she realizes she will never get him out of her heart. She comes down to the village longing for death and in the end is killed by him. It is a very bitter tragedy and so full of passion that Puccini had once meant to make an opera of it. I used the same powerful image of the dark, hollow-eyed woman in the shawl that I'd had in *Cavalleria*. The photograph of Anna in that shawl, sombre and fierce, is one of the best production stills I know.

La lupa opened in Florence on 26 May at the Teatro La Pergola, the same theatre where I had first met Luchino all those years ago. There were problems: Anna could hardly project her voice as far as the back of the stalls, but none of that seemed to matter. To three generations of Italians Anna Magnani was a symbol of survival, the woman who fights against all the odds, who's always getting the rough deal but who soldiers on. She had been famous since before the war and there was a huge audience willing to put up with any drawback in order to see her again. And despite her problems of technique she did manage to communicate the power of the role. That night we knew that her come-back was assured, as was the future of our company.

We took both the plays to Paris for the Festival des Nations and although it was *Romeo and Juliet* that won the Grand Prix it was *La lupa*, or rather Anna, that caused most attention. It was impossible to get tickets for the opening night at the Sarah Bernhardt, though it was still difficult to hear her anywhere beyond the closest seats. But I could tell she was making progress; she was slowly but surely finding her way back to the theatre. She was an old trouper with all the survival mechanisms that that entails and she was working on her voice at every performance in order to conquer the problem.

Initially she had said she would only tour *La lupa* for three months as she didn't want to get stuck in theatre. The company went on to Zurich, Vienna, Warsaw, Prague, Moscow, Leningrad, before opening in Rome but by then Anna could not bear the thought of giving up the part and a further season was set up. In any case she had fallen for one of the actors in the company, always a good incentive. Eventually we had great difficulty in getting her to abandon the role three years later. I suspect she would have gone on doing it for ever. It was the perfect role for her and she never found another like it.

It was very satisfying for me to have contributed to saving her from the oblivion into which she had been shunted, but I was having less success with my other great lady. Just as Anna was struggling to master her projection before a Paris audience, Maria was entering the final rounds of her life-long battle with her voice. I should have known from the increasingly neurotic way she was behaving that there would be trouble with the

206   four remaining performances of *Tosca* for Covent Garden. Sure enough, a
the last moment she announced that she could not do them. This was bad
enough but to compound the damage the final night on 5 July was to have
been a Royal Command Performance for the Queen.

When Maria sent word she could not go through with them, panic broke
out at Covent Garden, where people had been queuing for nights to get
tickets and where preparations for the Royal reception were in full swing
People were also angered by photographs in the newspapers showing her
at parties and in nightclubs. David Webster went to see her in Paris and
begged her at least to do the Royal Command Performance. She was in a
state of absolute panic, it seems, but in the end she reluctantly agreed, and
I set about rehearsing Marie Collier, who was to be her substitute for the
first three nights.

As soon as Maria arrived in London I knew this would be the end. I
called all my friends – John Osborne, Penelope Gilliatt, Kenneth Tynan –
and told them to come to Covent Garden by whatever means, that I was
certain this would be the last chance to see Callas in an opera. I was right
She arrived for that evening weary of the whole business, exhausted with
the struggle between Maria the woman and Callas the *diva*, between her
will to dominate a part and 'the Voice'. She got through it respectably and
the audience was generous with applause, but that was it: without any
great crisis, no cracked notes or sudden temper, neither collapse nor glorious
performance, it was on a down-beat, fading note that Maria surrendered
the stage at last.

After her come-back in *Tosca* and *Norma* some of the more intelligent
critics had, while celebrating her return, urged her to look on the changes
in her voice not as a tragedy but as a new challenge. There are a whole
range of operas that do not tax the upper register in the way the major
Italian classics can. They rely, however, on great powers of interpretation
and that was Maria's strength. Regrettably she would never entertain these
counsels. Instead she continued to be preoccupied with her declining affair
with Ari and to look on any engagement as a hideous encounter to be either
wrestled with or avoided.

Since the assassination of the President of the United States in 196;
Onassis had made himself available to join the Kennedy clan, though who
knows when he first conceived the audacious notion of marrying the world's
most famous widow? We may assume that by 1966 he had at any rate
decided firmly against marrying Maria, though at that point he may have
seen no further than a sort of shuttle taking place between the two famous
women. But Maria herself must have begun to have more than vague
doubts even as she clung to that vapid society world to which Ari had
introduced her. That year she asked me to escort her to the choicest event
in Monte Carlo, the Red Cross Ball at the Casino, it being one of those

occasions that were deemed by Onassis to merit public duplicity about heir relationship. He himself escorted the redoubtable Maggie van Zuylen, her husband the Baron Egmont van Zuylen van Nyevelt (to give him his full honours) being wisely averse to such occasions. As a one-time Belgian diplomat he'd probably had enough of public conversation, but Maggie seemed to thrive on any sort of party. She was amusing and lively and always got the best out of everybody, though her talents were sorely tested that night. Despite the pretence, once their entrances on the arms of others had been duly noted, Ari and Maria sat at the same table. Surrounded by princes and duchesses, they carried on as usual: he talked about money, she about herself. There is something riveting about such single-minded self-obsession, but not for long.

'Come on, Franco,' said Maggie after a particularly tiring monologue. Let's get out of here, we don't belong.'

She led me into one of the vast gaming rooms in the Casino and up to a roulette table. She occasionally placed a small bet and then suddenly she reached over and asked for her winnings on a chip.

'Excuse me, madam,' said an old gentleman. 'You are mistaken. That bet is mine.'

'Nonsense,' said Maggie, and the croupier raked the money towards her.

She played for a while and then did it again. I was astounded. She was so convincing and I wasn't entirely sure she was cheating and nor were the other players, who simply backed down. In the end she managed to accumulate $2,000, half of which she rather over-dramatically stuffed down her cleavage. The other half she gave to me, presumably as my share of the loot.

No matter how much Maria appeared to want to sink into this sort of rich life and no matter how definitive that final *Tosca* had seemed, I was not prepared to let the greatest stage talent I have ever known slip through my fingers so easily. I felt strongly that this was the end so far as stage performances were concerned, at least for the foreseeable future, but I reckoned there were other possibilities. The knowledge that I was going to be making *The Taming of the Shrew* with Elizabeth Taylor and Richard Burton had radically changed my status. I was now a property in the cinema industry and there were signs that other offers were in the pipeline. Harry Saltzman had already suggested that I direct the life of Nijinsky for him with the recently defected Nureyev in the title role. He intended to approach Edward Albee with a view to his writing the script. My own feeling was that, if I could film Shakespeare, why not opera, and why not Callas in *Tosca*? Now that I was to work with Taylor and Burton, her earlier objections to my inexperience, which had led her to turn down a film of *La traviata*, were no longer valid.

Maria suggested I join her and Ari on the *Christina* so that I could discuss

208   the proposal with the great man himself. I knew what the attraction of the
movies was for Maria: it was her Audrey Hepburn fixation. Hepburn was
the ideal and she saw herself singing *Tosca* while posing like Hepburn in
Roman Holiday. Whatever the reason, I was delighted. To capture her
Tosca would surely be one of the artistic monuments of our time. Onassis
was apparently eager to help as were Lord Brabourne and Tony Havelock-
Allan of British Home Entertainment, the government-backed film
company. They went out before me and were already on the *Christina* when
I flew to Athens. I transferred to Onassis' private sea-plane, the one in
which his son was later killed, and flew out over the uncountable islands
until we spotted Scorpios. As its name implied it was the shape of a scorpion
with its limbs spreading into the sea. It was beautiful, set in the bluest
water, protected from the swell of the sea by a string of bigger islands. And
there we could make out, like a child's toy, the pure white yacht. We circled
and landed on the water and immediately a Chris-craft came across to us,
and to my surprise Onassis himself was aboard, all smiles and back-slapping.
He seemed in great good humour and eager to please. Given that I had
often made my views known on the subject of his treatment of Maria, this
was puzzling. My luggage was brought out, but he ordered his men to put
it in another boat and, taking control of the Chris-craft, he sped us away
for a tour round his island, just the two of us alone.

There was a marvellous late June sunset and Ari behaved like a man
who has a treasure to show to someone who can fully appreciate it. I had
been on the *Christina* before in Monte Carlo, but I had never seen Scorpios
I observed my guide, his eyes hidden behind those famous thick spectacles
It was easy to write him off as a moneyed brute, but suddenly he would
surprise you, as now, when he unexpectedly quoted Dante:

> *Era già l'ora che volge il desío*
> *ai naviganti e intenerisce il cuore.*

> (This is the hour that turns towards rest
> and breaks the hearts of men at sea.)

Why did he say it? Had he learned it parrot-fashion to impress? Was he a
genuine lover of poetry? I was never able to fathom the man, and was
already left with the uncomfortable feeling that he was a mass of con-
tradictions – hence his peculiar fascination for Maria, who was herself an
uneasy blend of artistic genius and *petit-bourgeois* sillyness.

We wove our way in and out of every cove. He would switch off the
engine so that we could hear the sounds of the island and the pleasant
murmur of water on the rocks. He had turned a barren rock into a garden
of Allah. Two tankers daily shuttled water from Ithaca. The place was a

riot of plants – here daffodils, there roses – and a zoo of domestic animals –
white sheep, pigs, turkeys. After his quotation from Dante Onassis said
nothing; he simply withdraw behind his glasses, looking at his island.
The *Christina* was a splendid ship, decorated in French eighteenth-
century style with fabulous furnishings, carpets, pictures. Each guest had
a suite named after a Greek island. Guests would gather on the main deck
for drinks and food – needless to say, the chefs were of the best – and it
was there that I joined John Brabourne and Havelock-Allan having drinks
with Maria.

'Franco darling,' she said, 'I was just telling John and Tony that I'm
only doing this because Ari insists I should go into movies. You know,
Franco, I've been through hell all my life, worked like a slave and look
what happened – Meneghini stole everything. So is it really worth it? I've
had everything an artist could wish for, yes. But if Ari insists I do it, I'll
do it, though I'd rather stay here and relax.'

The three of us looked at each other as she prattled on. She was capable
of keeping up a constant stream of nonsense, as if trying to convince herself
as much as anything, but while she was in full spate Onassis came on deck:
'Listen, darling, save your voice for when you go on stage, because that's
when you certainly need every bit of it.'

Marie fell silent while we shuffled with embarrassment. It was to this
that the great love affair had descended. We were all suddenly genuinely
frightened for her. One had heard rumours of how these Greek tycoons
treated their unwanted women, stories of violence and even murder.

We went in to dinner and Maria quickly recovered her former manner.
She indicated the sumptuously laid-out table; the elegant china, cutlery
and glassware; the attentive servants.

'You see, Franco, I have all this, why should I bother with work. Don't
you think I look pretty in this dress, and what about my suntan? You
know, darling, for years they wanted me as white as the camellias in
Traviata, but can you play Violetta all your life?'

John, Tony and I steered the conversation round to filming *Tosca*. She
continued to say that she didn't need work, but it was clear that the idea
appealed to her immensely. More difficult to gauge was Onassis's attitude.
He was supposed to be willing to back the project, yet now that we were
getting down to discussing it he seemed to be rather ambiguous. I was
suddenly aware that it could all be another of his vicious tricks: to lead
Maria on and then let her down.

The main difficulty for us was that Herbert von Karajan had acquired
the film rights to the opera and was insisting on producing it with his
company. This would never tie in with the Covent Garden production,
which we wished to use as the basis for the film. Nor was it likely that he
and Maria would work together. They had done one or two productions in

210   the past including a memorable *Lucia di Lammermoor* at La Scala, but
Karajan was on record as describing Maria's voice to be like a knife scraping
across a plate; he said it gave him goose pimples. He had also recently
compiled a list of the greatest singers he had worked with for a magazine
article and he had left out Maria. That was the sort of thing *La Divina* did
not overlook and never ever forgave.

'Two *prima donnas* in a show are too many,' she said. 'If Karajan is
involved then I'm not interested.'

Sensing a battle, Onassis suddenly began to take an interest. 'We'll buy
him out,' he said, as if the conductor of the Vienna State Opera and the
head of the Salzburg Festival were rival shipping magnates.

We three visitors were debating the possibility of Karajan, a notably
difficult person, surrendering his rights. John Brabourne, with his international connections, thought we had some room for manœuvre. All at
once, there was a quite unexpected outburst. Maria and Onassis had been
talking together in Greek as they now did constantly, when suddenly he
yelled something at her with almost a snarl of rage. While the three of us
watched in blank amazement, a full-scale Greek row took place – shouting,
arm-waving – until Maria burst into tears and ran from the deck.

Without turning a hair, Onassis amiably resumed our conversation. He
poured brandies and a fairly heavy drinking session began. I forget what
we discussed, probably nothing, and eventually we all made our excuses
and left Onassis at the table, the decanter before him.

I tiptoed down the corridors to Maria's suite. When she let me in I saw
how swollen her eyes were from weeping. She fell into my arms and sobbed
her heart out. When the first spasm ended she started to talk through the
racking sobs, telling me about Ari, how he was the first to make her feel
like a woman, the first really to make love to her, and how afraid she was
of losing him.

'I am', she said, 'quite simply at his mercy.'

I comforted her as best I could and left her calmer but still miserable.

The next morning Onassis announced that the project must go ahead
and that he would give me $10,000 development money. It was a sign of
how he viewed the project. The pre-production costs of a film run to
hundreds of thousands of dollars; by giving so little, he could appear to be
promoting Maria, while actually ensuring that nothing happened.

I was, however, so determined to make the film that I got Renzo Mongiardino to begin designing the sets and Marcel Escoffier the costumes while
I began to write the script with Suso Cecchi d'Amico and to research the
locations. One day a rather shady-looking Greek called to see me and
handed me a bag containing $10,000 in cash, all very hush-hush, no receipt
nothing. We had, of course, already spent it, and the lot was handed over
to those who had been setting everything up.

Then the axe fell. Karajan flatly refused to part with the rights of *Tosca*.
I called Maria and told her the bad news.

'So send me my money back,' she said.

'What money?' I asked. 'You know where it's gone – production petty cash. $10,000 was nothing and, in any case, it was Onassis's money.'

'It was my money,' she said, her voice rising. 'He made me pay it out of the little I have left.' Then she was screaming. 'Give me my money back, give it to me, you understand?'

It was the other Maria, the woman who hoarded cash with Meneghini; the Maria who resented paying her father's hospital bills and who loved shopping in Woolworth's. I told her that I was out of pocket on the project and could not nor would not cough up the ten thousand dollars. She slammed the phone down and that was that. My attempts to help her and save her for her art had ended in acrimony and estrangement. It was a miserable feeling, which clouded a period that should have been full of pleasant anticipation.

I decided to cheer myself up at the expense of my sworn enemies, the Rome theatre critics. Just after that trip to the *Christina, Romeo and Juliet* had opened at the Teatro Quirino in Rome and had been mercilessly savaged by that bunch of cretins. On my arrival back from Greece it was the turn of *La lupa* and I was in such a belligerent mood that I decided to have some fun. I refused to send out any press invitations for *La lupa* and I let it be known that, if any critic wanted to see the play, he or she would have to pay for a seat like anyone else. They were incensed at this insult and, instead of just buying tickets and then savaging the play, they decided to attempt a sanction. They held a meeting and issued a press release saying they would refuse to review any play of mine in the future. If they had had any sense they would have realized that the resulting publicity would have the opposite effect to that which they intended. The run of *La lupa* was a sell-out, with tickets going for incredible prices on the black market. When the run had to end, because the theatre was being redecorated and we had to move to Milan, I took full-page advertisements in the papers thanking the Roman audience and especially the Roman critics, whose silent co-operation had made the success of *La lupa* so overwhelming. They never forgave me. They never will.

THIRTEEN

Shakespeare Backwards

At forty-two I hadn't caught up with myself, I hadn't stopped to catch my breath for five minutes – I had had little sense of time going by. Even allowing for vanity, I still looked good and there were certainly plenty of people around to tell me so. I suppose I thought I would always be young and attractive, and that life would continue to offer me new and exciting things to do. If this sounds insufferably arrogant then my only excuse is that all the evidence pointed that way. After all, you only have to imagine what it was like for someone who only a few years before had been squeezed into tiny hotel bedrooms, turning out opera sets for a miserable, insufficient fee, to find himself being flown by personal jet to Gstaad for an afternoon's discussion with Liz and Richard about our film. In fact, there was quite a lot of jetting around as the project was finalized, though it wasn't all champagne and caviare.

Richard was adamant that we should produce something worthy of Shakespeare. At one point he asked me to go and see his old schoolteacher Philip Burton, the man who had taken him under his wing and nurtured his talent, even giving the aspiring young actor his name. Philip was a Shakespearean scholar and Richard's idol, and the point of the meeting was to ensure that nothing we were planning would offend the Shakespearean purists. I wondered if I was going to find myself arguing with some sort of dusty Welsh bookworm with petty notions of how the Bard should be preserved but thankfully I found a charming, well-informed gentleman, only too happy to listen to my ideas and quite entranced by everything we were planning to do. I found him most helpful in clearing up some of the difficulties I had with the denser parts of the text and I left feeling how lucky Richard had been to have had such a father-figure to lean on when he was starting out.

If Richard looked on our forthcoming film as a return to his cultural roots, Liz was more prosaic. *The Taming of the Shrew*, though prestigious, was just another film for her, and this difference gave rise to some of their more epic squabbles. Seeing himself on a higher thespian plane, Richard would often refer to her as a Hollywood Baby.

212   'A golden baby,' she would retort.

'Well, you certainly like gold and you're as plump as a baby.'
'There are countries where they like women with a little meat on them.
If they hadn't banned my films because I'm pro-Israel, those Arabs would
be drooling over me. Just take care I don't meet a rich sheikh.'

It was all fairly good-natured, with her having a dig or two at his constant
drinking, but underneath there were hints of bitterness – his resentment of
her as representing the Hollywood that was destroying him and her dislike
of his British actor's superiority. Yet all this was nothing beside what was
clearly a great passion that they shared.

He was so keen to make the film that in the end they put up most of the
money and the film was billed as a Burton-Zeffirelli production.

As 1965 ended, preparations intensified. My dear friend, the writer Paul
Dehn, had come to Castiglioncello that summer to work on the film script
and I was busily engaged in putting together the sort of team who would
make sure that the standards of production we Florentines had been setting
in the Italian theatre for the past ten years were transferred to the cinema.

There were other changes in my life as I prepared to make the quantum
leap from stage to screen, and probably the most helpful newcomer to our
'family' was a young English girl called Sheila Pickles. She had been
working for my London agent, Dennis van Thal, and, when she heard that
I needed a secretary-cum-personal assistant, she volunteered for the job.
She was the perfect counterbalance to my free-wheeling, disorganized Latin
spirit. Now that I was an international producer and soon to be a film
director more and more people were essential. I was, in effect, a small
business with offices and a staff, yet I still operated like a footloose kid,
never keeping records and still dashing about as if I'd just discovered the
thrill of big city life. That is until Sheila took on the onerous task of bringing
order out of chaos. That she did this without behaving like some dour old
harridan was the greatest joy of all. She knew how to have fun while
carefully prodding me on to the paths of order and action.

I suppose I ought to have been nervous at making my first major film
with two such superstars, but I knew the business of film-making from my
years with Luchino and my little effort with *Camping*. As for difficult
performers, there were my years with Callas and Magnani. No, Liz and
Richard didn't scare me, but it was more difficult to cope with their
entourage. They had a court of about twelve people, ranging from lawyers
to hairdressers, and this gossiping, opinionated set had to be mollified and
won over. They were unbelievably powerful, always whispering in each
other's ears, making it harder to reach any decision by their continual
gossip and innuendo. I always knew when this tribe was coming my way;
there was the telltale chink of gold bracelets and necklaces, and the distinct
jangling of chains as it approached.

We filmed in Rome at the new studios of Dino de Laurentiis, who was

Zeffirelli

214 tremendously helpful. We all felt the prestige of these two megastars being directed by an Italian in Italy. The fact that the whole film was shot in the studios gave it an air of unreality which matched the remoteness of the language. The magnificent sets were designed by Renzo Mongiardino and the costumes by Danilo Donati. This sparked off the first great battle with the Burtons' entourage. They had brought with them Irene Sharaff, a costume designer with a clutch of Oscars to her credit and a formidable lady, but not quite what was needed for the film we were making. To her Italy was a blur; it didn't matter where she got her ideas from, which city, which century, it didn't make much difference, as the film to her mind was an Italian fantasy. I soon saw that we were going to have a showdown.

Her worst mistake came with the very thing she ought to have concentrated on, the creation of the character of Richard – Petruchio. The man had a problem: he wasn't tall, had narrow shoulders and a large head. The only way to cope with this was to make everything larger than necessary, to give him loose, flowing costumes. Perversely, Sharaff dressed him in form-fitting dark outfits with tight vertical stripes and topped the lot with narrow shoulders and high pointed hats. He looked like Olivier in *Richard III*, an emaciated cripple. My attempt to make this point to her produced outrage amongst the courtiers, and provoked a storm of whispering.

Liz was loyally on Sharaff's side: 'Franco, this is an important artist, you must respect her.'

I went to Richard and tried to reason with him, explaining that I would always defer to his superior knowledge of Shakespeare, but in matters visual, especially when it concerned the costumes of my native country, he would be wise to listen to me. I knew he had not liked that tight black outfit, but Sharaff was Liz's protégée and he was unwilling to interfere.

What could we do? Shooting was about to begin. I called Danilo, who was in charge of all the other costumes; we summoned the seamstresses overnight and ran up five costumes for Richard in thirty-six hours.

On the morning of the first day's shooting Sharaff was on the set with all her costumes, but we had already hijacked Richard and persuaded him to try on one of ours. 'I don't give a damn,' he said. 'Just as long as it's light to wear.'

We put the first costume on him and he at once began to move, to gesture, to act, using the capacious sleeves as any instinctive actor would. He was happy because he felt right; the character of Petruccio was there.

'Good,' he roared in that amazing Burton voice, looking at himself in the mirror, 'I feel like a lion.' Before we knew it, he was striding on to the set.

Sharaff was speechless. She assumed that we had been secretly making the costumes for weeks instead of virtually overnight, as was the case. The eventual compromise was that Richard would wear Danilo's costumes, and Liz Sharaff's.

That was our sole major area of conflict, though it wasn't the only problem. The main difficulty was Italy itself. The two of them loved it, their beautiful villa, the attractions of Rome, the food and the company. They were having a high time, loving, quarrelling and partying. Later Liz told me it was their only real honeymoon and the best time in their lives. Regrettably for me, I was the killjoy who had to make them work.

The crux of my difficulties was that they were not synchronized in their habits: Richard was the staunch theatrical professional who turned up at 7.30 every morning, was dressed and made up by 9.15 and ready for the first take at 9.20. Unfortunately, we then had to hang around until nearly 11 am waiting for Liz, whose morning was given over to her famous face – skin massage, eyebrow-plucking or whatever. In her defence it must be noted that she is not called one-shot Liz for nothing. We only reshot anything for technical reasons, and to understand what that means it's necessary to realize that for many shots an average of fifteen takes is not unusual.

We'd work that way until 1 or 1.30 pm, and then came disaster – the lunch party in their dressing-rooms. The whole feast would stretch until 4 pm, when they'd saunter back for a couple of shots, inevitably the worst of the day.

I suggested that we work French hours, that is, we'd start at 12 noon, having eaten, and work through till 8 pm with only a tea-break at 5 pm. It was not an easy proposal, as Italians don't like French hours. The grips and others on the unit would have to set up in the morning anyway, and would then have to stay on till after 9 pm, which meant that they'd never see their families. We eventually compromised by starting at 8 am and finishing at 3 pm with no break. Liz didn't like it, but in the end she agreed.

The positive side of their relationship was the way each counterbalanced the other's lack of experience – his in film technique, hers in Shakespeare. He helped her interpret the role, and she showed hom how to play down his large, stagey style. Her great skill is the ability to achieve the maximum effect doing almost nothing except raise an eyebrow or highlight a moment with a slight nod. She truly understood the camera.

For my part I'd already decided to make use of Richard's expansiveness by opening the play out, as one can do on film. Thus, I had him chasing her around the great house and on the roof, and even added a dose of slapstick when they fell through the roof into the woolshed. It was all very Douglas Fairbanks, with lots of athletic action, yet never lost sight of its classical origins.

Then Liz surprised us all. I had assumed, as I imagine had Richard, that when we did the notoriously controversial final scene in which Katherine makes her act of submission not merely to Petruchio but on behalf of all women to all men, she would do it in the now accepted ironical way. The usual trick is for the actress to wink at the audience as much as to say, 'We all know who really has the upper hand, don't we?' Amazingly, Liz did nothing of the kind; she played it straight:

> ... Thy husband is thy lord, thy life, thy keeper,
> Thy head, thy sovereign; one that cares for thee,
> And for thy maintenance commits his body
> To painful labour both by sea and land,
> To watch the night in storms, the day in cold,
> Whilst thou liest warm at home, secure and safe;
> And craves no other tribute at thy hands
> But love, fair looks and true obedience;
> Too little payment for so great a debt.
> Such duty as the subject owes the prince,
> Even such a woman oweth to her husband;
> And when she's froward, peevish, sullen, sour,
> And not obedient to his honest will,
> What is she but a foul contending rebel,
> And graceless traitor to her loving lord?
> I am ashamed that women are so simple
> To offer war where they should kneel for peace,
> Or seek for rule, supremacy and sway,
> When they are bound to serve, love and obey. ...

And she meant it.

Full of that Welsh passion, Richard was deeply moved. I saw him wipe away a tear. 'All right, my girl, I wish you'd put that into practice.'

She looked him straight in the eye. 'Of course, I can't say it in words like that, but my heart is there.'

Coming at the end of the film, this helped to make up for a sadder moment earlier on. One day, while we were filming, news came that Montgomery Clift was dead. Liz was devastated; Clift had been one of her closest friends since they'd been young stars in *A Place in the Sun*, and later she'd virtually picked him up and got him going again after his terrible car accident.

Although I had nothing like her reasons for grief, I was saddened by the memory of the handsome young star on whom I had tried to model myself. I remember the hours of practice in front of a mirror trying to smoulder as he did. Courageously, she decided to continue, but a couple of days later she suddenly burst into tears in the middle of a scene. As Richard held her close, he explained that it was about then that Monty's funeral would be taking place in Los Angeles. She had wanted to go, but such a rupture in the schedule was unthinkable to a professional like Liz. Even that day, after her sobbing had died down, she went on the set. By one of those awful coincidences, we had been shooting one of the main comedy scenes, where Petruchio is bringing back his tamed wife to her father and they stop at a fountain to let the horses drink. They are joined by another character and there is a lot of idiotic fun about the moon, the stars and the sun, as Petruchio gets Kate to agree to anything he says, no matter how ludicrous. As usual, one-shot Liz did the whole thing perfectly and gave us one of the funniest scenes in the whole film.

For all the superstar grandeur, the party-going and the flamboyant quarrelling with Richard, Liz was an observant, sensitive person, quick to notice when those around her were having problems. Much as I tried to hide it, she soon guessed that all was not well with me. Since my break from Luchino, I had led a pretty carefree life with occasionally a deeper commitment, but now I had made the classic error of falling in love where there was no possibility of its being returned. This is a humiliating, wretched feeling most of us experience at some time, and Liz, unbeknownst to me, decided to see if she could put matters right. You may imagine the surprise of the person involved to receive a phone-call from the most famous woman in the world with an invitation for a drink, and then to receive a sort of Agony Aunt's counselling session. But Liz was no blind romantic: when she told me what she had done, she also made it clear she thought it was hopeless and handed me a set of gold cufflinks with two cupids in turquoise for 'my blue-eyed boy'. I still treasure them.

The person Liz and Richard loved most was Aunt Lide. In fact, she was one of those responsible for the lunchtime feasts; she would send over Richard's favourite dishes, particularly Tuscan tripe or the soup with vegetables and beans that he adored. A production car would travel between our home and the studios bearing these treats, for Richard had a passion for simple domesticity quite belied by his roaring-boy image.

Liz soon saw that my aunt loved a small white Pekinese she had. They are extremely rare and Liz had my assistant Sheila go to great lengths to find one for her, eventually tracking down a specialist kennels in England. She was rich enough to hand out diamonds as presents, but she was also generous enough to want to put thought and effort behind her gifts, and my aunt certainly treasured the little white dog.

With two stars such as the Burtons I can hardly be said to have had much influence over the cast except in one case. Michael York played some of the small parts in *Much Ado*, notably that of a Sicilian in a black wig and moustache; singing, dancing and generally clowning around. Despite the smallness of his roles, I could see that the boy had real talent, and there was a good-looking freshness about him that I knew would gain him a following. When I asked Larry Olivier if he had any plans for Michael, he said he was going to let him simmer for a while. That used to be the National Theatre policy: Olivier would pick talent at a series of really tough

218   auditions, and then give the kids a chance to develop. Nowadays, when some tiro plays Hamlet in his local theatre company, he thinks he can never go back to lesser roles, but under Olivier he carried a spear for a year or two.

Nevertheless, I believed that Michael was ready for bigger things and my mind turned to the role of Lucentio, the young man whose visit to Padua and whose desire to marry Katherine's young sister is the opening of *The Taming of the Shrew*. It was a crucial role, where a foot wrong would cripple the film from the start. We tested three or four actors, including Michael, and I agonized over my decision. Eventually, I took Richard along to see the rushes and his reaction when he saw Michael was ecstatic: 'My God, that boy's good. What are you waiting for? Take him.'

I was overjoyed, it was what I wanted to hear. I shall never forget when I told Michael, who was only twenty-two or twenty-three, and his eyes shone with happiness. He was a breath of fresh air in the part and his career was well and truly launched.

We filmed from the end of March until June and during the shooting I took my two stars to the reopening of *La lupa* at the Quirino Theatre in May. In June we were invited to the home of the Princess Pignatelli to meet Robert and Ethel Kennedy. They were a charming couple and he seemed genuinely interested in the problems confronting young people in the 1960s.

Our group went on to dinner and then a night-club, until Richard began to get irritated by the noise. We accompanied the Kennedys to their hotel and it was on the way back that the most extraordinary competition began, I don't know how. The two men, Burton and Kennedy, began to compete as to who could out-recite the other in Shakespeare's sonnets; it was an astonishing feat as they both had quite remarkable memories. They continued reciting as they got out of the car and walked into the lobby of the Hotel Eden, but it was then that Richard delivered the *coup de grâce* – he threw back his head and using all the force of that amazing golden voice he recited the fifteenth sonnet backwards, starting at the final word and ending on the first. We all stood dumbfounded at this insane achievement and Robert Kennedy graciously conceded defeat. Liz, who until then had shown little interest in the matter, was suddenly radiant with pride. 'Isn't it awful', she said, 'to have to tolerate this monster?'

Towards the end of filming Liz, Richard and I decided to have a celebration and to indulge a common passion, football. We had a television brought on the set so that the whole crew, Italian and British, could watch the historic World Cup Final between Britain and West Germany. What an occasion, and what passions were unleashed. It soon became clear that the Italian referee favoured the British, and a certain amount of booing broke out, in which Richard and I joined. Liz was furious. She may have adopted America and converted to Judaism, but at heart she was and is an unthinkingly patriotic Englishwoman.

'How can you side with the Germans?' she snarled. 'After what they did in the war.' It was hopeless to point out that this wasn't Arnhem but a game at Wembley; like many others in that stadium, Liz saw it as a simple extension of history.

The main filming was now over, though a slight delay meant that I had to leave for New York to prepare for the reopening of the Met with some covering shots still to do. As these were not particularly difficult, Richard gladly undertook to direct them himself. I no sooner arrived in America than I was plunged into a series of crisis meetings. I had already had premonitions of disaster when early sections of the score of Sam Barber's new opera had arrived in Rome and I had asked an elderly maestro to play them on the piano for me. I had at first thought it was the man's advanced years that was making the music so slow, but when I pointed this out, he insisted that that was the correct speed. As each new section arrived, it became increasingly clear that Sam was writing a pleasant chamber piece and not at all the grand epic we had all been anticipating. It began to appear as though it was not going to be suitable for such a big night. I had already expressed my doubts to Rudolf Bing before I left for America, but I arrived to find that the composer had made few changes, being determined to do it in this small-scale way. As rehearsals got going, it became increasingly obvious that the grandiose settings we had devised would be totally at odds with the music, and a further series of crisis meetings was held. I pointed out that the first-night audience at the opening night of the opera house in Bayreuth hadn't liked *Tristan*, so what chance did we have? But the others merely laughed. At the end of August I suggested to Bing that we move the opera to later in the season and open the House with a gala evening crammed with as many international stars as we could commandeer – there was just enough time to organize it. In any case, I argued, the opening-night audience weren't coming for the opera, they were coming to flash their jewels. But Bing wouldn't hear of it, he couldn't bear the thought of disappointing Sam and the cast, who were so looking forward to the honour of launching the new theatre.

Rehearsals were hellish, like cracking a whip over a dead horse. We also had serious technical problems due to conditions in the new Met, the worst of which concerned the revolving stage. I had designed my entire second act around this, but it broke during rehearsals and needed months to repair. I therefore had to reconceive entirely the whole act with its battles, pyramids and elephants. I worked harder on *Antony and Cleopatra* than I had done over the spectacular *Aida* at La Scala. We opened on 16 September and, worse than being simply tedious or inept, there were actually places where it was unintentionally funny: during the battle of Actium we had a

220   vast revolving golden pyramid, six barges, twelve horses, four elephants,
one hundred and twenty Romans with a huge crowd of other players all
milling around to the thin reedy music of two clarinets. The audience
giggled and who can blame them, it was ludicrous. I stayed in New York
for the second performance in order to keep up the spirits of the cast, but
it was clear that so inept a production was doomed and sure enough the
Met quickly threw in the towel and cancelled the run. I'm happy to be able
to say for Sam Barber, who was a subtle, gentle person, that the opera has
since been revived in Spoleto as a chamber work, at which level it was a
deserved success. Unfortunately for us, it was hardly the great spectacle
we had needed for such an important night.

The nicest thing to come out of the whole business was a telegram
saying: 'If you have to fail, do it on a grand scale. You did it. Bravo.
Congratulations. Liz and Richard.'

With relief I returned to Rome to begin editing *The Taming of the Shrew*,
but I'd no sooner got under way than another disaster struck, though this
time far more tragic than a mere first-night flop.

It was six in the morning on 4 November when my sister Fanny called
me at home to say she was a virtual prisoner in her house because the Arno
had burst its banks and Florence was flooded – a catastrophe of apocalyptic
proportions. I tried to calm her as best I could, then dressed and drove to
Florence at once to see what I could do.

I made a wide detour, avoiding the valley of the Arno, and approached
the city from the higher ground to the north. Looking down on it was
incredible; Florence had become a sort of Venice. I have to admit that at
that distance, with the early morning sun reflected on the water, the scene
was eerily beautiful. But, when I abandoned the car and began cautiously
to make my way through the outskirts, the picture was very different. The
sewers had burst and, because it was November, everyone had stocked up
with heating oil, which had been flushed from the tanks to add to the
filthy torrent. Cruelly, earlier heavy rains had caused the river bank to be
reinforced with sandbags so that the flash flood was perfectly channelled
through the city until it reached the Ponte Vecchio. This wonderful old
bridge, which even the Germans had spared, was now the city's downfall,
because its famous span of shops and houses acted as a dam and forcing
the waters back across the city. The surge overturned cars and swirled
them through the streets, smashing through lower windows and doors, and
carrying oily garbage into churches, libraries, palaces and museums.

The flood was still in full spate when I arrived, with cars crashing down
sidestreets and wave upon wave of water forcing its way over the barricades.
I realized at once that it would be possible to film it, either as a record or
more positively as a way of showing the outside world what was happening
to the city so that we could raise help. I telephoned the president of the

national television corporation, the RAI, and asked for his authority and help to film. I made my way to the local office of RAI and found a film crew waiting for me. I immediately commandeered a small rowing-boat and we set off. *En route* we were joined by the British journalist Sidney Edwards, who edited the arts page in the *Evening Standard* and was a great lover of Italy and its culture. We also found some freelance television people who were able to help out. Thus we were able to record the flood virtually as it happened and capture the extraordinary scenes of devastation. It was a week before the water subsided, and we made an extensive record.

I visited my family whenever I could and met old friends who were able to fill me in on the human side of the tragedy. Miraculously, almost no one had been killed. A few old folk had died from shock, but, given the scale of the disaster, this was minor. The real tragedy was economic. Naturally, the world saw the ruined art works, the oil-stained Madonnas and the perished volumes, but the Florentines witnessed the destruction of their livelihoods.

Over 6,000 shops were destroyed, most of them packed with goods for Christmas. Countless people had their homes and cars wrecked wihout any possibility of insurance covering this so-called act of God.

That first week was bad, but when the water went down it became worse. Then we saw the extent of the horror – the line of oil round every sculpture, the living-room with a dead cat and a child's toy side by side, the priceless family treasure in pieces, the Renaissance fresco smeared with glutinous filth. A friend of mine, an artist, had kept the work of a lifetime on the ground floor of his house because of an injured leg which prevented him from using the stairs. He lost all his paintings, everything he had ever done. He was sixty years old and he never painted again.

When the water finally receded, there were the most amazing cameos: a jeweller and his entire family scrabbling in the black mud trying to find the missing gold from his shop; an old lady sitting in a battered armchair as if on the surface of the moon; a priest saying mass surrounded by incalculable losses to the artistic heritage of mankind.

Of course, the tragedy drew the world to us, not merely in the form of the huge and generous financial aid but also the unbelievable stream of elderly professors and concerned young people, art-lovers and Italophiles with a vast knowledge of Italian cultural artefacts and how to restore them, and of those who just thought they should lend a hand. We filmed them at work: ordinary people carefully helping the experts to lift down the Cimabue Madonna, and hitchhikers and librarians delicately blowing talcum powder into the priceless volumes in the National Library. They were wonderful and we Florentines will never forget them.

There were risks of infection from the sewage and oil, but the young kids took this in their stride, sluicing theimselves down with alcohol brought in by units of the Italian army which had been despatched to provide shelter

222 and supplies for the helpers. Despite the sorrow, there was also an air of purpose: people of all sorts, nationalities and backgrounds doing an unequivocally good act. There was an air of freedom about it all. I remember seeing a young girl making love with a young soldier near the tomb of Michelangelo in Santa Croce, happily deconsecrated at the time – it seemed quite beautiful, though not entirely appropriate. Just the year before, Joan Sutherland had sung the *Messiah* there and, as I turned to leave them to each other, I seemed to hear the music echoing round the basilica.

The most tragic episode I witnessed was the loss of the Crucifix by Cimabue, the greatest individual disaster caused by the flood.

A group of students and volunteers gathered at the foot of the crucifix in the convent of Santa Croce as the waters gradually receded. The crucifix, one of the treasures of Florentine Gothic art, had been ravaged by the water and most of the paint had flaked away from the wood, but the tiny pieces were miraculously still there in the mud below. The students rescued most of the paint flakes and religiously laid them on a piece of metal sheeting they had found.

Later soldiers and firemen arrived to find the place deserted; they were equipped with high-pressure waterhoses, with which they had been ordered to clear the mud. Quickly and cheerfully they began to clear everything, and one of them grabbed the metal sheet on which the priceless fragments lay and used it to scrape mud off the floor. I arrived just as the pieces had been scattered once more over the floor and, before I could stop them, the firemen turned on their hoses and flushed one of the greatest examples of human genius literally down the drain.

One person who of course came to help was the very man who had already done so much to save Florence – Frederick Hartt. In the years since the war, when I had worked with him in Livorno trying to save the Medici harbour buildings, he had become an internationally recognized expert on Renaissance art. Now he was again to prove invaluable to our city and he agreed to take part in my film.

When I took the film back to Rome, I knew we would be able to make a stunning documentary. When I saw Richard Burton again and he asked me if there was anything he could do to help Florence, I told him there was, he could be the narrator. He came immediately and set to work. The film went out on 4 December, exactly one month after the disaster, and was quickly sent around the world. In the end it helped raise over $20 million for the city, its treasures and its people. Most went on restoring our glorious works of art, but the citizens too were given something to cover their losses. A subsidy was provided to Fiat to provide ten thousand cars, but more important was the money spent in a mammoth campaign of tree-planting in the hills around the city to rectify the soil erosion which was the original cause of the flooding. Hopefully, a disaster on that scale will never happen again.

I was immensely grateful to Richard and so were all Italians. His presence in the film added enormously to its effectiveness, and his eagerness to help was typical of the man. I am still sorry we never had the chance to work together again and that he seemed to waste such talent on so little. The waste appeared worse when one remembers that he was a man of considerable culture and learning, and was always enthusiastic and encouraging wherever there was a project he felt was worth while, even if he himself was not directly involved. He did everything he could to promote the idea of a film of *Romeo and Juliet*, even though there would be no part in it for him. The idea came up while we were filming *The Taming of the Shrew*, for it seemed to all of us to be the only logical thing for me to do next. We were agreed that that youthful production at the Old Vic had somehow to be translated on to film for the vast international audience we felt sure would flock to see it.

Normally, today, there is quite a gap between films for a director. It usually takes a long time to set up the project, yet astonishingly there were barely three months between the release of *The Taming of the Shrew* and the start of work on *Romeo and Juliet*. Little credit for this goes to the moguls of the film business, who, as ever, had no sense of history at all. Despite the fact that the stage productions of *Romeo and Juliet* had pulled in an unexpected new, youthful public, the backers went on insisting that Shakespeare was bad box-office. Even after *The Taming of the Shrew* came out, they fell back on the argument that such success as it was having was due entirely to the appearance of Richard and Liz, and that as my interpretation of *Romeo and Juliet* implied that the leads would be played by two unknowns it was a recipe for disaster.

At first I had little hope of convincing them otherwise, and indeed my agents found almost every door closed to them in their search to find a producer. I was not too worried. I still had the offer to direct *Nijinsky* and, as 1967 began, I started seriously to discuss the project with Sam Spiegel. Unfortunately for us, much of the prospect for the film rested on whatever script Edward Albee might produce. There seemed little cause for worry here: following *Who's Afraid*, he had written the marvellous *A Delicate Balance*, which I was about to produce in Italy. What none of us knew at the time was that Albee was now struggling to develop a new style, a sort of theatre of the abstract, and his script was definitely in this new mode. His Nijinsky was a creature of dark despair. Of course, Nijinsky's story was a tragic one, the tale of the century's greatest dancer whose career was blighted by his mental problems, but Edward's script seemed to concentrate on particularly dark areas. It opened with a true event: the day when the dancer Serge Lifar tried to shock Nijinsky out of his madness by improvising

224   a ballet performance in the asylum in the hope that Nijinsky would join in. The result was awful, as the poor man lumbered round the room like a drugged bear, childishly imitating the polished movements of the young dancers. It was a powerful way to begin the depiction of a life so rich in talent, but unfortunately little else in the script lightened that aura of vile darkness. Sam and I both agreed that the project was doomed from the beginning – it was better to let poor Nijinsky rest in peace, at least for a while.

At the end of February *The Taming of the Shrew* opened at the Odeon Leicester Square with a Royal Command Performance and a week later in New York at a Gala Performance, to which Robert Kennedy came. I returned to open Albee's *A Delicate Balance*, and then went to Florence for my own private Italian launch of the film. My rather eccentric notion was to show it first at the Odeon in Florence, where all those years ago I had seen Olivier's *Henry V*. I insisted it be shown first in the English version, so that any remnants of the old English ladies, our *scorpioni*, would be able to enjoy it. Miraculously, some of those old girls were such survivors they were able to come, though most were by then in wheelchairs. Time had not diminished their appetite for whingeing about Italy, and before the lights were down, I was able to catch the remembered whisper of complaining voices – they did't like certain changes to the décor and the lighting in the cinema, the new fashions the girls were wearing were outrageous, and as for this idea of Elizabeth Taylor in Shakespeare, well, really! But as soon as the film had started I could sense that they were loving it. This was their Shakespeare. Of course there was the slight irritation of there being an Italian director – though, as a Florentine, not typically Italian – but as almost everyone else was English that could be overlooked. I wished them well and hoped the evening brought them joy and happiness. They were as precious to me as the ancient stones of my city.

Any idea that the success of *The Shrew* – and indeed it was an immense success – would lighten the task of raising the money for *Romeo and Juliet* was instantly dispelled when my agents reported that doors were still being closed in their faces. But Dennis Van Thal was not so easily thwarted. He eventually brought together John Brabourne and Tony Havelock-Allan of British Home Entertainment, who had been keen to produce my *Tosca* with Callas. Dennis completed the deal by putting me in touch with a remarkable man called Bud Ornstein, who was Paramount's head of productions in Europe. He was a fan of the English theatre and had seen my stage version of *Romeo and Juliet*. 'If this man can put one-tenth of the energy from that stage play on screen then we ought to do it,' he told Dennis. But his bosses in America were more than sceptical. They only agreed to let him have his way as long as the film was a no-risk low-budget affair that could recover its costs with an art-house audience and television sales. Paramount was owned by Gulf and Western; the moneymen set the financial limit at the derisory sum of $800,000. Determined to shoot the film at any cost, I rashly agreed.

Cinema has to be more cautious than the theatre because such huge sums of money are involved, and, even for a low-budget film like this, it was insanely risky not to have a big-name star somewhere on the billing. On top of that, the cinema with its huge close-ups exaggerates everything, and my principals would have to be extra beautiful and exceptionally talented to pull off so difficult a feat. There was certainly no lack of choice. Agents, mothers and fathers all pushed their clients, sons and daughters forward when they heard we were casting for the ideal Romeo and Juliet. Paramount weren't sure how to handle it. On the one hand they were worried about the idea of unknowns playing the lead in the film; on the other, they didn't know what to make of me since I appeared to be successful and to know what I was doing. Unable to cope with something so far from their experience, they left me to it for the time being. I tested various combinations of boy and girl, trying to find a pair who worked really well together.

The boy turned out to be less of a problem than I feared. Lila de Nobili, who was in London designing a production for Peter Hall at Stratford, told me to and look out for a young actor called Leonard Whiting. I did so, and, sure enough, he seemed ideal. He was beautiful in that Renaissance page-boy way that was revived during the 1960s; he could probably act; and, as was obvious when I met him, he was very ambitious.

The girl was more of a problem. I had seen Olivia Hussey early on in the tests. She had some talent, but she was unfortunately overweight, clumsy-looking and bit her nails constantly – hardly the delicate Juliet I dreamt of. My first choice was a really beautiful girl who stood out because of her sensational hair, a golden cascade that was her best feature. I called her back a month later for a second test, but, when she walked in, my heart sank. The unisex era was just dawning and she had had her golden locks trimmed to look like a boy's. I was almost in tears, not merely because I had lost my Juliet but also because she had lost her chance of a lifetime. When I asked her why she'd done it, all she could say was because her sister had. She begged me to let her wear a wig, but I knew she could never cope with the role in such an artificial way. (However, a director is not God, merely one of his many instruments, so perhaps this was all for the best for her in the long run.)

The other parts were less difficult. I cast Robert Stephens as the Prince with Natasha Parry as Juliet's mother, Pat Heywood as the formidable nurse, Milo O'Shea as the Friar and John McEnery as Mercutio. Michael York was delighted when I asked him to join us, though he was taken aback when I told him that I wanted him to play Tybalt.

'Not Romeo ... Mercutio?'

'No, Tybalt. But you won't regret it. Even with only twenty-four lines,

226   it will be a major role when you see what we will do.'

He agreed because he trusted me, and that left me with my last major headache, Juliet. In desperation I summoned back some of those I had earlier rejected and that was how I stumbled on the amazing transformation of Olivia Hussey. She was a new woman: she had lost weight dramatically. Her magnificent bone structure was becoming apparent, with those wide expressive eyes and her whole angular self. She was now the real Juliet, a gawky colt of a girl waiting for life to begin. I had my cast.

As often seems to happen when I'm about to begin a major project, I ran away to do something totally different; this time it was a curious trip to Egypt. The person behind this escapade was my friend Rosemary Kantzler, who had a stake in Ford Motors. The Ford Foundation had underwritten the opening of the new Met, and Rosemary had agreed with me that it was sad so much hard work had come to nothing. She was intrigued when I rather offhandedly suggested that we ought to have spent the money on a film of *Aida*. She liked the idea because it fitted into one of her pet schemes: what might be called the saving of Egypt. There were several powerful Americans who were saddened by the fact that Nasser's Egypt had been pushed into the Soviet camp over the Israeli question and who hoped that something could be done to improve Egypto-American relations. To someone like Rosemary the only avenue possible for such a move was the cultural one, and so she unexpectedly took me up on the idea of filming *Aida* with the proviso that this be done in Egypt. Naturally I was delighted and so, on 20 May, a group under Rosemary's leadership flew to Cairo. I was bowled over by the country, by everything from the expected beauty of the pyramids and the city of Cairo to the unexpected grace and charm of the Egyptians themselves. I was convinced from the start that *Aida* was a certainty. And then, a week after our arrival, I noticed something strange: there were suddenly no international newspapers on sale, only the local press. I whiled away my spare hours by visiting museums and writing postcards to friends, but, when I went to buy stamps, I found something very unnerving: what they sold me were large, gaudy stamps with the head of Nasser in the foreground and behind him a burning city. I asked the concièrge at the hotel what it was that was burning so brightly on the stamps and he promptly told me it was Tel Aviv. I nearly had a heart-attack. Had all this happened during the few days we were away visiting the pyramids? Ah, no, the man explained, that was what was *going* to happen soon. I went to Rosemary and once and told her I had the most terrible premonition. I suggested we should leave at once. We hastily assembled our group and caught the first – and – last plane back to Italy. The day after we returned, all hell broke loose as the Six-Day War began – though it was certainly not Tel Aviv that burned as a result of it.

We had assembled for work on *Romeo and Juliet* at the end of May, though not in the conventional way in rehearsal rooms. I had for some time been dreaming of getting out of the centre of Rome, which increasingly had come to seem dirty, crowded and inconvenient. Of course, I'd had fun there as a young man enjoying big city life with friends of my own age, but now I wanted something more open, which I could share with my increasing herd of pets. I had discovered a small estate, really a sort of park, on the outskirts of the city not far from the ancient Appian Way. The owner had built a group of pleasant country-style homes, each far enough away from the other to appear isolated, in effect lost amongst the trees and gardens. It was ideal; near enough to the city for work, far enough for the sort of country existence I now wanted. I rented first one house and then later another larger home, where I still live today. That May I moved my entire company: not just Aunt Lide and Vige but also the principals of *Romeo and Juliet*. There we all were, during the hot summer, living as if in a cheerful, busy commune; Olivia and Leonard rehearsing on the lawn; Nino Rota writing the music in the salon; Robert Stephens and Natasha Parry learning their lines or swimming in the pool – it was a dream world.

I was lucky to have my old friends Tony Havelock-Allan and John Brabourne involved. Tony was a very experienced film man, who had done a lot of work with Carol Reed and Anthony Asquith. Curiously enough, the latter's *Orders to Kill* had been based on a wartime story by Donald Downes, who knew him well, and the script had been produced by Paul Dehn, who had worked on my *Taming of the Shrew*. All rather incestuous.

I was grateful for the support of Tony and John as well as the loyalty of Bud Ornstein, who assisted in the arrangement of finance so that I could start building the sets at Cinecittà even before we were sure we had a cast. These were not to be on the same scale as those of the *Shrew*. Because of our limited funds, I had spent a lot of time searching for locations in Tuscany and central Italy for exterior filming. I wasn't sorry about this, as I welcomed the idea of doing something different and knew that we had some truly magnificent backgrounds to use.

Before we started shooting, there was a particularly good omen: Christine Edzard, one of Lila de Nobili's protégées, and Richard Goodwin, the associate producer of British Home Entertainment, who met for the first time during our 'commune', fell in love and later married. It seemed the perfect start to *Romeo and Juliet*.

We opened filming on 29 June in the beautiful town of Tuscania, about thirty miles from Rome; then we went to Pienza near Siena and thence to Gubbio. We had one week's summer break in August and then went on filming until the middle of October. Although that is a fairly average filming schedule, it is still a long time to be thrown together so intimately with a group of people, and of course there were the inevitable tensions.

I found myself in the role of a father to the kids, trying to help them off

228 screen as well as on. Olivia needed this more than anyone else as she came from a broken home and was looking for a father-figure; she responded beautifully to my direction. By the same token, Leonard was the typical teenage boy trying out his ego. He always had to be allowed to do it his own way first and I had to be patient, only stepping in when he stumbled. It was a struggle. He was frightened of seeming to be my puppet in front of the others and was over-keen to remind us that he had had some experience. This was exacerbated by the fact that I never needed to tell Michael or John McEnery, who was Mercutio, what to do. Leonard chafed at this until I pointed out firmly that they were far more experienced actors than he and that he had better stop making comparisons, which in the end were unfavourable to himself. That aside, his looks were perfect for the role; he was the most exquisitely beautiful male adolescent I've ever met.

For his part Michael was having a wonderful time. A photographer called Pat had come from the *Sunday Telegraph* to do a story on us and – another good omen for *Romeo and Juliet* – the two of them were soon inseparable. They eventually married and have always made a wonderful couple, with her doing much to promote his career. I have more than a soft spot for Michael, I love and admire him. He has been in most of my films and I know of no one better to work with.

As soon as I had some rushes I quickly put a couple of sequences together and showed them to Richard and Liz.

'I wish I was young enough for this,' she said. She was truly moved by Olivia's performance and the energy of the whole cast.

'You've got problems with the verse,' said Richard. 'But perhaps it doesn't matter – you're probably right. It certainly looks great.'

My real problem was more prosaic. My pathetic budget had run out and we were just half-way through. The only thing to do was to throw myself at the feet of Charlie Bluhdorn, the head of Gulf and Western and therefore Paramount. He was no movie-maker and notoriously unsympathetic to the problems of directors, but only he could authorize more funds.

He made a visit to Rome, where a screening of my first cut sequences was arranged, and I awaited the great man's arrival with some trepidation as our future was in his hands. He was a boisterous fellow and, as I found later, very lovable in his crazy way. He burst in with his entourage and never stopped barking orders and yelling down the telephone to Hollywood. I suppose he meant well, and he had a reputation for trying to beef up the film business, but what was going on on in front of him was obviously not within the range of his experience. He constantly turned to talk to his aides about other matters, the telephone rose and fell; *Romeo and Juliet* passed unheeded. My heart sank then suddenly a thin, reedy voice struggled to make itself heard.

'Will ya shad-up, Daddy?'

Everyone fell silent, it was Bluhdorn's son Paul, who was being taken round Europe by his father. He was the exact opposite of his progenitor – small, thin, bespectacled, with a teeth-brace, aged about fourteen or fifteen. Bluhdorn was obviously impressed by his son's anger.

'D'ya like this?'

'Sure.'

'He likes it,' said Bluhdorn in a shocked voice to the others. Then, turning again to Paul, he asked, 'D'ya understand it?'

'Sure.'

'He understands, well can ya beat that! An' I thought we were gonna haf to dub it.'

From then on he watched it in silence, or rather he half watched the film and half watched his son. By the end of the few scenes the boy was in tears, he thought it was wonderful.

And that was it: all because of the kid the money we needed was found. The picture was finished for a mere $1\frac{1}{2}$ million. But the punchline was even better; it eventually grossed $50 million, the highest ratio of investment to earnings in the history of the studio. It virtually saved Paramount. Bluhdorn had been on the point of closing down the studios because of all their recent flops, but my Shakespeare film kept them afloat and spread confidence and excitement once more. They went on to make *Love Story* and *The Godfather*. But no one ever remembered Bud Ornstein, whose faith in me had made it possible. There was one of those periodic corporate reorganizations and he was no longer needed, but that's Hollywood.

One by-product of the filming was my first chance to work with Laurence Olivier. While we were shooting, he was on a neighbouring sound stage making *The Shoes of the Fisherman* with Anthony Quinn as the Pope. Naturally he felt an almost proprietary interest in any film of a Shakespeare play. The contrast between the rather boring film on which he was working and the glorious text we had at our disposal obviously affected him. Eventually he asked me if there was any way he could join in, and I, delighted at the chance, asked him if he would voice the prologue.

'Of course,' he said. 'But isn't there anything else?'

I think he would have played Romeo if he'd thought there was half a chance. In the end I got him to dub Lord Montague, who'd been played by an Italian with a thick accent. By now unstoppable, Larry insisted on dubbing all sorts of small parts and crowd noises in a hilarious variety of assumed voices. The audiences never knew just how much of Laurence Olivier they were getting on the soundtrack of that film.

Even in my most self-confident moments I could never have predicted the enormous success of *Romeo and Juliet* with audiences all over the world. From the Bronx to Bali, Shakespeare was a box-office hit. The effect on me was stunning. It made me a lot of money, transforming me from someone

230   who'd always lived at the limits of his income to someone who could be
described as rich, and it elevated me (if that is the word) from being a
European celebrity to someone who was famous internationally. Innumerable interviews and television appearances came in the wake of the film's
opening in country after country. With my secretary Sheila I trailed around
with Olivia and Leonard from city to city, from press conference to television studio. I knew that I had crossed over from one state to another,
that in ways I could not yet foresee I would now operate on a different
plane.

Now is the time to voice another of my superstitions – not an especially
unique one, as I think it's probably the most commonly held of all – that
a run of good luck is often followed by a period of bad. The film opened in
America in September 1968, where it had its greatest success – but then
the bad news came. That September Aunt Lide had gone home to Florence,
and friends called me to say that she had collapsed in the street. I went at
once and was told the appalling news that she had known she had cancer
for some time, but had refused to let anyone tell me while I was enjoying
that moment of triumph. She had collapsed before, but that was at a
dinner-party with close friends who had been able to take care of her. I
find it impossible to write down what I felt. It is enough to remember that
of the three women who took care of me she was the longest-lasting of my
'mothers'. She had convinced my mother to give me life, had saved me
when I was alone and had seemed all that stood between me and that 'no
name' illegitimate state. I was consumed by an irrational determination
that she would never die. I brought her back to Rome and put her in the
Salvator Mundi Hospital, where I was told she would have the finest
specialists. They informed me that she had an incurable cancer, but I
flew to New York to see Bill Cahan, a friend who was an internationally
acknowledged cancer expert, and arranged to take her there to see him.
However, when I got back to Rome, everything seemed tinged with foreboding. One morning we missed one of the dogs, Oliver, a little Peke,
the mate of Liz's gift. He was eventually discovered drowned. Mystery
surrounded the event and made us all more miserable than ever.

Aunt Lide could not be moved and New York was out of the question.
Of course, I knew she was dying, but I would not accept it. It was impossible
to concentrate on the idea of a film. Throughout the last months of 1968
projects came and went, but my mind was only half on all this. I was flying
in doctors from all over the world and trying desperately to stave off the
inevitable. Aunt Lide died on 28 October and I have never fully recovered
from the blow. For days I was in a state of shock and for weeks I could
think of little beyond my own sense of loss.

The cycle of disasters was, however, far from complete. One rainy night
I drove from Rome to Florence and passed along a stretch of motorway

outside Orvieto which was notorious for being grotesquely badly constructed. There was a bend built on a bank of earth, the soil of which washes down in bad weather to make a dangerous slurry where the curve is at its sharpest. That night my headlights just caught in time the looming outline of a big motorcoach slewed across the road. I got out and ran up as the driver staggered out. He was bleeding and crying: 'My God, oh, my God, look what's happened.'

At first I couldn't see what his problem was. The bus was upright and he was hurt but nevertheless alive.

'Inside,' he said. 'Please help inside.'

I climbed into the coach, but couldn't see anything. Gradually I made out low murmurings, which I slowly realized were prayers. As my eyes accustomed themselves, I saw the enormity of the tragedy: the coach was full. It had been carrying a party of Jesuit priests between Florence and Rome, and the skid had swept the bus across the double highway, where it jack-knifed to a shuddering halt. The occupants, most of whom had been sleeping, were thrown forward with shattering force. Some were dead and all were horribly wounded, with broken faces and smashed noses and jaws. Yet no one cried out; they simply sat where they were and murmured their prayers. I involuntarily crossed myself. Then a blind fury overcame me. I ran out onto the motorway and tried to flag down cars, many of which simply drove by. Swearing and yelling, I marshalled those who did stop, and together we carried out the wounded and began to ferry them to the nearest town, Orvieto.

The horror did not end at the hospital in Orvieto; rather it descended into black comedy. The nun who kept the gate at first refused to open up. Poor old creature, she kept shaking her head and saying how impossible it was because everyone was asleep. I ranted and raved at her obstinacy. Only when we lifted one of the wounded Fathers out from a car did she see how foolish she was being and unlocked the gates.

The hospital was rather plain, stark and old-fashioned. Full of so many wounded, it took on the air of a battle station, with the nuns scuttling about quite unable to cope, their faces still puckered with sleep. As soon as I had my charges settled, I drove back to Rome to the College of the Jesuit Order. I forced my way past the functionaries and demanded to see Father Arrupe, the Vicar-General. His lean, black-clad figure came sweeping down the imposing circular staircase. Of course, he had already received full details of the night's events.

'You are our Good Samaritan, thank you,' he said.

'Father,' I begged him, 'you must act quickly to get them out of that hospital. Those people are kind and they're trying their best, but they're not equipped for a disaster on this scale.'

He saw my point and instantly gave orders to his aides to organize a fleet

Zeffirelli

of ambulances to bring his colleagues back to Rome.

As he saw me out, he suddenly stopped and gave me his blessing. 'Thank you, my son,' he said. 'Whenever you have suffering, God will be there.'

It was only later that his words came to have a very special meaning fo me and to take on the force of prophecy.

Out of all the possible hospitals, the Jesuit Fathers were transferred t the Salvator Mundi and my first visit to them brought back the painfu hours spent at Aunt Lide's bedside. That hospital seemed to be assuming a grim significance in my life. I already knew by heart its corridors an staircases, its odd byways and courts, as if it were some bleak ancestra palace that I would always return to and find my way round. I took gift to the injured Fathers and listened to them as they talked and prayed. Th chaplain of the hospital was, I think, called Father Callaghan, and I joine them when he said Mass in the wards. I did not understand my reasons a the time. After the intensity of religion during my schooldays I had, a most people do, let my faith fade as the business of life took over. Perhap it was watching the Fathers at their quiet devotions that made the mem ories of twenty years ago seem so appealing, or perhaps it was that hospita and the memory of Aunt Lide that made me long for something I had lef out of my life.

Christmas came and went, and I tried to be cheerful. My main enter tainment was football. I am a passionate fan and will go anywhere for match, so I was particularly pleased when Gina Lollobrigida rang up t ask me to go to Florence on 17 January to see our local team, who wer top of the league. I offered to drive, but she said that for her the whol thing was really a publicity stunt, so she'd have to go in her Rolls. Sh arrived looking splendid in a jaguar coat and I got in front beside her. Sh had two friends in the back and the four of us gossiped away. She wa supposed to be a competent driver and she seemed to manage, so I trie not to worry about the fact that she could barely hold the steering-whee because of her long nails. Anyway we laughed a lot. I remember stoppin at a gas station and, as we pulled away, a slender, fair-haired boy in ligh blue overalls smiled and waved at us. It is my last clear memory – tha golden boy, like the Angel of Death.

We were no sooner on the road than I realized we were approaching th bend where I had encountered the bus with the Jesuits. It also came to m in a flash that it was the accursed 17th! I turned to tell Gina to take car because of the muddy surface and saw at once that she had already los control. I leaned across partly to steady the wheel and also, instinctively to cover her face. And that is how the right side of my head received th full shattering impact of the windscreen as the car crashed to a halt at th barrier and I was thrown out across the bonnet and into the darkest void.

FOURTEEN

Through Pain

I think I remember dreaming about the young Angel of Death waving, waving, waving ...

Or perhaps at first I didn't dream at all. I can't remember being moved and I am not sure when I first came to ...

I can remember light hurting one eye, but not seeing anything. I shut out the pain ...

I dreamt that Aunt Lide was walking away from me and I was following her. She turned and said angrily, 'Why do you want to come with me? You have to stay. Stop behaving like a child. You have so much to do. ...'

When I awoke I could see out of that same solitary eye. There was a plump, middle-aged woman in white staring back at me. Then there was movement, two, maybe three, people lifting me, and the sound of scissors – they were cutting away my beautiful cashmere sweater I was so fond of. I started to scream: 'Don't cut it, don't cut it! I love it!'

I must have sunk back as they sponged me down, but as the dampness touched my face I woke again and saw the same plump woman dressed in white. Then I made out three members of my family. Vige was crying and I knew then that I was hurt and must be in hospital. My mind cast about trying to work out what was wrong with me and suddenly it acknowledged the most obvious fact: I was still seeing through only one eye, the left. My first thought was that I was blind in the right eye. There was no pain on that side of my face, it was dead. I tried to ask them what had happened, but oblivion returned ...

I opened my one eye again and there was the same peasant woman as before, but this time she was with Fanny and Sheila, my secretary. I told them I had to get to the football match, and they told me that the match had been on Sunday and it was now Tuesday. After a second I started to laugh, helplessly. Fanny was alarmed and asked for the doctor. I was too weary to explain to her that I was laughing because I realized that if I had died on that Sunday then this Tuesday would have been my funeral. The laughing fit exhausted me. I slept again ...

As I lay unconscious, a figure entered the room and stood by my bed looking down at me, and holding my hand for a while. When I woke, they

233

234   whispered to me that I had had an important visitor, Count Luchino
Visconti. He had hurried to Orvieta from Milan, where he was rehearsing
a play, and had only been able to stay a few moments. The knowledge that
he had come to see me after all that had passed between us was a tiny ray
of light in the darkness which enclosed me.

I woke up and knew it was night. The same woman was standing at the
end of the bed now and I saw that she was a nurse. I suddenly knew that
I was in the same run-down hospital that we had brought the Jesuits to. I
asked her for a hand-mirror. She objected, but I made her do it. Then I
saw the terrible truth. The right side of my face was a balloon gorged with
blood, a formless pulp that buried the eye. My mouth was a gaping wound.
I had so often studied my face in the glass and I had been rather proud of
it, as vain as any actor. Was my self-love so sinful that I had to be brought
so low? The woman gently lifted the image of that split and bloated thing
out of my sight and left me. This time oblivion refused to come. I lay for
hours trying to forget what I had seen.

Now I woke frequently and the pain intensified. Whatever had held
sensation at bay no longer offered that blessing. The agony, the throbbing,
unceasing ache was terrifying – a malign thing with its own independent
existence, always there waiting to strike whenever consciousness returned.
Friends came and went without coalescing into identifiable people. Only
my plump nurse seemed real. She became a nanny, mothering my childish,
helpless body. The doctors looked, prodded and appeared unsure. The nuns
tended to my needs or sat beside the bed and quietly prayed. I thought of
the Jesuits and began to puzzle over the words of Father Arrupe. The
coincidence was just too great to be ignored, but as yet I was unable to
work out what it might mean. I remembered other bizarre coincidences,
like the encounter with my 'brother' who saved my life and all the other
'chance' events which had changed the course of my life. Clearly, there was
something more than chance involved.

Sheila had been coping energetically with the situation. As I had done
with the Jesuits, she realized immediately that I must be moved from
Orvieto to a major hospital in Rome. When she came to tell me all this, I
got her to explain what had happened at the time of the accident. It seems
that, when the car slammed to a halt against the barrier, I had been thrown
sideways through the windscreen and so I did not take the impact on my
forehead, my nose or, miraculously, on my temple. Had I done so, I would
have been killed. It was the maxilla, the cheekbone, the strongest part of
the skull, that struck the windscreen and, in doing so, the bone shattered
as did the upper and lower jaw. There were eighteen different fractures and
seven teeth were knocked out, but the cranium and thus the brain seemed
to be undamaged. When Lollobrigida and her friends staggered out of the
Rolls, they laid me out on the road, believing I was dead. Cars were flagged

With Laurence Olivier as Nicodemus on the set of *Jesus of Nazareth*, 1976; beside Michael York as St John the Baptist; talking to Peter Ustinov about his part as Herod

Directing Robert Powell in *Jesus of Nazareth*

With Donald Downes in Positano in 1973
Dinner in Positano with Eduardo de Filippo,
Liza Minelli and Tennessee Williams, 1973

On a terrace of Villa Treville, Positano, and
(*right*) my collection of eighteenth-century
Caltagirone pottery in one of the sitting-
rooms
    Liza Minelli, author Kay Thompson and
Pippo Pisciotto, Positano, 1973
        (*Opposite*) At home in Italy with Ricky
Schroeder, who starred in *The Champ*, 1979

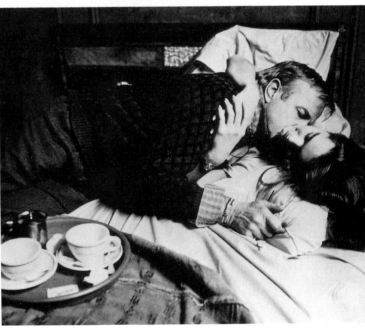

Directing John Voight in *The Champ*
Wholeheartedly directing Brooke Shields in
Endless Love, 1981

Working on set designs for *Otello* at La Scala,
1976
        Filming Placido Domingo as Otello, 1985

In the garden of my home in Rome
Bambina

down and the police summoned. When they arrived, they decided I was dead and threw a blanket over my head. All attention was turned towards Gina, the filmstar. She was bruised and in shock, and must be taken to hospital. Only when they came to lift my corpse into the ambulance did someone notice that blood was still pumping out of my wounds, that my heart was still beating. Then they panicked and headed for Orvieto with me as quickly as they could. I had nearly died twice over.

As before, it was clear that this local hospital was hardly the place to treat a serious accident like mine, but, when Sheila tried to have me moved to Rome, she came up against the worst of Italian bureaucracy. Only when Professor di Stefano, the man who had so gently cared for my aunt, stepped in did things begin to move. I was lifted from the bed to a stretcher and into the ambulance. Every shudder on the journey was seismic, jolts of fear and pain.

Thus I entered, yet again, the Salvator Mundi Hospital. Even lying prone on a trolley I could make out the familiar details; the place had entered my soul. I felt as if some grim destiny was being worked out. I spent a bad first night within these all-too-well-known walls and I again had the nightmare in which my aunt seemed to be angry with me because I wanted to join her.

The next day brought little hope. Professor di Stefano examined me and then broke the news as kindly as he could. No, I wouldn't suffer any mental damage, but – and this was the terrible part for me – my face was badly smashed and even the best surgeons in Italy could do little. He let the news sink in. Then he told me that, while he had wanted me to know the worst, there was one slight possibility: that a surgeon in England, Sir Terence Ward, who was an acknowledged genius in these cases, might be able to restore my smashed features into something reasonably acceptable. He promised to telephone him at once.

I waited anxiously while he went to phone and, as I lay there, I became aware that someone was standing beside my bed. I tried to turn and see who it was, and managed to make out the black robe of a priest. Suddenly, the figure leant closer and said, 'You have much good to do in your life, don't worry.'

I had no idea what he meant; it was as mysterious as Father Arrupe's words. Curiously, the man had no sooner spoken than he smiled and left. Later, when I tried to find out who he was, no one knew. He wasn't the hospital chaplain, but I'm sure I didn't invent him or his words. He must have been a patient or a visitor who wanted to comfort me.

When di Stefano returned, I knew at once that the news was bad. He explained that, though Sir Terence would be happy to treat me, he could only do so in England. That was impossible as I couldn't be moved, and it would be no use later when the bones had set. Di Stefano tried to reassure

Zeffirelli

me, saying that he would get the finest team he could.

When he left, I lay back and waited for oblivion, hoping that there would be no ghosts to disturb my sleep.

Di Stefano woke me later that same day, and he was very excited. Sir Terence Ward's secretary had phoned back to ask if I was Zeffirelli the opera director. Then a little later, Sir Terence himself had phoned; he said how much he valued my work in England and that he would fly out the following morning and, all being well, would operate the day after.

Sir Terence Ward arrived with his assistant, Sheila Lowry. He was everything a leading British surgeon ought to be, the embodiment of calm competence, as if the whole thing were a mere nothing that would soon be put to rights. Nevertheless, his examination was detailed and thorough, and there was a great deal of incomprehensible talk between him and the senior Italian surgeons, who had come to the hospital at di Stefano's alert to learn from the leading specialist of their day. I felt slightly put out. It was my accident and my face, and in a perverse way I didn't want it treated like just another run-of-the-mill operation; it had to be epic. All this chat among the specialists seemed to reduce me to the status of an object in a laboratory. When Sir Terence had made a few supposedly reassuring remarks about the following morning's labours, he left for further discussions with his Italian colleagues. I felt distinctly unhappy. I was used to being master of my world, the director, the focus of any action; now I was a lump of damaged skin and bone to be dealt with by experts. Although I would never have admitted it at the time, I was also desperately frightened. Despite Sir Terence's reassurance, I knew full well that the operation would be long, difficult and far from certain. I became nervous and petulant. I told Sheila Pickles to tell di Stefano that I must have my 'nanny', the old woman who had looked after me at Orvieto. Naturally, he and the matron objected. I had, they said, a perfectly capable nurse, a blonde German girl as efficient as could be imagined. I insisted; they refused. Despite the limitations of being bedridden I threw a memorable tantrum, worthy of Luchino at his most insensitive. They capitulated, and Sheila went to arrange matters.

I slept fitfully. They injected me and I drifted away.

I awoke vague and unsure, my face gripped as if in a vice. The nurse from Orvieto was with me, and I reached out and touched her. She was crying and this upset me even more.

'I didn't bring you here for that,' I said. 'You must stop or I'll send you back.' But even that mock threat didn't prevent her from sobbing.

Sir Terence came and explained what had been done. Rather than further damage my face by cutting it open for the operation, he had worked from inside. He had opened a passage to the left and right through the roof of the mouth, inserted his fingers into both sides and, using the left side of my face as a model, he had gently remoulded the right into an identical shape. This done, he had inserted a special compound of his own invention, something akin to dental filling, which he formed under the re-set bones on the right. This compound hardened like steel and provided an unyielding mould against which the still fractured bones would gradually knit, hopefully retaining the form he had so skilfully shaped for them. He had sealed this mould into my face and he would, he said, return within three weeks to remove it and complete the cosmetic part of the operation. He seemed pleased with his efforts, and I offered a silent prayer of thanks.

I dozed off again, but when I awoke the pain was unbelievable. The steel-like cast inside my skin felt as if it were a mountain. The grip of the vice intensified. My 'nanny' tried to comfort me, but I could not suppress cry after cry.

Despite sedatives, the pain was ever present and ever shifting as the bones settled and set against the mould. As the hellish days crept by, the pain seemed to increase. Weeks passed and still Sir Terence did not come back. I began to ask for him incessantly, but no one could or would tell me what was happening. Then, as the bones finally hardened, a new torture was added, a terrible itching just below the surface. The unbearable irritation made me want to scratch and claw at my face, tear open the flesh and yank out the concrete foundation that was driving me insane. The sensation was uncontrollable. They tied me down to prevent me hurting myself. It was the ultimate humiliation.

As I lay trussed like a prisoner in the very depths of degradation and misery, the hospital chaplain, Father Callaghan, asked if there was anything he could do – perhaps I would like him to read aloud to me something of comfort from the Bible. My mind was in turmoil, I couldn't remember anything from the Bible at all. Then, suddenly, I thought of the Sermon on the Mount: perhaps he would read that. It was a bizarre choice, almost as if I wished to add moral anguish to my physical suffering. After all, I belonged to a profession that takes pride in its vanities and worldly successes, and now here I was, racked and bound, listening to those solemn words lauding the poor and the meek above all others. Yet despite this incongruity, the words were comforting. I made an effort, I tried to pray even though the words were at first mechanical, thoughtless things learned in childhood. I forced myself to say them and, perhaps because I was for once in my life immobile and trapped, they began to have a point. Confined to a hospital bed, far from the distractions of a church – the ceremony, the paintings, the people – the very ordinariness of prayer suddenly became meaningful. When you are absolutely alone, you can talk to God.

I asked Father Callaghan to read to me anything from the Gospels as

238   often as he could. I had not listened to them since I was a child. I had been
a typical lazy Italian Catholic, an unthinking believer who performs the
minimum religious observance necessary to remain in the Church. I had
never thought to study or improve my faith. But now I listened carefully
to what was being said and I began to realize that my life, for all its busy
successes, was an empty, drifting thing. I was forty-five and I had never
stopped rushing about long enough to consider what I was doing. It all
seemed crazy and shallow when viewed from my bed.

Other people came to read to me, friends and family, a constant stream
to help take my mind off the continuing itching pain. Faithfully ever day
Suso Cecchi d'Amico came to sit by my bed in case I needed anything. A
fan letter came from a young man called Pippo, who'd read in the newspapers about my accident and asked if he could come and visit me. He said
in his letter that he had gone to see *Romeo and Juliet* several times and I
was his favourite film director. Now he too joined my group of readers and
his visits were the ones I looked forward to most. He was doing his national
service in the navy and was bursting with lively interest in the world of
theatre and cinema. One day, when my old friend Alfredo came to visit me
and saw Pippo in his sailor's uniform reading beside my bed, he later said,
'Do you realize your Uncle Gustavo was in the navy? It's Aunt Lide who
has sent you this angel.'

Seeing Pippo, all the suppressed longing to have a son to whom I could
pass on all that I had learned was aroused.

One night, after a visit from Pippo, I had a dream in which I saw my
patron saint, Francis of Assisi. It was one of those crystal-clear encounters
and, when I woke, I remembered the dream and knew with certainty why
he had come to me. I spoke to Father Callaghan as soon as he came on his
rounds and told him what had happened. He asked me what I made of it,
and I said I thought it was a sign that I had to do something positive about
these new religious thoughts which were preoccupying me. I told him that
I intended to make a vow to dedicate my work to God whenever possible.

I entered the fourth week. Still no Sir Terence. Again, I had to be
restrained from hurting myself in the throes of the itching agony. Like my
patron saint, I found only in animals perfect love and giving. I had a big
shepherd dog called Gosto at that time and I knew he was missing me
dreadfully, so I had my family take my used linen home for him to sleep
with before it was washed so that he could smell my scent and know I was
still alive.

The readers came and went. I spent happy hours talking to Pippo, who
was no simple provincial boy but a complex young man searching for his
way in life. I recognized a lot of my younger self in him.

One of the other cheerful things in that whole sorry period was the way
so many people tried to show that they cared. Letters, flowers and gifts

poured in. There were kind thoughts from friends like Liz and Richard, but also unexpected gestures like the bouquet of flowers from the Beatles, who were really only acquaintances. I'd met them in 1965, when I was in London for *Much Ado About Nothing*, and I'd seen them on and off whilst I was there. Their manager, Brian Epstein, wanted me to do a film with them and we'd sometimes talk about the possibility without getting anywhere. Then, as I looked at the flowers they'd sent, an idea began to take shape. The Beatles represented the generation of peace and love, the gentle era of flower power. Might they not somehow fit into my slowly unfolding plan to film the story of St Francis? Thinking of that helped me through the worst hours of pain.

One of those who came frequently to visit me was Donald Downes. He kept me amused in his usual forthright way with a stream of comment on the events of the day: the folly of politicians, especially American ones; the hopelessness of Italian doctors with the only possible exception of di Stefano, whom he knew and of whom he approved. For myself I was simply cheered by his presence. He always had something valuable to huff and puff about, whether it was the latest literary lion or the background scandal to some theatrical event. He was the most voracious reader I have ever met and that, combined with a natural intellectual arrogance, produced a wonderful raconteur.

After five weeks Sir Terence Ward returned. He pronounced himself satisfied and said he would operate the next day.

Although there was the inevitable degree of pain and nausea in the days that followed, that second operation, though it too lasted about five hours, was far less profound than the first. Once more through the mouth, Sir Terence removed the steel-hard mould against which the bone had set. When I came to, my face was swollen again, but this time I knew that underneath was something whole and living. Sir Terence had already gone, so I was spared having to try to express my gratitude. He had left a bill for his out-of-pocket expenses, and that was all. It was another act of kindness to put into that ever-expanding treasure-chest of my love of the British. It did seem that, at every turn in my life, it was they who came to my rescue. I had even more reason to be grateful for Sir Terence's generosity when it turned out that Lollobrigida had minimal insurance, quite insufficient to cover even my hospital bills. Afraid that I might sue, as indeed I should have done, she visited me with her lawyer and the usual gaggle of photographers; she asked me to sign a release. I just wanted to close the episode and forget the whole thing. I signed.

But it was a slow road to full recovery. My return home, though it delighted Gosto, was hardly a complete resumption of normality. I was still very ill and somehow I couldn't pull myself together. It was three months after the accident, yet I couldn't shake off my lingering weakness. The

240   worst part of this convalescence was the agony of keeping my damaged sinuses functioning. Sir Terence was adamant that his colleague, Dr Musgrave, should handle this aspect, and so for weeks I would fly to London on a Tuesday evening, have my sinuses drained on the Wednesday, then fly back to Rome. Those who have gone through the misery of having their sinuses drained just once in their lives will know what I was going through. But Dr Musgrave was good. I'd already heard about him through people like Maggie Smith at the National Theatre, where he was rhinologist to a lot of the actors.

My teeth proved a more worrying problem, until I found an American who could do the necessary cosmetic dentistry. After that, I began to feel that my familiar face was being returned to me. Despite that, the summer was not happy. I was lethargic and frequently ill; any bug or virus around seemed to find me a happy hunting-ground. Anyone else would be ill for a day; I went down dramatically. Eventually, on one of my trips to London, I went to see Sir Terence to ask if there was any way out of this impasse. He saw at once what was wrong – too many antibiotics and too many X-rays. So much medication and radiation had weakened me physically and were the cause of my depression. He ordered a complete end to all treatment, and that was when my recovery truly began.

By the end of the summer I was starting to improve. The first sign was a feeling of anger and fury at how much I had missed because of the accident. *Romeo and Juliet* had been nominated for a clutch of Oscars, but, because I hadn't been able to help with all the ballyhoo that precedes the judging, we only won two, for best costumes and best cinematography. It was a setback, as that year had really established me as an international film director. Still, Paramount was delighted with the prestige and the money they were making, and gave me an excellent five-year film contract. They may have had their doubts about my idea for a film about St Francis, but anyone who could turn $1½ million into $48 million in one year could be indulged. In any case, I put their minds at rest by telling them I would fill the film with music that would appeal to a young audience.

I searched out a lot of original Italian medieval music and we made a demonstration tape mixing it with jazz. It worked beautifully and I hoped that this would not only pacify the studio but would also tempt John, Paul, George and Ringo to come in on the project. They certainly liked the idea, and on my visits to London I would call round to wherever they were rehearsing or recording to try to nudge the scheme along.

As soon as I left hospital, I'd got a team of writers working on the story. The tale was simple enough, though clearly the emphasis would be on its contemporary relevance. St Francis was a holy revolutionary: his concept of a non-violent, pacific reversal of the greed and laziness that he felt had crept into the church and indeed the world of his day was obviously akin

to the spirit of the 1960s. If peace and love was the slogan of the decade
then here was a story to match it.

I liked the Beatles, though of course in different ways. I suppose at a
human level I found Ringo the most open and friendly, but I soon saw that
to get anywhere you had first to convince Paul of an idea, and then get
John to deal with the practical problems. I managed eventually to get that
far, but as soon as John and I began to work out a schedule, it was instantly
clear how impossible the whole thing was. They could film for two days
here, five there, then another three somewhere else – but never for any
consistent period. Reluctantly, we concluded that St Francis was impossible. How sad that now seems when one considers there is no record of them
in a full feature film. Dick Lester did a marvellous job with *A Hard Day's
Night,* but that was no more than a brilliantly-sustained sketch. It's a pity
they were never really given the chance to act together and it is a project
that I shall always regret not having done.

For the moment this setback seemed just another irritation to add to all
the others, mainly physical, which dogged me that year. I knew the film
would go ahead, but, like everything else at that time, it would have to
evolve slowly. There was to be no quick return to the days of overlapping
productions of six or seven operas a year! In any case, my new-found
interest in spiritual matters was forcing me to be more analytical about
what I was doing; I no longer wanted to dash from city to city, theatre to
theatre and bed to bed.

Sometimes, when I tell English friends about my religious feelings, they
comment ironically on my life-style and make it clear that they think I
must be at best a hypocrite and must somehow adjust the teachings of the
Church to my liking. But this is not the case. My private life is what it is, but
my religious convictions are unwavering. I believe totally in the teachings of
the Church and this means admitting that my way of life is sinful. The
Protestant with his conviction that there is nothing between himself and
God would find such a situation intolerable and would therefore be forced
either to renounce his worldly needs or his Creator. But Catholics believe
they have the Church to intercede for them and that the Church, being
both Divine and Human, will be forgiving. We Latins have always been
able to accommodate the rigours of belief with the needs of the body
without forgoing one or the other, and I see no reason for the Church to
bend to the easy solution of changing its age-old morality to suit the
promiscuity of our day. We can draw comfort from the belief that the sins
of the flesh are not mortal sins unless accompanied by violence or corrup-
tion. Of course, it helps being Florentine; we were the people who reconciled
the Humanism of the classical world with the faith of the Judeo-Christian
tradition to create the spirit of the Renaissance. It's hard for other people
to realize just how easily we Florentines live with that past in our hearts

242 and minds because it surrounds us in a very real way. To most people, the Renaissance is a few paintings on a gallery wall; to us it is more than an environment – it's an entire culture, a way of life.

I can remember playing football in the cloisters of the Convent of San Marco when I was a boy; there was some restoration going on and Professor La Pira came from behind the communicating door that led from the monastery to the museum and, seeing me, called me over and led me up a flight of stairs to the old dormitory. There before us at the top of the steps was the Annunciation of Fra Angelico and I stood looking at it, rather embarrassed, clutching my football, while La Pira gave me a gentle lesson in faith. He explained that the Annunciation was the most important point in the history of mankind for that was the moment of incarnation, when the Spirit of God becomes a man and takes on all that that means. It is the *initium*, the beginning of all – the beginning of the Nativity, of life, death and resurrection. It is the promise and covenant, and it renews itself naturally in every woman at the instant of conception. When I was older, La Pira told me of his horror of abortion, which makes it impossible for a foetus to achieve resurrection and eternal life. I was shocked when I felt he was more ready to forgive infanticide than abortion, but all this seemed logical, clear and poetical to me at the same time – and very Florentine. Then he went on to explain that Christ, the son of man, was like us all: he ate, slept, cried and laughed. He knew what it was like to be betrayed, He was afraid on the Cross, there were times when He did not understand what was happening to Him and times when He got angry. All this, La Pira explained, makes us feel a little less guilty about the sins of the flesh. We know God understands and forgives.

Of course, La Pira was an extraordinary man who did wonderful work with poor and abandoned people. He was a great hero in my youth and his influence is still with me. I suppose part of my feelings after the accident were caused by the awareness of just how close death is. I knew I would never marry, but somehow, without fully realizing it, I wanted to have a son. Looking back, I can now see that this was what Luchino had wanted me to be. Most of the great artists never bred children but they acquired them as pupils, whom they formed and who often surpassed them – Perugino had Raphael, Verrocchio had Leonardo. Without trying to put myself into that category, there was nevertheless an unspoken element of that desire for continuity in my relations with the young people around me. I was forty-five and the time was right. I began to see more and more of Pippo, and I tried to advise and help him wherever possible. He completed his national service near Rome and then went on to study accountancy, but I was certain, from the interest he showed, that one day we would work together and I would be able to teach him something of what I had learned.

My return to work was to be *Cavalleria rusticana* and *Pagliacci* at the

New York Met in December, but even that came under the black cloud of 1969. No sooner had I begun to find my feet in New York than the opera house suffered its worst and longest strike ever. I had been dashing around trying harder than ever to work up the production, fully aware that this was a test of whether or not I had lost my touch. I told no one. I tried to keep up my usual director's confidence but inside I was waiting to see if all was well. The disappointment when everything suddenly stopped was matched only by my unexpressed fears that perhaps the curse was still with me. All theatre folk are superstitious, and heaven knows I had reason enough to believe that, where before luck had been on my side, now it had deserted me.

When the strike dragged on everything collapsed. Led by the conductor, Tommy Schippers, all the principals left one by one to honour their next commitments. When the end of the strike came in sight, it appeared to be too late: there was no cast and no conductor. Then something inside me clicked. I wouldn't let them cancel; I had to do it or I might lose heart. I went to see Lenny Bernstein to beg for his help. I tried to disguise the fact that I was desperate to break the curse which seemed to be hanging over me, preferring to appeal to his loyalty to the Met, though no doubt he saw through that. *Pagliacci* had remained almost intact with Fausto Cleva conducting and the great American tenor Richard Tucker as Canio. But *Cavalleria* was a disaster. Happily, Lenny said he would conduct it and that seemed to break the spell. To our great delight Franco Corelli agreed to come out of retirement to sing Turiddu, thus turning the event into a major 'come-back' for a much loved singer and, equally happily, Grace Bumbry said she would sing Santuzza. In the end, miraculously, a disaster had been transformed into a star-studded event and I threw myself into rehearsals, desperate to prove I could still do it.

Now the situation was reversed: *Cavalleria* seemed able to take care of itself, but *Pagliacci* looked as if it needed working on. Richard Tucker had a reputation for being a great singer, but something of a cold fish as a performer, a man rather held in and unemotional. Throughout his career the critics had praised his voice and damned his acting with faint praise, referring to his 'businesslike' qualities, which made him sound like a Wall Street banker. I made a real effort to get inside the man, to talk to him and find out what had made him the way he was. It wasn't hard to discover that the struggles of a young man from a New York Jewish background to get into the difficult world of American opera had produced someone who felt that self-control was his best ally. Yet underneath all that was a deeply religious man, who, if you took the trouble to look, was of a surprisingly passionate nature. As the rehearsals progressed, he began to unwind and to let those passions show. When we opened on 2 January, there was a new, terrifying and heart-rending Canio that completely shook the critics, who had thought they had Tucker neatly pigeon-holed.

There was, however, one part of the story that was far more lighthearted. Richard wore an odd wig, a complete hairpiece, and not just on stage – he never appeared without it. It was an attempt to look younger than his years, but sadly it merely made him look like a sort of stage gigolo. I took him to one side and told him that, unfortunately, he was in many ways far too young for the part of Canio, who should be much older, bald in fact. Richard listened without comment except to say that he would talk it over with his wife, Sarah. A day or so later I met them both and she agreed with me that Canio should wear a clown's wig when he is made up, but that, when he removes his make-up, he should lift off the wig and be bald, a sad old man in effect. I was delighted and pleased, as I thought, to have seen off the embarrassing shiny black hair-piece. But I had not bargained on the unbelievable persistence of illusion combined with human vanity. Tucker's solution was to wear the clown's wig over a bald wig over his own wig! It looked rather peculiar to say the least, and was far too hot for him under the lights, but he simply wouldn't admit to his true baldness and there was nothing anyone could do about it. Of course, one night the inevitable happened: as he removed the clown's wig, he simultaneously pulled off all the others, and there he was, really bald, the way I wanted Canio to be.

Some time later, I happened to bump into him and we began to talk over old times. I mentioned the incident of the three wigs, and he looked me straight in the eyes and told me rather severely that he hadn't the least idea what I was talking about. I suppose I should have realized that this would be his reaction, because I had heard since that, when he went to his synagogue, which was rather cold, he would wear a second wig for warmth and then his yarmulke over that.

Even allowing for that slight diversion, the opening night of *Cav* and *Pag* was full of action. The part of Nedda was to be played by Teresa Stratas, my first encounter with the young Greek singer, who seemed to me to evoke echoes of Callas. From the beginning I knew we would one day do something important together, but for this first event her closest similarity to Maria was an unfortunate tendency to get thoroughly nervous before a performance. Teresa did what became a calamitous feature of her career. She cancelled at the last minute, leaving Lucine Amara to take her place.

Things were equally eventful with *Cavalleria*. Lenny had the idea of trying to resurrect the original tempos of Mascagni, which, because the composer took himself rather too seriously, were very slow indeed. The result leant dangerously towards self-indulgence, which was fortunately abandoned at later performances. More serious was the behaviour of Franco Corelli, who was not in agreement with Lenny's tempo and had done what Maria would never have done by taking the odd short cut. Unfortunately,

he hadn't bothered to warn anyone, which didn't please Lenny. There were
fireworks backstage in the interval. However, none of these details were
obvious to the audience, who simply lapped up the energy generated by all
this creative tension.

The ovations at the end of the evening were my best medicine. As I went
out to take my bow, I said a venomous goodbye to 1969 and indeed to that
whole bizarre decade. I knew that opera would always be there as a sort of
security, a bedrock that I could return to, but now there would be more
films and, importantly, more choices. In the future I would be more selective
and careful about what I chose to do – less running from one theatre to
another. When the rest of the production stepped forward to join me centre
stage and we took our bows together, I said a special thank you to Lenny,
who had helped to pull me out of the black trough into which I had been
sinking.

Out in the audience with Vige was Pippo. I had managed to get him a
pass from the naval authorities to come to New York for the first time, and
it seemed only right that he should be there as a new period in my life
began.

Saints and Sinners

Given the way much of my life had been led, especially during the 1960s, it would be reasonable to assume that my interest in religion was merely the result of a painful accident and a period of enforced introspection, but there was more to my reawakened faith than just remorse or mid-life depression. If, before, I had often considered that the role of destiny was important in my life, now I began to reinterpret this as providence, as if there was a guiding hand directing my decisions. Even I could never have foreseen how my desire to use what talents I have in the service of God would eventually turn out far beyond anything I might have predicted in 1970. But, looking back, it is possible to see that there was a pattern to events which led inexorably to the point where I was able to be of use to the Faith on a vast international scale.

Perhaps less surprisingly, it was the Church which first appeared on the scene. Because it had been announced that I was to direct a life of St Francis, I was approached by Monsignor Macchi, secretary to Pope Paul VI, who said that His Holiness wished to commemorate the bicentenary of Beethoven's birth with a performance of the *Missa Solemnis* in the Basilica of St Peter's. This was an extraordinary idea. Although the music is sacred, it is nevertheless given 'in performance' and is not in itself a religious ceremony. Until then the Basilica had never been used for anything other than the rites of the Church or for meetings of its consistories and councils. I was less surprised than most, because I had known the Holy Father when he was archbishop of Milan and was aware of his keen interest in the arts. His palace in Milan had been a sort of salon for some of the most talented people in the city and music had always been his first love. But, whilst I might have expected him to wish to celebrate a great composer, I was as surprised as anyone to learn that he was willing to let the event be televised and flattered to learn that he wished me to direct the entire event. Of course, I said yes.

There is no need for me to attempt to describe the magnificence of the setting, but it must be said that the performance was to match it – there were to be two full orchestras conducted by Wolfgang Sawallisch and two choirs, one from Munich and the other from Santa Cecilia. Among the principal singers was the young Placido Domingo, making one of his first major international appearances. The first time I met him, I found a nice, sympathetic, young Spaniard, rather shy, and as plump as a dumpling! Like Callas, he was to transform himself pysically and mentally. But even then he had a marvellous voice that one knew could only get better.

The performance was to be on 23 May 1970, and it was only when I went to St Peter's for the first planning session that the full scale of what I had to do was borne in on me. There was Bernini's enormous Baroque baldacchino covering the altar above the tomb of the apostle St Peter himself, and, behind it, the Papal throne. I shuddered at the thought of touching anything in that sacred place and turned my attention westwards. We could build a stage at the entrance and face the audience towards the great doors of the Basilica. Having almost decided this, I began to foresee difficulties; everyone would have their backs firmly turned to the altar, which, for all I knew, might be sacrilege. No one seemed able to help; the problem had never arisen before. There was only one way to find out and I asked for an audience with the one man who could decide. To my surprise, Pope Paul was completely relaxed about the whole thing and urged me to do whatever I thought best. I tentatively suggested raising a stage over the apostolic tomb up to the level of the altar and he concurred with enthusiasm.

As I left the audience, Monsignor Macchi drew me to one side.

'Don't let it worry you,' he sighed. 'This is not a place for prayers – not like our cathedral in Milan. But, if you want to create a big spectacle then this is the place to do it.'

Now I realized that we had the opportunity to create a most stunning *mise-en-scène* and I decided at once to go further than merely showing the event like a concert. I asked, and was instantly granted, permission to film the Vatican treasures, and I spent two nights in the Sistine Chapel filming through long lenses, seeing the frescos as only Michelangelo had when he painted them. I was able to pick out a detail – an eye or a hand – to see the brushwork and the finer points normally missed. The whole chapel tends to be overwhelmed by the *Last Judgement* on the far wall, but, able to isolate elements of the ceiling, I could see that even the solitary figures of the prophets, which often seem to be merely supporting decoration, are in fact equally powerful and majestic. It was then that I had the idea of making this a joint homage to Beethoven in music and Michelangelo in art. We went on to film Michelangelo's *Pietà* at night in the deserted Basilica, brightly spot-lit in the surrounding blackness.

I spent the 11th of May filming the great Bernini sculptures of the Papal tombs, the nights of the 12th and 13th in the Sistine Chapel, and the 19th with the *Pietà*. We documented this so well that, when later the sculpture was senselessly damaged by a madman, the restorers were able to use our

248   video tapes to see the work from every angle.

We had a final rehearsal on 22 May and on the afternoon of Saturday the 23rd the great event took place. It had been timed to coincide with the fiftieth anniversary of Pope Paul's ordination and he sat in the front row surrounded by hundreds of recently ordained young priests on the floor at his feet. They came from every continent – Orientals, Africans, Indians, Latin Americans, Europeans – every race and colour. It was a moving and powerful image.

The *Missa Solemnis* lasts one hour and ten minutes. We set the scene and lingered on the opening bars before mixing into our recorded sequences. I began on the trumpets in the orchestra, but ended in the Sistine Chapel with a hair-raising, spinning shot across the vault ending on God's finger reaching out to Adam's. It fitted the music beautifully, which was itself a minor miracle, as I'd timed everything to a recording conducted by Karajan. I'd just had to hope that his tempo wouldn't be too different from Sawallisch's.

The second sequence centred on the *Pietà*. It started as no more than a speck of light in the dark, a distant star; I had done the longest, slowest tracking shot imaginable so that the effect was of the sculpture gradually appearing out of nowhere, from dark space, approaching us with the mysterious music of the Incarnatus. As the statue came into full view, I mixed through to the heights of the dome of the Basilica, then down so that the Madonna and the body of Christ seemed to descend to the thousands of people watching below.

The awesome closing music was accompanied by images of the Bernini tombs, symbols of death and punishment with their golden skulls and skeletons – the transience of glory and power. We ended in the Basilica itself, an explosion of angels soaring round the dome, the shimmer of the golden mosaics.

I was excited by the way I could blend live with prerecorded sequences and could mix the whole thing together there and then. Unlike the film director, who works patiently and slowly through the skills of so many people, this was immediate, within my direct control. I was determined to do more work of this kind when the opportunity arose. The only sad part of it is the impermanence that goes hand in hand with the immediacy. Apparently today no one can find the tapes of the *Missa Solemnis* and the likelihood is that they have been destroyed.

The week after the *Missa Solemnis* I went back to London for a third operation. I was growing quite used to them by now. But I mustn't give the impression that all was doctor's waiting-rooms and sacred music; if God was served then Mammon was also in the picture. The continuing world-wide success of *Romeo and Juliet* was changing my life. I was rich. I had been doing increasingly well throughout the 1960s and could command

high fees for an opera or a play, but all that was as nothing compared to
the earnings from a movie hit. I'd never imagined such a thing; it was like
stepping out of one play and into another with an entirely different part.
All that money would have been meaningless, however, if a lot of other
things had not happened at the same time.

It's these happenings that convince me that some sort of plan is being
worked out in which we all fit. The sequence of moves was at first remote,
yet with odd tragic echoes of the event that had so disrupted my own life.
Not long after my own accident in May 1970, Bob Ullman, Donald Downes's
lifelong friend, was killed while driving back to Positano. It was shattering
for Donald.

They really were 'the odd couple'. Although never anything but friends,
theirs was a sort of marriage. They bickered the whole time and quarrelled
about everything from food to the books with which the villa was piled
high – Donald read about three a day. But if anyone else dared criticize
the one to the other, then let the third party beware. To the outside world
they presented a united front. It was a unique household, a mixture of
culture and eccentricity. There was a constant stream of literary and theatre
folk. There were bizarre fads like Donald's sudden aggressive dieting, or
excessive feasting, which meant that he had to have three entire wardrobes
for when he was thin, fat or just in between.

In many ways Donald was the dominant figure in the household. He
organized the wonderful meals and his forceful opinions always led any
conversation. It was also Donald who had turned the hillside into a Garden
of Eden. So it was a surprise to recall after Bob's death that it was he, and
not Donald, who had bought the villa from the Duchess of Villarosa all
those years ago. Of course, he had left the property to Donald, but the will,
inevitably, was rather eccentric. Bob left no money, but the will obliged
Donald to make financial provision not only for the servants but also for
the odd group of stray people who had collected around them in Positano.
This motley gang, all impecunious, some amusing and some just played
out, were entirely dependent on the two friends. The will was a disaster:
Donald's only solution was to sell the villa to settle the debts.

I told Donald to have the villa valued and that I would find him the
money to save it, but that he *had* to go on living there exactly as before,
bitching included. I would use the villa for holidays, as I always had. One
day, I imagined in the far future, I'd move in and make the place my own.

At first Donald was delighted. He continued to live in the topmost of the
three villas – oddly enough the most primitive and run down – to take his
leisurely coffee on the terrace with its spectacular view across the bay to
Positano, to read and read, and bitch and bitch. But of course it wasn't
the same. There was no one to argue with; no one, when one looked up
from a book, to discuss it with, no one with whom to complain about the

Zeffirelli

250   Americanization of Italy and the daily despoliation of the Costa Amalfitana. For Donald everything was declining; the new rich were building villas everywhere, the village was a tourist trap, and there was no one with whom to share his irritation. He was getting more and more like the old *'scorpioni'* in Florence, clucking away in Doney's about the shortcomings of the Italians. One day he suddenly announced that he no longer felt he could go on living in Positano and would like me to take over the place. At first I thought he was merely embarrassed at occupying somewhere he no longer completely controlled, and I insisted that the place was always his, but it soon became clear that he truly wanted to move. He hated the new Positano, because he loved the old one too much.

'I don't want the place to be a shrine,' he explained gently and perhaps sadly. 'I've had twenty wonderful years here. I'll keep coming as your guest, but I know the sort of person you are. You'll want to change the place and make it really your own, so go ahead.'

And I did. I had the masons there within days. Donald had guessed that with my love of decorating and creating theatre, I was frustrated at never having a place to transform. Now I could start creating my dream world out of the three villas which stepped down the terraced hillside. I named one Romeo, another Juliet and the third Mercutio. Each place had a different character: I kept the eighteenth- and nineteenth-century Neapolitan style of the upper villa; the red house that Diaghilev had used I also kept in period; while I lavished all my theatricality on the large main reception area below with its white cupolas. This became a large white space full of mirrors and palms, and all around I added terraces and verandas, stepped gardens and little secret walkways with hanging plants, flower beds and exotic shrubs. I constantly add to it: a grotto, a new bathing place, a vegetable garden, a games court.

There are about 3,000 plants now, some of them very rare, and for many of these I must thank Donald, who had already created a marvellous garden and gave his best advice whenever he came. He first returned the year following my building spree, and I was very nervous waiting for him to come down the steep, winding stairway that leads from the Positano–Amalfi road on the corniche above. I needn't have worried. He was in a mood of cynical good humour, and after looking at the white salon he said: 'Oh yes, very beautiful, but when can we see the second act?' He then took a breath and added: 'Looks a bit like the new Holiday Inn, Tunis.' We all laughed. he went on: 'It could have been a lot worse – a Casablanca Hilton.'

That was typical of Donald. His sharp tongue kept a lot of people at bay, but it wasn't just empty bitchiness. He was very well informed and had an extraordinary memory for dates and facts, which meant he could, and often did, demolish anyone he thought was being pompous or just vague. This didn't make him popular with the average chatterbox but I valued what he had to say. I list him as one, and in some ways the most important, of the three men who taught me most.

Luchino showed me the world of creativity in theatre and films, how to conceive an idea and how to bring together a whole world of culture that could embody it. He also taught me how to create theatre with designers, writers and actors; in other words, how to direct. Tullio Serafin taught me music, the depth of it both historically and technically, and how to interpret its most difficult expression, opera with its supreme economy, concentrating only on what matters most. Serafin passed on what he knew like the elder of a tribe teaching the young braves, and through him I became part of a line that stretched back through Verdi to Monteverdi.

But Donald was different. For one thing he didn't really do anything apart from write a little journalism and the occasional book. He was that rare thing, an intellectual; he led the life of the mind. And how he nourished it, or rather feasted it daily. I still have his library at the villa and I am quite used to foreign visitors looking at me with new respect when they see the scope of 'my' reading. What Donald taught me can't be as easily quantified as the others. They taught me skills, but his lesson was of an opposite kind. Whereas all my life I had been surrounded by people who did things, even though at a high cultural level, it was nevertheless within accepted patterns. Donald, however, questioned everything. In the space of a single conversation he would expose the folly of some fashionable literary idea and then dissect the latest disaster in American foreign policy. He was my antidote to the narrow theatrical world I moved in. Though I preferred to take my lessons in the villa, a walk into Positano with him was a walk through a minefield. Everything new displeased him and he would not hesitate to point out the shortcomings to whomsoever he could buttonhole. Children, in particular, irritated him and mothers were often upbraided for failing to discipline their offspring. I preferred to avoid those encounters.

His best bequest was Elia the cook (whom we always call Ali, because he has that Arabic Neapolitan look) and his wife, Giovanna, our house-keeper. Ali has lived at the villa since childhood and he and Donald were very close. Donald was a great gourmet, though oddly enough, given his choice of residence, he had little affection for Italian food.

I can remember being invited by Donald and Bob to join them on a motor tour from Amsterdam, where I was working at the Holland Festival, through northern France and down to the Riviera. I willingly agreed, thinking to improve my knowledge of the country in the presence of two so widely informed and entertaining people, but as soon as we set off I began to sense there was something peculiar about the itinerary. Our route was obviously meticulously planned, yet we never seemed to go anywhere. On the contrary, we spent hours in remote restaurants eating superb lunches

252   and dinners. It had been agreed that we would avoid Paris, but, when I discovered that we were not to see Chartres, I protested.

'What do you want to go there for?' demanded Donald.

'Well, surely we want to see the cathedral?'

'No,' said Bob.

'But I must. I've never been.'

They looked ruefully at each other and began to consult a book of notes.

'Well, I suppose we could,' said Donald. 'But it means missing the *quenelles* at that little place outside Rouen, though we'll still get the *poulet à la reine* at Annecy on the lake, if we're lucky.'

It was then I realized that the two of them had meticulously mapped out a circuit of the finest restaurants in France, carefully balanced to permit a light lunch to be followed by a heavy dinner or *vice versa,* and anything else – be it a palace or a museum – was completely irrelevant.

The same thing happened in the Loire valley, when I discovered that they planned to bypass the Château de Chenonceux. Distinctly bored with gorging myself, no matter how good the fare, I told them we would have to part for a while and that I would catch them up later. We compromised. They dropped me at the château and collected me after a copious lunch. Thus we made our way south.

Donald wrote three books on *haute cuisine* and he taught Ali to cook superbly. There had been an original cook, Tommaso, who was highly skilled, and Ali had been his kitchen boy. How they managed I do not know. The kitchen was a tiny downstairs room without proper ventilation, a little hell. When Tommaso left, Ali continued to produce wonderful food in that torture-chamber. One of the first things I did was build a place fit to work in that was light, roomy and allowed some means of ventilation.

Now, when he came to visit, Donald would survey his pupil's efforts with a proprietary air. If they fell below some mythical standard, he would reach out with his walking-stick and give poor Ali a whack. Had it been anyone else, I'm sure Ali would have walked out, but, like me, he loved Donald's irascibility and tolerated his moods.

As soon as I took over the villas in 1970, I invited friends from all over the world. Lenny Bernstein and his family were among the first to come and stay. Having reluctantly given up the idea of working with the Beatles, I needed to pull together the core of the music for *St Francis,* because that was an essential as the script. Following my ideas, two of Italy's best screen-writers, Lina Wertmuller and Suso Cecchi d'Amico, the latter Luchino's favourite writer and friend, had produced an outline which I thought magnificent. We had decided on a title taken from a prayer of the saint: 'Brother Sun, Sister Moon'. Now the problem was to find a British writer capable of developing the story and providing the English dialogue. This proved a nightmare.

The reason for the emphasis on music was that the achievement of St Francis found a parallel in the music of his day. As our story revealed, Francis was the son of a rough cloth merchant in Assisi, which reminded me of my own father with his textile business. He was typical of the late medieval world with its emphasis on hierarchy, power and money, and its fear of the unknown. Assisi, like all medieval towns, was a place of private turreted fortresses, locked away from the countryside by high walls and barred gates. But this uncultured merchant married a cultivated lady from Provence, which was then the centre of art and music. She brought to Assisi her lighthearted ways and the beautiful Provençal songs, the profane music of the troubadours, which celebrated dalliance and love. She passed on her culture and her music to her son; the boy was even named after her homeland. Francis was one of the first to reject the fearful medieval world with its dark view of God, the first to go out into the countryside and to see the work of the Almighty in the natural world – flowers and God's humbler creatures. As part of that new openness and lightness Francis composed new hymns, not in Latin but in Italian, which was an unheard-of provocation, and set them not as chants and dirges but to the popular tunes his mother had taught him. This was, of course, shocking to the traditionalists, the merchants and the Church of his day. But young people were entranced and followed him in their thousands. He was able to trans-form an entire way of thinking to the point where the Pope himself was obliged to acknowledge the rightness of the Franciscan mission.

How close this all seemed to what we felt in the 1960s – that the young would create a new world order based on love and gentleness after those fearful Cold War years. And how similar it seemed musically, with rock music being played in churches and the Jesus people singing on the streets. That was what I wanted to bring together: something that would unite the love-songs of Provence with the music of our day. Lenny was very excited by the early music, the 'Laudas', and worked hard at finding a modern form for them. At one point he collaborated with the poet and singer Leonard Cohen, but, like the script, somehow the thing didn't gel.

One British writer after another produced a script – we must have had twenty in all, all unsatisfactory, some outrageous. The problem was that they kept seeing Francis in Protestant terms. To them he was a pre-Lutheran revolutionary overthrowing the authority of the Pope, whereas the opposite was the case. Francis was in total obedience to the Church and would kneel in the mud as even the fattest, most corrupt priest walked by because he represented the authority of God. This duality of belief that we possess is completely alien to the Anglo-Saxon Protestant mind. Sadly we lost Lenny, totally disheartened by the hopelessness of the scripts we were getting. In the end Lina, Suso and I created the story, and took such dialogue as we needed from the various English versions. It wasn't ideal, but there was nothing else to be done. As for the music, early in 1971 I approached the folk- and pop-singer Donovan, and fortunately he came up with an inspired combination of old and new music that solved my problem.

That left only the inevitable headache of casting. Alec Guinness agreed to play the Pope, but the vexed question of who should play Francis stretched over months.

My first choice was inspired, even though it didn't work out. On one of my visits to New York, Tennessee Williams had taken me to see a performance of his play *Camino Real*. He thought the production was especially good and he singled out a brilliant boy who was intelligent yet extrovert in a very attractive way. It was the young Al Pacino, who with his Italian looks and a sort of winning charm struck me as someone who might play the saint. Paramount flew him to London, where we did a film test, which sadly didn't work out. He had pronounced features, which then seemed even more exaggerated, and he hadn't yet learned to moderate his more theatrical gestures for the camera. Film acting has to be very internalized, otherwise you're left with melodrama or farce. I told him this, but tried to reassure him that his day would come.

Later, during the filming of *Brother Sun, Sister Moon,* Charles Bluhdorn, who by then thought I could do no wrong, began to talk vaguely about the *Godfather*. He thought that the man who had made *Romeo and Juliet* so Italian would be ideal for a Mafia picture. I knew otherwise. I had met Italo-Americans in New York and been invited to their homes, so I had seen how folksy their Italianness is. It's not really Italy at all, but a sort of dream of turn-of-the-century life that has largely vanished. A real Italian would find it very difficult to create that world, but Francis Ford Coppola was the man to get it right. I suggested they show him my screen test with Al Pacino, and the rest, as they say, is history.

Following that test, I was still left with the problem of casting St Francis. I wanted Isabella Rossellini, the daughter of Roberto and Ingrid Bergman, to play St Clare, but the Rossellini clan said no. Ingrid, however, was furious that her daughter had missed such a chance. Eventually I settled on lovely Judi Bowker for Clare and the young Irish actor Frank Giles for Francis. We were so sure of Frank that we arranged for him to have his teeth fixed, but I was going through the motions of some final screen tests when in came a young unknown, Graham Faulkner, and that was it. We had to unravel the contract we'd signed with Giles and start putting our new Francis into the role. Whenever I go to the dentist, I have a twinge of conscience about Frank, but he's gone on to success, thank goodness.

Our locations were stunning: Assisi itself, San Gimignano, and Gubbio – the most beautiful and best preserved medieval city in Italy. We shot very little in the Rome studios. Our most impressive location was in Sicily, inside the eleventh-century cathedral of Monreale, whose Byzantine interior most

Saints and Sinners

255

resembled the sort of medieval splendour I needed for the papal court. The
Bishop of Monreale was so taken with our theme that he gave us *carte blanche*
to use his magnificent church. In return for this generous cooperation, I
brought in some of Italy's finest restorers, who returned the mosaics, the
finest in the west, to their former brightness and clarity.

That said, one would have thought that so sacred a project would have
been assured divine protection. But St Francis is known in Italy as a
particularly difficult saint. Although in the early part of his life, the part
covered by our film, he promulgated the simple, holy life in tune with
nature, his later years revealed a more complex, denser character. In old
age he became a rather tortured mystic, uncompromising and tetchy. He
passed into a realm of meditation and other-worldliness that often made
him harsh and unapproachable. It is the spirit of this later St Francis that
has a reputation for preferring to be left alone, and if you think this is
primitive Catholic superstition then you must find a better explanation for
the fact that this part of Italy was struck by eighteen earthquakes during
the period we were filming! We were planning to film in the ravishing
church of Tuscania, but a few days before we could do so a violent earth
tremor brought the apse crashing to the ground. While we were filming at
Monreale, a bus carrying forty of our crew began to run down a steep,
winding road out of control when its brakes failed. The chief electrician
called out: 'St Francis, save us!', and they bounced into a wall on one of
the bends, which broke their descent, but left them dangling over the
precipice with both front wheels spinning in mid air. So frequent were the
earth tremors that the film technicians from England were terrified and
insisted on being housed in caravans in an open field. Valentina Cortese, who
played the mother of the Saint, walked around with a pillow permanently
clamped on her head for fear of falling masonry.

Something of this air of saintly disapproval seemed to infect Graham
Faulkner. He began to throw tantrums and brood. Whereas all the other
young actors kept together as a rather jolly band, he stood apart from
them, almost as if he were touched by the spirit of the Saint in later life.
Apart from Michael York, I haven't always been lucky with the young
actors I've discovered and, like Leonard Whiting, Faulkner didn't follow
up our film and soon disappeared as an actor.

One success was Pippo, who, having finished his accountancy course,
came to work with me on the film as one of my assistants. At first I thought
he just wanted to enjoy himself and didn't realize how serious he was about
working in films.

Despite heavenly brickbats and earthly pride, our team persevered. As
the film unfolded, I knew that I had made something out of my own Italian
Catholicism, superstitious and childlike if you like, and not at all the sort
of thing with which the Protestant world can identify. It was something

Zeffirelli

256　born out of the Tuscan countryside of my childhood, the village where Ersilia took care of me, rather than an adult, intellectual view of Christian belief that masks sentiment in ritual.

When I'd finished shooting, in September 1971, I flew to New York for a medical check-up and I was thus able to witness the master classes given by Maria Callas at New York's Juilliard School. This was the first time she had surfaced since that last *Tosca*, and I couldn't miss the opportunity to see how she looked and how she would handle her pupils. We had tried to make up after our quarrel and had met once or twice, but they were hardly exciting encounters; she was then preoccupied with the misery of her life without Ari. Since the announcement of his marriage to Jackie Kennedy in 1968, she had led an embittered, reclusive existence in her Paris apartment. She occasionally toyed with proposals, but let them drop the minute there was any possibility of their being realized. That is why I was intrigued that she had consented to take on the Juilliard classes for, although they were not performances, there was still the old *frisson* of seeing *La Divina* centre stage.

It was wonderful to watch her trying to communicate her passion to the young singers. She corrected them technically, but obviously dearer to her was the need to instil in them her belief that the words and thus the drama had to be felt and expressed. Oddly enough, she seemed to gain most pleasure from teaching the male parts and I suddenly remembered she had once told me that she wished she could have been a baritone. She made quite a decent job of rumbling through the lower register.

Maria was soon engrossed in what was happening and before long, as one of the girls sang an aria, the voice of Maria could be heard, tentatively at first, singing along with her. It was more than just the inability to resist a good song. What was soon clear to those who knew her was that she was testing herself, seeing how her nerves would stand up to singing in public again by this first half-way encounter with an audience. The voice was certainly ragged, but it was still there. I suppose that was why I had come, as had the others I saw when I looked around: Tito Gobbi, Grace Bumbry, Placido Domingo.

Maria's search for comfort in the wake of the Onassis débâcle led to her involvement with her old friend and partner, the tenor Giuseppe di Stefano. In 1973 they attempted to co-direct *I vespri siciliani* (*Sicilian Vespers*) for the opening of the new Turin opera house, but, as the critics were quick to note, neither had any notion how to place a chorus or supervise scenery and costumes. There was only one thing Maria could perhaps still do, and that she was still too scared to attempt: singing.

I was now absorbed in editing *Brother Sun, Sister Moon*. As 1971 began and the film took shape, I started to have niggling doubts about what would become of it. Watching the various scenes cut together, I realized

just how much the film was rooted in the 1960s, yet now that the 1970s 257
were unfolding it was clear that a massive change had taken place. Young
people were no longer espousing peace and love; they were out on the streets
protesting against the Vietnam War, throwing bricks, burning draft cards
and fighting with the police. Since the events in Paris in 1968 a creeping
mood of anger and violence had spread through our major cities. *Brother
Sun* began to look almost naïve in the face of such cynicism.

The film opened in Italy at Easter 1972, and in the main reactions were
good. But I knew that this was the easiest hurdle, a Catholic audience
looking at the story of that most Italian of saints and the 'most saintly of
Italians', as Mussolini described him. Before the public opening I organized
a private screening in Florence for the poor, abandoned children whom
Professor La Pira took care of. He maintained a home for them. It was a
double delight for me to do something for those with whom I could
especially sympathize, given my own background, while at the same time
making an offering to the man who had taught me my faith. Professor La
Pira was himself something of a mystic. He was a devoted Marian and,
after that screening of *Brother Sun*, he laid his hands on my head in a
blessing. He told me simply and convincingly that the Madonna was my
mother and had watched over me in my own mother's womb, *my* incarnation. It was both wonderful and frightening. He had that sort of holy
madness that grips some very devout people, yet he was not a holy fool –
far from it, he was exceptionally clever, and it was this combination of
worldly intellectual and holy simpleton that made him so unnerving yet so
fascinating a character. Later, when he was mayor of Florence, he was so
horrified by the war in Vietnam that he flew to Hanoi to see Ho Chi
Minh in order to preach peace as St Francis had done with the Sultan of
Jerusalem, when he tried to end the horror of the Crusades. They both
failed, but the important thing was that such great spirits raised high their
voices against human madness.

I was happy to see that La Pira's audience enjoyed the film, but not
much reassured about the future. It would open in America at Christmas
and I wasn't looking forward to it.

The most cheering news had come, as ever, from England. Now that
filming was over, Larry Olivier wanted me to work for his National Theatre
troupe. His original idea was for a Goldoni or a Pirandello, and I went to
Brighton to stay with him and his wife, Joan Plowright, so that we could
exchange ideas.

Larry and I had remained friends since his work on *Romeo* and, whenever
he was filming at Cinecittà, he would come and visit or sometimes stay as
my guest for as long as he needed. There is a curious spice to our relationship;
to me he is the hero of my youth, yet I flatter myself that he is somewhat
intrigued by me, the Italian who had the nerve to film Shakespeare, an

258 activity once considered his personal preserve. I remember Larry coming to visit once when I was desperately trying to finish some much overdue designs for a new production. I explained the situation and asked him to excuse my absence, while I went to my studio to get on with the work. After about an hour or so, as I was leaning over my drawing-board concentrating on one of the sets, I became aware that someone, albeit silently, had entered the room. I glanced behind me and saw Larry watching my every move, quietly and intensely. I smiled and he came up to the drawing-board.

'Can I design something?' he asked, reaching for the felt-tip pens.

I gave him a piece of paper and tried to get on with my work. He began to map out something and then to colour it in. Inevitably, it was impossible for me not to want to see what the great man was so intently creating. Realizing that he had my attention, he explained in his gentlest voice: 'It's a rose garden I'm planning. I'm going to put this here' – he described a circle – 'pink roses, what d'you think? And at the centre, red roses. I'd like to paint with flowers to make a pattern you could look down on from the bedroom windows. See how exciting it is? God does it, of course. We just plan it and Nature does the rest.'

I had to smile. Like La Pira, Larry too has his childlike side – he had scribbled in the colours. But I understood him. He just couldn't bear being left out; it was like *Romeo* again, he had to join in and play a part. If I was designing then he must design too. This is what makes him the greatest actor of our time; it's in every cell of his body, the craving to emulate and participate. I've known many performers, but none who had that yearning to the extent Larry had.

In Brighton, in the two linked Georgian houses they had made their home, I got to know Joan. After supper, as we relaxed round the table we were unexpectedly caught up in an impromptu comedy. I knew Larry loved truffles, so I had brought some as a gift. Without thinking, I referred to them by the Italian word *tartufi* and Larry instantly picked up on the obvious connotation with Molière's Tartufo, the eponymous religious hypocrite of the famous play. Without hesitation, Larry launched into an Italian extravaganza, a sort of Commedia dell'Arte in which all the characters, beginning with the anti-hero Tartuffi, were taken from Italian cooking. Larry soon perfected all the parts, giving different voices and facial expressions to each. The story centred around a pretty maiden called Tagliatella with her maid, Pastatina. Sweet little Tagliatella was the daughter of old man Panettone and, oh, what trouble they had with their lovesick servants – Risotto, Tortellino and Spaghetto. Further complications were provided by a Neapolitan doctor, Maccherone, and the priest Don Raviolo. In truth it was the most convoluted tale imaginable and to thicken the soup further I proposed the arrival of three foreign suitors: Le Comte de Foie-Gras, Lord Salmon and Prince Kaviar – which

Larry seized upon with relish, because he could now add three strong foreign accents to the mix.

I haven't a notion how the hilarious drama worked out, but I do clearly recall the way that delightful family gathered round to watch entranced as their famous father performed for us: Julie Kate on her mother's lap, fighting back sleep, quietly sucking a thumb, which Joan would gently remove; Tamsin and Dick in their early teens, a perfect blend of their parents' features. It is a family for whom I feel so much affection, and never more so than on that magical first night.

I went to my room happily exhausted to find an unusual bed, which I later learned was from a shop that specialized in old-fashioned eiderdown mattresses. It was the most comfortable, reassuring thing ever, like a mother's womb. I sank into it and lay like a child at home in England, all pretty and cosy the way we foreigners like to imagine it. I slept awhile. Then suddenly I seemed to be dreaming. I was in the midst of Shakespeare's *Romeo and Juliet*: there was the old nurse, clucking about, drawing the curtains.

'Mistress . . . Why, lamb! Why, lady! Fie, you slug-abed. . . . What, not a word? You take your pennyworths now; sleep for a week. . . . Ay, let the County take you in your bed; he'll fright you up, i' faith . . .'

I thought at first that I must have dozed off at the theatre and then I remembered where I was. The nurse was Larry in pyjamas, slippers and dressing-gown with a towel over his head. It was morning and the man I'd always worshipped – Hamlet and Henry v, mixed in with my memories of newly liberated Florence – was waking me up with a private show. I snuggled down into that wonderful bed and relished the performance.

Later we got down to discussing what productions we might do. Kenneth Tynan had wanted me to do a Goldoni, *La locandiera* (*The Mistress of the Inn*), but I wished to do something contemporary, a Pirandello perhaps. It seemed to me that here was an author who had changed the face of theatre and yet had never been satisfactorily produced in England. Now, Kenneth joined us for our discussion and he had another idea. Yes, we should do a modern work, but why not Eduardo de Filippo, a Neapolitan actor and author who had always been so popular in Italy and elsewhere, but wasn't yet known in London. I thought it an excellent idea and I knew it would satisfy Larry, who was keen to find some good parts for Joan. She, it must be said, is a very clever lady and asked me which of de Filippo's plays were the best. I suggested *Filumena marturano* and *Saturday, Sunday, Monday*, two plays de Filippo had created for his sister, the great Titina. She then asked which was the better of the two and I replied *Filumena*. 'Right,' she said. 'Then let's do *Saturday, Sunday, Monday* first. If the public likes it, then we can give them something even better later.'

So it was agreed. It was also decided that Larry, Joan and the family

Zeffirelli

would come to Positano for both a summer holiday and more preparations for the autumn production. They came that July and it was to become a happy annual event centred round Julie Kate's birthday on 27 July, an excuse for an Olivier carnival.

They had no sooner arrived that first summer than I suggested they might help with an idea we had been trying to launch, an Arts Festival for Positano. Larry and Joan agreed to do an evening's reading for us and our 'festival' was made. News soon spread that the world's greatest living Shakespearean actor and his equally renowned wife were going to give a unique performance in the unparalleled setting of the harbour of Positano. People came from all over Italy: actors like Vittorio Gassman; the dancer Léonide Massine, who owned one of the nearby islands and had been part of the Diaghilev set who had stayed at Treville in the past; and Tennessee Williams, of course. Appropriately, given what we were planning, Eduardo de Filippo came from Naples.

I don't know which was more awesome, the performance itself, the ringing grandeur of the poetry under a tent of stars, or the subsequent encounter between Larry and de Filippo. Both were great planets in their own galaxies and it was fascinating to see them orbiting each other. De Filippo may have been a descendant of a line of travelling actors, a product of the noisy, often tragic gaiety of the Neapolitan slums, but he was by then one of the major figures of the Italian stage. Neither was going to concede an inch to the other, and their conversation hovered between formal politeness and theatrical bitchiness in a masterly way. As Larry, Joan and I returned to the villa by boat, I asked him what he had thought of Eduardo.

'Boring old fart,' said Larry, thus confirming that the encounter had been a great success.

In fact, Larry was memorably puckish all evening, much to Joan's irritation. One of the few sources of discontent between them was the familiar one of Larry's drinking. He would rise early, swim, do about three hours' solid work, lunch, sleep, work for another hour, then drink. He wasn't a heavy drinker, but he did like his booze, and that night Joan was rather sharp about it. Inevitably this was the cue for a new role, the poet of the whisky bottle – as soon as his glass was empty the performance would begin.

'Shall I have just a little of this splendid amber fluid, this nectar of the Gods? But who could say no to the tiniest splash, the smallest tear?'

He knelt in front of Joan, who was playing cards with us. 'My lady, will you grant me the smallest taste, a mere nothing?'

He picked up a soda bottle.

'But what is this? The tiniest little fizz, a sparkle to add to my golden glass.'

He kept it up until Joan was forced to laugh and told him to do what he wanted. When he'd had enough of the game, he filled his glass and announced he would go to bed. He stood at the door, bid us all a flamboyant good night and walked into the darkness. He was no sooner outside than there was a resounding crash and the noise of breaking glass. My assistant Dorino ran after him and was soon back in a state of shock.

'He's dying. Lord Olivier has fallen and he's dying.'

'Nonsense,' said Joan shrugging. 'He's just found a new role.'

The irony was that, although he was milking the scene for all it was worth and although he certainly wasn't dying, Larry had fallen quite badly and was lying outside bleeding from a small cut on the forehead, while we flatly refused to believe a word of it. This was poetic justice at the end of a day of poetry.

Later that summer Donald Downes came to stay, and he was to figure in a curious replay of an event from twenty years earlier. Just as Luchino had come to find me when I was swimming near his villa on Ischia in order to tell me of my father's stroke so now Donald was waiting as I stepped out of the water at Positano to say that the same thing had happened to Luchino himself. He had gone out to dinner at the Eden Hotel in Rome with Suso Cecchi d'Amico, but, before the meal began, he had collapsed. It was a major stroke; only later was it discovered that this was not the first and that he had hidden earlier, lesser warnings. Suso and his other friends managed to get him to the Clinica del Rosario, where his sisters joined them. After Donald had helped me accustom myself to the shock of this news, I hurried to Rome to be with him.

Luchino's sister Uberta told me that he had asked for me to be sent in at once if I came. They were having a difficult time keeping him relaxed. In recent years he had devoted himself to the young Helmut Berger, whom he had discovered as a waiter in a German hotel at which he was staying. Loyally, the sisters were trying to cover the fact that Berger had not come to the clinic, so my arrival was a useful distraction. I could barely disguise my sadness when I saw Luchino propped up on pillows looking so helpless. The stroke had removed control of some of his movements, most noticeably his eyes, which seemed to turn independently. It was a cruel sight, not made any easier by his proud attempt to ignore as far as possible what was happening to him and to go on talking as if he and I were simply planning some new production. I did my best to maintain the fiction.

Eventually his family and friends arranged for his transfer to a clinic in Switzerland with a reputation for this sort of problem. I kept in touch as best I could, but in September I had to fly to Vienna to direct *Don Giovanni* at the Staatsoper. Inevitably, Luchino was on my mind as I worked on the characters. Not inappropriately: there was a lot of the 'Don' about the

262 great Visconti – the arrogance, virility, charm, power and destructiveness were all common features. It seemed incredible that Luchino had never directed it.

It was a decade since that first Dallas production and I was now ready to expand my bleak vision of a ruined world into its final form. That burned-out wasteland in Dallas seemed strangely prophetic – by 1972 it was appropriate. The death of the hopeful, peace-loving decade of the 1960s and the sudden descent into the aggressive, cynical 1970s found its echo in the production. Imagine the moment when a bomb explodes, the blinding white instant in which everything is caught in stark silhouette, the elaborate *fer-forgé* balconies just beginning to twist in the searing heat, the metal only just resisting. This was the setting for my *Don Giovanni* and I think it went about as far as I could go. It was a conception that had nagged away at me over the years.

I am not a great Mozart fan except for this one unparalleled work; everything of Mozart is in it, as is much that went before and a great deal of what was to come after. It brings together a whole panorama of European culture: Spain, Austria and Italy, but somehow it always seems to defeat interpretation because the visual element is all in the words and music, and anything anyone adds is superfluous. It also has so many layers of meaning that any attempt to pin it down with costumes and sets to a particular time and place always diminishes it. I now think that, if I ever do it again, I'll stage it in a completely abstract way, on an empty stage just using lights, though that would hardly be what I'm supposed to be good at as, if I have any strengths in production, they are in the use of spectacle.

Donald Downes never sugared his criticisms and he always said my films were nothing compared to my theatrical work – to him I was a man of the stage. But that was to miss something of what I can do. I had worked in the cinema almost as long as in the theatre and had tried to bring some of the size, scope and glamour of the big screen to the stage. That's why they say I'm good at Hollywood-style productions of *Turandot* or the melodrama of *Tosca*. I try to make a simple, clear, interpretation that can be worked out in theatrical ways.

Luckily my next contract brought me back to La Scala and close to where Luchino had been moved, his family villa on the shore of Lake Como. He was paralysed on his left side and needed daily physiotherapy, but the room that had once been decorated by his beautiful mother, the tragic heiress Carla Erba, was equipped as a cutting-room. There Luchino, who had never found a woman to replace his beloved mother, could edit his story of the mad homosexual Ludwig with his uncontrollable passion for Wagner's music.

As soon as I returned to Italy, I went with Pippo to visit him. It was strange to walk again in the beautiful nineteenth-century park laid out around the imposing villa. There was a large Rolls-Royce Silver Wing parked in the drive, which his sisters had bought so that he could get in and out easily.

Only later did Uberta tell me the full story of how they had acquired so expensive a vehicle: it seems that, when they saw he would need a big car, they asked him what he would like. But when he told them, they were horrified – wouldn't he just make do with a Mercedes? He was adamant that the world had got to see that Visconti was still riding high.

'Before I could have done with a Fiat,' he said, 'but now it has to be a Rolls.' Then he turned to his sisters and implored them. 'All my life, have I ever asked you for anything?'

Had he ever asked them for anything? One really didn't know whether to laugh or cry. Here was the man who virtually beggared his family in order to pay for his productions and jewellers' bills, who had caused them to sell off one of the largest industrial fortunes in Europe in order to indulge his genius, and now he demanded to know if he had ever asked them for anything. Needless to say, they bought him the Rolls-Royce.

He was seated in a wheelchair on a veranda, propped up by cushions and surrounded by beautiful young nieces and nephews who'd come to read to him. There was a prim nurse in starched white and the usual rough-and-tumble of family dogs. The sisters sat, upright, aristocratic, patient, in a near semi-circle around him. A slight autumn breeze stirred the water on the lake and brought the occasional leaf down from the trees. I stopped for a moment in my approach, held by the idea that he had posed the whole thing, it was so much like a scene from one of his films. I went on, bent to embrace him and noticed that his left eye was hooded, less open than the right. I made no comment on his affliction and he offered none; that would have been intolerable to him. We talked about work, his work. He would do the Ring cycle at La Scala. Now that he had become so involved with *Ludwig* he felt the time was right. As long as I listened to him and did not dwell on his appearance I was utterly convinced that he could and would take on the enormous task, such was the power of the man. The Ring by Visconti – what a prospect. We talked until the light began to fade and it became chilly. We moved inside, and he insisted Pippo and I stay to dinner. We discussed the meaning of the cycle and the nature of Wagner's characters as if there were just the two of us sitting on the floor in front of the library fire in the Via Salaria. All the intervening years, the separation, the feuding and the bitterness had gone.

As we drove back to Milan that night I tried to convey to Pippo what he had been like in his great days. Even now there was so much power left that I was sure he could do the Ring, all that was needed was faith on the part of those at La Scala who would have to cope with his infirmities. I was due to work at La Scala on the opening production of the season, *Un*

264   *ballo in maschera,* and was prepared to help out if needed, but this was not to be. The morning of my first rehearsal I overheard the current gossip that the management had decided to call in another director for the Ring, Luca Ronconi. I was appalled at the thought of what this would do to Luchino and went to the Sovrintendente and angrily demanded an explanation Inevitably, they had their excuses ready: they had seized on the designs that Luchino had submitted. These had been done by Mario Chiari, whom he had used many years before. They were exactly what Luchino wanted but the management decided that they were somewhat dated and wrong They were clearly using this as an excuse to change directors. It was indescribably painful for Luchino and incredibly shortsighted on the part of La Scala, because what they could not see was that, despite his infirmities he was at the peak of his creative genius and was about to launch on a series of stunning productions, to my mind the best of his career. They foolishly lost for ever the chance to have the Visconti Ring cycle; it's a tragedy.

It was Suso Cecchi d'Amico who kept Luchino going. Even though he was too ill to attend the première of *Ludwig* in January 1973, she used all her influence to get the National Theatre in Rome to let him direct the Italian version of Harold Pinter's *Old Times.* The result was extraordinary Luchino took Pinter's play as a mere outline and virtually created his own play within it, endowing what had been a story about a family with elements of lesbianism and nudity never envisaged by the author. As for the staging, it was as if Luchino was trying to show that, despite his afflictions, he would never take the easy way out. He'd rearranged the whole theatre, turning the stage into a ring in which his own grotesque idea of the family could be enacted in glaring focus like an unending fight. He had a box to himself at one side, from which he was watching the production, and asked me to join him there after the show. It was a touching occasion, for so much of Italy's theatrical life came to give him an ovation Anna Magnani, Rina Morelli, Andreina Pagnani, all shortly to die. The box became a shrine, with lines of people trooping up to shake his hand and show their love. I arrived first and he asked me to stay with him. I stood beside his chair, careful to see that he was not too tired. I kept thinking of that night at La Scala when he had hugged me to him and tried to fight off anyone who came near me.

Luchino's production of *Manon Lescaut* at Spoleto the following June was the finest version of that Puccini opera I have ever seen and a good slap in the face for La Scala. He persuaded Lila de Nobili to come out of seclusion in Paris to create the sets and he had Piero Tosi design the costumes. In a way he was surrounding himself with all the talent he had launched and they, in turn, repaid him with their greatest work. As I watched, I marvelled that a man by now virtually immobile and so easily

exhausted should still have seen to even the tiniest detail of the interpretation, costumes and set in the way that had always been his hallmark and
which he had taught us all. Perhaps it was his disabilities which for once
cleared his mind of some of the clutter that often bedevilled his work. To
Manon he brought only clear thinking and clear interpretation, and thus
created a brilliant production. I was happy for him, but also sad when I
thought of the physical suffering he had gone through to create his triumph,
one of the last truly happy moments in his life.

My own production at La Scala of *Un ballo in maschera* had given me a
second chance to work with Placido Domingo. What a transformation he
had undergone since the *Missa solemnis*! He had lost weight and was
no longer a chubby boy, but an attractive man. Suddenly, he showed a
tremendous authority. He had an underlying sensitivity that came with
his intelligence. The comparisons with Callas are obvious, both in the way
they took control of their bodies to create their own physical appearance
and in the informed way they approached the meaning of their roles. I have
found that it is only the truly great performers such as Callas, Simionato,
Domingo, Olivier or Magnani who listen to a director no matter how green
he is because the great are always ready to learn, always absorbing ideas,
listening, observing and digesting. Of course, they may in the end reject
what they are given, but never out of hand.

It was while I was working on the opera that my agent, Dennis Van
Thal, called me from London to say that everyone in the film business was
talking about an incredible project, a truly vast film and television tie-in
which would for the first time present with majestic scope and dignity the
life of Christ. He kept emphasizing the scale of this project, the huge sums
of money, the prestige, and he went on to say that mine was one of the first
names on the list of possible directors. I was far from bowled over. I could
imagine how long a list they must have and I was extremely sceptical about
anything coming of it. In any case, I felt I had now fulfilled my vow; I had
made my film of St Francis and was surely free to move on, perhaps to
another Shakespeare film or to some other giant like Dante, whose *Inferno*
might furnish a subject for the epic of epics. I was not to know that destiny
or providence had not yet done with me so far as religion was concerned.

That I was less enthusiastic about religious productions was no doubt
due to the treatment I received in New York. The Christmas opening of
Brother Sun, Sister Moon was in some ways worse than I'd anticipated. The
Vietnam protests had intensified; this was the time of flag-burning and
guilt. I went to the previews and watched the reactions. Some were ugly;
there was mocking laughter at the idea of love and gentleness. Just as
Romeo and Juliet had struck the right note at a time when young people
were creating a cultural revolution, so *Brother Sun* went totally against the
grain of the new cynicism. The humiliation of what I had always viewed

266   as an offering to my patron saint for help in time of trouble was deeply painful to me. Needless to say, the critics did not flinch from putting in the knife. The only bright spot in this gloom was Tennessee Williams, who was loud in his defence of the picture, writing in the newspapers that he was ashamed people could not appreciate beauty and innocence. At the end of the year, one of the papers, the *New York Times* I think, asked various people to list their top ten films of the year and Tennessee picked *Brother Sun, Sister Moon* as his first choice. But his was a solitary voice; most of the comments were derisory. As I flew back to Italy, I tried to convince myself there was no point being miserable over what such people say. But it never works; one always is.

The only thing that gave me strength was the memory of Chanel and how abused she'd been at the time of her first comeback. As I kept telling myself, she'd won through in the end.

Again, I was to find myself in one of those troughs which every life goes through, that weary succession of collapsing projects every film-maker has to get used to. First to go was the plan to film Dante's *Inferno*, which was cancelled in January 1973.

I turned again to the idea of making a musical version of *Much Ado About Nothing* with a delightful score by Nino Rota, and went to New York to see if Liza Minnelli would be interested in a film version. There is a great rapport between us, but I could sense at once that she was not particularly attracted to the project. Then I began to talk about various ideas I had, including another try at *Camille*. I told Liza I wanted to remake the film. I even had a preliminary script by the writer Hugh Wheeler which embodied some of my ideas. My *Camille* would not be Garbo's romantic heroine, but a more earthy turn-of-the-century woman, a lady of the night. She would probably be a cabaret singer rather than a courtesan, and her lover would be the son of an important politician. There was to be a political scandal in the background with echoes of the Dreyfus affair.

As I was telling her this, I could see that Liza was completely entranced. 'I want to do it,' she exclaimed in that intense way she has. 'You must find a way. It's a deal.'

She had just done *Cabaret* and was the biggest box-office draw at the time, so I was elated. The whole thing seemed unbeatable, Minnelli as Camille. We agreed that she would come to Positano that summer so we could work on the idea with a view to filming in the autumn.

Before then there was the Easter opening in London of *Brother Sun, Sister Moon*. It was greeted with no more enthusiasm, though with less derision, than in New York. As expected, the critics were merciless. The only joy I have had out of the whole business is the affection the film has found amongst those in the world where faith means more than supposed sophistication. Since it was made, not a day has gone by when it is not shown somewhere in the world and now it has become a cult movie. Once, when I was in South America, I was asked to go to Lima to attend a showing. I set off from Rio by plane, but technical trouble turned us back. We set off again five hours later, expecting to arrive at eleven at night. I hardly imagined that anyone would be there to meet me, yet, when we landed, a vast crowd was waiting at the airport. They burst into cheers and applause, and began to chant the theme from the film as I was led towards them, It was an astonishing experience when I think of those New York audiences.

My summer in Positano with Liza was a pleasant interlude, much of it due to her zany humour and raw enthusiasm for everything she is engaged in. But it was not to be. *Camille,* like so many other ideas at that time, never got off the ground. Grimaldi, who had produced *Last Tango,* wished to make *Camille* into a 'red-light' movie and, since we couldn't possibly agree to such an interpretation and he refused to compromise with us, the deal fell through.

Some force seemed to be at work determined to clear away all my projects, to ensure that I would move in a certain direction. I know I risk sounding unhinged, but it is necessary to realize just how many good ideas which had big stars attached to them and solid financial backing suddenly faded away, often for no discernible reason, in order to understand why I was becoming so superstitious.

Having accepted that we were not going to be able to go ahead with *Camille,* Liza went off for her autumn concert tour, while I went to London for my National Theatre production of *Saturday, Sunday, Monday.* I had been brought up on de Filippo. Back in the 1930s we had always gone to see his touring company; he was a theatrical institution in Italy. The Neapolitan theatre has deep roots. It comes out of the Commedia dell'Arte tradition and most of the Neapolitan theatrical families are related in some way. De Filippo was the natural son of Scarpetta, who was the great figure in Neapolitan drama at the turn of the century. De Filippo, with his brother and sister, acted from childhood, lived in theatres and was always on the road. He once told me the reason he had such a strange, fascinating voice was that when he was eighteen or nineteen he'd been doing a particularly strenuous part and returned sweating to his dressing-room, where there was a cold draught. His voice went and never really came back. He had developed a sort of coarse rasp, little more than a rough whisper, but it worked beautifully; whenever he opened his mouth, the audience had to shut up and really concentrate to hear what he said. It gave him a reputation for great presence, when the truth was that he couldn't project. He was in good company, for the same thing had happened to the great Eleonora Duse.

De Filippo was a sort of Goldoni. He wrote plays for his company and thus, by extension, for his family, so that his work tended to be about Neapolitan family relations. He worked up the individual characteristics of his players in a very natural way. They were simple, earthy and, at their best, alive with human insight. *Saturday, Sunday, Monday* was typical: three days in the life of a tight-knit family. But what brilliant characters. The ordinary husband is so much in love with his plain wife that he jealously imagines her to be pursued by one and all, especially their neighbour above. On Saturday the ground is laid; on Sunday everyone gathers for the family meal, when the drama breaks; and on Monday there is the reconciliation. Nothing much happens, there are no earth-shattering events, but the play reveals a great deal of truth. I had seen it first in 1956 and had been bowled over by it.

I was more than delighted when Ken Tynan came up with the idea of doing it in London, although I realized from the start that conveying the true Neapolitan atmosphere without making it a gross Italian caricature was going to be difficult.

Our strengths were, as ever, our actors. Larry wanted to do it for Joan, and she was certainly just right as the symbol of adoration who is not immediately, conventionally beautiful to the others. When they came to Positano to prepare the piece, it was amazing to see how Larry absorbed the manners and gestures of the people in the village. One day, at rehearsal, Larry turned up with a manual of Italian gestures – heaven knows where he'd got it. Inside were the hand signs for 'I love you', 'I'm hungry', and a host of less polite expressions. Larry, as usual, was full of that over-polite humbug which he liked to affect.

'Excuse me, Franco darling,' he said. 'As you are Italian, perhaps you could kindly help me by explaining what this means?'

I was content that he should use gestures, but less happy with the sort of accent he started to spread about. Once Larry began using mock Italian it was infectious, and soon everyone sounded like Scottish ice-cream sellers. I was determined to stop this, and that raised the question of directing a man like Olivier. I was experienced enough not to be daunted by the task, but equally wise enough to know that you don't just charge in and try to remake the man according to some image of your own. In any case he would't let you. I knew this would require skill. Great actors like Olivier will absorb ideas and then transform them into speech patterns, gestures and expressions which they know instinctively will work for them. You cannot totally remould them, but you can do a great deal by stealth, almost by deception. You can trick them into finding things in themselves they didn't know were there. It's fair game, because someone like Larry is such a wonderful old fraud; he'll thank you for your advice, praise you for your insight, bless you for helping him in this way, and then go and do it exactly as he wants. Inexperienced directors might get mangled.

Anna Magnani comes to mind in this context because, while we were rehearsing, a friend called from Rome to say that Anna had been taken to hospital with cancer. I had known that Anna was not well, but this sudden decline was a bad shock. On recent occasions, when she had come by to sample Vige's cooking, she would tell me about this or that doctor she was trying; one would have a novel treatment, another would be giving her pills of various sorts. In retrospect, it is clear that, because she changed doctors so often, none of them ever got near to diagnosing what was wrong with her until it was too late.

A few months before I left for London, she had asked if she could dine with me alone, as there were always too many people around at my parties. I said yes, of course, and left it at that. But stars seldom appear in the heavens alone and later that day I was rung up by Maria Callas, who was then preparing her only attempt at direction, *I vespri siciliani,* for the Turin opera. She was in Rome at the costume-makers and said she desperately needed my advice, an unusual confession which meant she was really in trouble. There was no refusing her.

'Why don't you come round tonight?' I said.

I had no sooner hung up than I remembered my promise to Anna. I knew it would be hell with two such *prima donnas,* but I could see no way round it. Magnani arrived first and was in a foul mood. She complained about the traffic and about how far I lived from the centre of the city. Then she said, 'Well, at least it's going to be a quiet evening.'

'Absolutely, Anna,' I said. 'There will only be four of us – just you, me, Maria Callas and Giuseppe di Stefano.'

'What?' she hissed. 'That Greek bitch with no voice left?'

I forbore to tell her that Maria might consider her an Italian bitch which no career left, and led her into the main room, full of foreboding about the meeting of these two sacred monsters. What happened was unnerving. Maria, when she arrived, was in one of her humble moods. She was the adoring fan, the little girl meeting the great star and almost knelt at Anna's feet.

'What a pleasure,' she gasped. 'I watch all your films, I learn so much. Your Medea on stage was perfect. I've sung it many times, but you act it so much better than me.'

I tried to detect any hint of sarcasm, but there didn't seem to be any.

Anna was caught unawares. 'Well, you too are wonderful, you've done incredible things.'

I had no sooner breathed a sigh of relief than I realized the next hurdle would be the dinner table. Who should sit on my right? I waited until Anna went to powder her nose, then I said to Maria:

'Listen, darling, Magnani is so much older than you. I'll have to put her on my right, if you don't mind.'

'You must,' she said firmly.

Zeffirelli

270   The meal was incredible: the two of them just prattled away. Every time I tried to speak they were deaf to me.

In some ways my housekeeper, Vige, was more nervous than I. Maria was a notoriously difficult person to cook for, as you could never be sure if she was on one of her rigid diets. Anna, on the other hand, was supposedly a typical Roman with a passion for rich food. Vige agonized over the menu and in the end the meal consisted of several subtly alternative dishes. There was a lightweight dish of spinach balls with egg and, side by side, the same thing wrapped in pasta leaves; some were cooked in sage and butter, others in a mushroom sauce, and others just boiled in water. There was an especially fine dish of veal in white wine and, beside it, a spicy *stufatino alla cacciatora*. In the end everything was thrown out of gear when Anna nibbled delicately at all the unfilling diet food, while Maria scoffed the heavy rich dishes like a trooper. Vige, who was spying at the door, could hardly believe it.

Finally, I left the two of them alone. I occupied myself with di Stefano and the problems they were encountering as they tried to cope with their first production. That was the last time I saw Anna.

In London, when the news of her illness came, I was desperate to help. Again, I turned to Bill Cahan, who was director and first surgeon of New York's Memorial Hospital. He had just married Grace Mirabella, the chief editor of American *Vogue,* and the couple were honeymooning at the villas in Positano. Bill had given me so much help when Aunt Lide had been dying that now, although I hated to bother him, I rang to beg him to call Rome to ask the doctors there what the situation was. When I called again, Grace told me he had not merely telephoned but had left for Rome. Such was his international reputation that the Italian doctors were not offended by his offering a second opinion. But, when he called me, the news was not good. He concurred with Anna's physician that she had an inoperable cancer of the pancreas. I spoke to her one last time on the telephone.

'There is a time to . . .', she was saying, but her voice disappeared and her son Luca came on the line to explain that she was too ill to speak.

I was told later to what lengths they went to keep her alive, until in the end she struck one of the nurses who was giving her yet another injection and begged her to let her die. This story reminded me of little Luca all those years ago screaming at his mother because of the endless painful treatments he was put through as a child. It was as if the whole thing had come full circle. When she finally died that September the poor boy was distraught. They had had the most intense, even passionate, relationship and her death was unbearable for him. He wanted her corpse embalmed but it was not permitted, so he had her hair dyed its former raven black and her make-up done by the people who had worked with her on so many of her films.

I left rehearsals and flew to Rome. I saw her lying there just as I'd known her, that near-savage woman who had been the symbol of Rome since before the war. And yet, appallingly, she received little official recognition. An actress of her merits should have lain in state on the Capitol, yet because she had no political allegiance no one bothered to arrange it. Not for her the thirty-six metre tricoleur that hung above Colette as she lay in state at the Palais Royal. But the ordinary people of Rome honoured her by their millions. They laid siege to the clinic where she had died. It was such an event that the Italian President felt obliged to make a gesture, but when he tried to approach the coffin, he got more than he bargained for: Luca screamed abuse at him for not giving his mother the honour he believed she deserved, and indeed he was right.

Though she was not given a state funeral, the private ceremony at La Minerva, the artists' church near the Pantheon, was a great and moving occasion. Her last years had been sadly empty, but now it was possible to remember how she had dominated not only Italian theatre and cinema but Italian life for two generations. I remembered the grand actress I'd known as a young man who just wanted to kick off her shoes and sit up talking all night. She was unique. Even the last act in her story had an element of passionate drama about it, thanks to the one great love of her life, Roberto Rossellini. While her grave was being prepared, he offered Luca a temporary place for Anna in the Rossellini family sepulchre and Roberto himself took charge of the interment. It was an amazing scene. Ingrid Bergman laid a bouquet of vivid scarlet roses on the coffin, there was Rossellini's first wife alongside his present wife, the Indian Sonali Das Gupta, with their child; and a girl who everyone knew was Rossellini's latest mistress. He was like an oriental potentate burying one of his harem, and the odd thing was that none of the others seemed to think it was odd!

Back in London, after only two days away, I was surprised to discover that I had crossed one of those invisible lines which so upset the otherwise tolerant English. No one, it seems, may halt a rehearsal even for the funeral of a close friend. I remembered how Richard Burton had stood out against Liz going to the funeral of Montgomery Clift, as such a thing was contrary to his standards of theatrical behaviour. Here was a real culture clash; but we survived the crisis.

In the end, I swayed the production away from jokey Italian accents, arguing that they wouldn't do Chekhov in funny Russian voices or Molière with French ones. We got a real Neapolitan atmosphere by a clever ruse: when the family gathered for its Sunday lunch, we had a huge pot of real Italian ragout simmering on the stove. The aroma of tomatoes, peppers, garlic and oregano wafted round the Old Vic. It was irresistible, and it was very funny to overhear members of the audience as they left the auditorium suddenly deciding that they wanted to run to Soho for an Italian meal.

Zeffirelli

272   De Filippo came over for the opening and was delighted. As an old trouper he was impressed by the way Olivier had captured every detail of gesture and speech – he had created an authentic old Neapolitan fool.

While de Filippo had not bothered us during the production because he trusted us, now that he was enjoying such success he was determined his play should be done in New York. I, who knew the signs better than he, was more cautious. I was aware that, as usual, a lot of leading New York theatre people had flown over to see the production, but I also knew that none of them had expressed interest in an American version. They could foresee, as I could, the problem. There is a large Italo-American population in New York with their own brand of English, much parodied in Mafia movies. That would have been quite wrong for this Neapolitan play, but it would have seemed equally strange to have the actors speaking straight English, as we had in London. There was a sense in which this tiny difficulty was insurmountable. But de Filippo was adamant. The following year directed it in New York with Eli Wallach and Sada Thompson, and, as foreseen, the impact was far less strong than in London.

There was to be one unpredictable by-product of *Saturday, Sunday Monday*. While we were rehearsing, my agent again brought up the possible film of the life of Christ. The idea had apparently originated with Italian television. Looking for a co-production deal, they approached Lew Grade of ATV, who had previously produced Burt Lancaster in *Moses*. Sensing a winner, Grade had immediately gobbled up the project as his own and hurried off to Rome, where he contrived a papal audience with Pope Paul VI, who gave him a sort of official Catholic imprimatur on the whole thing. This effectively took the production out of the hands of Italian television chiefs, though they were still determined to have a say in who would direct the films. Typically, they could not agree on an Italian director; their favourite candidate was the Swede Ingmar Bergman, and a respectable sum of money was handed over for him to produce a treatment. When this arrived, it turned out to contain a sensational 'own goal' – Jesus and Mary Magdalene were little short of lovers. Collapse of the Italian faction!

Now, it seemed, Lew Grade was pressing for me. He knew about my religious leanings but, more germanely, he came to see *Saturday, Sunday Monday* and not only loved it but helped arrange its transfer to one of his West End theatres. We met for the first time since the television transmission of *Tosca* almost ten years earlier and I was immediately impressed by two contradictory elements in the way he behaved. On the one hand he was blunt to the point of dismissal: 'If you don't do it, someone else will.' An obvious point, but one that always gets attention. On the other hand, he was touchingly thoughtful about what needed to be done. Because of the length of the film (there would be over six hours of television in all) there was an unparalleled opportunity to tell the life of our Lord without recourse to the clichés and theatricality which had turned Hollywood's attempts into the crude epics with which we were all too familiar. The most winning argument he didn't have to make: that here was a Jew talking persuasively of the need to reaffirm traditional Christian values in a time of moral laxity. I remembered how moved I had been in 1965 when Pope Paul VI had made the declaration *Nostra aetate* (Our Times), which finally laid to rest the notion that the Jews were responsible for the death of Christ. It was a plea for racial tolerance and human brotherhood. After the meeting with Lew Grade, my mind kept turning over the possibilities of so vast a subject. I thought of my time in hospital and of my decision to try to use whatever talents I had in the service of my faith. Here, surely, was the best opportunity I would ever get; but more to the point was the fact that anything which might have stood in the way of my taking on the task had mysteriously fallen by the wayside. I see little reason to doubt that someone somewhere had brought me to it and I have no doubt as to who that someone is. A few days before Christmas 1973 I cabled my acceptance; it was perhaps the most important decision of my professional life.

SIXTEEN

One Star

The project was to take over two years of my life. I was to produce a series of films for television which would convey the life and words of Christ taken quite literally from the commonly agreed texts of the New Testament without recourse to legend or tricky cinematic mysticism. The reality which film can create was to be used to show the humanity of Christ. It was as simple as that. It was also dauntingly complex. Generous finance, several remote foreign locations and a cast list like a *Who's Who* of the acting profession all had to be managed like a military operation. On top of that, there was the need to satisfy an international audience with very different perceptions of their 'Lord'. Lew Grade was emphatic that the films should be acceptable to all denominations. It was an unnerving thought that for once I would not simply have a producer to contend with but church leaders, theologians, historians and even the ordinary faithful. Also much of the potential audience would be unbelievers who, without the forgiveness of faith, would readily find any bad dialogue or over-sentimentality ridiculous. All those Hollywood epics were stacked in the background ready to provide an all-too-easy batch of clichés and schmaltzy scenarios. If any hint of that should creep in we would be pilloried.

My experience with *Brother Sun, Sister Moon* now had an unexpected relevance. Any wish to popularize the story, to introduce a contemporary interpretation, to add songs or any other show-business elements had been thoroughly exorcized by that wounding episode. If there was to be any interpretation it would be more backward-looking than fashionably contemporary and was to come from the feelings I'd had after my early conversations with Lew Grade. The point I wanted to make most evident was that Christ was a Jew, a prophet who grew out of the cultural, social and historical background of the Israel of his time, with its farms and small villages, each with its cramped little synagogue; an Israel occupied by an arrogant enemy and always smouldering on the edge of a civil disorder. More than that, Christ's words had to be seen as a continuation and fulfilment of centuries of Jewish religious teaching. It is not at all an original notion that Christ behaved, thought and spoke as a Jew of his time, but it is one that is often overlooked. We are surrounded by images of the New

Testament which were reinterpreted in ways relevant to their day: the
touching medieval nativities sparkling with northern snow, the Renaissance
crucifixions watched over by Florentine bankers in the dress of the period.

Both the words of Pope Paul's *Nostra aetate* and the need to create
cinematic reality led to the decision to try to show the historical Jewish
Jesus. Of all the attempts to capture the life of Christ, the most successful
in my opinion was the spare, beautiful film by the French director Julien
Duvivier, shot in the 1930s entirely on location in Provence. That was to
be a clear inspiration.

Thus, at the beginning, I faced two different problems: first the need for
a basic story with dialogue that was speakable yet still acceptable as the
words of Christ, and second the need for locations that resembled as clearly
as we could imagine the Holy Land of Christ's day. Later would come the
whole question of actors; at first it was words and places that mattered.
The size of the project precluded the normal working method of writing a
script and then finding locations and getting sets built. These two elements
would have to progress in tandem. Fortunately, the prestige of the project
and the sums of money pledged meant that in all fields we could turn to
the finest talent alive. For our script we approached Anthony Burgess, who
seized on the commission with relish. He simply took on board our idea of
the Jewish setting and disappeared to get on with the writing. With relief
I put that side of things out of my mind and set off in search of Christ's
Israel, a journey which was to take all of 1974 and much of the following
year.

I knew before I started out that Israel today bears little relation to the
Judaea of the Gospels. I had visited some of the holy places when I'd
directed opera in Tel Aviv in 1959 and 1962, and was aware how depressing
most of them are nowadays. But I had to be sure. Perhaps I would find a
village that could be Nazareth, a fortress that could be Herod's palace or
a lake that could be Galilee. In a sense it was a wasted journey, but at least
it cleared my mind and showed that there would be no easy answer, no one
location.

Returning from location search in Jordan, I was welcomed – if that is
the right word – at the other side of the Allenby Bridge by a delegation led
by the Israeli Minister of Communications. He was, naturally, an urbane
and cultivated man, and I remembered the knowledgeable audiences in the
Mann Auditorium, so quick to notice the least fault in a performance. His
greetings were effusive, but I could tell that there was something worrying
him.

'It's a pity you've come here for a project like this,' he said after the
exchange of courtesies was over. 'Why not Shakespeare or Verdi, something
a little less problematic?'

It was so evidently a truthful remark which just slipped out that I felt

Zeffirelli

I had to put his mind at rest. I told him my aim was to show that Christians and Jews shared common roots, that we were, via Christ, all sons of Abraham, and that I, personally, had always considered the Jews my elder brothers. But I could see he still harboured doubts about what we were doing and he explained that films about Christ usually rekindle old hatreds. I tried to reassure him and, though I may not have fully succeeded, the incident certainly strengthened my resolve to make this Jesus a man who was clearly a Jew, a man of Nazareth and no enemy of his own people, then or now.

I tried the surrounding areas: Jordan, Syria and Turkey, but even where there was a possible site the politics of the area or the logistics of filming in remote places ruled them out. I crossed off the Middle East and headed for Egypt. Many of our most imposing scenes would be set in the Temple of Jerusalem and my first task was to find a comparable building which could be dressed to the period. Curiously, early Islamic architecture was not modelled on early Egyptian temples or Roman buildings but on Hebrew structures, and some of the great mosques were clear replicas of the Temple, with its colonnaded halls, outer courtyards and fountains for ritual ablutions. There were such mosques in Cairo, some absolutely perfect like that of Toulun, but again the politics were against us; the notion of masking the Islamic symbols with Hebraic decoration and filling the sacred site with people wearing traditional Jewish garb was clearly anathema to too many people. One thing emerged, however, from my visit: it pointed me firmly in the direction of North Africa, which was eventually to prove the right solution. The sort of building I had in mind had its finest expression in Islam's fifth most sacred shrine: the Great Mosque of Kairouan in Tunisia. That, too, proved untouchable, but the countryside yielded some sensational locations: the interior of the fort at Monastir with its watch-tower became the Roman garrison in Jerusalem; the hill before the *ribat* or fort in nearby Sousse was Golgotha; and against the ancient walls we would build our own temple.

Thoroughly entranced by the Mahgreb, I went to Morocco and there I found the exteriors I needed, the unspoilt landscape so reminiscent of Galilee. On the fringe of the desert the ancient fortress at Ouarzazate would be Herod's palace in Judaea. The people themselves, living in a way unchanged for centuries, were ideal for the crowds which came to hear Christ preach. Only one thing was missing, Nazareth itself. I was loath to build a stage-set, yet nothing seemed quite right. Then, in April 1975, a fortunate détour provided the answer. I was travelling with my production designer, Renzo Mongiardino, when we decided to indulge in a spot of tourism, a trip to the impressive Roman ruins of Volubilis near Meknes. We passed through the village of Moulay Idriss, a holy place named after its local Moslem saint, and as we continued on our way I saw above us on the hills a little settlement of white Berber houses. We went up to explore and there it was – my Nazareth, square, mud-brick houses with their walled courtyards, a well where the Berber women drew water, the smell of baking bread, the men weaving baskets. It was ridiculously impractical for film-making; there was no electricity, no modern installations of any kind, but it *was* Nazareth and I wired Lew Grade that I had found the place.

Back in Tunisia I was taken to the Isle of Djerba off the eastern end of the coastline. It is associated in legend with Ulysses' isle of the lotus-eaters. More pertinent for me was its ancient Jewish community, descendants of refugees from the Babylonian invasion of Israel, whose synagogues main-tain the oldest and most authentic Jewish ceremonials. The patriarchs of this thousand-year-old community with their flowing white beards could not have been invented by any make-up department. I explained what I was doing and asked if they would take part in our filming. Everything was solemnly translated into ancient Hebrew and formally discussed. They agreed and suddenly, with all the childlike innocence of the truly holy, they began to laugh; it turned out that they were delighted to be going on holiday on the mainland.

That was mid-1975, just before shooting was due to begin in Morocco. Anthony Burgess had come up with his script. It was predictably a *tour de force*. Anthony has an amazing, almost sponge-like capacity to absorb what he reads and had obviously drawn on a wealth of sources, Biblical and Rabinbical, to weld the sometimes patchy history that the apostles have left us into a homogeneous story. There was a price to pay for such a spontaneous way of working in that some of his recollections of Christ's words were not exact, but these were minor matters which I knew we could iron out. Anthony had given us our framework and he left us to flesh it out. In fact, we often finalized the precise dialogue while shooting, offering the actors a set of paraphrases of the Gospel sayings amongst which they could choose in order to find speakable words.

I was helped in all this by Suso Cecchi d'Amico and Emilio Gennarini, who came to work on the Burgess outline. It was a strange time for Suso, as she was still occupied with the task of rescuing Luchino from the decline into which his illness had led him. She cajoled him and those around him into working. She arranged meetings, talked to producers and encouraged everyone to believe that, despite the weakness in his body, the wheelchair and the humiliation felt by that most independent of men, he could do what he set out to achieve. She was loyal, loving and tireless. Her greatest achievement was encouraging him to film *Conversation Piece*, which she helped write, and still she fought on, persuading him to film d'Annunzio's *L'innocente*, even though he was getting weaker and weaker.

Sadly, he had given up the house in the Via Salaria where we had lived. That part of Rome had been ruined by developers and traffic, and the beautiful villa was stranded among concrete blocks. it was impossible to imagine anyone else in a place so imprinted with his personality. I, of course, remembered the library, the fireplace, the beautiful things. When I spoke to him, he would wave such memories aside; he loved precious objects, but he was never really attached to them. He had bought a rather gloomy house by a lake near the papal summer residence at Castelgandolfo, but he was only happy at his villa on Ischia. He had come to Positano once and said how much he loved it. Half jokingly, he suggested one or other of us should give up his villa so that we could combine our talents to produce one glorious place. The idea was no sooner proposed than we laughed it away: the thought of our two superegos together again was too much to take, even as a joke.

Suso was a wonderful help to me with *Jesus of Nazareth,* as we were now calling the production, to emphasize its Jewish roots. It was unusual and rewarding to have so much preparation time, a luxury compared to my earlier rate of a dozen or so stage productions a year. Apart from the film, my only other work in 1975 was the New York staging of *Saturday, Sunday, Monday* in November and another papal commission to direct the televising of the opening of the Porta Sancta in St Peter's to mark the beginning of Holy Year. It seemed fitting, given the new project I was working on, that I should have been involved in the sacred ceremonies that Christmas Day. His Holiness was naturally interested in the film and at an audience he spoke to me about the effectiveness of modern techniques in communicating, as he put it, as a missionary. He ended by saying: 'Any new creation God allows man to conquer can equally easily become an instrument of Evil. May God always see that you are not seduced into temptation by the new media.'

I realize that there will be many people who no longer share my religious faith and who will simply find those words unctuous or even empty. I realize too that there will be a temptation to think that I'm somehow 'putting on' a religious act, perhaps to justify making the film. The problem is that it is almost impossible to explain any faith to those who don't share it. The ecstatic and joyful expressions on the faces of young believers look merely cretinous to the jaded unbeliever, who can only imagine that they have taken leave of their senses. That is why blindness is often used as a metaphor for disbelief. How can one describe sunlight to someone who has never seen it? And yet throughout those two years I was frequently surprised to find evidence of faith in the most unexpected people. The most recalcitrant old roués would turn out to cherish a long-suppressed belief in God, often at an almost child-like level. Of course, as I have already pointed out, acting folk are traditionally the most superstitious people on earth and a healthy fear of somehow getting on the wrong side of God is no doubt part of their nervous view of fate. But even allowing for that, the sight of famous people, well-known actors and actresses, suddenly gripped by the meaning of our story was to be one of the most startling things about the filming.

It was these hidden memories of faith which led to our famous cast in the first place. Of course, there was a move to have only unknowns, on the not unreasonable grounds that any famous face brings along the shadows of previous parts which may conflict with the sacred role now being played. Could someone well known for playing a whore play the Virgin Mary, so the argument went. It was one that had to be reckoned with when I remembered that sacred plays, the Mysteries or the Passion, are usually acted by virginal girls and men of good character in their village. I rejected this argument, not because I wanted to stuff my film with stars; rather, it was because I saw what we were doing as an offering in the way the Renaissance painters looked on their work, and thus only the best in acting was possible. I wanted each part played by an acknowledged master of theatre and film, but I had to recognize that even our generous budget would not run to casting the New Testament with the favourite sons and daughters of the William Morris Agency. It was here that Laurence Olivier came in. Olivier was one of those who keep a lingering affection for the Biblical tale and he was eager to take part without any thought of glory and without haggling over money.

'I'm too old for all that horse riding, so I can't be Pilate. I'm not Jewish enough for Caiaphas. Just give me those two little scenes as Nicodemus.'

The associate producer on the series was Dyson Lovell, who had worked with me ever since *Romeo and Juliet,* when he had done such a good job on the casting. He now dreamed up a brilliant scheme whereby all stars would be paid $30,000 a week, no more and no less – and that really isn't much in film terms. He called it 'most favoured nations' – don't ask me why, but it was with Larry that we established this principle.

As soon as word got around that Olivier was in the film, the enquiries started: 'I suppose he's playing Pilate? No? Only a small part. And the fee?'

Moved, I liked to think, both by these latent religious impulses and certainly by the presence of Olivier as the doyen of their profession, the stars rushed to join us. Anthony Quinn as Caiaphas, Ernest Borgnine as the Centurion, Peter Ustinov as Herod, Christopher Plummer as Herod Antipas, James Mason as Joseph of Arimathea, Ralph Richardson as Simeon ... and so many others. I wanted Elizabeth Taylor as the Magdalene, but she was unwell, so I enquired about Ann Bancroft, the perfect actress, but rather reclusive; she asks for fairly high fees in order to discourage unwanted producers. To my astonishment she agreed. One of the few who hummed and hawed over the money was Marcello Mastroianni, who had been offered the role of Pilate. Mercifully, as it turned out, because

280   we finally got Rod Steiger, who was magnificent. And, of course, I wanted Michael York as John the Baptist.

When the avalanche of talent had settled, I was left with the greatest problem of all – casting Jesus and Mary. It is pointless to recount the details of the search and the weary number of times we auditioned, tested and rejected.

For Mary, who has only a small amount of dialogue, the obvious thing was to find a young girl, perhaps a young Moroccan. But even without words the face of the Madonna has to speak eloquently, and the Berber girls had obviously no training in expressing themselves with looks and gestures even when their jealous brothers would allow them to try. The next idea was to have the veteran Greek actress Irene Papas play the elderly Mary, and so we auditioned dozens of young girls in Athens who could have been her at fifteen. Again, no luck.

Then I thought of Olivia Hussey. She had become like a daughter to me and, indeed, she called me Daddy or by the rather pointed nickname of Bloaty, a reference to the fact that I was putting on weight. We were very close indeed. Since playing Juliet eight years earlier, she had married and divorced, and was the mother of a beautiful boy. Although she could still look angelically young, there were now reserves of sorrow and knowledge to draw on. A screen test showed that she was able to play Mary the girl and Mary the weeping mother, but perhaps more extraordinary was an un-expected ability she revealed. Like many of her generation, she had tried to find some refuge from the unhappiness of her love life in eastern mysticism. She had a guru and practised meditation – not my cup of tea, but it actually helped magnificently. When we filmed the Annunciation, I obviously re-jected the idea of having an angel with wings and a halo. Instead, God's message comes in the form of a silent beam of light that passes through a high aperture in the little mud-brick room to fall on the face of the young Madonna. Olivia simply went into a trance and the effect was heart-stopping.

Later, in Tunisia, when we filmed the Pietà, she became so transported that without instruction or help she threw herself forward and lifted the recumbent body of Christ, a seventy-kilo man! For me, with my memories of that terrible morning in 1944 when I had watched the mothers keening over their sons hanged by the Germans, it was doubly moving. Olivia was shaking and weeping, and after the filming we had to carry her away. It had been pouring with artificial rain and, because of spots on the lens and other technical hitches, the four camera operators felt it would be wise to cover ourselves with a retake. When they called Olivia the tension was such that she fell to the ground and began screaming as if possessed. Unsure of how to handle this, we tried to bundle her out on to the set. She was laughing hysterically, stumbling and shouting. Appalled, Ann Bancroft walked up and slapped her in order to end the hysteria.

'That's enough,' she said looking directly into Olivia's eyes. 'We can't go 281
on like this. You're ruining everything, you're being irresponsible.'

But really it was beyond the poor girl. She hadn't been acting, she had
been living the part, and all we could do was to drape her over the dead
Christ, to whom she clung as if drowning. Awesomely, when I saw the
rushes, this image of the Mother of God clasping her dead Son to her was
so moving I knew at once that it had to be in the film.

There was much else in the whole enterprise which simply imposed itself –
including the lead, who in a way appeared by accident. I was testing Robert
Powell for Judas and, as usual, I was concentrating on his eyes, always
central to any screen performance. I happened to remark that they were
good enough to be the eyes of Christ, and this provoked a rather irritable
remark from one of my producers about how I could consider the same
actor for two roles as different as the Devil and holy water. Perhaps stung
by his sarcasm, I insisted on giving Powell a test for Jesus. Impulsively, I
also resolved a major dilemma we had been struggling with – what should
Jesus look like? Should he be the classical handsome Nazarene of western
high art, bearded, with long hair parted in the middle, and dressed in a
white Middle-Eastern robe with a red cloak draped over one shoulder? Or
should he be, as many have argued from strong religious commitment,
not merely ordinary, but actually physically unprepossessing? We had
considered Dustin Hoffman, who is short with irregular features, and Al
Pacino, who has a Byzantine face. Now, without weighing the pros and
cons, I simply told the make-up people to part Robert Powell's hair in the
middle and give him a beard. I asked for a seamstress to fix him up
with the conventional robe and cloak. I barely paid attention to these
preparations, but then, when it was almost ready, I went over to my
photographer Armando Nannuzzi, who was adjusting the camera. I bent
down and looked through the viewfinder into darkness, when suddenly
Armando lifted away the lens cap and there was Christ. It was stunning.
Then the seamstress, noticing a stray thread, ran on to the set to remove
it and, seeing the full effect for the first time, said: 'Oh, my God,' and
crossed herself. Who was I to argue?

In truth, it was sometimes quite worrying how closely our actors and
actresses became identified with their roles. It is not widely known that
Moslems accept the truth of the virginity of Mary, the mother of the prophet
they call Issa. After nearly a month of filming in the little Moroccan village
there was a scandal when Olivia arrived one day dressed, unexceptionally
to us, in tight jeans and a T-shirt. A village elder came to see me to beg me
to ask her to dress modestly because of the reverence they had for her.

For the procession to the cross, Robert Powell insisted, for the sake of
verisimilitude, on carrying a heavy wooden beam rather than a fake one.
He was clearly exhausted by the task, but then he had to be strapped to

the cross in cold rain, his arms stretched out immobile. It was clear that he was truly suffering and, while watching this, some of the most cynical members of the crew found themselves crying. At the moment when Christ was nailed upon the cross there was a palpable feeling of gloom and fear among the cast and crew. Strangely the hundreds of Tunisian extras began to react in a way we had never seen before.

At first there was merely a lot of worried muttering and shaking of heads, but this soon gave way to something akin to anger and distress. Then hysteria broke out so violently that I thought we might be in danger. All at once it was borne in on me that these people had no idea what we were really doing. They knew the story of Christ in only the most sketchy fashion and they had even less knowledge of the techniques of film-making. As far as they could understand it, we monsters had taken a rather nice young foreigner, had beaten him up so that he was awash with blood and had then, horrendously, nailed his hands and feet to pieces of wood. No wonder we now looked so shamefaced.

Their distress became so palpable that I had to get our Tunisian production team to go about explaining what was really happening. Eventually, everything was sorted out when Robert Powell, who was freezing cold upon his uncomfortable perch, told us to get a move on – plus the use of a four-letter word a little out of keeping with his awesome role.

I shall never tire of saying how wonderful Robert Powell was. How rewarding it was to work with someone so determined to ensure that every inflection was true to what must surely be the most terrifying role any actor could play. It became clear that something more than acting was required: a deeper personal commitment was needed and Robert gave it. For me, the task of directing that international *Who's Who* tested me to the limit. Each one was a great performer with his or her own way of doing things. Each arrived with an idea of how that bit of the script should be played, and each had to be guided to an interpretation that would lock into the overall picture. A clear example of this was Rod Steiger's Pontius Pilate.

Steiger was one of the first to offer his services without any consideration of money. As a veteran of the Actors' Studio, the centre for 'method acting', he had meticulously prepared his role before he arrived. His Pilate was a tortured man thrust to the centre by a powerful historical destiny. His confrontation with Christ must be an earth-shattering event, a turning-point. The problem was that this hardly fitted our interpretation of the Gospel story in its Hebrew setting. The truth must have been that, except for its reputation as a troublesome, 'backward' sort of place, Judaea was hardly central to the Roman Empire. Few Romans were stationed there (which is why the story of the Centurion is so important, as he must have been a man of note) and for Pilate the place must have seemed like a

punishment post. We know that Pilate had already blotted his copybook
by provoking a riot in Jerusalem when some of his troops defiled the
Temple, and it's likely therefore that his only thought was to keep the
peace. Hence he let the Jews themselves decide Jesus's fate; Pilate wasn't
bothered. It must have been something like Monday morning in any city
magistrates' court, when the weekend miscreants are rushed through, while
the justice of the peace hardly looks up as he sentences the usual line of
drunks and brawlers to a small fine or a day or two in jail.

If I had any fears that Steiger would be unwilling to 'unpick' his interpretation, they were groundless. I suggested he read Anatole France's story of
the elderly Pilate, who, when asked in his exile in Marseilles about the
Galilean prophet, simply cannot recall the incident. Rod took the point
and Pilate's slightly bored, unconcerned attitude that is slowly unnerved
by Christ's presence was the perfect interpretation. Far from being a monster whose hands are stained with the blood of the innocent, Steiger gave
us the representative of a civilization whose ethics bend under political
pressure; a figure truly representative of our own time, rather than some
neatly divided tale of good and evil that probably has never really existed.

It would be quite wrong, however, to paint a picture of a group of
high-minded ascetics, dedicatedly constructing a religious offering in an
atmosphere of monastic calm. It is true that there was a great spirit among
us all, whether in the wilds of Morocco in 1975 or in the relative comfort
of Tunisia in 1976, but the atmosphere of an evening was more jolly than
worthy and certainly no one could complain about the company. Even our
most passionate moments were lightened by comic relief. Our producer,
Lew Grade, arrived while we were filming the crucifixion. He gawped, taken
aback by what must have looked like half the population of Tunisia whirling
about in ancient dress. He took me aside and, waving his arms in the air,
he described a large rectangle.

'It isn't cinema, you know, Franco,' he said in a soft paternal voice.

Then with his hands he made a small square.

'It's television, just a little box. How many people can you get on a
television screen?'

Realizing that what was done was done, he asked me what I was doing
the following day. By the curious vagaries of a shooting order, I told him
we were filming the scene in the Garden of Gethsemane.

'Who's in it?' he demanded.

'Jesus and the twelve apostles,' I explained.

'What!' he exploded. '*Twelve* apostles? Can't we make do with less?'

I hasten to add that I've never had a better producer. Although I had
been impressed at our first meeting, I had many doubts about how our
relationship would work out. In many ways he seemed to be a typical brash
theatrical manager, wheeling and dealing, and more concerned about the

284   business side of things than anything else. I suppose I envisaged having to fight every inch of the way to get my film as I wanted it. How wrong that impression turned out to be. Lew was entirely with me and did much to sort out my initial difficulties. These arose because of the residual interest Italian television still retained in the project, which meant that the rushes we were shooting went to Rome to be seen by the producers at RAI. There were still those who wanted an interpretation other than mine: Christ as the common man, Christ as someone indistinguishable from those around him. Those that held this view sniped away at my film for turning Christ into a star and for surrounding him with the famous faces of Hollywood. It was a pernicious argument and one that was likely to prejudice the outcome of the filming. Away on location it was disturbing to receive echoes of this controversy. When Lew Grade found out what was happening, he instantly took charge. He stopped the rushes from going to Rome and supervised them himself. From then on, the messages I received were entirely encouraging. Most supportive was Lew's wife Cathy, who, unlike her husband, was a Catholic and, more than anyone else, completely devoted to what we were doing. She, too, would try to see the rushes and backed me in every way possible.

When it became clear that we were shooting marvellous footage, I begged Lew to consider releasing a cut version as a cinema film. Quite rightly, I now believe, Lew refused. This was a story that people should experience in their homes, he argued, a story that should be told in full and not edited down to suit people on a night out. He would have made easy profits if he had accepted my suggestions, but that was not his way, as I happily discovered.

For me, one of the best discoveries of the filming was a new role for Pippo. It might have been difficult for him amongst all these stars, but his natural good humour meant that he was always popular. When filming began, he had asked if he could work with me again; then, just as shooting started, the First Assistant fell seriously ill and Dyson Lovell suggested Pippo for the job. When I expressed surprise at the idea, Dyson told me just how much Pippo had been learning; he had, unbeknownst to me, been interesting himself in everything from camerawork to direction, so I thought well, here goes; let's give him a chance. He turned out to be very good and was launched on his career.

In some ways, it is perhaps unfair to single out Pippo for praise amongst a team such as we had. Many were people I'd worked with for years, some I'd helped pick out when they were young and had trained in theatre design or costume making, others were brought in because they were famous in their own field. But one person alone did more than anyone to make his mark on the film: David Watkin, the lighting cameraman. When I lost my former cameraman, Armando Nannuzzi, who had left to become a director, we were lucky to find David available. It was he who created that look of Old Master paintings, a feeling of deep, rich oil-colours lit by a sudden direct light through a small window or the chink of a door. Each set became a succession of brilliant still lives. He did it by perfecting his own peculiarly complex lighting technique. A barrage of powerful arc lights was positioned behind translucent white panels, giving a gentle, diffused light all over the set; slits were cut in the panels so that the desired points within it could be highlighted by an intense beam. No one knew how much time he would need to set up – sometimes it took him five minutes, and sometimes even days to light what was otherwise the simplest scene. Worse still, the exposed lights there in North Africa raised the temperature unbearably. Often the cast would have to stand around in heavy costumes and make-up while this was going on. Even among professionals used to hanging about on film sets, rebellion was in the air. The worst day of all was one of Larry Olivier's. Larry, who was suffering from a series of ailments, had to wait hours while Watkin lit the scene. I could see the pallor under Larry's make-up and when, at last, everything was ready, he simply couldn't do it. He tried to speak, but that great, finely tuned voice had given up on him. It was an awful moment. We wrapped for the night and the next day Larry was able to go ahead.

Afterwards he came to warn me: 'Franco, you know how much I care for you and love you, but you are going to lose the picture if you don't fire this man. He doesn't know what he is doing.'

I did my best to placate him, but I was determined to stick it out. When we saw the rushes, Larry was the first to admit that it was a stunning achievement, though he understandably insisted we remember how much he had suffered for each shot. 'Of course, nothing compared to the sufferings of Our Lord,' he added with a sigh.

Undoubtedly, David Watkin's finest moments were the scenes in the temple when the Sanhedrin met under Caiaphas, the High Priest, to interrogate Christ. Of many memorable moments, this was for all of us one of the high spots of our two years' work simply because of the sheer glitter of the people involved – Anthony Quinn as Caiaphas, with Olivier and James Mason among the Pharisees. It must have been a testing moment for Robert Powell, almost as if he were on trial himself before this jury of great actors. What took the awe out of the occasion was the inevitable banter between shots. One thing that Lew Grade had made clear during his visit was that we were going to over-run, so rather than have intractable editing problems he suggested it would be better if I cut back on some of the scenes now. All well and good, except that these famous players had forgone financial reward for the glory of appearing in this holy work. How to get them to reduce their parts? Fortunately, Larry came to my aid again. Acting as a sort of shop steward, he rose from his council seat and addressed me.

'Darling, I'm going to offer you a little flower, a couple of flowers. Can I cut these two lines altogether?'

Taking their cue from him, the others were soon following suit.

'I think I can make more of this with less,' James Mason offered.

Ian Holm said: 'I've very little here, but I can do with even less.'

Everyone helped, except Anthony Quinn, who sat on his throne, head in hands, brooding. We waited.

'I think,' he said slowly, 'I think I honestly don't feel there is anything to be cut in my role.'

There was a groan and Larry spoke up waspishly. 'Surely, my dear boy, if you read it more carefully, you'll find a lot you can do without.' This gave notice that it was now open season for a spot of bitching. 'Don't rush, take your time. We can wait, can't we, Franco?'

We started off, but, whenever Quinn said a line, Larry and James Mason would start wringing their hands in horror.

Quinn pretended to ignore them and went on brooding. We tried for another take.

'Darling,' said Larry, 'are you sure we show enough respect to Our Lord if we pronounce His title Lorrd? Why not try God instead?'

Quinn considered this and then nodded, but, when he eventually spoke, the result silenced even Larry. 'Our Gaahd,' said Quinn in exactly the same accent as before.

Larry and James shrank into their costumes.

'Never mind,' said Larry. 'I've learnt one thing – that a great actor can do a lot more with less. In any case, no matter what we do, in the end Franco has the scissors.'

The point made, Larry and James sat back and let the work continue.

The weeks we spent on those Temple scenes would have been among the most exciting and happiest of my career had it not been for news from Italy. It came on 17 March, the accursed day. I was coming back from a screening of some rushes when I was taken aside and told the news that Luchino Visconti had died. My feelings cannot be expressed.

I did not want to see him dead, so I left for Rome the morning of the funeral accompanied by members of the film crew who had worked on many of his pictures. There was something indisputably theatrical about the funeral itself, almost a dramatic confrontation. In the square before the beautiful church of Sant'Ignazio, the Communist party held a secular funeral for one of Italy's most illustrious noblemen. The mayor of Rome and the secretary general of the Party delivered the eulogies. It was sad that even at his death there was this confrontation between politics and the Church. After the singing of the Red Flag the coffin was carried inside the church where family, friends and an immense crowd were waiting and the funeral proper began. He was to be cremated later and the coffin remained on its bier afterwards. I stood by it for nearly half an hour surrounded by those who had been nearest to him all his life. After a moment I looked up and saw his sister Uberta, who had loved him perhaps more than anyone. She was crying and that was more than I could bear, and I too began to cry. Then suddenly there were photographers pushing forward, trying to get a picture of me in tears by the coffin. Wally Toscanini tried to come between me and the flashlights, Luchino's nephews and nieces hurried round to shield me from their squalid act. Surrounded by a wall of people, I was allowed to mourn my friend.

I flew back to Tunisia the same night, and the day after we resumed the shooting of the Sanhedrin, but at the exact moment on the morning when he was to be cremated we stopped for two minutes' silence. Luchino might have orchestrated his last rites between the Communist Party and the Church in a manner he no doubt found spectacular, but in the end I had created my own last farewell to him. There in a temple which I had caused to be built, out of sympathy with me the world's finest actors and film technicians stood in homage to the man who was undoubtedly the single greatest figure in my life. This wasn't just empty pride on my part. He had been my mentor, and all of this – the set and the people – was a tribute to what he had helped me achieve. But there was another thought in my mind: he may have looked on his religious funeral as merely a way of hedging his bets, while I was offering him a re-creation of the Bible, a scene of great piety, out of true conviction that his soul might rest in peace.

SEVENTEEN

Hollywood

One person notably absent from Luchino's funeral was Maria Callas. She sent flowers and wrote me anguished, confused messages, but she who had once loved him so passionately could not bring herself to travel to Rome. Onassis had died the year before and she was already drifting into a world of shadows, where Luchino's death must have seemed just another unreality. There were pills to help her sleep at night, while in between the days drifted by quite without point. Often she would not leave the protective luxury of her apartment in the rue Georges Mandel for days on end. She was alternately confused and regretful. Sometimes she was happy enough slouching around watching westerns on television, at other times she complained bitterly about the emptiness of her life. One of her few pleasures was listening to pirate recordings that had been made illegally during her performances and which her devoted fans now sent to her. They were the only echoes of some of her greatest moments and she would listen to them, while sifting through the equally unofficial snapshots of her which she had done so much to prevent at the time. In such an atmosphere it was hardly surprising that she alienated her oldest friends, as she dwelt on imagined slights.

Inevitably, I had not seen her for some time as I moved around North Africa filming, and was only aware of her condition from news passed on by mutual acquaintances. After so long a haul it was almost impossible to believe that *Jesus of Nazareth* was nearing completion and that I would at last be able to resume my former life and take up with old friends like Maria again. What I did not realize was that, during the two years I had been so completely absorbed with that vast project, things had changed with her to a point where I could be of little help. We finished filming in May 1976, and the incredible army of stars with our legion of craftsmen and technicians finally split up. We had shared a sort of life together, we had aged, gone through good times and bad, known periods of illness and celebrated our birthdays and mourned our dead. To work as a group over such a prolonged period is very unusual, at least for Italians, and produces difficulties of its own; it's a sort of mass marriage in a way and one of the worst things about it is that, when it ends, there are undoubted withdrawal symptoms. They manifest themselves when the security of this family is no longer there and the real world beckons. It was going to be hard to adjust to my old life again.

My first work after the film, even while the editing was going on, was to be in Paris, so I assumed I would see a great deal of Maria.

I was keenly looking forward to working in the French capital again, a city that had proved lucky for me in the past. My Italian versions of *Romeo and Juliet* and *Hamlet* had received the Prix des Théâtres des Nations, and my French production of *Who's Afraid of Virginia Woolf?* had been one of the major talking-points in recent French theatrical life. Add to that my work at the Paris opera with Callas in *Tosca* and *Norma*, and with Sutherland in *Lucia*, and you can see why I felt I had the place in my pocket. I was returning to the city at the invitation of Pierre Dux, the director of the Comédie Française, who not only knew my French productions but had also often visited London in the past to see what I was doing at the Old Vic and elsewhere. Dux wanted to do what Benthall had done and get some of my Italian-ness into the Comédie. There were three possible productions: Beaumarchais's *The Marriage of Figaro*, the *Oresteia* of Aeschylus or de Musset's *Lorenzaccio*. Even before *Jesus of Nazareth* had been completed, discussions were under way and the clear favourite was soon *Lorenzaccio* – the entire company wanted a chance to participate and de Musset's play has a cast of over eighty. The other good reason was that I, a Florentine, would presumably feel some affinity with a play about the Medici.

The occasion was to be awesomely spectacular – the state reopening of the refurbished Salle Richelieu, which had been closed for five years. For a foreigner to be asked to undertake so prominent a production in a country famous for its cultural chauvinism was an unexpected honour. I had already experienced the grandeur of French formal occasions four years earlier when Mme Pompidou invited me to attend a charity screening of *Brother Sun, Sister Moon*. I had noted that this was to be held at the Sainte Chapelle, but had thought no more about it until the hired car brought me to the entrance. Then, of course, I remembered that the Sainte Chapelle is one of the great monuments of medieval France, the mausoleum of the French kings, a soaring Gothic edifice famous for its unparalleled stained-glass windows. As I arrived I was less struck by the ranks of armed Gardes Républicains lining the red carpet under its canopy than I was by the presence of a contingent of ordinary soldiers manning searchlights. The reason why they were there only became clear as I stepped inside to join Mme Pompidou on the receiving line. As daylight faded, the searchlights outside were trained on to the stained-glass windows, creating a jewelled kaleidoscope of flickering colour over the interior. The guests, far from being theatre or jet-set people, were that discreet, semi-private inner group

290   of truly influential people, in which the women were dressed simply but elegantly in dark greys and deep blues set off by the occasional subtly coloured scarf in fuchsia or green and the almost imperceptible fine diamond brooch. As if to protect the eyes from any stress, the white cinema screen was covered with a velvet curtain which silently parted at the moment ordained for the screening. I, who thought myself a master of theatrical spectacle, had to admit to certain feelings of envy at the way so moving a 'show' had been put together. I have never seen any of my films presented in such glorious surroundings. After the performances, we went into the sepulchre below, where, among the tombs of kings and queens, the élite of the Republic dined on food from Maxim's to the strains of medieval plainsong.

If they could do all that for my little film, what would it be like when they reopened a part of their major theatre? I decided it was better not to think about it.

I have mentioned the cultural chauvinism of the French, but really it goes much further; their snobbery and arrogance can sometimes be breathtaking. In truth they wear their arrogance as a public act: it is cosmetic, it covers what they really are and presents a face that they wish the world to come to terms with. In other words, it is an art which they have mastered as nobody else can. If the ordinary Frenchman is arrogant, then, dear Lord, try the actors at the Comédie Française! Anyone working there is at the summit of French cultural life and knows it. Everything about the place reinforces his or her sense of ultimate superiority. The actors are called *sociétaires* and are partners in the company. It was set up by Louis XIV expressly to create an élite centre of French excellence and the very building accentuates their separation from nornal life. Not for the *sociétaires* the squalid, unkempt dressing-rooms of the English theatre. Each of them has a *loge,* virtually a separate apartment in that great rambling building, which they may decorate themselves and where they have their maids, friends and even their dogs. Of course, there is a strict hierarchy, and your exact social position is clear from the location of your *loge.* Inevitably, the place is a hotbed of warring, gossiping factions that puts La Scala in the shade. Again, the building aids this by being a warren of corridors and almost secret staircases where groups can gather to conspire.

Given that they already tear each other to pieces, you can imagine what it was like for a foreigner to be thrown to these wolves. I, poor innocent Florentine, had no idea when I arrived. I had been nervous of the Old Vic before going there and had found nothing but help and consideration, so I naïvely assumed that the Comédie, being an equivalent institution, would operate in the same way. I was soon disabused. My first problem was that in some ways Pierre Dux, the director, had almost too much faith in me.

Michael Benthall, all those years ago in London, had brought me in when
I was still building my career and had made sure of carefully guiding me
through the shoals of British theatrical life. In any case, I had already quite
a wide knowledge of the British stage. I had no equivalent knowledge of
French theatre, but Dux regarded me as an established, highly experienced
director who might resent any interference. Not being very *au fait* with the
rising talent in Paris, I asked if I could have the film and theatre star
Claude Rich as the lead, and Dux agreed. As it turned out, although Rich
was superb, there were young actors in the company fit for the task and,
in fact, when Rich finished his run, he was replaced by just such a one,
Francis Huster, who was wonderful. What I had not fully comprehended
was that, unlike the relatively small British companies, the Comédie has a
reservoir of between 140 and 150 actors of all ages, and they can call upon
retired *sociétaires* if need be. There is simply no need to look elsewhere. I
had no idea that this was the case, so I blundered on. The result was that
even before rehearsals began I had alienated this insular company by daring
to pass them over in favour of a fellow outsider.

From day one of rehearsals I seemed to be getting it wrong. But what
was *it*? I tried to explain to them that, as is my wont, I had not come with
a set of ideas about the play or the characters already locked in and that
this was to be something of a workshop production in which we would all
strive to bring the piece together during rehearsals. This was a method
which had worked very well in London and Italy, but it appeared that
nothing could have been more calculated to earn the displeasure of the
sociétaires. They would simply stand around waiting for me to tell them
what to do. To add to it all, I realized that language was the main issue.
Just as I had had little to contribute to the great labour of enunciating the
awesome majesty of Shakespearean speech, so I had even less to give to
what I now saw was the equally moving language which was the very
reason behind the Comédie. The exquisite perfection of French was borne
in on me and, whereas with English I had a good command of the language,
my French was of the schoolboy variety. Insecurity began to creep in; and
the company soon sensed it and played on it.

'I don't understand you,' said one of the younger actresses at an early
rehearsal. 'To me the whole point is the beauty of the language and you
just can't inspire me.'

As I had just come from inspiring half the major actors and actresses in
the world, my first inclination was to give the young strumpet a piece of
my mind. But I forbore: she had a point. De Musset was more of a poet
than a great dramatist. *Lorenzaccio* is not an easy work to produce; it is
very wordy and has little to break up the piece. I took a deep breath and
thanked the young lady for her kind observation. I asked her to kindly
consider the fact that we were producing a play rather than an opera and

292   that, while I did not doubt the force and beauty of the language, never-theless it could not be compared to the glory of Shakespeare, with whom I was somewhat familiar and that in any case we were concerned here with drama and *that*, if she would kindly allow me to say so, was something I happened to know about.

The incident was typical of many displays of overbearing French arro-gance, the like of which I never witnessed in the English theatre, where, as long as you don't bullshit, you will be listened to. Only one thing stopped me from walking out, the knowledge that underneath it all these people were the very best representatives of a very great culture and it was up to me to win them over.

In some as yet unrealized way I recognized their mannerisms. The way they behaved recalled something or someone in my past. And then one day it dawned on me – it was Visconti. This was just the way Luchino had behaved, the same shell presented to the outside world, the carapace that meant 'take me as I choose to present myself'. After all, Luchino had learned that style from the French, when he was young. Now that I recognized it, it suddenly ceased to bother me. I saw now that if I had arrived that first morning and absolutely laid down the law as to what and how we were going to tackle the play, if I had absolutely refused to consider any suggestion by any of them as to what we were doing, if I had snubbed them and treated them as inferior to those I was used to working with, then I would instantly have been given their respect and cooperation. But this realization had come to me too late; the moment had passed, and in any case I don't work like that. All I could do was go on as I had begun – smile when they goaded me and hopefully wear them down.

All these problems and dilemmas meant that I had no time for socializing. As the opening night in November crept nearer, and the press began to build up the spectacular event, which President Giscard d'Estaing would attend, it was clear that I had to put everything else out of my life in order to pull the performance together in time. I tried to make this clear to Maria when we parted after a pleasant dinner with some friends at her apartment. After all, she who knew better than anyone the nightmare of state theatrical occasions should have sympathized. Instead, I detected an air of offended pride each time I refused an invitation. I suggested she come to my rehearsals – surely she would enjoy that – and we could talk during the breaks or have a quick bite of lunch together. But even that seemed to annoy her, as if it was below *La Divina's* dignity to consort with mere actors. I gave up and tried to concentrate on my work.

Happily, as I had hoped, the reluctant company slowly began to see what I was doing. Gradually the unwieldy pageant started to take on dramatic form. They saw that here was a vehicle in which they could really act, not just recite great poetry, and as that dawned there was a sea change in their attitude towards me. The whispering and the clannish meetings on staircases and in corridors seemed to diminish, the bitchy remarks addressed to me on stage dried up and there was, at last, a willingness to follow me in trying different ways of putting together a scene rather than having a solution handed down from on high. Also, as I explained to one of the actors who asked how I could remain so calm, 'No matter how bitchy you all are, it's far less than I expected.' I was much helped in all this by the older performers, the *anciens sociétaires* who had been brought in to swell our numbers. Typical was Annie Ducaux, one of the doyennes of the Comédie. She had had much experience outside the theatre, having been a famous movie star of the 1930s; she was far more willing to set aside the mannerisms of the company and recognize that my approach of going to the heart of the drama could produce results.

Despite all the agony, the opening performance gave me more pleasure than almost anything I have done in the theatre. It has been one of the satisfactions of my career that I have been able to cope with the cultures of other countries and tackle major works by the sacred figures of other lands in their holiest shrines. Now I had added France to the list that had begun with Britain over ten years earlier. And what a show that opening night was. The British are unbeatable at those dignified state occasions like the lying-in-state of Winston Churchill, but the French are on their own when it comes to the flamboyant social event. Again it's the arrogance. They just seem to be able to strut around, supremely self-confident that theirs is the best of all possible worlds and the rest of us – overawed by the ambience of such a gorgeous and glittering occasion – have little choice but to go along with them.

The only irritation on that spectacular opening night was Maria's refusal to come. She gave no reason and I, totally preoccupied, asked for none. It was sad that dear Maggie van Zuylen had died in 1970, for she would surely have made clear to me how bad Maria's situation was. Without Maggie, we were isolated in our separate worlds. In any case things were moving at such a pace I could not conceive that anyone had come to what amounted to a full stop in the way Maria had.

I hardly had time to enjoy my success in Paris before I had to hurry to Milan for what was to prove another landmark production – *Otello* at La Scala for the opening of the 1976 season.

This was the first time I was to do it with Placido Domingo in the lead and Carlos Kleiber conducting. The event was the brainchild of Paolo Grassi, who for years had been head of the Piccolo Teatro and who was now in charge of La Scala. Knowing that Placido was maturing into what was being recognized as the Otello of our time, he was determined to assemble the finest production around him to ensure that La Scala could claim the glory of ascending that summit along with him; this was to be

Zeffirelli

the Otello. With Mirella Freni and Piero Cappuccilli as Desdemona and Iago, we were sure of a magnificent supporting cast. I set about creating what was to become a major interpretation of the piece and one which was to have a significant effect on my future and that of Placido.

There is a curious anomaly in the part of Otello and of the original Othello. Shakespeare seems to have got the story, as so often, from the Italian original by da Porto and it is likely that the translator misinterpreted the Italian word *Moro,* which can mean simply a swarthy person rather than a fully-fledged Moor. However, Shakespeare and subsequent generations have chosen to make Othello an African. We both saw Otello not as some black savage with a veneer of western civilization easily ripped away by Iago's poison but as a truly cultured man of the Renaissance whose goodness makes him blind to the sheer force of evil that is brought to bear on him. Mine was a Catholic view of the opera – a religious struggle with Otello finally surrendering the western faith he has adopted and returning to his African roots, to the faith of his own people and the religion he possessed before being taken into slavery. Iago represents the cancer that eats away within Christianity, his evil is all our failures to truly act upon our beliefs. His destruction of Otello is no less than that which white society had inflicted on so many other cultures by failing to live up to the very standards it purports to represent.

It was awesome to work with Kleiber for the first time. Here was a man who exacts from musicians the very highest standards and who brought the La Scala orchestra and chorus along with Domingo to a pitch of perfection. All this nervous energy was reflected in what happened outside the theatre on the opening night. Supporters of extreme left-wing factions had singled out La Scala for a showdown, on the grounds that the 2,000 people in the audience represented an élite, which was a provocation to their egalitarian beliefs. There had already been several incidents; some of the previous seasons had opened with eggs being pelted at people as they arrived at the theatre and some were thrown from the gallery into the stalls. Now a worrying rumour spread that a major demonstration was being planned with as many as 20,000 people involved. It began to look as if there would be as much drama on the streets of Milan as there would be on the stage of La Scala.

Oddly enough, whoever was behind this protest had misinterpreted the situation. Far from being an élite event exclusively offered to the bejewelled rich of Milan, Paulo Grassi had decided that for the first time ever an opening night at La Scala should be televised live. Millions would thus have the opportunity to share the experience of Placido Domingo in his greatest role. As I had previously done a number of live broadcasts from La Scala, it was obvious that I should direct this historic performance. Thus I added the strain of camera rehearsals to the already mammoth labours involved in bringing the stage production to its peak. I had even designed the massive sets of wood, metal and stone to evoke the grim masculine garrison world of the Venetian troops, further emphasized by heavy costumes in leather, metal and wool. This was the brooding, embattled atmosphere in which the tragedy unfolded, an atmosphere enhanced by the tales of what was building up outside.

However, Paolo Grassi was not a man to be intimidated by bands of young hooligans. As soon as he learned what they intended to do, he alerted the police and the army, and got them to put several thousand men into the city centre to apprehend the various bands of troublemakers as they converged on the theatre.

Because the streets were sealed, many of our audience had to abandon their vehicles up to nearly two miles from the theatre and wend their way through police and army cordons. All afternoon television and radio carried reports of scuffles and arrests as the demonstrators attempted to defy the blockade. I doubt whether any other first night in recent years has attracted such attention. Either you watched the opera as I was directing it on one channel or you watched news of what was taking place outside the theatre on the other. To switch from the performance to the news was to move between one of the highest expressions of culture on the one hand to scenes of mindless barbarism on the other. Nothing could better have countered the argument of those who wished to denigrate what we were doing at La Scala.

When the curtain went up, none of us knew whether or not we would finish the opera. If only a handful of rioters had penetrated the theatre the performance would have been ruined. I was struck by the thought that somehow Maria would have loved the challenge of facing the rioters and freezing them with a look. In the end we, and by that I mean the entire civilized community, succeeded. The vandals were held at bay; *Otello* was a triumph.

The whole experience brought home to me certain truths. This was undoubtedly a television event, with or without the attendant demonstrations, but I had so far only touched on the possibilities of bringing opera to a wider audience. That night I sensed just how great those possibilities were; twenty-four million people in Italy and Europe had watched *Otello* on television. Balancing this was an awareness of just how unsatisfactory live transmissions are; no matter how well you prepare and rehearse, it is always a matter of luck. While the thrill of 'being there as it happens' can compensate for a lot, I as a perfectionist was always left vaguely dissatisfied with the final result.

How I wished Maria had been at that opening, but she was still sulking over my 'unfaithfulness' in Paris. Her worst 'punishment' for my behaviour was her refusal to attend a charity preview of *Jesus of Nazareth* which

296 Princess Grace organized in Paris for Unicef just before Easter. Tragically, I had not realized that Maria's behaviour was a cry for help. I must also admit that I was not blameless. I was having a run of success and could not bear the thought of wasting an evening rehashing the past. Unaware of the seriousness of her condition, I didn't realize how painful for her my refusals were. Her failure to turn up at rehearsals or at my premières I put down to pique, and, heaven knows, I had enough reasons to believe that this must be the case; great performer though she was, Maria was incredibly petty in private. An evening with Maria was an evening talking about Maria; how good she looked; how nice her hair, her dress; how she really must make a come-back, etc., etc., etc. Frankly, it was frequently very boring and only my memories of *La Divina* on stage, when she was transformed by her art, were enough to get me through it. Nevertheless, had I known, I would have tried to do something. Today I often regret not having guessed what was happening to her, but with Easter came the long awaited televising of the *Jesus of Nazareth* films and inevitably I was caught up in the excitement generated throughout the world. The films were transmitted in America, Britain and Italy at different times over the Easter period. Other countries followed on various days, but everywhere the viewing figures were astronomical. In Italy between 80% and 83% of the population watched the programmes. In practical terms this meant that only babies, the blind and the otherwise infirm did not see the films. The police reported that theft dropped to near zero, which gave rise to my fantasy of a bunch of hard-bitten crooks in the back room of some sleazy bar gazing remorsefully at the flickering television. For the first time the Pope referred to a television programme when he said in his Palm Sunday message to the world: 'Tonight you are going to see an example of the fine use which can be made of the new means of communication that God is offering man. But keep in mind that, whatever good feelings and effects this experience will have on you, this must only mark the beginning of your search for God. Only the beginning.'

In fact, it was recorded that many churches saw a dramatic increase in attendances during the period when the films were transmitted. Many countries have now shown them several times and millions have seen them on video cassettes. Each time they are shown I receive scores of letters from all kinds of people telling of a faith renewed, a marriage saved or a suicide avoided. Priests and ministers write to tell me of converts made, suffering eased and the bereaved comforted. I am very grateful for each one.

Some of the results were in many ways disturbing. I was used to being famous and being recognized in streets and restaurants, but the success of *Jesus of Nazareth* brought a different dimension to all this. I remember stopping at a village in southern Italy and going to a café for a drink. There was a sudden commotion; the waiter had called down the owner's wife, who appeared dishevelled and anxious, with that look on her face as if a miracle were happening. She ran out and began to call in the women of the village. 'He's here,' she shouted at them. Suddenly I was surrounded by a crowd of little old ladies in black; some of them were pulling scarves and handkerchiefs over their heads as if they were in church. Others tried to kiss my hand. It was unnerving.

I was to have similar experiences all over the world, as if I had done something on a higher plane than simply make a film. I had to keep reminding myself of a wonderful remark by Laurence Olivier to a *New York Times* interviewer during the shooting: 'There is only one star here, the star of Bethlehem.' It helped me see the whole thing in perspective even while I was being mobbed by people who seemed to think that I must somehow be in touch with God Himself.

Almost the first person to congratulate me was Callas. Typically, she had watched the films on television in the womb-like safety of her apartment with Bruna and Ferruccio. When she telephoned, I could hear how moved she was and talking to her again brought back all the sadness so many of us felt at her denying us *La Divina* on stage. The new director of Covent Garden, John Tooley, wanted me to do a production for them and, when we met in Rome, he suggested that we try to entice Maria back. Naturally we were both excited at such a prospect and we talked about the possibility of Monteverdi's *The Coronation of Poppaea* as a vehicle for our plan. We came up with the somewhat *risqué* notion of having her sing the lead in *The Merry Widow* too. John rang her and, when she didn't reject the notion out of hand, I followed up his call and told her that I was coming to Paris the next day. She wanted to know what parts we were thinking of, but I refused to tell her until we met. She was irritated by this teasing, which was just what I wanted. I took her out to lunch and started proposing *Poppaea*.

'But Poppaea doesn't have the biggest part,' she protested. 'Nor the best aria, "Addio Roma".'

I forbore to tell her that this was one of the reasons we'd come up with the idea, in order to give her a lead role with less strain, but she went on, preposterously, to suggest that we could transfer some of the other singers' arias. She knew no one could agree to that, which was her way of scotching the whole thing. Undaunted, I began to talk about *The Merry Widow*.

She interrupted: 'Callas, in musical comedy? Me in an operetta?'

'Why not?'

'Franco, please. People would laugh at me wasting my time on such a thing.'

I told her that, far from being easy, the role of the Widow is very demanding and needs a damn good voice, and I emphasized how wonderful

298 she would look in the Belle Époque costume. She was definitely attracted to the idea, but she was already preparing her excuses. Yes, she would consider it, but she was so busy; however, she would be in touch. I began to get a little irritated and told her she should trust her friends and stop wasting her time and talent. Perhaps I ought to have seen what was happening to her and realized that she was beyond such pleading. I had noticed that her once beautiful hands now looked transparent; you could see the veins below the skin. Then, as I walked her back to her apartment after lunch, I was appalled to realize that she was actually afraid. She kept close to me, terrified that she would come into contact with passers-by, she hesitated at crossings, looking wildly about her until I led her firmly forward. This was partly due to her usual problem of being unable to see without her spectacles, but now it went deeper. She kept on talking about how dangerous the world had become, that terrorists were everywhere and she would never go back to Italy because of all the kidnappings. From time to time she gave a little involuntary shiver. It was beyond any normal distress at the present state of the world, it was paranoia. Though I could see this evidence of her mental state, I was unaware of just how far her physical decline had gone. When I left her at her apartment, she had recovered her poise sufficiently to promise to consider John Tooley's offer but I think I knew in my heart that it would never come about.

That summer the Oliviers came to Positano again. Joan had been very moved by *Jesus of Nazareth*. For my part, proud as I was of all the praise and attention the films were getting, I now felt the need to move on. But where to go next? *Jesus of Nazareth* had been on such a scale in terms of performers and audience that anything else looked like a come-down by comparison. Happily, I had our second de Filippo play, *Filumena marturano*, to direct, and that was set to be a pleasant interlude while I thought things over.

Through the summer holidays I worked on the play with our adaptor Willis Hall, and with Joan as Filumena, ready for the West End in the autumn. The story is a classic tale, which Eduardo dressed up with great skill into an amusing piece. The lead was a role ideal for Joan's comic gifts. The Filumena of the title is the ageing mistress of a man who has just fallen in love with a younger woman. Filumena plays the old trick on him of pretending she is dying so that he will marry her on her death-bed, then as soon as the priest has gone, she leaps out of bed and he realizes his mistake. That is the moment when the play opens, with the old man banging his head and shouting: 'Fool, fool, fool!'

But the tricks have only just begun. Filumena now reveals that she has secretly had three children, one of which is his. In the end he is obliged to accept that he must take all three as his children, which is exactly what Filumena wanted all along.

After the holidays in Positano we rehearsed in London, then opened out of town in Norwich, before moving to the West End. The audiences were again entranced by de Filippo's charm. He came to Norwich for the opening and was convinced that he could now look forward to a hit in America. However, when we opened in London I was once more aware that the usual procession of American agents and producers was not leading to the sort of enquiries that normally precede an offer – they could see, as before with *Saturday, Sunday, Monday,* that this Italian charm might work on the English but would have little hope in New York.

Joan and Larry came to the villa in Positano twice more, in 1978 and 1979, and I can remember one especially bizarre arrival. There had been the usual tiring journey, by air to Naples then by car to Positano – it's the sort of day every parent dreads. Anyway they had made it and staggered down the many steps to my gate. I went up to greet them and was confronted by a ghastly spectacle: Larry, deathly pale, almost bald but with what remained of his hair bright red. He looked like a made-up corpse. Only when he began speaking in a perfect American accent did it dawn on me that he was working up a role. In fact, he was preparing a film about General MacArthur and those summer weeks with us were punctuated by a tape-recording of some of MacArthur's wartime speeches, which Larry would then impersonate. He went at it over and over again. Unfortunately for the rest of us, they weren't awfully interesting speeches and by the end of the hundredth repetition I thought I and my other guests would go mad.

When he got bored with MacArthur, Larry would come amongst us, usually improvising his favourite role – the geriatric English gentleman. This involved a great deal of breathless huffing accompanied by excessively doddery gestures. He would emit sad little sighs and remarks like, 'Don't worry about me, old boy, I shall manage, truly I shall.' He would accept a glass or a plate with, 'How kind, how very, very kind,' as if everything were for the last time. Whenever he saw me approaching he would come forward, slightly hunched, and grasp my hand in both his, whispering: 'Dear, dear Franco . . . so kind [sigh] . . . so very, very kind.'

It was all so convincing I began to think he might expire at the villa, and when Ali told me that Lord Olivier rose very early to go for a swim from the rocks below, I was terrified. I told Ali he must follow him down and watch in case he came to grief. But Ali was mystified at my concern and told me there was no problem, that Olivier dived straight into the sea and swam strongly. The next morning I got up early and crept down to watch. Sure enough, along skipped Larry and dived straight in. I was waiting for him as he clambered out of the water. As soon as he saw me he hunched up and slipped into his role. 'Dear boy, how nice for an elderly gentleman to get a little exercise. . .' What could one say?

While *Filumena* had been a totally happy occasion for the Oliviers, it

300   was marred for me by something that, yet again, occurred during rehearsals. Looking back, I see now that I ought to have expected it and should have been prepared when it happened. On 16 September Maria Callas had a stroke and died. In effect, she had been dead to the world for some time but I, who had shared many of her most vibrant moments, had not seen it and was shocked by the news. First Magnani, then Luchino, now Maria – I had been accustomed to a world of giant talents that was no more.

I flew to Paris and went to rue Georges Mandel to look for the last time on that extraordinarily powerful face which had expressed with unparalleled skill Violetta, Lucia, Norma, Tosca. What ghastly lives the Muses sometimes visit on those with genius. The cold body on that bed had been two people: Maria the woman who wanted to be loved and Callas the *diva* who was a Vestal at the altar of her art. They had seemed to battle it out within her and in the end both lost; all that had been left in those last years was little more than the shell which was laid out in that darkened room. Her maid, Bruna, stood by her body, obsessively fussing over her dead mistress: first she would gently comb her long tresses, then she would smooth her precious lace nightdress or brush away some imagined speck, then she would stop for a while and pray a little, then she would begin again, combing, combing, combing. It was a sublime image of the dead Violetta.

Like Luchino, in her declining years Maria had attracted an unappealing batch of acquaintances. What with them and the frenzied media attention being given to a woman whose life had combined high art, operatic scandals, Onassis and the Kennedys, I could see that the funeral was going to be a tasteless circus. I flew back to London and got in touch with her friends around the world. We decided that, on the day of her funeral in Paris, we would hold memorial services in Milan, Rome, New York and London. I helped Sydney Edwards, our old friend on the *Evening Standard,* organize ours at London's Greek Orthodox Cathedral in Moscow Road. I read the lesson and am glad that we were able to make it a dignified farewell. The Paris funeral was, as predicted, a shambles, with newspaper photographers shoving their way forward in the church and no one paying much attention to the ceremony. It was the sort of botched job an ultra-professional like Maria would have hated. She who regarded any appearance as a duty to the public could never have condoned so sorry a débâcle.

The deaths of Luchino and then Maria, and the way *Jesus of Nazareth* brought a full stop to a strand in my life, combined to make it clear that 1977 was going to be one of those turning-point years. There were other outside factors that were also pushing me towards something new. This was a strange period in Italian life, the apogee of the Red Brigades and what looked like the imminent collapse of public order. The first night of

Otello at La Scala was only one of many incidents. All too often the terrorists succeeded; kidnapping, bombing, all were daily occurrences. Italy is still a young democracy without many of the built-in safety devices against subversion that you get in Britain and America. Having had experience of the Communists during the war and afterwards with Luchino, I knew better than most that the Italian Left is no respecter of the rules and that many of them, as became clear, would stop at nothing. While I was not afraid personally, as Maria had been, I nevertheless found myself becoming increasingly incensed with the situation, angry at the daily reports of further atrocities. Knowing there was nothing that I could do personally to improve matters, it occurred to me to take a break from the claustrophobic atmosphere of decay and violence which seemed to be suffocating my country.

I had been a frequent visitor to Tunisia after working there on *Jesus of Nazareth* and the idea began to form that I could do something that would add a substantial reason to my going to live there.

It is not difficult to explain why I liked Tunisia so much. There are more beautiful places in the Mediterranean, but few with a population as charming and welcoming as this North African country. It is so different from its neighbours, untouched by dogmatism and free of the violence that mars so many Islamic states today. In which other Arab country could a Jewish producer have financed a film about Jesus Christ and found nothing but a desire to see the project succeed? Not over-blessed with raw materials, the Tunisians have placed a lot of faith in tourism to fund their national economy, but are ever on the lookout for new development ideas. Having been made so welcome, I was determined to help, if the opportunity presented itself. This came in the form of an ambitious young Tunisian called Tarak ben Amar, a nephew of the President's wife, who had worked as associate producer on *Jesus of Nazareth*. He had been bitten by the film bug and conceived ambitious plans to set up a Tunisian cinema industry. It was not as far-fetched as it at first appeared; Tunisia has a superb climate, with sunshine almost every day of the year, yet it is near Europe. There is also a large, inexpensive workforce, along with skilled craftsmen, many of whom have had experience as immigrant workers in France or Italy.

It was a combination that could prove attractive to film producers fed up with soaring European or American costs and the ever-present risk of strikes and other industrial unrest that plagues the film industry. I had been decorated by President Bourguiba after our filming and granted honorary residence in his country. I now had a house and an office there, and undertook to persuade as many of my fellow film-makers throughout the world as possible to consider using the facilities the country offered. The effects of our labours were immediately obvious, with Italian, British,

302 French and American film-makers coming to Tunisia. Perhaps the biggest coup was persuading Steven Spielberg and George Lucas to film there.

Although I stayed in Tunisia whenever I could, it was never my intention to work there permanently. What Tarak and the other Tunisians involved in the film business wanted was that I should act as a sort of roving ambassador, spreading the word about what the country had to offer. With the Italian situation driving me to work elsewhere I began to wonder whether the time had not come for me to look to America.

These were only vague thoughts that might have led nowhere except for a bizarre combination of circumstances, which brought me to believe that destiny was taking a hand in my affairs again. Even before the release of *Jesus of Nazareth* MGM had asked me to do a film for them in Hollywood. They had contacted me while I was dubbing the *Jesus* films in London, but with my mind still fully occupied I just said 'great' and left it at that. Then, one truly miserable February evening, I'd returned to the flat where we were staying. I was cold and wet; Pippo and my assistant Bianca had gone to the theatre, so I cooked myself a little pasta and switched on the television. As I began to eat I realized that I was watching King Vidor's *The Champ* with Wallace Beery and Jackie Cooper, the same film I'd seen as a child back in 1931. And, just as I had forty-six years before, I cried; it was partly the film and partly the memories of my mother, Ersilia and Aunt Lide. I cried so much that, when I took a mouthful of spaghetti, it was salty with tears. When the others came back, they thought I was ill, I looked so pale, with my eyes swollen. It was ten o'clock in London, so I called Stan Kamen, my agent in Los Angeles, and told him I had an idea for the film MGM wanted me to do – it would be a remake of *The Champ*. He told me to call the head of MGM, Dick Shepherd, at the studio. Shepherd admitted that he'd never seen the King Vidor original, so I pointed out that it was their film, they presumably had a copy somewhere in the archives and maybe he could check it out. He called back the next day and said they'd had a screening. He was worried it was too much of a tear-jerker for a modern audience, but I insisted that this was precisely the point. If I, a cynical, worn-out Florentine, could be reduced to tears by that simple, sentimental tale then so would millions of other people. I thought he had taken the point.

At the end of 1977 I made my decision. I would go to Los Angeles and see whether there was a place for me at the centre of the American film industry. I was aware of the fact that Hollywood has a reputation for making fools out of creative people who are sucked into its maw, but I was feeling very confident after *Jesus of Nazareth* and ready for the challenge.

Having arranged my contract with MGM, I flew to Los Angeles and moved into the then unheard-of Beverly Comstock Hotel. Perhaps under the impression that this was some secret new 'in' place, people started to drop

by, so that today it has become a star hotel, which always makes me smile.
I was introduced to the Hollywood class system by a famous agent called Sue Mengers, a lovely, witty lady who was trying to entice me away from Stan Kamen at the William Morris Agency. She gave a welcome party for me which was very carefully graded: first a small supper for the A class, about twelve people – senior production people, major directors. Then, after dinner, came the super-A class: about twenty people, including Gregory Peck, Barbra Streisand and Jack Lemmon, rather grandly looked in for coffee. Then the B class, hundreds of people on the verge of making it, came round for a late-night dance. I doubt the Viennese court was quite so rigid in its protocol and I never really understood the rules. Being a rather sloppy Latin, the idea of a social engagement booked months ahead was inconceivable. This flaw in my character led to several horrible *faux pas*; one of the worst being with Pat York, Michael's wife. In June 1978 she invited me to a party in my honour for the following September. I was at home in Tunisia that August and she rang to double check that 16 September was still OK. Of course, when I returned to Hollywood, I completely forgot. For weeks afterwards I received reproving looks and admonishment from the *beau monde* for my unforgivable gaffe – they had all stood around waiting for me. Why somebody didn't just ring me up the day before to remind me I'll never know, but that's social life in Tinsel Town.

My first months in LA were great fun. I rented a lovely house in Beverly Hills and brought over my family and my dogs. Forget about Hollywood sophistication, about cocktails by the pool, about fashionable drugs and fast living; this was Italy on the West Coast. Vige was soon making the best pasta in town and people were dropping in round about mealtimes. Before long Vige was queening it over a loyal band of film people; she's had more success with her cooking than the average *femme fatale* has with her body.

My view of Hollywood may disillusion some people. I loved the place because it offered such a healthy, open existence. Beverly Hills is a suburb of spacious houses surrounded by large gardens bursting with flowers all year round. The rooms inside are nearly always filled with cut blossoms, which is a thing I adore. I also found it a wholesome place, for people exercise a lot and any myths about the *louche* lifestyle of the cinema world can be discounted; if you're working, you're up before dawn to get to the shoot. The only ones who live any sort of infamous night-time existence are those who are out of work, and in Hollywood terms that means failures. The truly big stars are never out of work and are very careful how they use their time and energy. When not involved in actual film-making, most of them have business interests that take up their time and are normal family people. Typical were Gregory Peck and his adorable wife, Veronique, who had a large, sunny English-style home. I was delighted to see that it was

304   surrounded with columbines, one of my favourite flowers, and, when I saw how they cherished a dog that had lost a leg in an accident, I knew we were bound to become close friends.

In the years that followed they often came to Positano with their children, usually at the beginning of September. On one occasion they arrived with the best gift they could have brought – Claudette Colbert. She was one of the actresses I most admired in my youth. She was celebrating her eightieth birthday and I was rather concerned about the number of steps she had to climb or descend whenever she wished to go to the town or the beach.

'Don't worry, dear,' she reassured me with her inimitable smile, 'my doctor has told me not to take the elevator if I can, but rather climb the stairs. It's good for your heart and circulation. The only thing you have to do is climb three steps and rest while you count to three, or climb five and then rest while you count to five, or whatever number you choose. It depends on your health and age.' She smiled again. 'I'm all right. I climb seven and rest seven!'

And thus she went up and down all the steps feeling wonderful and never out of breath, with that expression on her face which made her so unforgettable in *It Happened One Night*.

The Pecks were also there one summer with Liza Minnelli and a special group of friends to celebrate her husband Mark's birthday on 4 September. At the impromptu party organized for the special day Liza sang her whole repertoire accompanied by the local Neapolitan musicians and singers. I wish I had taped it. At one o'clock in the morning she sat on Mark's knees, wound herself around him like a cat and sang, very softly and gently with a touch of humour, 'It Had To Be You...'

I so loved the life of gardens and open-air living, which reminded me of Tunisia, that I contemplated moving to Hollywood permanently. All the omens for *The Champ* seemed so good and I felt on top of the place. Hollywood and I seemed made for each other. Admittedly there was none of the cultural life I was used to, virtually no theatre or opera, but set against that was the sensation of being a major director in a town where this means belonging to the ultimate inner circle.

Clearly, the only way to win with a film like *The Champ* was to have the insurance of some big names on the billing. Everyone was plugging Ryan O'Neal for the father and as he was one of my favourite younger actors I was happy to go along with that. The way he had managed to break every heart in *Love Story* ten years earlier made him an ideal choice, but unfortunately he proposed his own son, Griffen, for the child. He wanted to try the same gimmick with him as he had with his daughter Tatum in *Paper Moon*. Griffen was a nice kid, but he was a little too mature for the role. In any case, there was already another candidate.

Following his promotion on *Jesus,* Pippo was working as my casting director in New York with the main task of finding a small boy who could do a modern Jackie Cooper. Obviously he would have to have cute looks, but he must also be able to act and take direction. It was this last requirement that led Pippo to concentrate on children with some experience of film work. That was how he came across the then six-year-old Ricky Schroeder, a bright-eyed, tousle-haired kid who had featured in a couple of successful television commercials. As soon as I met the boy, I knew he was absolutely right for the part. He had nothing of the hard-bitten theatre brat about him, he wasn't a sort of premature adult dragged around the studios by an over-ambitious mother. In fact, he was almost worryingly innocent and trusting. It was these qualities which shone through in the screen test we did and which netted our main star, Jon Voight.

With the departure of Ryan O'Neal the Hollywood gossips were beginning to predict my early downfall. It was breaking all the rules to reject a star like O'Neal and his son. However, I was happy and lucky to have Jon interested in the project. I had always respected him and the success of *Midnight Cowboy* and *Coming Home* had not only made him good box-office but also given him status with radical America. It was perhaps a consciousness of this that initially made him have doubts about our story, which was hardly intellectually heavyweight. But when he saw Ricky's screen test, Jon was overwhelmed. He insisted we give the boy a chance; we absolutely had to make the film so that Ricky could play the part. It was typical of Jon to think of it that way.

With a big name like Jon Voight in the film, the rest was easy, and soon we had Faye Dunaway as the mother, ideal as the hard-bitten, self-centred bitch whose return sparks off all the trouble.

I felt very responsible for young Ricky. He had his seventh birthday as we began filming in March 1978 and I was aware of how impressionable and sensitive he was. He often came with his mother and sister to our house and soon became part of the family. Vige mothered him and Pippo was like a big brother. Sometimes it was worrying to see how he hung on every word I said as this curious mix of father-figure and film-director. I remember him sitting in a corner when I called out jokingly: 'Who's that creature over there?' He began to cry. I was stunned and, when I asked him why, he said it was because I'd been nasty to him by calling him an animal. I had to show him my copy of St Francis's *Canticle of the Creatures* before I could convince him that a creature was really a very nice thing to be.

Despite his sensitivity, Ricky was a tough professional on set and quite capable of standing up for himself beside a big name like Jon Voight. Jon had this sort of anguished New York style of acting, endlessly trying to feel his way into a role, always questioning what the motivation is behind the words and thus always improvising. On the first day's filming he did just that; he spouted an invented speech at Ricky, who simply froze.

306   There was a silence, and then Jon said to Ricky, 'You have to speak now.'
'No, I'm waiting for you,' Ricky replied.
'But I've said my line.'
'You haven't.'
'But I said it. You got the message.'
'What message?' asked Ricky forcefully. 'You're supposed to say your line as it's written, then I speak.'

So much for the sensitive little boy. But for all his confidence on set I was always conscious that it would be difficult to get him to retake scenes over and over again as an adult professional can do, particularly those involving great emotion. The very last scene of all was especially difficult. Jon Voight, the boxer, dies in the ring at the moment of his victory. Faye Dunaway, the mother, comes to reclaim her child, but then it's over to the boy. The father is carried to his dressing-room, the doctor comes in, listens to the heart and says, 'I'm sorry'. There's complete silence, and nobody notices that the boy is there. He pushes through the crowd and starts to tug at his father.

'Let's go,' he insists. 'Wake up! Wake up! Let's go home.' And then he begins to shake the dead body desperately, furiously, trying to rouse his father. My God, what a scene!

I knew we'd have to do it in one take and fortunately we had a marvellous cameraman, Fred Koenekamp. He was both very professional and extremely good with Ricky, who adored him. Fred cleverly lit the scene from all angles, somewhat like a television studio, no easy task when you consider most film lighting is monodirectional. With that 'open' lighting we were able to cover the action with five cameras.

However, even with that safeguard, there was still the problem of getting Ricky into the right emotional state. He'd had to cry in earlier scenes and I'd used various, more or less outrageous, tricks to get him going. The most effective was arranged with Pippo, whom Ricky adored. After pretending to be totally dissatisfied with Pippo's work, I began to shout abuse at him and then I pretended to fire him. Ricky was horrified and burst into tears; we rushed him on to the set and started filming. Between shots, the poor little boy would tearfully beg me to relent and to take back Pippo, who was sitting glumly watching us from a corner of the studio. Curiously, a Hollywood old-timer told me that King Vidor played a similar trick to make Jackie Cooper cry.

When that charade was played out, I then told Ricky the moving story of my grandmother's death, how she had prepared little gifts that we each had to open but that just as we began to take out her last presents she closed her eyes and died. That did it and he was in floods of tears again.

But I didn't want to do something like that for this final scene. I wanted

Ricky to show what he was capable of as an actor. Diane, his mother, a wonderful woman who was ever on hand to help, agreed with this, so she took him into a corner to help him prepare. I had noticed that one thing which made him cry more was the sight of himself crying, so I arranged for a mirror to be set up. Although keeping well away, I could nevertheless see him looking into the glass and concentrating hard. After a moment his mother indicated with a light wave of her hand that we should run the cameras and on set he came, a true little professional, crying his heart out. Ricky gave one of the most moving performances imaginable for any actor of any age. I think he deserved an Oscar.

Recently, I was looking through my diary and remembered it was Ricky's birthday, so I rang him up. After *The Champ,* he had a string of successful films and now hosts a major American television show, yet it was strange to hear his mature, confident voice at the end of the line.

'Do you know how tall I am?' he asked, thinking I would have a mental image of a seven-year-old. 'I'm five foot six. When are we going to work again? But you mustn't think of me as a baby any more.' His voice went deeper and deeper as he spoke.

'What about girls?' I asked.

'I can't tell you, my mother is around, but they give me a lot of trouble.'

His mother for the film, Faye Dunaway, was certainly the source of much of the trouble in the plot. There were also difficulties off camera. Faye is a highly-charged woman, a fanatical over-achiever who has fought her way to the top, and sometimes it tells. We had two filming sessions with a break for her between them and, when she returned for the second bout, she had noticeably put on weight. I was very concerned: the scenes would never cut together. She was fully aware of the problem and swore she would diet as hard as possible. That was when she really showed what she was made of. She lost an incredible ten pounds in a single week. Only a will of iron could have enabled her to do it. That bizarre incident indicated what had put her up there amongst the leading female stars of our time. There's no nonsense with Faye, just the real stuff. That supreme self-control was what made her such a joy to direct. A great actress like Faye will assume any interpretation required, she wills herself almost physically into the lines she is saying. And she will never do the easy, obvious thing; she will always come up with an unexpected and exciting solution – a habit which, of course, both angers and delights a director. Another of her remarkable gifts is her elegance and style. I am surprised that Hollywood has not used her more for high-class parts in the Marlene Dietrich tradition. Nobody could reflect Marlene's magic better than Faye; they even have the same rivetting cheek bones and long, fine, almost transparent hands. But does anyone in Hollywood know or care?

The hiccup over Faye's weight was really our only significant problem.

308 It was a lovely film to make and, whilst I knew the critics would find it too unmodern in its unashamed sentimentality, I was confident that the public would want it. Inevitably, Jon Voight, who had been the darling of the radicals for *Coming Home,* took most of the flak for daring to appear in a 'popular' film which was also a tear-jerker. I was worried for his sake, but when he brought his family to a screening and they loved it, he was moved to tears and dismissed what the critics were saying.

Once again I was confronted by the ludicrous contradiction that the radical tradition ought to be a popular one and yet, if one tries to create a work for the mass audience which honestly appeals to their best instincts, the Leftists, of all people, can't resist the temptation to be snobbish about such a work.

Some of the comments of these confused critics were insidiously hurtful – that we had exploited a child, given cheap emotional solutions to complex family problems, and so on. As an antidote one had to go to the cinema and see the public's reactions. I got a real thrill out of watching people caught up in emotions they obviously felt. Kenneth Tynan, who had kept in touch since the Old Vic days, was now living in California and he came to an early showing. He, of all critics, might have been expected to find *The Champ* a sentimental horror.

'This film is the opposite of everything I've ever liked,' he said. But he went on to admit: 'You won. You just blew up my tear ducts.'

Oddly enough, it was also the only one of my films which Donald Downes ever liked. 'This is real film-making,' he said, 'not just playing with Shakespeare, but dealing with a modern classic – I think you made it! Perhaps you're a film director after all.'

In the end it was one of those films that succeed despite everything written about it. MGM raked in a staggering $146 million, if my information is correct, for an outlay of a mere $9 million. I should have been the darling of the studio, with scripts and offers arriving by the truckload, but it was not to be. Every so often the American film business goes through a seismic upheaval and people are toppled from power. Byzantine corporate mergers take place and new waves of businessmen arrive to take control.

My dear friend Dick Shepherd left. The new management took over and swallowed the millions of dollars we had made for them with no thanks, no acknowledgement and no offer; on the contrary, there was almost resentment. Is that Hollywood? I am not sure.

On the one hand, you have an infrastructure for the mass-production of films that is second to none, with the finest craftsmen, from carpenters to costume-makers, and a huge selection of acting talent. If you want to cast a small character part, the agencies will send round a dozen people absolutely perfect for the role. In that sense it's a director's paradise. But on the other hand, it's also a quagmire. The 'majors', the big studios, are now merely purveyors of sound stages and equipment, they hardly produce anything daring or personal any more. The decisions are generally in the hands of moneymen, people with backgrounds in accountancy who see films as risk investments. Their period in power is limited to two or three years, then they move on. It's like our governments in Italy – they are never sure how long they are going to remain in power so there is no possibility of developing a policy. All too often the profits made from films are not reinvested in more films but are syphoned out of the industry into real estate. The cinema survives because people in America still go to the movies. Cinema attendances are pretty low in Britain and Italy, though France has a viable audience for its home-made product. Yet in America that huge public, far from allowing the industry to take risks, has led to the relentless search for safe stories which fit a predictable market profile, anything that will make a killing at the box-office over the first weekend.

I'd been remarkably fortunate to have Dick Shepherd and Ray Wagner as producers. It was Dick who'd first invited me to Hollywood and who had gone along with what I wanted to do. When we'd found young Ricky, but hadn't yet decided who the father should be, I had come up with the idea of trying to do some filming at the famous Miami race track on Flamingo Day. This was a unique annual event named after the flocks of pink flamingos near the track, and on that special day all the ladies and some gentlemen in the crowd dress in pink. It's an incredibly lively spectacle and I wanted it as background for the opening scenes of the film. The problem was that, without a star in the leading role, there was as yet no film. Dick and Ray, seeing that I really wanted these precious shots, found the money somewhere so that I could start. They were real film people.

When I think of how the majors treat talented film people like Dick Shepherd, I am reminded of one of the nastiest and saddest sights I have ever come across. It was when we were filming at the Miami race track. Away from the main stables, where all the proud winners of the moment were kept, was a place for abandoned horses. These too were noble thoroughbreds, often owned by a syndicate, but they had started to lose and their owners no longer found them a profitable investment. One day they would be coddled, stroked, exercised and lovingly taken care of; the next they were cast off like lepers. These proud animals, with their high-stepping grace and aristocratic toss of the mane, now hung their heads, lonely and confused. Most of them ended up in the knacker's yard, victims of that equine Hollywood!

Perhaps I should have packed up and left LA but something needled me. I am as stubborn as my grandfather on occasions and, in any case, I was still in love with life in Beverly Hills. No, I would stay and deal with the system somehow.

EIGHTEEN

Love Stories

There is a curious experience which can only be described as a sort of 'advance dream'. It's a vision of a place one has never been to or seen pictures of, but which one knows for certain exists somewhere. I have often created stage sets of such imaginings, only to find myself confronted with the reality later – a square in a peasant village, the interior of a stately room. I suppose an out-and-out rationalist would insist that I must have seen a photograph at some time and had simply forgotten about it while retaining the image in my subconscious. But I'm not so sure. I think there are advance dreams, glimpses that come to us while we sleep and which aren't so easily explained. I had had such a place in my mind for some time; almost like a beach in a tropical country, a place of waving palms and limitless sand. At first I thought it was just a hazy image of California, but then I wasn't so sure. It was the palm trees that puzzled me, countless identical palms all in rigid lines stretching to the horizon. Far from being vague this seemed very precise. It was puzzling.

With *The Champ* launched, I returned to my home in Tunisia to rest and brood on what I should do next. I had two operas planned: *Carmen* in Vienna at the end of the year and *Traviata* in Rio de Janeiro at the beginning of 1979, but my mind was never far from film-making. I was soon involved with Tarak ben Amar again, making plans to improve what was by now Tunisia's burgeoning film industry. I was enjoying the excitement of watching something that I had seen start from nothing grow so well.

At one point Tarak took me on a journey to the far interior of the country, where the Sahara begins. There the unending stretch of undulating dunes is punctuated only by the occasional astonishing oasis of palms and water, which has always captured the visitor's imagination. It reminded me of my dream but not quite, though it was sufficiently alike to stir memories of another time in a different North African country. Slowly I realized I was thinking more and more of that visit to Egypt in 1967 with the Ford Foundation, when we were contemplating producing a film of *Aida*. Why hadn't I remembered it earlier? After all, the Camp David agreement between Israel and Egypt seemed to have totally transformed the situation in the Middle East. It might now be possible to film in Egypt again, and with Tarak's experience the Arab world might be interested in being involved in an international project of this calibre. Verdi had been asked to compose a work to celebrate the opening of the Suez Canal, linking the Islamic world to Europe, and the opera still remains a symbol of the Egyptian longing for cooperation with Europe. Now that global *rapprochement* was in the air, might not this be the ideal film to make?

I was somewhat tentative as I suggested it to Tarak; after all, opera is a very European art form and not one that people from other societies and cultures can take to easily. However, as with most educated Tunisians, he happily copes with two cultures: the older Islamic one and the later colonial French version. Tunisians are proud of being bilingual and bicultural, so he readily accepted my invitation to come to the opening night of *Carmen* in Vienna.

Far from being put off by the experience, he was as entranced as I had been at *Die Walküre* in Florence all those years ago. I knew what he was feeling: the excitement of a world not fully comprehended, but which has nevertheless struck one with consuming force. He listened readily to my thoughts on what we might do with *Aida*. After all, filming opera was no more than a way of bringing together the two sides of my life, and it seemed to be an idea whose time had come.

Television had accustomed us to the idea of the camera nosing around a stage performance, but the possibilities of film, of the opera re-set specifically to allow the language of cinema to take over, to be either as realistic or as fantastic as the director wishes, this had been only tentatively explored. Early films of operas had been done 'live', but recent attempts had settled for filming to playback after a studio recording of the opera. I could see that this would probably form some sort of battle line in the future, the 'live' against the 'recorded' schools of thought. But I could also see endless permutations of the two schools; say a basic recording for most of the action with some close scenes done live. One might even use the old Hollywood device of great, though not especially photogenic, singers doing the recording while more appealing performers mimed on camera. Such an idea will no doubt be anathema to the purists, who have lost all sense of opera as a popular medium.

These were certainly ideas whose time had come: Bergman had filmed *The Magic Flute*, there was Losey's *Don Giovanni* and the work of Jean-Pierre Ponnelle with operas like *The Marriage of Figaro* and *Tosca*, which were made directly for television and not taken from a stage performance.

But, first, much of 1979 and the early part of 1980 was to be taken up with promoting *The Champ* as it opened in different countries throughout the world. It was a pleasant interlude and allowed me time to ponder various schemes. My agent, Stan Kamen, suggested I read a very interesting

312   new novel called *Endless Love*, written by Scott Spencer; apparently there
were backers for a film of the book. I was intrigued by the story, which in
some ways was an update of *Romeo and Juliet* – two young lovers whose
romance is doomed through parental interference – but very much a part
of the post-1960s permissive society.

The story took the same simple, sentimental line as *The Champ*, but I
wasn't afraid of that. If I'd thought more about that earlier mould-breaker
Camille, which had flopped because it pre-dated a shift in fashion, I might
have been more cautious, but the tenacity that is sometimes a virtue in me
turned into a dangerous pigheadedness and led me to accept help from
those I should perhaps have kept at a distance. The rights to *Endless Love*
were in the hands of financier Keith Barish, who had put together a package
that included the young actress Brooke Shields, one of the most stunningly
beautiful women I have ever seen. Barish had touted the package round
Hollywood until he got a sympathetic response from Jon Peters, the attractive husband of Barbra Streisand. All this sounds complex, but it was no
more than the average wheeling and dealing that goes on in Los Angeles.
Jon Peters wanted to be the overall producer of the film, and together he
and Barish sold the idea to Peter Gruber, a young executive at the record
company Polygram. This whole Byzantine operation was now offered to
me as director and, because I liked the book, I closed my eyes to the
somewhat convoluted package attached to it. I thought Stan Kamen was
a sufficient guarantee.

While I was considering *Endless Love*, I still pursued the idea of Egypt
and *Aida*. Uppermost in my mind was my loss in never having filmed Callas.
I ought to have made *Traviata* with her and that lost *Tosca* rankled more
and more. In the summer of 1980 Tarak and I went so far as to undertake
an extensive tour of Egypt in search of locations. He had seen the potential
for using the actual sites of that ancient land; everything from the awesome
temples to the simple villages would be perfect for our project. I flew from
New York to Cairo and we travelled up the Nile by private motorboat; we
were thus able to stop and explore whenever something struck our fancy.
In this way we encountered numerous little villages, untouched and well
off the usual tourist circuit, occupied by simple peasant folk almost perfectly
dressed for the film in their djellabas. It was so reminiscent of *Jesus of
Nazareth* and Tunisia that I felt instantly at home.

We allowed ourselves detours up small canals, through the high papyrus
stems in the marshlands, then out across mirror-like lakes broken only by
the boles of sunken palm trees. To see these things in the violent Egyptian
sunsets was to witness magic.

Then, one fortunate day, we left our boat and followed our guide away
from the river for several hours. Slowly we found ourselves engulfed in line
upon line of palm trees. We had entered an extraordinary date plantation,

hundreds of years old and consisting of rigid lines of gigantic palms that stretched for miles in every direction. It was one of the most imposing sights I have ever seen and I knew at once that this was precisely the place prefigured in my dream. There was one broad central avenue crossed by another, the ideal setting for the triumphal march as the Pharaoh's army led by Radames brings the captive Aida to her fate, and his.

Excited by everything we had seen, Tarak and I returned to Cairo to arrange the practicalities of filming. Happily, his father was a personal friend of President and Mrs Sadat and had arranged meetings for us. We first met Mrs Sadat in the Ministry of Culture and were delighted to find how enthusiastic she was that our project should get off the ground. Later, when we met her with her husband at their official residence, they made it clear that their dearest wish was to end the isolation of Egypt from Europe, which had been a result of the lingering Arab conflict with Israel. They saw *Aida* as a way of emphasizing the cultural links between North Africa and the rest of the Mediterranean basin.

One of the things which particularly struck me when I met the Sadats was how unusually handsome they were as a family, with perfect features, sparkling dark eyes and almond-white teeth, as well as being grace-ful movers; parents, sons and daughter all seemed to have the beauty which comes from an awareness of belonging to an ancient and civilized race.

Back in America I set about organizing the music. There was only one ideal conductor for me, Lenny Bernstein. We had planned to do *Aida* in Vienna once before, but that had not come off; now I was determined that we should bring it about. As soon as I got back I saw him in New York and told him everything I'd seen and done. He was fascinated and promised to make a decision as quickly as possible.

In the meantime, the discussions about *Endless Love* were coming to a head. Although I was excited about the story, I was understandably worried about the rather strange team that came with it. It was not that men like Jon Peters were inexperienced – indeed he was in many ways one of the true denizens of Hollywood, with a deep knowledge of its ways. He and his associates felt they instinctively knew what the public wanted, and that ultimately they understood how to target a film to its audience. I felt it was a dangerous delusion on their part and one which I had begun to suspect quite early on as they talked about how they viewed the story. To give myself some protection I insisted that, if I directed the film, the day-to-day producer working with me should be my old friend Dyson Lovell, who had already worked on practically all my films. They agreed, and on that basis I accepted their offer.

While all the details were being finalized, I spent my weekends with Lenny at his lovely home in Connecticut. Over those idyllic weekends in

314   his study looking out over marvellous countryside we produced one of the most detailed working film-scripts I've ever seen. It was accompanied by my sketches for the shot-by-shot storyboard, sets and costumes. When Tarak saw it, he was astounded by the lengths to which we had gone, but it was only the visual evidence of the extraordinary discussions and the range of the ideas which Lenny and I had covered. His best idea was that we should have a young unknown black singer in the leading role; naturally we wanted Placido for Radames. A girl called Leona Mitchell was one possible candidate, but Lenny was also willing to consider someone not necessarily trained in the operatic tradition, who would be susceptible to the necessary schooling. This was the sort of thinking only possible by a man whose career had spanned La Scala and Broadway. Both of us were ideally suited to cope with the idea of making opera a living, popular medium again. Neither of us was hidebound by the conventions of grand opera and both were willing to bring show business ideas to bear on that still rather dusty art form.

For the moment we felt we had done as much as we could and, while Tarak set about putting together the finance, I turned to *Endless Love*. Filming began in New York State on 9 September and from the first I was aware of the flaw that ran through our package. We should have had young unknowns as our two leads, but the deal had been put together on the basis of having a box-office draw in the person of Brooke Shields.

She had already made *Pretty Baby* and *Blue Lagoon*, and was enjoying international success as a model. The problem we didn't think through was that she would come to us with a fairly well-defined persona to which I would have to adapt, rather than the other way round. Worse still, she had been the darling of the press for the last couple of years, which usually means that at some point the pendulum will swing the other way as they inevitably start to debunk the idol they have created. There was nothing wrong with Brooke either as an actress or a person – on the contrary, I couldn't have asked for a nicer, more cooperative young star.

With Brooke as the girl we felt we could risk the unknown Martin Hewitt as the boy. He was fine. I had no problem getting him to respond as I wished, but almost from the beginning of filming I could see that Brooke was wrong for the role. She was too established, popular and experienced an image to play convincingly the role of an insecure teenager. My instinct was to scrap the story and do something totally different, like transfer the whole operation to Paris and create a different story around Brooke herself, perhaps set in the world of fashion modelling of which she was a part. She was made for something glamorous, not for this tremulous personal drama. But, of course, that was out of the question. The rights had been bought, money laid out on the production, we were locked on to the treadmill and the only way off would have been for me to quit. I was psychologically and ethically incapable of such a thing, and so we soldiered on. One way I devised to counter the faults I saw in Brooke's performance was to concentrate on the wider drama taking place inside the family and thus broaden the action. One consequence was that, when filming ended on 19 December, we were left with an unwieldy amount of rushes which were sufficient to make a five-hour film. I could see that there were going to have to be heroic labours in the cutting-room before a manageable film appeared

Still, I wasn't unduly worried at that point. Despite my misgivings about some of the performances, I felt certain that there was gold amongst all that footage and all I had to do was quarry it. Half my mind was still on *Aida*, which was looking more and more hopeful. Although it would be expensive to shoot, the cooperation of the Sadats meant that we could probably count on the 'loan' of Egyptian soldiers as magnificent unpaid extras, a fantastic bonus. With that we could probably keep our budget down to $10 million, a sum Tarak felt confident he could raise.

Then, suddenly, there was a totally unexpected shift of focus: I was able to make my first opera film almost immediately. Even while the editing of *Endless Love* was going on I had an old commitment to produce new versions of *Cavalleria rusticana* and *Pagliacci* for La Scala in January 1981.

Italian television wanted me to do another of the first-night live transmissions that we'd started with *Otello*. Seizing the opportunity, I told them I didn't want to do just another live television broadcast with all its missed shots, imperfections and bad improvisation. What I did want to do was film the operas. We could do it in the theatre, but without the audience. I could place several cameras at different points to cover every scene and, if we wanted to, we could even film some scenes outside on location in order to increase the visual spectacle and broaden the scope of it. The German company Unitel saw at once that they would have a very marketable product on their hands. The scheme was further boosted by the presence of Placido Domingo in both operas, but one thing I saw straight away was that *all* the leads had to look good, that was the whole point. I told the people at La Scala they should abandon whichever soprano they had signed up for *Pagliacci* and get Teresa Stratas, the Greek singer I had worked with in that earlier production with Richard Tucker at the Met. I wanted her because she alone had the looks to carry off the role on film, as well as being a superb actress. As she was not an especially well-known singer in Italy, they were not enamoured of the idea, but I persuaded them.

After the normal opening of the operas to the theatre public, I got on with the new task of filming them. We would have two days per opera: a Monday, when the house was closed, and a ten-hour session the following day, when we would have to move out before the evening performance. We built a platform over the front of the stalls as our working area, on which I placed my film cameras.

316   As a magazine of film lasts only ten minutes, we had to divide the opera into small segments, which we then shot bit by bit live with the orchestra, just as the first musicals had been done before the war. Sometimes I would move a camera on stage to get the angle I wanted and sometimes we cleared all the cameras off the platform in order to get as wide a shot as possible from the back of the theatre. We completed most of the work in those two double sessions except for the odd missing elements, which we shot in a small film studio in Milan.

Much of the credit must go to the conductor Georges Prêtre, with whom I had created productions of *Tosca* and *Norma* at the Paris Opera. He had the unenviable task of gearing the orchestra to play in ten-minute bursts. Imagine having to inject feeling into a performance which not only keeps stopping and starting but which has also to be repeated over and over again, with each retake being exactly the same length. As for the performers, one might perhaps have expected Placido to be less suited to the role of the young Turiddu in *Cavalleria* than he was to the ageing, overweight Canio in *Pagliacci*, but one can never be totally sure with him. In the end he was fantastic in the latter. Canio is one of his major roles and one of his greatest contributions to the opera of our day. Understandably, as most tenors do who have played the role, he felt that Canio is the centre of the piece; the girl only exists to feed his part, as it were. He was therefore quite surprised to discover that I read the composer's intentions differently; to me it is the girl who is the pivot of the tragedy. It is her suffering and ordeal which give meaning to the story, not merely the pathetic misery of the old clown hidden behind his smiling make-up. There is a three-minute intermezzo in the opera and I used this music to illustrate the girl's moment of crisis – should she run away with her lover or not? I filmed Teresa as she underwent that spiritual trial until in the end, her heart breaking, she comes to the little tent where the circus folk live. She sees the clowns darning their costumes and eating a simple meal of bread and cheese, and she knows that she cannot leave them. It was perhaps the most cinematic section of the film, the sort of sequence impossible on stage, which fully justified our filming it in the first place. But Placido was a bit put out when he realized that the opera had been taken away from him and even today he often reproaches me, though only mildly, for in the end he is too intelligent and generous an artist not to see the truth in what I was getting at.

After that January production I returned to America and my film editing to discover increasing signs of difficulty. As I had suspected, some of the performances were less than brilliant and no matter how we cut them together there were still some very worrying moments. Happily, I had Dyson Lovell on my side rather than one of those stonewalling money men and he agreed that we had to reshoot some of the scenes.

I was beginning to have my first real doubts about the film, but as yet could not exactly pinpoint what they were. I put these thoughts out of my mind for the moment and joined my *Cavalleria* people in Sicily, where we were to film some of the peasant scenes and the great Easter procession, one of the best moments in the opera. After the worries over *Endless Love* it was a relief to be back in those pretty villages and that stunning countryside I remembered so well from days of filming *La terra trema* with Luchino.

We finished our Sicilian filming on 19 April, and I returned to America to see the first full rough-cut of *Endless Love*. This lasted just under three hours, but I was immensely relieved when I saw it. We showed it to Ned Tannen at Universal and he and his wife loved it. As neither were easy people to please I was well content with the way things were going. But it was now that the real struggle began; the film had to be drastically edited down to under two hours and it was certain that something would have to go. I was all for trying to keep it as the story of two families dragged into tragedy by their inability to cope with the intense passions aroused by their children. Only this approach brought any light and shade into the film: the father's jealousy of the young man who is making love to his daughter, the mother's longing for the boy who is satisfying in her daughter the needs she herself feels. Sadly, Jon Peters and his associates did not see it that way; they wanted a youth movie with everything concentrated on the two kids. To them this was a simple story of thwarted juvenile passion provoked by old-fashioned, unsympathetic parents, the sort of story with which every suburban teenager in America is supposed to feel some kinship. While I had control of the final edit of the film, I was nevertheless remorselessly dragged in the direction in which they wished the film to go. Whereas I should have calmly pursued the story I knew had to be made, I politely listened instead to their insistent advice and only succeeded in confusing myself. Their cleverest move was to organize a series of screenings of different versions of the film before invited audiences. In fact, what they did was pull in young kids off the streets. They heckled and laughed throughout the showings. It was ludicrous to accept their reactions as typical of what any proper audience might feel, but Polygram insisted on drawing conclusions which inevitably favoured the interpretation they wanted. The film was cut and recut, hacked to shreds.

One day, as I was walking to the cutting-room, I was overcome by a cold fury. How on earth had I allowed this to happen, I who had directed Callas, Magnani and Olivier, the operas of Puccini, Verdi, etc., who had handled tempestuous superstars like Elizabeth Taylor and Richard Burton, who had made a box-office hit out of Shakespeare? But it was no use thinking like this, things had gone too far. I finished the film in a way that can only be described as a total compromise, if not a complete surrender: it was

318   neither the well-crafted family tragedy I had wanted nor quite the mindless soap opera I had been encouraged to make. The producers now rushed to get the film released: it would open in Chicago on 15 July and in New York the following evening.

The critical reception for *Endless Love* made that for *Brother Sun, Sister Moon* seem positively jovial. Most critics seemed to take pleasure in insulting Brooke Shields as if it never crossed their minds that, whatever her qualities as an actress, which I think are remarkable for her age, she was an adolescent at the time, and the sort of wounding remarks aimed at her were frankly disgusting. Predictably, the film made a fortune: something between $70 million and $80 million.

However, there were precious few satisfactions to be salvaged from the affair. I felt guilty towards those who had put their skills in my hands, and was deeply grieved when Ned Tannen's wife asked me what on earth had happened to the beautiful film she and her husband had seen at that first rough-cut showing. How could I explain to her the agony of all those months of editing? All I could do was thank God for my two films of *Cav* and *Pag*, which were now ready.

Both operas went down well in Italy, but that was nothing compared to their success on Channel 3 in America. *Pagliacci* was eventually awarded both a Grammy and an Emmy. The surprisingly large viewing figures and the deluge of enthusiastic letters and telephone calls revealed a larger audience for opera than anyone had dared believe existed. It confirmed what I had been thinking, that if it was released from its rarified opera-house atmosphere and was done with all the glamour and skill of the great musicals, which are after all the true inheritors of the nineteenth-century operatic tradition, then opera could have its place again.

All this pointed me squarely in the direction of *Aida*. Unitel were interested and said they would put in half the budget. British, French and Italian television were all negotiating; it all looked hopeful, so how could we fail?

How? Oh, so easily, as it transpired. I went to Argentina for the opening of *The Champ*, which was beginning its tour of Latin America, and so it was appropriately in an unfamiliar land, in a strange hotel, as far from Egypt as it is possible to get, that I heard the appalling news that President Anwar Sadat had been senselessly gunned down while presiding over a military parade. It was one of those moments when the world seems to miss a heart beat. I could visualize all too clearly the profound distress of Sadat's lovely family; seldom have I felt so ashamed of belonging to a species which kills its own kind so insanely. So many hopes had been raised by that man, so many dreams of peace in the Middle East, of a *rapprochement* between Europe and the Arab world, of a new beginning in the Mediterranean, of new dreams that the people of Egypt would take a leading role in international affairs – all dashed to pieces. And there among the shards was my little dream, perhaps not as vast nor as earth-shaking as those others I have mentioned, but in its own way a part of them; there, broken irreparably, so it seemed, was *Aida*.

I telephoned Lenny, but couldn't find him, so I wrote him a letter that became a grieving lament for Sadat, the man and the leader, which Lenny later told me forced him to tears.

Without the cooperation of the Sadats all our well-laid plans were just so many pipe dreams. When I managed to contact Tarak, he confirmed that it was pointless even to think of going ahead in the present climate of turmoil which had developed in Egypt.

It was in a gloomy frame of mind that I returned to New York in November to direct *La bohème* at the Met; there seemed to be little that was truly exciting ahead of me. *Aida* was lost and only the sour taste left by *Endless Love* remained. Yet these are feelings which I, of all people, should have by then learned to reject. I should know that, when God takes away, He will surely give back, that there is always a balance which compensates for the disasters in our lives.

The swing of the pendulum began in November 1981. I was back in Rome and had been invited, along with other show business people, to go to the lovely medieval town of Viterbo for an annual gala to raise money for animals in need. It was hoped that our presence would attract the well-to-do, who would donate money to the cause. The principal beneficiary was to be kennels where over two hundred strays were taken care of. The main fundraising event was to be a variety show, part professional, part amateur, in the beautiful eighteenth-century theatre.

As Viterbo is just north of Rome, the organizers sent a car to collect me. The driver was a quiet, respectful young man who said his name was Luciano. As he spoke only when spoken to, I imagined the journey would pass in silence, and yet something about him, perhaps a certain *gravitas* beyond his years, made me draw him out. He was only twenty-one, had recently finished his schooling and was having difficulty finding work. Unemployment was bad in Viterbo, so it appeared, hence his temporary job as a chauffeur. He wanted more than anything to find a role in life and I found myself sympathizing with him as he explained his difficulties in getting ahead in a small town with few openings. However, it was only when we drove back to Rome, after what had proved to be a charming and I believe a profitable show, that he began to tell me the full story of his life.

You may imagine how I felt when he told me that he was illegitimate and did not know his father. Because his mother, to whom he was devoted, had been unable to care for him, he had spent the first fifteen years of his life in an orphanage. There had been no Aunt Lide to take him in and no one to offer him the assurance that he had someone to whom he alone could

320   cling. Now all he was asking out of life was something to do, a role that would give him an identity. He had had little formal training and did not expect life to offer him great things.

Did he, I enquired, like driving? He said he did and so the matter was easily resolved; it was about time I had a driver anyway. However, at the back of my mind was the hope that I could perhaps help him find his way in life and give him some of the guidance and support he had missed – could perhaps be the father-figure he'd never had.

The next swing of the pendulum came in New York with a new production of *La bohème*, which turned out to be an exhilarating experience. No matter how many times I do an opera there can still be one that suddenly clicks into place. One critic called it a revolutionary interpretation, but I demur; most ideas that seem revolutionary are really already there, embedded in the play or the opera. The only revolutionary claim any director can make is to have seen what no one has bothered to see since the author compiled the work. Everyone thought that my decision to make *Romeo and Juliet* with young people in the starring roles was daring, yet it was no more than what Shakespeare must have done, and with a fourteen-year-old boy playing Juliet, let's not forget. Similarly with *Traviata*: to begin the opera at the end, as I always do, is nothing more than an elucidation of what is clearly there in the music.

What so intrigued the audience about my new *Bohème* was the way I treated the role of Mimi, the waif whose last love-affair, as she dies of consumption, is the subject of the opera. Every production I had ever seen had had Mimi arrive at the artist's studio (where she meets the poet Rodolfo) as a beautiful, radiant young woman. Only later does she succumb to her illness. This seemed to me to make a nonsense of the piece. Why, I asked, does she immediately faint in front of him? The problem in other productions has been that the average soprano is just too big and healthy to do what the libretto and the score demand, so the truth is usually fudged. But I had Stratas again and, as no one else before, she could be both beautiful and waif-like. We researched the whole nature of the consumptive, once a major theme in European art, now happily a thing of the past. Puccini in *La bohème*, as indeed Verdi in *La traviata*, was familiar with all the details of the illness and of the way its sufferers behaved. The consumptive was often granted a pale, ethereal beauty which many found very attractive. Apparently some robust young men claimed to derive particular pleasure from making love to these dying creatures. Consumptives had strange patterns of behaviour that both operas play on. There would be unexpected remissions in the decline of the sufferer, who would suddenly experience a surge of strength and well-being, only to see it slip away again. That is why *Traviata* and *Bohème* are both about false hopes which are dashed. Both also use the fact that female consumptives were often given to great passion; there was a need to cling on to those with life and health as if to draw support from them. It is strange to recall the influence that now defeated illness had had on my own life; if my mother's husband had not been bed-ridden with it, would she have fallen in love with my father? If her daughter's husband had not suffered from it, would they and not Aunt Lide have taken me in?

The illusion of tubercular people was that love can save you; love is care, warmth and the security of not dying alone and unaided. Thus, when Stratas as Mimi entered the studio, she was already clearly dying: pallid, coughing and feverish, she fainted dead away, and only when Rodolfo has carried her to the fire and sings *'Che viso da malata'* does he see that beneath her pallor she is beautiful. It is then that false hope is raised, and, because we had admitted the audience to the truth, they were able fully to experience the tragedy. Only the petite and haunting Teresa Stratas could have got away with it, and only José Carreras looked youthful enough to set beside her. It was an extraordinary and unique combination, and one I doubt I shall see bettered. It set off many trains of thought. Where would I find again such a pair and why didn't I do something now that I had them, meaning of course a film? How many opportunities had been lost as I planned, discussed and prepared. Callas was never filmed and *Traviata*, *Tosca* and *Aida* had been cancelled along with a dozen or so less advanced schemes. If I had what I needed then why not go ahead? I called Tarak and told him I had the perfect duo for *La Traviata* and that we should forget *Aida*, at least for the moment, and just go ahead and do it.

Why a young Tunisian producer, who by then had built up a flourishing business in his own country, should have been as inspired by the idea as I was I'll never fully comprehend. But inspired he was, and soon he was in contact with financiers in the Arab world to raise the money. We were not going to be awash with cash, but there would be just enough, and as soon as we were under way Tarak was able to get Universal to agree to distribute the film.

We would have a tight twelve weeks to film at the studios of Cinecittà in Rome and a further two weeks on location in Normandy, with another week in Paris. Despite the limitations, I was delighted. At last, by sheer effort of will, I was to make my first full opera film.

When I first approached her with the idea, Teresa Stratas warned me not to go ahead.

'Watch out,' she said. 'You might be in serious trouble with me. I want to be fair to you, Franco, because I like you.'

Everyone who knew her also advised me to take care. I remembered that opening night at the Met in 1970, when she had refused to go on, and I knew her reputation for pulling out at the last minute and creating havoc. But I thought that we could handle it. She had been no trouble at La Scala

322 or at the Met in *Bohème* and I hoped that was because we were in tune with one another. Perhaps with me she would relax and get on with the job. Anyway, what was I to do? The entire notion sprang from her; it was her combination of voice, looks and acting talent which had led me to dream of a film of *Traviata* in the first place. It was pointless to think of changing her.

Because of *Bohème* at the Met, I wanted to have José Carreras as Alfredo. His youthful looks would be the perfect foil for Teresa. Unfortunately, his Spanish agent foresaw complications and he turned the offer down. Whatever the reason, this left me with only one choice, in many ways a better one: I approached Placido Domingo and he agreed to do it. We had discussed the possibility before, but he had always said he thought he was past the age for that character.

'Franco, I'll do it for you,' he said, 'but I count on you to help me look convincing.'

Placido, as his name implies, is an island of calm amidst the stormy operatic seas. Given the problems we were to have, his placidity was to prove essential to the survival of our venture.

Because this opera is so much a part of me, this time I had a particularly clear idea of what I wanted to do. With *Cavalleria* we had introduced an element of realism into the production: we used real villages with real Sicilian peasants, something entirely appropriate to the opera's origins as a story by Verga. But this was not how I saw *La traviata*. I don't really believe that realism and opera can ever be completely happy bedfellows; it seems better to accept the artificiality of people singing and use the world of illusion to best advantage. This *Traviata* would complete a circle, for I had explored the possibilities of the cinema as regards time shifts and flashbacks in my stage production; for instance, Violetta lies dying, yet watches the guests assemble for a party she gave several years earlier. Now those cinematic ideas would be turned back into cinema. To add to the layers of illusion, there would be exterior shots of the countryside where Alfredo's sister and her young fiancé live, and where they risk separation if her brother continues his affair with Violetta, the Parisian courtesan. This 'window' on the story was, of course, something Verdi could not have contemplated, but had certainly dreamt of, as with the scene of Alfredo and Violetta enjoying their country idyll before his father comes to beg her to leave him. All these ideas, I knew, would irritate the purists, but they would do exactly what I wanted: they would appeal to a wide cinema audience used to visual variety and unwilling to support the limited theatrical staging which opera-lovers accept in order to experience great singing. Beauty, drama and emotion were what I was after.

Despite occasional exteriors, much of the action inevitably took place in Violetta's Paris apartment and here I let my skills as a set designer run riot. The walls, ceilings and doors were made of translucent Perspex painted, but left clear at the edges, so that the lights caused a shimmering sparkle to fall on the room, as if the flamboyant *fin de siècle* gas chandeliers were glittering on every surface. The dining-room and the main corridor were a riot of Victoriana, some of which I'd collected over the years.

I think Placido Domingo, who was magnificent, will forgive me if I say that the whole enterprise depended on Teresa Stratas as Violetta. It is Violetta who suffers and dies, it is her sacrifice and religious sense of self-denial for a higher and impossible love that must ultimately make us weep for her. Callas had achieved that, and it was astonishing for me to see just how similar in many ways the two women were. There was that same fanatical attempt to enter the part, the same draining emotion and, perhaps in consequence, the same insecurity and need to be reassured and comforted. Such performers are never easy to work with, but usually they are the only ones worth it.

But, oh, what problems we had! The trouble began at the very start, at the music recordings in New York with Jimmy Levine conducting the Metropolitan Opera Orchestra and Chorus. Teresa, who, I was told, was barely over bronchitis, was frankly not in great voice during the recordings and she knew it. Nevertheless, she generously did all she could to provide a viable soundtrack. The result was that, when we filmed and refilmed, when we then did cut-aways and repeats, she was forced to hear herself over and over again, a constant reminder that her singing had not been of the best. This was not as bad as it might seem, for it is standard practice to re-record parts of the music to fit the final version of the film. It was possible for her to retape any part of her performance she wanted. However, this did not alter the fact that someone who was so conscientious about her performance was being forced to listen hourly to something substandard. Worse still, she was constantly in the commanding presence of Domingo, a singer at the height of his powers, and this too seemed to overwhelm her.

She became very edgy, even more nervous than normal, but at first I put this down to her usual passionate striving for perfection. It came to a head when Piero Tosi, who was designing the superb costumes, asked her to try on the dressing-gown she was to wear in the final deathbed scene. It was an elaborate and voluminous affair and, as Teresa is so tiny, Piero had made a pair of ministilts on which she would have to perch in order to carry off this splendid creation. Piero wasn't being flippant; his thinking was that the flamboyant robe would represent Violetta's last valuable possession when all else had been sold off to pay her debts and doctors' bills. That gown alone she had guarded and thus, when her lover Alfredo returns, too late to save her, her wearing it would be all the more poignant. It seemed a brilliant coup to me, so I was astounded when Teresa threw the thing to the ground.

324   'It's not for me,' she screamed.
'Believe me, you must wear it,' Piero said.
'Why?'
'Because you have to,' he insisted. 'If you had seen what Maria did with it, you're too intelligent an artist not to agree with me.'

Teresa stared at him with loathing and all at once I knew why she had been growing increasingly agitated as the days passed. Almost everyone on the film had at one time or another worked with Callas. To us she *was* Violetta and in making the film we were somehow giving ourselves a second chance to make the film with Maria. I was as much to blame as anyone: every gesture I had asked of Teresa and every detail of interpretation, no matter how I tried to disguise it, had been inspired by the work I had done with Callas so many years before. Now along came Piero trying to resurrect, through her, the many memories and emotions Maria had given us.

'I'm not a ghost,' she shouted. 'Just because I'm Greek and can sing, I'm not a ghost.' Then she went deathly calm and quiet as if dragging what she was saying out of her most secret inner self. 'I have to thank you for the honour, yes, thank you. But I'm not Callas, could never hope to be. Look at me. All I've got to offer is my little skinny body. There's not much of me, but that's what we can use, what you *must* use. I really could make people believe I'm dying of consumption. Just give me a thin chemise like a little girl and let everyone see how emaciated I am. And,' she added emphatically, 'let me be barefooted.'

I was very moved by what she'd said and was determined to try to see things her way. But then I made a fatal mistake: in order to reassure her I let her see some of the rushes. Directors don't often do this, as rough shots can give a false impression to the untrained viewer. Again, many stars like Faye Dunaway refuse to look at them on the grounds that they can interfere with their thinking about a role. I simply hoped that Teresa would feel reassured and more a part of the team if she joined in our sessions, but the result was disastrous. She became overwrought. She hated the way she looked and blamed our director of photography, Ennio Guanieri, as well as Piero Tosi and the make-up artists. The truth was that she couldn't bear hearing herself, but refused to admit it. No, it had to be the way Ennio filmed her eyes or some other quibble.

One day, shortly after, we came on set to find her gone. She had bolted.

Shooting was stopped for several days while we tried to track her down. We were almost on the point of collapse when we discovered that she was in London with a friend of hers. Tarak flew to London to persuade her to return. Fortunately, her friend made the point that dozens of innocent people would be thrown out of work if she persisted in running away. She was finally convinced and allowed Tarak to take her back to Rome.

All through the film we argued and compromised. What agony and strain she put herself through. If she wasn't in a particular scene, she would disappear to the studios of International Recording in Rome, where she would attempt to redub her voice on to the orchestral tracks. One day I slipped in secretly and spied on her; only then did I fully comprehend her fanatical striving for perfection.

'*Ancora, ancora,*' she would scream at the sound engineers as she tried yet again to better what she had done. I could see she had only limited means, but she was intelligent and tireless in making the best use of the instrument she had. This was not the first time she had behaved like this. I remembered a joke that went the rounds when she recorded a wonderful *Salome* that Karl Böhm conducted – 'Ah, yes,' said the wags, 'but Böhm and Stratas never met, you know.'

If so, then it was no more than what she was doing in that studio in Rome. No wonder she was so tense on set; there were no days off and no chance to relax at all. It was even worse than just recording for sound only; here she had to dub the performance she had already given for the camera.

'*Ancora, ancora!*' The words echoed in my ears as I slipped away. That night I wrote her a note saying how right she had been in knowing what was best for her Traviata.

Despite our attempts to rethink the way we handled her, Teresa refused to compromise with us. Piero was her enemy, or so her behaviour towards him indicated, and he wasn't the only one on the team to feel the power of her resentment. More worrying was the way she was already working up an avenue of escape from the film, getting her excuses ready to show that we and not she were to blame for any flaws in her performance. I had already heard her suggest that she had ruined her voice forever in order to give me the sound track for the film.

As may be imagined, by the end of filming I was heartily sick of my leading lady and her antics. Her moods had become a bore and her nit-picking attempt to do the impossible with what God had given her had passed all comprehension. Only when I began to cut together the film did I have cause to look back on her behaviour with a little more gratitude. That final scene as she approached Alfredo, tiptoeing on bare feet and with her emaciated arms stretched out towards him, was heart-breaking. She had been absolutely right about it.

The film was ready by the end of 1982 and had its first showing at a private party in Los Angeles given by Gregory Peck, who was then chairman of the Motion Picture Academy. The guest-list was pretty impressive: Jimmy Stewart, Cary Grant, Johnny Carson, Fred Astaire, George Cukor, Vincent Minnelli, Jack Lemmon, Diana Ross, Barbra Streisand, Bette Davis. . . . I discovered the latter sitting on a staircase after the viewing, almost overcome by what she had seen. Bette was totally bowled over by Stratas's performance and kept reiterating that it was amazing that she

326   not only sang so well but also gave one of the best acted performances. Everyone, from Bette Davis on, supposed that Teresa would now launch herself into an acting career; there were certainly plenty of people at that screening who would have been delighted to give her a chance. But she was still brooding on the whole affair. She totally refused to take part in any of the publicity and I heard that she was considering a press conference at which she planned to denounce the film when it opened in New York on 20 April 1983. She was only restrained from doing so by the ecstatic reviews she received. All the critics praised her great talent as an actress and predicted that a career in films obviously lay at her feet. All to no avail. Teresa disappeared: no press conferences, no future plans, nothing. It was as tragic as the story of Violetta herself.

My main concern was how the ordinary public would react. If this turned out to be a well-received art-house movie patronized by the regular opera-going crowd then I had achieved nothing. Although I had been looking at the film for weeks during the editing, at the opening in New York there was something fresh about watching it *en masse* in a crowded cinema. Watching those familiar scenes – beginning in the deserted apartment where Violetta lies dying, then her memory of the dinner party with the first steps of the doomed love affair, on to the country dream shattered by the father's arrival, the ball with its horrendous confrontation between the angry Alfredo and the shattered Violetta, and then the final reconciliation, which ends tragically in her death – looking at it all afresh, I knew that originally this was Maria's film. Dear Teresa had known it from the start, but what a challenge and what a triumph for her in the end. Despite the differences in physique, voice and personality, Teresa had done what Callas had not, and perhaps could never have done: she had created an everlasting, memorable film portrait of Violetta.

In the darkness of the theatre I gradually realized that there was a noise like a distant tide from the audience. People were crying quite openly, and not just the women. In the half-light, I could make out people fumbling for handkerchiefs and tissues as they fought to control their feelings. I looked back at the screen as Violetta struggled to convince Alfredo and herself that she was not dying, that she could get up, and that they would be able to live together again. Then I knew that, despite all the odds, Teresa had created the Violetta we had all been dreaming of. I looked at *her* wide, dark eyes begging for a little more time to live and love, and then I realized that I too was crying, quite helplessly.

NINETEEN

Otello

In September 1985 disaster struck Mexico City – an earthquake of massive force shattered large areas of the city. Because of faulty construction many apartment blocks crashed to the ground, trapping hundreds of people under dust and rubble. Placido Domingo's father had moved from Spain to Mexico when Placido was a child and many of his family had joined them. Now he found himself hurrying back to Mexico City with the dreadful news that the aunt who had helped raise him as a child and three other members of the family were buried beneath their home. For days he struggled with his bare hands in the filth and dust to save his relatives, but all to no avail. When he finally gave up the struggle, he was a changed man. His voice had been temporarily damaged by the dust, but this was not the reason for his decision to retire from opera performances for a year. It was true he wanted to raise money for Mexico by giving a series of concerts, but also the experience made him realize that the whirlwind of international per-formances had to stop sometime, that there are moments in one's life when one has to take stock of what one is doing and why. I had tremendous sympathy for him, not only because of the deaths of those he loved but also because I remembered how I, too, had had a dramatic change of attitude after my accident.

It was a disturbing period for me. As Placido was struggling so manfully to disinter his relatives, I was waiting with an army of scene builders and film crew in Barletta in south-eastern Italy for him to arrive. We were due to begin my second full-scale film opera, *Otello*, and, inevitably, Placido had the starring role. For one awful moment it looked as if the tragedy might force him to cancel the film. The work of months would have come to nothing.

The story stretched back to March 1985, when we had been doing *Tosca* at the Met in New York. Placido asked if I would be interested in filming another opera as he had had an offer of finance from a leading production company. I was, of course, intrigued; finding money for opera is not the easiest business, as I know. I had longed to do a film of *Carmen* for ages and by rights we should have done it with Stratas, who would have been perfect in the part. But her antics during *Traviata* had made it impossible

328   for me to find anyone to back her in a film. I can forgive her moods and her walk-outs – there is nothing I don't know about theatrical nerves – but I cannot forgive her for making it impossible for me and for her to create a work that we had every right to do. Stratas and *Carmen*, Karajan and *Tosca* are sadly missed opportunities.

So, of course, I was interested to know who these people were. They turned out to be a pair of American-Israeli film producers called Menachem Golan and Yoram Globus, whose company, Cannon Films, had sky-rocketed to major status, first as film distributors and then as film-makers, in only a few years. I had met them once, but had hardly thought of them as producers of opera. As far as I knew they specialized in down-market pop and action films. Placido's news seemed doomed from the start.

How wrong I was. I should have remembered the Mann Auditorium and my work in Israel with those audiences of deeply musical Jews, aware of any fault. Placido had spent some time in Israel with the Tel Aviv opera and was very popular there – Golan and Globus are great fans of his. Having made money out of popular films, they were ready to do what they really wanted. They dreamt of producing an art film.

Their names were at first a little difficult to remember, so I dubbed them the Gamma-Globulins, but when I met them again, I realized that here was every serious director's dream: cultivated men with money to back their hunches and the will to make quick decisions. It was the speed that impressed me most: anything they wanted to do they just got on and did it. Indeed, they turned out to be as beneficent to the health of the film business as gamma globulin is to the blood.

The two years before Golan and Globus appeared in my life had been very frustrating. Following *Traviata,* I should have gone straight on to another major film, yet as so often before there was a sudden, inexplicable stasis. Tarak was willing to find finance for another project, but there was a stumbling block: we had ideas but no script. Hundreds of thousands of dollars were wasted on paying writers for scripts we couldn't use. As every film director knows there is a dearth of writing talent.

As usual when film projects fail, I turned to theatre. One high spot was *Maria Stuarda* at the beginning of 1983, and *Turandot* at La Scala at the end of the year, but the gaps between were large. There were gala openings for the *Traviata* film in various countries, but no prospect of another movie. Fortunately, there was my work in Tunisia, building studios, training new people and devoting my time to promoting the new North African Hollywood. However, only at the end of 1984 did things really begin to look up. I directed my first Pirandello play, *Right You Are (If You Think So)*, in October. Then came a new production of *Traviata* destined for the Met in New York, but first presented that December in Florence. It was conducted by Kleiber and sung by a new young soprano, the stunning

Cecilia Gasdia. This production was to move to Paris before going on to America; and the fact that so elaborate a co-production had been arranged meant that I could create sets and costumes on a cinematic scale. I was determined that, after the film of *Traviata*, this stage version should not look thin. Conscious that it would transfer to Paris, I worked hard with my old Florentine friend Anna Anni to capture the rich *fin de siècle* world of gilded stucco and heavy velvet drapes, that plush coffin in which the frail Violetta is entombed.

With this production of *Traviata* the pace of work began to quicken. The year 1985 opened with a radical departure – my first ballet. I'd always steered clear of that particular world, as I felt I would have little to contribute, it seemed so specialized. Ballets are directed by choreographers, so where would I come in? It was only when I realized this was a myth that I was able to accept La Scala's long-standing invitation to move into this field. The key that unlocked the gate was the recollection that this century's greatest director of ballet was Diaghilev, who certainly wasn't a dancer or choreographer. Having accepted that, it was easy to see how ridiculous the situation has become in the world of dance; after all, we don't let voice-trainers direct operas, so why let feet-trainers direct ballet?

All this brought me to *Swan Lake*. Of the great classics, this was the one which captured my imagination most, yet it was clear that, as it is performed by the world's leading companies, it is a severely flawed work. In fact, it proved my point about choreographers as directors. *Swan Lake* as it is usually done derives from the later versions put together at the Imperial Russian Ballet and subsequently amended by more recent choreographers – some of genius, like Sir Frederick Ashton. But I had the feeling that, with all these changes, the whole work had somehow lost its way. Tchaikovsky's original score had been severely cut over the years. The original production in St Petersburg had not been a success, and it was only after the composer's death that Lev Ivanov rechoreographed part of the second act for a gala memorial. This was so popular that he and Marius Petipa decided to try and salvage what they could of the entire work. They were much influenced by Saint-Saens's ballet *La Mort du cygne,* a fairytale containing fluttering ballerinas with swan-like gestures which Ivanov and Petipa transposed wholesale into their *Swan Lake*. In a sense they succeeded triumphantly; their ballet became the greatest jewel in the Russian repertory and, as such, it has been passed on to every major classical ballet company. But at what cost!

Whenever I have seen it done I have been struck by how shallow the story seems. Why does Prince Siegfried fall in love with Odette, the princess who is clearly half-swan, an absurdity, and why is Odile, the creature of the evil Rothbart, danced by the same ballerina, a foolish and confusing convention if ever there was one? It was obvious to me that years of

Zeffirelli

330 adaptation had pushed the work so far from what must have been in Tchaikovsky's mind that only a radical return to his original concept would do anything to clear up the confusion.

As is my wont, I went back to the early score, trying to piece together the music before it was chopped up to make the selections Ivanov and Petipa wanted. I also had research done into the sort of ideas currently in the air when Tchaikovsky was working on the composition. The discoveries were astonishing. Listening to the original score and reading the research notes revealed a world far removed from the fairytale ballet we are all used to. Here was a gloomy Northern folktale retold in the moody symbolist manner fashionable in the 1870s – the world of Gustave Moreau, Puvis de Chavannes and Odilon Redon. This was the age of half-whispered passions, of aestheticism and decadence, of Oscar Wilde's *Salome* and a belief in beauty as an end in itself.

In the original, captured peasant maidens and princesses have been doomed by the spells of Rothbart to spend their days as swans. Only at nightfall, by the cold light of the moon – a prominent feature of much symbolist art – did the tragic creatures become girls again, passing their time in a melancholy half-life until dawn returned them to their feathered state. Here was a mystical dream, not a brightly-coloured circus! Prince Siegfried falls asleep while out hunting. The swans land and become maidens; the prince wakes and sees Odette; they pass a night of love together, but when the dawn breaks and the evil spell comes into effect the Prince sees the beginnings of the transformation and faints away. Thus he cannot be certain that he has not dreamt the whole thing.

The spell can only be broken if someone is willing to die for love of one of the swan-maidens. In order to protect his evil plan, Rothbart sends his creature Odile, disguised as Odette, to a birthday ball given by the Prince in order to confuse him into choosing the wrong maiden. This he does, and the heartbroken Odette throws herself into the lake, where she drowns. Realizing his error, Siegfried follows her and the spell is broken. The underlying theme of Tchaikovsky's original work was that Love triumphs over Death, and it seemed worthwhile making the effort to restore that noble vision.

What an opportunity this presented to me. Now I could do with ballet the sort of things I had tried in opera and cinema. Instead of dancers in stiff tutus and feathers, I used special effects, lights and back projection, with film and slides to show real swans swooping down to the lakeside. As they approached, they spiralled into a swirling mist from which appeared the maidens – not a neat regiment of identical automatons but real girls, individuals in the loose mid-calf-length ballet dresses of an earlier age. It was these effects which most polarized the audience; there were those who hated what they saw as an assault on the great tradition and those who were willing to acknowledge that here was an attempt to revitalize a moribund art form. It was much as La Scala had been in the 1950s, when opera was being transformed and the warring factions were as unforgiving and as noisy as ever.

The opposition front-of-house was no more than that which had surfaced as I tried to assemble the production. We had originally hoped that Mikhail Baryshnikov would dance the Prince, but, when he discovered this was not going to be just a new ensemble of sets and costumes by Zeffirelli with everything else unchanged, he pulled out. What really upset him was the absence of tutus, that silly circus costume first taken up because it shows more of the ballerinas' legs. It has become a symbol of the old-style classical ballet and a rallying point for all those who do not wish to see any change in the world they are familiar with. Thank God, we had Maurizio Bellezza of the La Scala company as the Prince, with Alessandra Ferri as Odette and Carla Fracci as Odile. One of the high spots in our production was a *pas de trois* between the three protagonists which we introduced. This so clearly fitted Tchaikovsky's music that it was impossible not to believe he had intended it to be used that way. Also true to the composer's wishes was the aura of symbolist horror which infused the piece: when Siegfried unmasks Odile, he tears away her disguise to uncover a hideous, vile creature. Likewise, at the end, the theme of the triumph of love was heightened by a final scene in which the Prince and Princess, after a fabulous scene change, are shown living dreamlike and free beneath the moonlit waters.

Directing my first ballet proved exhausting. La Scala was bedevilled with strikes and our opening was much delayed, but in the end it was worthwhile. The excitement of breaking new ground was just the fillip I needed. I'm not sure whether or not I will do more; *Nutcracker, Sleeping Beauty* and *Giselle* all seem fully worked out, leaving me little room to manoeuvre. I would, however, like to tackle a Stravinsky ballet, perhaps *The Rite of Spring*. For the moment, that first *Swan Lake* was a satisfying beginning and one that launched 1985 as one of the most creative years of my life.

So there I was in New York for *Tosca*, with Placido proposing another film. But which opera were we to do?

The original idea of Golan and Globus was *Trovatore,* but I quickly pointed out that the first rule of filmed opera is that the story should be universally understood; it would be madness to attempt to put over one of those convoluted opera stories. It is far better to go for an opera that comes from another well-known source such as a classical play. In any case, we had the solution in front of us. Placido is acknowledged as the greatest living exponent of Verdi's *Otello*. The story is known to millions and it combines intense passion with high drama and adventure on an epic scale. They needed no convincing.

33² We immediately announced the forthcoming production at the Cannes Film Festival in May 1985; then I set about recruiting the other principals.

The second hard rule of filmed opera is that the singers must look good, be believable and not merely be able to act but able to act for the film camera. Placido, of course, was no problem, but which soprano was beautiful enough to play the young Desdemona? This was no time for long agonizing. Infected with the Golan-Globus quick-fire enthusiasm, I settled on the Italian soprano Katia Ricciarelli, and she accepted just as quickly. But who was to play the difficult role of Iago? Someone who could look innocent, not a twisted villain whom Otello would see through at once. Who could act, really act? I considered a lot of singers, but no one seemed to fit. Then Placido suggested a friend of his, the Puerto Rican bass-baritone Justino Diaz.

I knew Justino, though not under the most favourable of circumstances – he had sung Anthony in the ill-fated *Anthony and Cleopatra* which had reopened the Met. He'd worked with me later in *Carmen* and *Don Giovanni* in Vienna; he always seemed to be on the edge of international stardom, yet never quite there. I had my doubts, but was unable to come up with anyone else. Persuaded by Placido, I decided to risk him. I did a screen test in Rome and was astounded by how quickly and naturally he adapted to the camera; better still, he had a great sense of humour, which, on a long filming schedule, is a godsend.

We assembled in Milan at the appropriately-named Conservatorio Giuseppe Verdi with the orchestra and chorus of La Scala to record the music. Initially, Carlos Kleiber, who had so brilliantly handled our original stage *Otello*, had been going to conduct, but, when he dropped out, we were fortunate to get Lorin Maazel.

Lorin is absolutely in tune with the problems of filming opera; he knows that the director must have variations of the same music, as it is impossible to predict absolutely how a scene will be shot – for instance, will the singers need to be close and intimate or distant and loud? In addition, he is sympathetic to the fact that the opera will have to be cut. Apart from its overall length, which is too much for a cinema audience, there's much unnecessary repetition in nineteenth-century opera, which holds up the action. By contrast, the director may need to insert bridging passages to extend the action on occasions, and Lorin was willing to help orchestrate those. We knew the purists would howl with rage, but in the end all we were doing to Verdi and Boito was what they had done to Shakespeare – cutting and adapting to turn a work of art in one medium into a work of art in another. After all, cinema *is* an art form and has its own techniques and constraints.

After recording the music, we spent three months designing and building the set, and recruiting the actors and crew. Thus I was waiting at the castle in Barletta for news from Mexico that might or might not put an end to the whole dream.

It was with immense relief and gratitude that I received word that, although he planned to cancel all other engagements, Placido would go ahead with the film. He knew that too many people were now involved for him to be able to pull out. The singing would be no problem, as the music had already been recorded. What a relief it was for opera lovers everywhere that the opportunity to see in action the greatest Otello of our day was not lost.

We were both very conscious that this was a unique opportunity, for the money from Cannon was such that for the first time an opera could be filmed on the scale of a Hollywood epic. In those three months I had scoured the old Venetian trading empire to find sites that would correspond to the Venetian Cyprus where the action takes place. Unfortunately, politics excluded several candidates. The crusader castles in the Lebanon were out of the question and even my beloved Tunisia had become unsafe for an Israeli company to work in, thanks to the presence of the PLO. I finally decided on the castle at Barletta because its interiors had the harsh feel of the garrison world to which Otello and Iago belonged. The castle has magnificent domed rooms linked by echoing arched passageways. For the main exteriors I chose the port of Heraklion in Crete because many of its old Venetian harbour buildings are still usable. Nevertheless, we would be obliged to construct virtually an entire castle keep with its monumental entrance. Our intimate interiors we would shoot in the studios of Cinecittà in Rome, which still left the problem of Otello's ship to be dealt with. Months of hard work lay ahead, but we launched off with a will as soon as Placido joined us.

From the first it was obvious that Placido wanted to purge all thoughts of Mexico from his mind by plunging into the part. He threw himself almost violently into his first scenes, in which he and Iago chase round the castle corridors as the hapless Otello is tortured by his jealous thoughts. It was also clear that, when the action called for Otello to break down, Placido was barely acting – his tears were real. It was obvious to all of us what he was suffering, yet, true professional that he is, he worked harder than any and demanded no concessions. Because he had to be made up as an African, his call time was hours before anyone else's, yet this he bore without complaint. If anyone imagines that all opera stars are querulous, over-sensitive freaks they should think of Placido Domingo and change their minds.

Equally satisfying was the work I saw all around me, the truly magnificent sets, produced by a team which I had helped train over the years. This *Otello* was to be the consummation of many talents. People who'd started out as assistant painters or seamstresses on things I'd done years ago now answered the call to show how their talents had developed over the years. These were people who'd watched Lila de Nobili, Piero Tosi and Renzo Mongiardino at work. Watching them reconstruct the glory of Venetian art in those barren castle chambers, I felt very proud of them.

Not that the sets were to be mere backdrops to the action; to me they were part of my attempt to reveal the nature of the characters. I filled Otello's studio with Renaissance scientific instruments such as astrolabes and lenses which a great navigator of the period would have collected around him. My purpose was to show his intelligence and culture. As in my stage production, he is no way the usual conception, a savage with a light veneer of Western civilization easy to push into primitive behaviour at the first contact with Iago's lies. Rather, Otello to me is the perfect embodiment of European culture, so much so that he exists on a plane where he is unable to cope with the satanic evil of a monster like Iago. Otello has accepted the West, but its mindless evil destroys him. All this was reflected in the set, for I used the great magnifying lenses, so typical of the science of the period, to give dramatic force to the poison Iago is pouring into Otello's ears – as the two of them circle the studio Iago's face is captured in those lenses. It is magnified and distorted into a thing out of Hieronymus Bosch, something not out of the Renaissance of Otello but out of the Dark Ages which preceded it.

Happily, Placido and I were at one over our interpretation of the role. He has done many Otellos, but I know that the one we did at La Scala remains closest to his heart. He told me that, whenever possible, he tries to use the costumes from that production, even in other opera houses with other directors, because those are the ones in which he feels most comfortable.

The risk we took with Justino Diaz was fully justified from the first. He proved not merely a good actor – most opera singers can act after all – but he also turned out to have an instinctive feel for the exigencies of the camera, such as the small facial gestures that scream louder than words, and the need to do little in order to say a lot.

My greatest worry was our Desdemona, Katia Ricciarelli. She had difficulty in adapting to a situation in which dozens of technicians were standing around staring at her while she attempted to mime her part. All her opera-house tricks and gestures were completely wrong for the camera. Fortunately her main scenes would be later, in Crete and Rome, and there was still time for her to settle in.

It wasn't merely a matter of training professional singers to act: there was the opposite as well. We had to train actors to sing or, at least appear to do so. Again, one of the advantages that filming can give to opera is the facility to replace singers who are unsuitable physically with actors miming to their voices. I doubt this should be done with the principal roles, as the public would probably consider this cheating, but lesser roles can be enhanced in this way. The obvious case in *Otello* is Cassio, the young officer who is used by Iago to waken Otello's jealousy. It is necessary that Cassio be young and handsome enough for Otello's suspicions to be aroused. My image of Cassio was of a young Venetian aristocrat who is probably a childhood friend of Desdemona, which is why she so frequently and disastrously intervenes on his behalf, confirming her husband's worst fears. Two carefree, young, upper-class Venetians like Desdemona and Cassio would have had a pretty easygoing attitude to sex. There would be jokes and games, none of which would mean anything to them. But to Otello, who has adopted Christian morality in a wholesale way, this would be intolerable. I chose as Cassio a blue-blooded Italian youngster, Prince Urbano Barberini, who, as his name suggests, is a descendant of dukes and princes and whose ancestors include a Pope. He, too, was blond like Desdemona, giving them a physical affinity to contrast even further with Otello.

While we filmed in the domed chambers of the castle, Prince Urbano was being trained in sword fighting on the castle battlements or given a crash course in opera in his hotel room by one of our music directors. I don't have any qualms about using dubbing; in fact, at one point in the film I made an absolute virtue of it. At the moment when the lying Iago tells Otello that he has overheard Cassio talking in his sleep of his love for Desdemona, I showed a naked Cassio on the bed mouthing the words that Iago is singing – a double dub, as it were.

Having completed our scenes in Barletta, the entire production, craftsmen and performers, were flown by special charter on 9 November to Crete. The weather was glorious, the harbour set constructed in advance was breathtaking and the omens were good. On one side of the harbour was the main set; on the other, an old Venetian castle, which served as a general headquarters for the teams of dressers and make-up people who would have to handle the army of extras which was being recruited on the island. Here they would be trained to sing and fight, would be dressed, made up, fed and tended if hurt. Pippo and my other assistants had recruited young people, most of whom were holidaying on the island. I hadn't realized that Crete is such a crossroads for the young. Our extras were Canadian, Norwegian, French, Moroccan, everything. There was a cheerful atmosphere, because they were so enthusiastic and keen to shine no matter how minuscule their part in the action. Of course, we didn't just want the young, and here we were particularly fortunate in being on Crete. There are some amazing faces amongst the island peasants, faces that show the Cretans' Phoenician origins. We recruited in the villages, and every day busloads of black-draped ancients were brought to Heraklion, itself an adventure for them, to be taught to sing Verdi. Heaven knows what they made of it all,

336 but they seemed to be enjoying the experience, like the elderly Jews of Djerba had done when we made *Jesus of Nazareth*.

Our first main scene, out on the harbour, was the opening moments of the opera, the great storm scene in which Otello's boat manages against all odds to land and bring back the Venetian troops who have just saved the island from a Moslem invasion. The boat itself we would do later, though where I did not as yet know. This was to remain a nagging problem until the end of filming. For the moment we would film all the action on the harbour: the milling crowds, the waves dashing against the soldiers as they tried to haul in the galleon, and Desdemona and her courtiers hastening down from the castle to greet their lord. And, of course, all this action and spectacle had to be done in a storm. For that we had three Cretan fire brigade trucks to shower the entire scene with gallons of water pumped from the harbour. It was incredibly difficult and uncomfortable work as we shot and reshot in drenching conditions. I had bonfires built so that we could attempt to keep warm between takes, but even so it was all we could do to keep up everyone's spirits.

Despite the miserable conditions, I was beginning to realize that something absolutely extraordinary was taking place. I could tell from the rushes on video tape that this was beyond anything I'd done before. It was almost frightening, and suddenly the responsibility seemed even greater.

We moved on to the scenes showing the pomp and splendour of the arrival of the Venetian ambassador and the feast in his honour, which ends in chaos as Otello attacks Desdemona and collapses in a jealous fit. Many have found Otello's reactions too extreme, forgetting that at that time, especially in garrison life, most men were riddled with syphilis. The disease was a plague and one of its symptoms was sudden fits of uncontrollable fury.

After the harbour scene came the first occasion when Katia as Desdemona was really called upon to act, and it was then that the transformation became clear. Professional that she is, she had studied everything around her and had been particularly attentive to how Placido worked – after all, he is now the opera singer with the most experience of film-making. It was clear she had not only mastered the tricks of performing on camera but was actually extremely good at them. It was when we moved into the hair-raising scene in the armoury, where Otello first accuses her of infidelity and she is forced to beg and plead with him, that the full force of what she was now capable of came through. I knew it while we were filming, but was even more astonished when I saw the rushes. I realized that she was able to convey the most heartrending emotions without recourse to the elaborate histrionics we accept in the theatre. However, I wasn't alone viewing the rushes. Justino Diaz joined me and afterwards I noticed that he was very pensive. Later I overheard him talking to Placido at the bar in our hotel. 'We can't sleep quietly any more,' he was saying, as he explained to his friend that any idea they might have had of being the only stars of the film was now over.

All this should have made me feel wonderful, but something other than the performances was preoccupying me. After the drenching storm scene a number of the crew had gone sick with a rare sort of bronchial infection. This took the form of a sore throat and fever with a couple of days' unpleasant flu. Not everyone succumbed at once, but the wretched virus slowly wended its way amongst us, picking off different people at different times. I seemed to be immune, but on reflection this was probably the protection afforded by all the nervous adrenalin in my system as I struggled to energize all those singers and craftsmen. Sadly, there was a limit to this protection and, as we approached the end of filming in Crete, I began to feel more and more fatigued. Just as we were going to pull up stakes and transport the whole operation to Rome for the final days' shooting that December, the worst possible thing happened: I collapsed with pneumonia. There was nothing to be done; I was too sick and feverish to continue. The effects of the virus were exaggerated by the months of unremitting work, often long into the night, day after day. As the production closed down in Heraklion, I was flown to Rome and a bed, inevitably, in the Salvator Mundi hospital.

I was to spend the final fortnight of 1985 recuperating, while beyond the clinic walls the producers struggled to hold together our crew and performers. All our stars had firm engagements elsewhere and were soon heading towards the four corners of the world to fulfil them. I myself was committed to transferring *La traviata* from Florence to Paris in mid-January. Then on top of everything, Katia, who had been having a whirl-wind romance with the Italian television star Pippo Baudo, suddenly married him and the two left for a honeymoon in Russia, where Katia had a series of concerts arranged.

For one dark moment it looked as if these spinning atoms could never be reassembled; then once again the calm good sense of Placido found a way. He took the lead in cancelling all other engagements and rallied the others behind him. By the New Year, although still weakened by antibiotics, I had to go to Paris to supervise the transfer of *Traviata*.

Paris turned out fine. Although this *Traviata* had begun in Florence, there was a feeling that the opera was somehow coming home to the city where the story is set; and, indeed, it was now settled into the very theatre whose gaudy splendour had done so much to inspire the look of the production. Its reception was a wonderful boost after the depression that comes with illness and hospitalization, and I felt much refreshed when, at the end of January, we all met up again at the Cinecittà studios in Rome.

Zeffirelli

338   What confronted us now were the most intimate scenes of all. Set in
the castle bedchamber, there was first the love duet between Otello and
Desdemona, and then the final death scene in which he murders her. In a
way, it seemed that the Almighty had granted us a blessed respite rather
than an inconvenient delay. We had all had the chance to take stock of
what we had already done. I had been able to get my film editor, Peter
Taylor, to make a rough assembly of what we had shot, so that we knew
whether certain scenes needed to be redone. For a work on this scale, it was
a fortunate opportunity which seldom occurs.

Because of the way we had ordered our work, both Placido and Katia
were at full peak and both were absolutely in tune with the camera's needs.
Still it was a great strain, especially for Katia, as my interpretation of
the role envisages Desdemona, not as the wilting virginal girl sometimes
portrayed, but as a full-blooded, sensual young woman who has the courage
to stand up to her father's opposition to her marrying the Moor. This means
that the love duet in the bedroom was a highly passionate, almost erotic,
scene, and that is never easy to play before the unblinking gaze of dozens
of technicians. To make matters worse, one of those pestilential *paparazzi*
photographers managed to get into the studio, climb on to one of the
catwalks and take intimate photographs of Katia and Placido in bed. These
were published in such a way as to suggest that Katia was being unfaithful
to the man she had married only a few weeks before. Pippo Baudo, being
Sicilian, was not best pleased and, at his insistence, we had the set guarded
and cleared of all but the most essential crew.

That love duet is, to me, the emotional pivot of the opera. When Verdi
and Boito adapted the Shakespeare play, they dropped the first act and
plunged straight into the action on Cyprus. This made the opera much
more dramatic than the play, but left the composer with a problem: how
to explain the background of Otello and Desdemona's love and marriage?
Boito's solution was to have them reminisce during the love duet about all
that has happened between them, starting with the way Otello first
described his childhood and youth to her and leading up to their meeting
and subsequent marriage. It is, in effect, a sequence of musical flashbacks
and the perfect opportunity for me to insert the whole story visually. Thus,
after we finished in Rome, the plan was to move to Venice, where we would
recreate the scenes of their early life together, which would be cut into the
great duet. This was one of the most evident examples of what can be done
when you move from one art form to another. When, as I expect, some
critics pull the film apart because of it, they may care to remember the
'liberties' that Verdi and Boito took with Shakespeare. They added the
love scene in the first place; there are none in Shakespeare. They are only
begun or ended, as in Romeo and Juliet, for the simple reason that girls
were played by boys and it would have been unseemly to attempt to show

them intertwined onstage. Freed from that constraint, Verdi could improve on Shakespeare; he would hardly object to my humble attempts to improve on him.

After the love duet, we went on to the death scene. It was in the lead-up to her murder that I was able to bring to the part of Desdemona the interpretation which hovers over and within my entire film, for my Otello is a very Catholic affair. Otello's struggle is in a very real sense a religious one. As Desdemona prepares for sleep on her final night, Verdi has her sing both a version of the Shakespearean 'Willow' song and his own 'Ave Maria'. This delays the action drastically; one of the two had to go, otherwise the audience would, so my choice was to drop the song and give greater emphasis to the 'Ave Maria'. After all, despite the fact that he has just despaired of the Christian faith, Otello insists that Desdemona assure him that she has said her prayers and is thus in a state of grace before he puts her to death. Despite everything, the essential morality of the man remains intact.

The death scene was physically exacting, especially for Katia, who had to be manhandled to the ground and strangled. I think only the fact that we all knew we were nearing the end of a work we might never see the like of again kept her and the rest of us up to it.

At each stage of the filming the already high budget had crept up and up. Not because of any profligacy, but because all of us saw how special the film was going to be and wanted to enrich it as much as possible. When he first saw our rushes, Menachem Golan sent me a cable saying: 'Each frame looks as if it were painted by God! Nothing less than that!' And he, more than anyone, insisted that the needs of the film should override all other considerations. The final act of generosity of my Gamma-Globulins came in the matter of Otello's galleon. We had scoured Europe to find a period boat in a suitable location where we could film Otello's arrival and his first triumphal aria. This would be intercut with the storm scene shot in Crete. Naturally, we hoped to find a galleon built for some other film which we could adapt to ours. There were various possibilities, but they came to nothing. In the end, when we had finished in the studios, Cannon agreed to let us construct a section of a Venetian galleon on the coast just north of Rome. Although it would appear for only a few fleeting seconds, at a cost of some $80,000, Cannon insisted our film should have the visual richness necessary to captivate an audience from the earliest moment and thus, I trust, discourage anyone from trying to film *Otello* again for at least twenty years. Understandably, I wanted my *Otello* to be definitive.

Thus in March, despite the risk to our health, we were again being sprayed with gallons of sea water in order to simulate that tempestuous moment. It was the last day's shooting with Placido, almost exactly a year to the day from when we had first decided to do the film.

TWENTY

A Portrait

As I complete this book, *Otello* is about to open. I am, as usual, confident and uncertain in equal measures, and also sad – it's like watching a child grow up and leave home. How strange it is to think back to those days over half a century ago when Mary O'Neill introduced me to Shakespeare, and Uncle Gustavo took me to my first opera. I trust they can see me now.

Thanks to my Gamma-Globulins, this time I will perhaps avoid the hiatus that has often followed my major productions. At sixty-three, I feel that a whole new world is opening up to me. As usual my diary is filled with operas for the next four or five years, but that is not what I mean. *Otello* has proved to me that all the skills I have learned from so many talented people are at their peak, and I must use them to good effect. Whether this means more opera films, more Shakespeare or entirely new material is irrelevant; I have to go on, because I am now sure that there is a wide audience out there which likes what I do with film opera. *Traviata* succeeded in making opera a popular success; audiences everywhere took easily to the story of the doomed courtesan. It's still running in many countries and the video cassette sales are amazing. But the real pleasure for me was to combine the skills I had learned over the years. Now I want to push back the frontier a little further and give this new audience for opera something a bit more difficult. *Traviata* is really the best musical ever, full of well-known, detachable hit numbers, but *Otello* is a more difficult experience for any audience. Yet think of the spectacle – the storm scene, the parade of the Venetian ambassador and the brooding crusader castle – and the emotions. I think a wider public than before can be enticed to the later Verdi.

When *Otello* was previewed at the Cannes Film Festival in May 1986, one American publication wrote of it: 'All production credits are of the very highest order. Every frame has the magnificence of composition as well as the color shadings of Renaissance paintings of the Italian School. There is nothing in this film that does not serve the purpose of high drama, musical, cinematic or otherwise, to ultimate perfection.' So perhaps I will succeed in pulling in a new audience for a complex work.

I don't want to claim a sense of mission, as if I have singlemindedly been

340

striving all my life to give opera back to the people, but now that the chance has come, I am happy to have done it. I have always been a popularizer and have always regretted that after Puccini the mass audience has been neglected, even on occasions despised, by modern composers. I have found it an irritating irony that those who espouse populist political views often want art to be 'difficult'; and the supposedly *avant garde*, while being politically left-wing, has often proved culturally élitist. Yet I, who favour the Right in our democracy, believe passionately in a broad culture made accessible to as many as possible. I am wary of critics who think it smart to pour scorn on my productions because, as they put it, they are aesthetically self-indulgent. In all honesty, I don't believe that millions of young people throughout the world wept over my film of *Romeo and Juliet* just because the costumes were splendid.

Perhaps I am beginning to wear down the opposition. While I was at the Cannes Film Festival, I was interviewed by *La Stampa* columnist Lietta Tornabuoni. Lietta is a wry, left-wing journalist who has hardly been one of my most ardent supporters in the past; in fact, we've often crossed swords. This time, however, when I had finished outlining my future plans, she expressed astonishment at what I was proposing.

'Everyone here is so exhausted and disenchanted,' she said. 'You're the only one left with any optimism. Just like a beginner.'

Recognition at last!

I have, throughout my career, been giving the world's major opera houses new productions of the great classics which will act as their standard repertoire for years to come. Of course, we have to have *avant-garde* interpretations, of course we can have modern-dress versions of eighteenth-century operas and all the other fun and games, but recently it did look as if that was all we would have. Surely, every generation must also see the great productions as their creators truly wanted them done, not as pickled museum pieces but as honest, living intepretations of the author's wishes.

Theatre is not like a painting, which hangs on a wall and only has to be restored from time to time; theatre is still alive and depends on the people who work in it, who must have a culture broad enough to comprehend and reinterpret for their generation what the original author intended. I suppose that in some ways I am the last standard-bearer of a great craft and tradition which I inherited from people like Serafin and Visconti. If so, then I am proud of it.

One thing is certain: I enjoy my life whole-heartedly; I am not tortured by self-doubt or driven by creative *Angst*. I rather like being famous. I know I ought to pretend that it's a bore being recognized in the street and asked for my autograph, but it isn't. It's rather pleasant. I dread the day it might not happen. I try to remember that the press is another fish in the sea I swim in. I readily admit to being loquacious and to holding trenchant opinions on everything from sex to football, so I'm quite happy to deliver them on television or in newspaper interviews, often creating unnecessary hostility around me. I am genuinely happy when I am given awards and I was deeply honoured when the Italian President made me a Grand Officer of the Republic.

None of this, however, stops me from falling flat on my face from time to time. 1983 was an election year and the Christian Democrats were worried that their long period in office would lead to a massive popular reaction. It seemed possible that the Communist Party might at last break through. One tactic the government dreamed up was to ask celebrities who supported the Christian Democratic Party to stand for election, in order, so they hoped, to maintain popular support. They asked me to stand in Florence, my home town, and two things persuaded me to go along with the idea. Firstly, I was in the middle of those two empty years when nothing seemed to get off the ground and when the idea of being a Deputy was rather attractive. Secondly, I genuinely thought I could use the post to realize a long-standing dream: to use my cultural connections and make Florence the European capital for the performing arts. Surely, I argued, its past entitled the city to such a role. Florence has a unique position not merely in the cultural history of Italy but also in that of Britain and France. My proposal was that, with the help of Unesco and the EEC, Florence could undertake such an ambitious scheme. Of course, access to political power was essential for anyone trying to bring this about and that was why I needed to get elected.

It was hardly surprising that the whole world of politics turned out to be inimical to me. I, who am used to speaking my mind whenever I need to and am used, as a director, to having my own way, suddenly found myself confronted with the need to compromise on every issue and seek the allegiance of people with whom I had nothing in common – in other words to be a politician. Needless to say, I was not a great success in these endeavours and I soon came to see that winning would be a disaster for myself more than anyone. Fortunately, the campaign was wonderful. Every day I set off with my party supporters into the Tuscan countryside to canvas votes and thus I inadvertently recreated the days of my childhood, when my friends and I would set off on bicycles to explore the villages and churches surrounding Florence. It was a moving experience to visit places I had not seen since those far-off days with the partisans, or even longer ago with Father Spinillo. Sometimes, with all the changes of the intervening forty years, it was hard to recognize the exact spot where this or that event had occurred. On the other hand, I occasionally came across somewhere totally untouched, vivid with memories of the Scots Guards or the head-strong, romantic Polish boys, terrifyingly alive with remembered danger.

One day our cavalcade stopped in Borselli, surely the most moving occasion of all. The villagers had abandoned the old village I knew and moved further down the valley. I was able to peer into the houses I remembered so well and was surprised at how tiny they were compared to my memories. Unfortunately, whereas I would have preferred the place to crumble quietly into dust, the old Borselli had been taken up by week-ending professional people from the city who were doing up the houses in 'antique' peasant style. I left them to it and went to the old cemetery to search out Ersilia Innocenti's grave. As I stood gratefully recalling all her kindnesses to me, I couldn't help but wonder what she would have made of me now. There I was at sixty, a world-famous stage and cinema director being paraded about the countryside kissing babies for votes. That helped convince me of the foolishness of what I was doing. That and the memory of Robert Kennedy, who had shown me what the finer qualities of a politician can be.

In the end, despite a respectable number of votes in my favour, I just missed being elected. I was left first on the reserve list. It was a relief really, though I live in mild terror that one of our Florentine politicians will have a fatal accident or retire, which would propel me into parliament, where I doubt I'd shine.

Donald Downes had once begged me not to be so foolish as to think I could be a politician. For him, as for me now, you had to be a Kennedy to be in politics. After leaving Positano, Donald had moved to London, largely for the cultural world he loved, but his health rapidly declined. The whole machine was wearing out and London began to irritate him.

'It's a mess,' he announced, when I went to visit him. 'It's no longer what it was.'

This was during the years of the Labour governments, which he scarcely found sympathetic, but the underlying reason was that he was looking for a nest in which to settle down and die. He moved to California in 1978 to live with his widowed sister-in-law, Polly, so I saw a lot of him during my Hollywood years. He was never reticent in his opinion of my work.

'You're much better at theatre than movies. You're too quick-witted, the movies take too much time. They encourage vanity and stupidity, and those are the two sins always lying in wait for you,'

He was always telling me to be more serious, less of what he called 'a jet-set boy'. I remember when he visited the hospital after my accident and learned that Gina Lollobrigida's driving had almost killed me, the first thing he said was: 'That'll serve you right. You shouldn't even shake hands with those movie tarts.'

I loved him for it. I remember him telling a top executive of MGM that he ought to be ashamed of the junk he was putting on the market.

'You are succeeding brilliantly,' he told him, 'in bringing up a generation of apes.'

344   In his last years he was not in good shape financially. He could barely afford a nurse and his sister-in-law was also old and unwell. When I was leaving Hollywood, I begged him to come back to Positano with me. He said yes, but, when I tried to make the travel arrangements for him in the summer of 1981, he raised every possible objection.

'I won't go on a plane that stops in New York. I swore I'd never visit that filthy city again.'

'You don't need to,' I objected. 'You just change planes at the airport.'

'No, no,' he said. 'The stench of the city will get into the plane.'

I was determined not to give up and tried to route him via Washington, but there were other objections there. And Boston? 'My God!' he said, 'I was born there, for my sins.' Even a stop-over in Milan was unacceptable, because of the debased character of the Milanese. The truth was that he was by then afraid to travel.

'I'll come one day,' he said. 'Don't worry. If I don't come myself, my ashes will.'

And that was what happened. I flew to California when I heard of his death and went to see Polly. He had made no will and everything had to be put up for sale. An auctioneer from the court came and put pathetic stickers for $25 or $30 on all the familiar things I remembered from my younger days in Positano. I offered Polly enough money to buy them all back, so that I could take them home where they belonged. His belongings returned with his ashes, which I buried on the terrace where he used to take his coffee every morning. His spirit looks out over the bay he loved so much, and I think he is at peace.

The year 1983 also witnessed Tennessee Williams's death, though he had long since passed out of our lives. The once vibrant, nervous, sparkling personality had descended into a depressive life of pills and alcohol, which gradually isolated him from the world. He had, so it seemed, outlived his talent, leaving only his vulnerability and depression. I think if I ever feel that whatever creative spark I possess has deserted me, then I will retire and take up building, gardening and looking after my animals as a full-time occupation. I think I would be perfectly contented.

I like to believe that Donald's spirit also watches over me as I continue to work on his villa. Building a new room or even just adding a garden wall gives me the sensation of being part of the flow of history, joining those who went before, and leaving something for those who will come after. The first thing our Roman ancestors did when they conquered new territory was to build; the legionaries were masons as well as soldiers. Only when they saw the magnificent works they had built did they fully accept that they had mastered a place. At Positano I feel like an emperor in my modest domain. It's a constant preoccupation. I'm always on the look-out for old tiles and fittings from buildings that have been demolished in the area,

because my real pleasure is to make whatever I have added look as if it has   345
always been there; again, this notion of belonging both to the past and the
future pleases me so much. When I succeed, I feel I have defeated time
and, while I'm working with my builders and carpenters, I am at my most
creative, and a corner of my mind will be working on future productions –
films, castings, designs. I may be laying out a pattern of tiles on a floor,
but I'll also be dreaming up a new *Turandot*.

People sometimes ask me why I have never created a home in Florence,
the city to which my heart and mind, indeed whatever clay I'm made of,
are so attached. But I have no wish to come to terms with the Florence of
today. I can tolerate vulgarity and stupidity almost anywhere but in
Florence. Somehow it doesn't seem quite so bad in a city like Venice, which,
as a sea-port, was created on the premise of travel, commerce, and the
chaotic mixing of races. But the ethos of Florence was always discretion,
style and harmony. The endless queues waiting to see Michelangelo's David
or milling like vagabonds round the ancient streets opening their Coca-Cola
bottles against the stones of our glorious buildings seem by their very
presence to destroy that which they have allegedly come to admire. I am
forced to smile when I imagine what Donald would have said about them.

I mean to exorcize the ghosts of the city one day by making a film that
will be the consummation of all I inherited from its ancient squares and
galleries, its cloisters and libraries, its language and people. My mind
constantly turns to the idea of filming *The Florentines*, an idea I have had
for a decade or more, which would show just how it was that in one brief
moment, at the very start of the sixteenth century, a single town could
have housed such towering geniuses as Leonardo da Vinci, Michelangelo
and Machiavelli. I imagine a film full of the beauty and pageantry of the
period, yet also vibrant with the profound cultural ideas which surfaced
during that all too fleeting explosion of talent. Frankly, I feel that at sixty-
three, with Shakespeare and Verdi and in particular *Otello* to my credit, I
am ready to undertake an epic of the Renaissance. Perhaps, if I make the
film, I will find it easier to love again the city of my birth.

However, my separation from Florence comes not merely from my wish
to escape the city's past; it comes also from a desire to distance myself from
my own past. In 1983, just after the election campaign, my last truly close
relation, Fanny, died. Her son had died the year before, a final tragedy for
her. She had continued to live in my father's old home; it had been rented
to our family for more than half a century and the owner offered it to me,
but when I went back after the funeral, I was appalled to rediscover the
tragic atmosphere of the place. The darkened rooms seemed stained with
all the anguish and self-sacrifice that had been suffered there. I declined
the offer and simply took away the paintings of my family which had been
left to me on my father's death.

346   I suppose the truth is that I have become a theatrical gypsy, travelling the world, going wherever my work takes me. Maybe it will be Brasil next for the story of the young Toscanini that I am planning as my next picture – a tale which combines the beginnings of the great man's career in music with the awakening of his manhood. Or perhaps a film of George Sand and Chopin in France? Or I might return to Hollywood once more to face the excitement of dealing with the monsters of the film business. Who knows?

I often think I should settle permanently in Tunisia, where 50% of the population is under twenty years of age. They are a new nation, humble, gentle and hopeful; everything lies before them and they are not over-shadowed by the monuments and traditions of earlier generations. Then again, I sometimes move in the other direction and wonder whether London should not be my home; after all I owe so much to the British for my early chances. One problem is the quarantine laws, which prevent me from travelling to England with my dogs. I strongly believe the period of quar-antine could easily be dropped from six months to three weeks. Even allowing for that, I wonder whether London, with its poorly subsidized theatres and nervous West End managers, has a place for someone who works on a grand scale and who is not much enamoured of committee meetings and schedules.

No matter where I go, I will always return to Positano, to the home I have made. When each new year begins, I invite friends to help plant trees and flowers with the first moon of the year. Everything is a process of new beginnings; there are so many things still to do. I am helped in all this by my faith, with its assurance of rebirth and renewal; as things pass out of my life, so new people and opportunities are offered. At that dark hour when I put out the lights, say my prayers and thank God for the day He has given, I am delighted to realize that I am still learning things which I did not know that same morning.

As time goes by, I find myself missing Luchino Visconti more and more. I often remember things we said or did. There seems to be no one around today of his heroic stature. When I started on this book, some of the things I wrote about Luchino were coloured by the bitterness I felt at his behaviour after we parted, but gradually, as the story unfolded, I found myself more tolerant, even flattered that the great Visconti should have been so angry at my leaving that he struggled for years to punish me. Anyway, judge not that ye be not judged, and looking back, I've done enough mean-spirited things to remove the right to condemn others. Today, I tend to dwell on Luchino's virtues rather than his faults, particularly when I see how those he worked with – people like Suso Cecchi d'Amico and Piero Tosi – are still so devoted to his memory. For his great strength was the way he formed a team who stayed with him. He was an educator, a maestro in the old Renaissance sense, surrounded by devoted apprentices and collaborators;

he seldom paid them, they earned their money where they could and worked for him in order to learn.

I, too, have people around me who have grown up working on my productions, though I've moved too much to keep a team with me at all times, as Luchino did. I do not teach directly; rather I always imagine that someone will learn by watching what is happening rather than by my telling them what to do. Pippo is now well launched on his career in film production, working mainly in America, and yet we are closer than ever before; he is my first 'son' and whenever he has problems he comes to me.

Close to me today is Luciano, the story of whose orphaned childhood so moved me the day we drove to Viterbo. He too now works as an assistant, helping me as I travel the world, seeing that my life has some order. It has been my privilege to give him the reassurance of personal support and affection which he had missed, and I have already begun the legal process that will enable me to adopt him.

It is in the closeness of the people I live with that I am most fortunate, more so than in the success I have had or the money it has brought. Vige is still with me, as well as my long-time helper Dorino. Ali and Giovanna are in Positano, and my friend and assistant Bianca has the unenviable task of managing my often chaotic affairs. One of my dearest friends is my ex-assistant Sheila, who went back to England and married. If Pippo and Luciano are my sons, then Sheila is my daughter.

In the early 1970s I had an idea which eventually brought together several strands of my life. The two old gentlemen who made Penhaligon's perfumes, including Luchino's favourite Hammam Bouquet, came to the end of their working lives. They only made enough to satisfy their grander patrons and there was every likelihood the business would die with them. I suggested to Sheila that she acquire the Penhaligon name and formulae from them, and then open a discreet business which would preserve the wonderful perfumes so dear to five generations of kings and princes of England. I helped raise the finance and she seized the opportunity. What a success she has made of it. When I look at the shop she set up in Covent Garden or at the one in Burlington Arcade, with their old-fashioned wooden shelves and neat rows of flagons of Hammam Bouquet, I think of Luchino, who wore it all those years ago. By another strange concidence there was a flat above the shop in Wellington Street and who should have rented it but dear old Sergeant Martin, who presided over the foyer of the Royal Opera House until his death in 1984. He always recalled his 'interrupter' whenever he saw me.

My closest friends remain the oldest ones: the actor Alfredo Bianchini, the designers Anna Anni and Piero Tosi, and the other Florentines who still survive. They won't be insulted if I mention them in the same breath as my dogs, for who could resent those loyal creatures? Recently Pippo

348   brought Bambina, a Jack Russsell, to the house and I promptly stole her –
it was love at first sight. She has recently starred on the cover of the *Sunday
Times Magazine* and seems set on a glittering career.

Some people drift in and out of one's life; others disappear, though
perhaps not forever. I suppose Harry Keith and Jimmy are around somewhere, grandfathers most certainly. Perhaps the two Germans who let me
cross the bridge with the dog Mussolini are prosperous businessmen today.
As one gets older, such thoughts make for tolerance. As I reread this
manuscript I am struck by the fact that the one person who remains
unforgiven is the woman whose nightmarish image so haunted my childhood – Corinna, my father's wife. Now, as I complete the story, there seems
less reason for such unyielding resentment. After Fanny's death, I took
away the two portraits of my father and Corinna. His I hung on one side
of the window of my study in the villa in Rome, hers I consigned to an
attic. Today I had it brought down and hung on the wall, so that they are
together again. She, poor woman, never had the chance to forgive me for
being part, albeit innocently, of the tragedy of her marriage; I, at least,
have been given the grace to forgive her. And after all why not? She did
what she did because she was in love, and we can all do such dreadful things
when driven by what should be the gentlest of emotions.

Index

349

Index

Index

Index

Index

VERDI — OTELLO — ATTO I°